New Testament Commentary

# The Gospels and Acts

F B Hole

**Scripture Truth Publications**

## THE GOSPELS AND ACTS

First published as articles in the magazines "Edification" 1937-39 and "Scripture Truth" 1940, 1942-44.

The commentary on the Gospel of John published in 1954 as "The Gospel of John, briefly expounded" by the Central Bible Truth Depot, London.

Hardback edition first published in November 1985 by Central Bible Hammond Trust Limited, Wooler.

Transferred to Digital Printing 2007

ISBN: 978-0-901860-42-2 (paperback)

ISBN: 978-0-901860-46-0 (hardback)

© Copyright 1985 Central Bible Hammond Trust

A publication of Scripture Truth

All rights reserved. No part of this publication may be reproduced, stored in a retrieval system, or transmitted, in any form or by any means, electronic, mechanical, photocopying, recording or otherwise without prior permission of Scripture Truth Publications.

Scripture quotations, unless otherwise indicated, are taken from The Authorized (King James) Version. Rights in the Authorized Version are vested in the Crown. Reproduced by permission of the Crown's patentee, Cambridge University Press.

Cover photograph ©iStockphoto.com/ofbeautifulthings (Tim Robbins)

Published by Scripture Truth Publications
Coopies Way, Coopies Lane,
Morpeth, Northumberland, NE61 6JN

Scripture Truth is an imprint of Central Bible Hammond Trust, a charitable trust

Printed and bound by Lightning Source

# CONTENTS

| | |
|---|---|
| Matthew | pages 1-70 |
| Mark | pages 71-135 |
| Luke | pages 137-207 |
| John | pages 209-317 |
| The Acts of the Apostles | pages 319-387 |

# MATTHEW

## CHAPTER 1

THE WORDING OF the first verse of the New Testament directs our thoughts back to the first book of the Old, inasmuch as "generation" is the translation of the Greek word, *genesis*. Matthew in particular, and the whole New Testament in general, is "The book of the *genesis* of Jesus Christ." When we refer back to Genesis, we find that book divides into eleven sections, and all of them save the first begin with a statement about "generations." The third section commences, "This is the book of the generations of Adam" (5: 1); and the whole Old Testament unrolls for us the sad story of Adam and his race, ending with terrible appropriateness in the word, "*curse*." With what great relief we can turn from the generations of Adam to "the generation of Jesus Christ," for here we shall find the introduction of *grace;* and upon *that* note the New Testament ends.

Jesus is at once presented in a two-fold way. He is Son of David, and hence the royal *crown* that God originally bestowed on David belongs to Him. He is also Son of Abraham, hence He has the title to the *land* and all the promised *blessing* is vested in Him. Having stated this, we are given His genealogy, from Abraham, through Joseph the husband of Mary. This would be His official genealogy, according to Jewish reckoning. The list given is remarkable for its omissions, since three kings, closely connected with the infamous Athaliah, are omitted in verse 8; and the summary as to the "fourteen generations," given in verse 17, shows that it is not an accidental omission, but that God disowns and refuses to reckon the kings that sprang more immediately from this devotee of Baal-worship.

It is remarkable also, inasmuch as the names of only four women are brought into it, and those not all such names as we might have expected. Two of the four were Gentiles, which must have been somewhat damaging to Jewish pride: both of them women of striking faith, though one of them had lived in the immorality which characterized the heathen world. Of the other we know nothing but what is good. The other two came of the stock of Israel, yet of both the record is bad, and of neither do we know anything which is definitely creditable. Indeed Bathsheba's name is not mentioned; she is merely "her . . . of Urias," thus proclaiming her discredit. So again all is damaging to Jewish pride. Our Lord's genealogy added nothing to Him. Yet it guaranteed His genuine Manhood, and that the rights vested in David and Abraham were legally His.

But if the first 17 verses assure us that Jesus was really a man, the remaining verses equally assure us that He was much more than a Man, even God Himself, present among us. By an angelic messenger Joseph, the betrothed husband of Mary is told that her coming child is the fruit of the action of the Holy Ghost, and that when born He is to bear the name of Jesus. He should save His people from their sins, therefore Saviour is to be His name. Only God is able to name in view of future accomplishments.

# MATTHEW

He can do so, and how fully has this great name been justified! What a harvest of saved humanity will be garnered in days to come, all of them saved from their sins, and not merely from the judgment which their sins deserved! Only *"His people"* are saved thus. To know His salvation one must be enrolled amongst *them* by faith in Him.

Thus was fulfilled the prediction of Isaiah 7: 14, where a clear indication had been given of the greatness and power of the coming Saviour. His prophetic Name, Emmanuel, indicated that He should be God manifested in the flesh—God amongst us in a far more wonderful way than ever He was manifested in the midst of Israel in the days of Moses, far more wonderful also than the way in which He was with Adam in the days before sin entered into the world. The two names are intimately connected. To have God with us, apart from our being saved from our sins, would be impossible: His presence would only overwhelm us in judgment. To be saved from our sins, without God being brought to us might have been possible, but the story of grace would have lost its chief glory. In the coming of Jesus we have both. God has been brought to us and our sins being removed, we have been brought to Him.

## Chapter 2

THE OPENING VERSES of chapter 2 throw a strong and searching light upon the conditions that prevailed in those days amongst the Jews found in Jerusalem, the descendants of those who had returned under Zerubbabel, Ezra and Nehemiah. The King of the Jews was born in Bethlehem and yet for weeks they knew nothing about it. That Herod the king should be in ignorance was not at all surprising, for he was no Israelite but an Idumean. But of all people the chief priests should have been apprized of this great event for which they had been professedly waiting—the birth of the Messiah. We find in Luke 2 that the event was made known from heaven, within a few hours at the most, to humble souls who feared the Lord. The Psalmist has told us that, "The secret of the Lord is with them that fear Him" (25: 14), and this is exemplified in the shepherds and others; but the religious leaders in Jerusalem were not among these, but among "the proud" whom men called "happy." (See Malachi 3: 15, 16). Consequently they were as much in the dark as the wicked Herod.

But there is worse than this. It is not surprising, again we say, that Herod should be troubled when he heard the news, for here was apparently a rival claimant for his throne. We read however that "he was troubled, *and all Jerusalem with him.*" So the advent of the Saviour produced not jubilation but consternation amongst the very people who professed to be waiting for Him! Evidently then something was terribly wrong, since it was as yet just the recoil of their perverted instincts. They had not seen Him; He had as yet done nothing: they just sensed that His advent would mean the spoiling of their pleasures instead of the fulfilment of their hopes.

# MATTHEW

Yet these men were well versed in their Scriptures. They were able to give a prompt and correct reply to Herod's enquiry, quoting Micah 5: 2. They had the knowledge that puffs up, and so they knew nothing as they ought to know it (see 1 Cor. 8: 1, 2), and they placed their knowledge at the service of the adversary. The "great red dragon" (Rev. 12: 3-5) of the Roman Empire, the power of which was vested locally in Herod, was ready to devour the "Man Child," and they were ready to help him to do so. Theirs was the wrong kind of Scripture knowledge, and they serve as a beacon of warning for us.

The scripture they quoted presents the Lord to us as "Governor," who should rule. In Micah only Israel is in view, but we know that His rule will be universal; and this is the third way in which He is presented to us. In JESUS we see God come forth to *save*. In EMMANUEL we see God come forth to *dwell*. In GOVERNOR we see God come forth to *rule*. It was ever His thought to dwell with men, governing everything according to His pleasure, and to accomplish that He had to come forth to save.

When the Young Child was found in Bethlehem there was the pledge that all three things would come to pass, and though Jerusalem was ignorant and hostile there were Gentiles from the east drawn to His rising, and they recognized the King of the Jews in Him. Do we realize how terribly they condemned the religious leaders in Jerusalem? The shepherds of Luke 2 knew of His birth within a few hours; these eastern astronomers within a few days, or weeks at the most; whereas several months must have elapsed before the priests and scribes had the smallest inkling of what had come to pass. First by a star and then by a dream God spoke to the wise men, but to the religionists in Jerusalem He did not speak at all, and there had been days when the high priest in their midst had been in touch with God by means of the Urim and Thummin. Now God was silent to them. Their state was as is portrayed in Malachi, and probably worse.

In Herod we see unscrupulous power allied with craft. When thwarted by the action of the wise men, he took, as he thought, no chances in his murderous onslaught on the children of Bethlehem. The fact that he fixed the limit of exemption at two years would indicate that the period between the appearing of the star and the arrival of the wise men at Jerusalem must have run into months. His ruthless and wicked action brought about a fulfilment of Jeremiah 31: 15. If that verse be read with its context it will be seen that its final and complete fulfilment will be in the last days, when God will finally cause Rachel's weeping to cease by bringing her children back from the land of the enemy. Nevertheless what took place at Bethlehem was the same kind of thing on a smaller scale.

Herod however was fighting against God, who defeated his purpose by sending His angel to Joseph in a dream for the second time. The Young Child was taken into Egypt, and thus Hosea 11: 1 found a remarkable fulfilment, and Jesus began to retrace Israel's history. How easily did God

# MATTHEW

frustrate Herod's wicked design, and just as easily not long after did He deal with Herod himself. Matthew does not waste words in describing his end: he simply tells us that "when Herod was dead," for the third time the angel of the Lord spoke to Joseph in a dream, instructing him to return to the land for death had removed the would-be murderer.

Joseph's first intention evidently was to return to Judaea; but tidings as to Archelaus succeeding his father having reached him, fear made him hesitate. Then for the fourth time God instructed him by a dream. Thus he, Mary and the Young Child were shepherded back to Nazareth, whence he had originally come, as Luke tells us. It is instructive to see how God guided all these early movements; partly by circumstances, such as the decree of Augustus and the tidings about Archelaus; and partly by dreams. Thus the schemes of the adversary were foiled. The "porter" held open the door into the "sheepfold" in order that the true Shepherd might enter, in spite of all that he could do. Also the scriptures were fulfilled: not only was Jesus brought out of Egypt but He became known as the Nazarene.

No Old Testament prophet predicted that He should be "a Nazarene," in so many words, but more than one said that He would be despised and an object of reproach. So in verse 23 it is "the prophets," and not one particular prophet. They had said He should be an object of contempt, which in our Lord's time was expressed in the epithet, "a Nazarene." In Darby's New Translation—large edition with full notes — there is an illuminating comment on this verse, as to the exact phrase used regarding the fulfilment, as contrasted with the earlier expression in chapters 1: 22, and 2: 17; showing the accuracy with which quotations from the Old Testament are made. It is a note well worth reading.

Nazarene is the fourth name given to our Lord in this opening Gospel. He is, as we have seen, Jesus, Emmanuel, Governor; but He is also the Nazarene. God may come amongst men to save, to dwell, to rule; but alas! He will be "despised and rejected of men."

## CHAPTER 3

THE THIRD CHAPTER presents John the Baptist without any preliminaries as to his birth or origin. He fulfilled Isaiah's prophecy; he preached in the wilderness apart from the haunts of men; in clothing and food he was apart from the customs of men; his theme was repentance, in view of the nearness of the kingdom of heaven. It was a very unique ministry. What other preacher has selected a wilderness as the geographical sphere of his ministry? Philip the evangelist went indeed to the southern desert to meet a special individual; but the power of God was so with John that the multitudes flocked to him, and were led to his baptism, confessing their sins.

In this Gospel there is frequent mention of "the kingdom of heaven," and for the first instance is here. No explanation is offered by Matthew, nor does he record any explanation as offered by John; the reason being doubtless that the coming of a day when "the God of heaven" should set up a kingdom, and all should see that "the heavens do rule," had been predicted in the book of Daniel. Consequently the term would not be unfamiliar to his hearers or to any Jewish reader. The same prophet had a vision of the Son of Man coming with the clouds of heaven and taking the kingdom, and the saints possessing it with Him. Now the kingdom was *at hand* inasmuch as "Jesus Christ, *the Son of David*", was found amongst men.

When there is a genuine and powerful work of God, men do not like to be apart from it, especially if they are religious leaders: consequently we find both Pharisees and Sadducees coming to John's baptism. He met them however with prophetic insight. He unmasked them as having the characteristics of the serpent, and warned them that wrath lay before them. He knew that they would boast of being in the proper Abrahamic succession, so he knocked that prop from beneath them, showing that it would not count with God. Nothing would do but repentance, and his baptism was with a view to that; but it must be genuine and manifest itself in fruits that were suitable. James, in his Epistle, insists that faith, if it is real and vital, must express itself in suitable works. Here John calls for just the same thing in regard to repentance.

These verses in the middle of chapter 3, give us a glimpse of what was wrong. The true Son of David and of Abraham having arrived, the kingdom was near, and no mere successional connection with Abraham would avail. Moses had given them the law: Elijah had recalled them to it, after it had been forsaken: John simply issued a blunt call to repentance, which was tantamount to saying, "On the basis of the law you are lost, and nothing remains but for you honestly to own it with humble sorrow of heart." The great mass of them were not prepared for that, to their ruin.

John also announced the coming forth of the Mighty One, whose forerunner he was. There was no comparison between them, and he confessed his sense of it by saying he was not fit to carry even the sandals of His feet. He also contrasted his own baptism with water and the baptism with the Holy Spirit and fire. The great Coming One should exercise perfect discrimination, sifting the wheat from the chaff. *These* He will baptize with the Holy Ghost, and *those* with the fire of judgment; and the issues will be eternal for the fire will be unquenchable.

These words of John must have been tremendously searching, and they will be fulfilled when the millennial age is about to be introduced. Then the Spirit will be poured upon all flesh, and not the Jew only—that is, upon all that have been redeemed. On the other hand the wicked will be banished to everlasting fire, as the end of chapter 25 of our Gospel will show us. Meanwhile there has been an anticipatory fulfilment of the baptism of the Spirit, in the establishment of the church, as Acts 2 shows. The context here decisively reveals that "fire" is an allusion to judgment, and not to the tongues of fire on the day of Pentecost, or any similar action of blessing.

When Jesus came forth for His ministry, His first act was to come to John's baptism, and that in spite of the objection which John expressed. The objection served to bring out the principle on which the Lord was acting. He was fulfilling righteousness. He had no sins to confess, yet having taken man's place it was right that He should identify Himself with the godly, who were thus taking their true place before God. Men of God in earlier times had done the thing in principle—Ezra and Daniel, for instance—confessing as their own sins in which they had but very little share, though sinners themselves. Here was the sinless One, and He did it perfectly; and lest there should be any mistake, at the very moment He did it, there was the opening of the heavens upon Him, the first great manifestation of the Trinity, and the voice from heaven declaring Him to be the beloved Son, in whom the Father found all His delight. In form as a dove the Spirit descended upon the One who is to baptize others with that same Spirit.

## Chapter 4

JESUS WAS NOT only taking man's place, He was more particularly taking Israel's place. Israel was called out of Egypt, then they were baptized to Moses in the cloud and sea, then they entered the wilderness. We have just seen Jesus called as God's Son out of Egypt, and now He is baptized; then as we open chapter 4 we find the Spirit, who had come upon Him, leads Him straight into the wilderness to be tempted of the devil. Here we find a contrast, for in the wilderness Israel tempted God and failed in everything. Jesus was Himself tempted and triumphed in everything.

Yet the temptations, wherewith the devil assailed Him, were similar to Israel's testings in the wilderness, for there is nothing new in the tactics of the adversary. Israel was tested by hunger, and by being lifted up in connection with the things of God—seen more particularly in connection with Korah, Dathan and Abiram—and by attractions that might lead them to worship and serve another beside Jehovah, and they fell, worshipping the golden calf. Jesus met each temptation with the Word of God. On each occasion He quoted from a small section of the book of Deuteronomy, wherein Israel is reminded of their responsibilities. In those responsibilities they failed, and Jesus fulfilled them perfectly in every particular.

The devil always sows doubts of the Divine Word. Contrast 3: 17 with 4: 3 and 6, and note how strikingly this comes out. No sooner has God said, "This *is* My beloved Son," than the devil says twice over, "*If* Thou be the Son of God." The little word "if" is a great favourite with the devil! Jesus appropriately met him with the Word of God. That Word is indispensable to Man's spiritual life just as bread is to his natural life. And man needs *every* word that God has spoken, and not just a few special passages only.

Are we all finding our spiritual life in "every word that proceedeth out of the mouth of God"?

The temptation of Jesus by the devil makes it plain beyond all dispute that a personal devil exists. From the days of Genesis 3, he had been accustomed to seduce men by appealing to their lusts and pride. In Jesus he met One who had neither lust nor pride, and who met his every onslaught by the Word of God; defeated consequently, he had to leave Him. His conqueror was a true Man, who had fasted forty days and forty nights, and to Him angels ministered. They had never before served their God after this wonderful sort.

The casting of John into prison, as verse 12 shows us, was the event which led the Lord to enter fully upon His public ministry. Leaving Nazareth, He took up His abode in Capernaum, and Isaiah's prophecy found its fulfilment, at all events as regards His first advent. If we turn up the passage (9: 1-7) and read it, we shall notice that both advents are in view, as is so often the case. His coming shone like a star before the prophets, but they did not as yet know that it was a double star. Galilee will yet see the great light of His *glory*, just as then they saw the great light of His *grace*. The forerunner having been silenced by imprisonment, Jesus took up and enforced His message of repentance in view of the kingdom being at hand. John's Gospel shows us that the Lord was active in service before this time. He had disciples, and He visited Judaea when "John was not yet cast into prison" (3: 24).

This being so, the calling of Peter, Andrew, James and John was not the beginning of their acquaintance with Him. That came earlier, and is recorded in John 1. Evidently also there were times when they or other disciples went about with Him before they were definitely called to leave their secular occupations and give all their time to Him. Following Him, He would make these fishermen to be fishers of men. By diligence and study men may make themselves into good preachers, but fishers of men are only made by Him. He was supreme at this Himself, and walking in His company they would learn of Him and catch His spirit.

In the three verses which close chapter 4, Matthew sums up the early days of His ministry. His message was "the gospel of the kingdom." It must be distinguished from "the gospel of the grace of God," which is being preached today. This has the death and resurrection of Christ as its great theme, and announces forgiveness as the fruit of the expiation He made. That was the glad tidings that the kingdom predicted by the prophets was now brought to them in Him. If they would submit to the divine authority that was vested in Him, the power of the kingdom would be active on their behalf. As proof of this He showed the power of the kingdom in the healing of men's bodies. All manner of bodily sickness and

# MATTHEW

disease was removed, the pledge that He could heal every spiritual ill. This display of the *power* of the kingdom, coupled with the *preaching* of the kingdom, proved very attractive, and great crowds followed Him.

## CHAPTER 5

THE LORD THEN began to speak to His disciples, though in the presence of the multitude, instructing them in the *principles* of the kingdom. First of all He showed what kind of people are going to possess the kingdom and enjoy its benefits. In the kingdoms of men today a man needs plenty of self-confidence and pushfulness if he is to be a success, but the opposite holds good for the kingdom of heaven. This had been already indicated in the Old Testament: Psalm 37, for instance, especially verse 11, plainly states it; yet the Lord here gives us a much enlarged view of this fact. He really sketches for us a moral picture of the godly remnant who will finally enter the kingdom. Eight things does He mention, beginning with poverty of spirit and ending with persecution, and there is a sequence in their order. Repentance produces poverty of spirit, and there all must start. Then comes the mourning and the meekness induced by a true sight of oneself, followed by a thirst for the righteousness which is only found in God. Then, filled with that, the saint comes out in God's own character — mercy, purity, peace. But the world does not want God or His character, hence persecution closes the list.

The blessing, contemplated in verses 3-10, is to be fully realized in the kingdom of heaven, when it is established on earth. In each beatitude save the last the godly are described in an impersonal way: in verses 11 and 12 the Lord speaks personally to His disciples. The "*they*" of verse 10 changes to the "*ye*" of verse 11; and now, speaking to His disciples, reward in heaven is promised. He knew that these disciples of His were to pass on into a new and heavenly order of things, and so while reaffirming old things in a clearer light, He began to intimate some of the new things that were soon to come. The change in these two verses is striking and helps to show the character of the "Sermon on the Mount," in which the Lord summarized His teaching, and related it to the old things given through Moses. In John 13-16, which we may call "The Sermon in the Upper Room," we find Him expanding His teaching and relating it to the full light He would give when the Holy Ghost was come.

In persecution for His sake His disciples were to be blessed, and they were to recognize this and rejoice. Naturally we shrink from persecution but history proves the truth of these words. Those who are identified with Christ fully and boldly have to suffer, but they are sustained and recompensed; whereas those, who try to avoid it by compromise, miss all the recompense, and are miserable. And further, it is when the disciple is persecuted by the world that most definitely he is "the salt of the earth," and "the light of the world." Salt preserves, and light illuminates. We can-

# MATTHEW

not be like healthful salt *in* the earth if we are *of* the earth. We cannot be as a light lifted up *in* the world if we are *of* the world. Now nothing more helps to keep us distinct and separate from the earth and world than persecution from the world, no matter what form it takes. Persecuted for Christ's sake, the disciple is real salty salt, and he also emits a maximum of light. Does not this word of our Lord reveal to us the secret of much of our feebleness?

Notice too that the light is supposed to shine in things practical, not merely in things theological. It is not that men recognize it in our clear or original teachings expressed in *words*, but rather in our acts and *works*. They should certainly hear our good words, but they must see our good works, if we are to be light to them. The word for "good" here does not mean exactly *benevolent* but rather *upright* or *honest*. Such actions find their source in the Father in heaven: they shed His light and glorify Him.

From verse 17 to the end of chapter 5 we find the Lord giving the connection between what He taught and that which had been given through Moses. He had not come to annul or destroy what had previously been given but rather to give the fulness of it—for such is the meaning here of the word, "fulfil." He corroborated and enforced all that had been said, as verses 18 and 19 show, and not one word that God had spoken was to be broken. And moreover as verse 20 shows, He insisted that the righteousness which the law demanded had in it a fulness which far exceeds anything known or recognized by the superficial scribes and Pharisees of His day. They rendered a technical obedience in ceremonial matters and ignored the real spirit of the law and the object which God had in view. Their righteousness did not lead to the kingdom.

Consequently He proceeded to show that there was a fulness of meaning in the law's demands that men had not suspected, referring to no less than six points as illustrating His theme. He spoke of the sixth and seventh commandments; then of the law as to divorce in Deuteronomy 24: 1; then as to oaths in Leviticus 19: 12; then of the law of retribution as given in Exodus 21: 24 and elsewhere; and lastly of such a sanctioning of hatred towards enemies as is found in Deuteronomy 23: 6.

As to the two commandments He quoted, His teaching evidently is that God has respect not only to the overt act but also to the inward disposition of the heart. What is prohibited is not merely the act of murder or adultery but the hatred and the lust of which the act is the expression. Judged by this standard, who is going to stand before the holy demands of Sinai? The "righteousness" of the scribe and Pharisee utterly collapses. Yet in both cases, having exposed this fact, He added some further instruction.

In verses 23-26, He showed two things of importance: first, no offering is acceptable to God if it be presented while there is unrighteousness manward. We cannot condone wrong towards man by professed piety towards God. Only when reconciliation has been effected can God be approached.

# MATTHEW

Then, second, if the matter which causes estrangement is carried to law, the law must take its course apart from mercy. The Lord's words here doubtless have prophetic significance. The Jewish nation was about to prosecute their case against Him, turning Him into their "adverse party," and it will issue in their condemnation. They have not even yet paid the uttermost farthing.

So with the next instance: here He shows us that any sacrifice is worthwhile, if it but leads to a deliverance from the hell that lies at the end.

In the third and fourth cases (31-37) He again shows us that what was ordained through Moses did not express the full mind of God. Both divorce and swearing were permitted, and thus the standard that men had to attain was not made too severe. Both matters are here set in a fuller light, and we see that only one thing is to be permitted to dissolve the marriage bond; and then that men's word should be so unequivocal and binding, that taking strong oaths, by this or that, is not needed. The man, who backs nearly every assertion by an oath, is a man whose simple word is not to be trusted.

Then again the law stipulated retribution of a very even kind for injury inflicted. It enjoined what we should call "tit for tat"; as also, while calling for love to one's neighbour, it permitted the hatred of an enemy. This the Lord reversed. He inculcated forbearance and the grace that gives, rather than the insistence upon one's rights; and also the love that will bless and do good to the enemy. And all this in order that His disciples may be quite distinct from the sinners of the world, and come out in the character of God Himself.

God is presented to them not as Jehovah, the Lawgiver, but as "your Father which is in heaven." That is to say, He is now presented in a new light. It is this that governs the teachings of the Lord here, for if we know Him in this new way, we discover Him to be marked by benevolence towards the unjust and the evil, and we are to be in our measure what He is. In the ministry of Jesus a new revelation of God was dawning, and it entailed a new standard of perfection. We are to come out practically as sons of our Father in heaven, for the perfection of a son is to be as the Father.

Eight times over does He say in this chapter, "I say unto you," and on six of these occasions the words are preceded by the word, "But," throwing His statement into contrast with what the law had previously said. We may well ask, "Who is this that quotes the holy law of God, and then calmly says, "*But I say unto you*"—so and so? He actually alters and enlarges the law; a thing that no prophet had ever dared to do! Does this not amount to terrible presumption, bordering on blasphemy?" Yes, indeed, and only one explanation will lift this charge from off Him. But that one explanation is true: *here we have the original Lawgiver, who once spoke from Sinai.* Now

# MATTHEW

He has come forth in Manhood as Emmanuel. Emmanuel has gone up another mountain, and now speaks not to a nation but to His disciples. He has every right to enlarge or amend His own law.

## CHAPTER 6

HAVING INTRODUCED HIS disciples to God in this new light at the end of chapter 5, we notice that all the teaching in chapter 6 is in reference to it. The expression "your Father," in slightly varying terms, occurs no less than twelve times. The teaching falls into four sections: almsgiving (1-4), prayer (5-15), fasting (16-18), earthly possessions and the necessary things of life (19-34). All four things touched the practical life of the Jew at many points, and their tendency and habit was to take up the first three in a technical, perfunctory way, and to lay all the stress and pay all the attention to item number four. The Lord Jesus sets them all in the light which His earlier words had shed. In chapter 5. He had shown them a God who deals with the inward motions of the heart as much as with outward actions, and yet that God is to be known as a heavenly Father. Still we notice how He repeats, "I say unto you." He does not teach as did the scribes, basing their assertions on the traditions of the ancients, but we have to take what He says, just because He says it.

If tradition rules us, we may easily get into just the position in which the Jews were found in regard to their alms-givings, their prayers and their fastings. To them it had all become a matter of outward observance, as meeting the eyes and ears of men. If we, on the other hand, lift our thoughts to the Father in heaven, who has an intimate concern as to us, all must become real and vital, and be done for His ear and eye. Three times over the Lord says of the mere formalist, "They have their reward." Their reward is the approbation and praise of their fellows. This they *have;* it is all in the present, and there is nothing more to come. He, who gives or prays or fasts unknown to men but known to God, will be rewarded openly in the day to come.

As to prayer, He teaches not only *secrecy* but *brevity*, which lies at the heart of *reality*. A man, who asks with intense reality and earnestness, inevitably goes straight to the point with the fewest words. He cannot possibly wander in a maze of circumlocutions. Verses 9-13 give us the model prayer, exactly suitable to the disciples in their then circumstances. There are six petitions. The first three have to do with God; His name, His kingdom, His will. The second three have to do with us; our bread, our debts, our deliverance. The heavenly Father and His claims must be first, and our needs second. The blessing of men on earth depends upon His will being done on earth, and that will only come to pass when His kingdom is established.

The forgiveness spoken of in verses 14 and 15 is connected with the debts of verse 12. In the heavenly Father's holy government of His children the unforgiving spirit comes under His chastisement. If someone commits an offence against us and we refuse to forgive, we shall miss God's governmental forgiveness. It is not a question here of forgiveness for eternity, since those to whom the Lord was speaking were disciples, with whom that great matter was already settled.

Very searching words as to earthly possessions are next spoken. No tendency is more deep-seated with all men than that of pursuing, grasping at, and laying up treasures upon earth, though they waste under the action of natural forces as well as the action of violent men. If we really know the Father in heaven, we shall find our treasure in heaven, and there our heart will be; and we have only to have the single eye to see this, and to see all else clearly. Then too our bodies become full of light: that is, we become luminous ourselves. We shall either be dominated by God or by mammon, for we cannot serve two masters. God and mammon are too utterly opposed for that.

Serving God, who is indeed a heavenly Father, we come under His watchful and kindly care. He knows all our needs and concerns Himself about them. We are impotent; unable to add a cubit to our height, or to array ourselves like the grass of the field. Our Father has infinite wisdom and power, and cares for the humblest creatures of His hand: we may have absolute confidence therefore in His loving care for us. Hence we are to be free from all anxious care. The men of the world are grasping at the treasure of this world which wastes so quickly, and they are full of care as to its preservation and use. We are to be resting in our Father's care and love, and therefore free of anxiety.

Now this is mainly negative. We are to be free of the anxious care which fills so many hearts; but this is in order that we may be free *to seek the kingdom of God*, and to seek it *first*. Instead of peering into tomorrow with apprehension, we are to be filling up *today* with the things of the kingdom, and that kingdom leads us in the ways of righteousness.

This was God's pleasure for the disciples who followed our Lord during His days upon earth: it is no less His pleasure for us who follow Him now that His work is fully accomplished and He is gone into the heavens. The spirit He thus inculcated was quite foreign to the religion of the Pharisee of His day, as also it is foreign to outward and worldly religion today.

## Chapter 7

THE LORD'S TEACHINGS, recorded in chapter 6, were designed to lead His disciples into such relations with *their Father in heaven*, that He would fill their thoughts, whether in regard to their almsgiving, their prayers, their fastings, or their attitude to the possessions and needs of this life. Chapter 7 opens with teachings that would regulate their dealings with *their brethren*, and even with *the ungodly*.

# MATTHEW

The judging of one's brother is a very deep-seated tendency in our heart. The judging of things, or of teaching, is not forbidden, but encouraged— as we see, for instance, in 1 Corinthians 2: 15; 10: 15 — but the judging of persons is forbidden. The church is called upon to judge those who are of it, in certain cases, as 1 Corinthians 5 and 6 show, but, apart from this, the judging of persons is a prerogative of the Lord. If, in spite of the Lord's forbidding, we indulge in it, two penalties are sure to follow, as He indicates here. First, we ourselves shall come under judgment, and have measured to us just what we have meted to others. Second, we shall drift into hypocrisy. Directly we start judging others we become blind to our own defects. The small defect in our brother becomes magnified to us, all unconscious that we have a big defect of a nature to impair our spiritual eyesight. The most profitable form of judgment for each of us is *self-judgment*.

Verse 6 has in view the ungodly, insensible of good and unclean in their tastes. Things that are holy and precious are not for them; and if foolishly we present them to them, they are despised and we may suffer their violence. It is right that we should be givers of God's holy things; but not to such.

But if we are to be *givers*, we must first *receive*, and of this verses 7-11 speak. To receive we must draw near to God — asking, seeking, knocking. A response from our Father is certain. If we ask for necessary things we shall get them, for He will not give us instead something worthless like a stone, or injurious like a serpent. We may rest assured that He will give us "good things," for His Fatherhood is of heaven. His standard therefore will not fall below that of earthly fatherhood. We may apply Isaiah 55: 9 to this, and say that as the heavens are higher than the earth so are His Fatherly thoughts higher than our thoughts. We of necessity cannot come up to His standard. Hence in verse 12 the Lord did not then demand of His disciples a standard above that set by the law and the prophets.

In verses 13 and 14 the Lord evidently looked beyond His disciples to the crowd. Before them there were the alternatives of the broad way and the narrow way, of destruction and life. We cannot say that the grace of God is narrow, for it has come forth for all men; it is the way of self-judgment and repentance which is so narrow. Few find that way, and but few proclaim it. The majority of the preachers prefer to prophesy smoother things.

The warning against false prophets follows. They are to be known not by their fine words but by their fruits. Fruit is the result and crowning expression of life, and it reveals *the character* of the life that it consummates. The false prophet has a false life, which must reveal itself in false fruit.

But there are not only false prophets but false disciples—those who loudly profess allegiance to the Lord, but the vital link of faith is lacking. Vital faith, as the Apostle James tells us, must express itself in works.

# MATTHEW

Everyone, who really comes under the lordship of Christ in faith, must of necessity be set to do the will of the Father in heaven, whom He presented. Judas Iscariot furnishes us with a terrible example of verses 22 and 23. Evidently he performed works of power along with the other disciples, but it was proved at last that no link of real faith ever existed and he was but a worker of iniquity.

And therefore the Lord closed His words with the parable of the two houses. Both builders, the wise and the foolish, were hearers of the words of Jesus but only one was a doer of them—and that one was the wise man. The parable does not teach salvation by works, but salvation by *that living faith which leads to the works*. If we cast our minds back over the Sermon on the Mount we shall realize at once that nothing but genuine faith in Him could induce anyone to do the things which He taught. We shall also realize how fully His teachings verified His own word in chapter 5: 17. He has given us the fulness of the law and the prophets, while adding fresh light as to the Father in heaven; thus preparing the way for the fuller light of grace that was to dawn as the fruit of His death and resurrection. The authority with which He announced these things was what struck the people. The scribes relied upon the earlier Rabbinic teachings, while He spoke the things that He knew from and with God.

## Chapter 8

AFTER THESE THREE chapters filled with His teachings, Matthew gives us two chapters occupied with His works of power. It was not enough for Him to enunciate the principles of the kingdom, He displayed the power of the kingdom in a variety of striking ways. There are five main illustrations of that power in chapter 8, and again in chapter 9. In each case we may say that the miracle the Lord performed in connection with human bodies, or with visible and tangible things, was a proof of how He could deal with the deeper-seated things of the soul.

The first case is that of the leper; a picture of sin in its *defiling, corrupting* power. The poor man was convinced of the power of Jesus, but not fully persuaded of His grace. Yet the Lord instantly delivered him by His touch and His word of power. Only five words, "I will; be thou clean," and the thing was done; a witness to the priests—if the man did as he was told—that the power of God was present amongst them.

The second case was that of the Gentile centurion and his servant; a case illustrating the *impotence* which is induced by sin. Here again is emphasized the power of His word. The centurion himself emphasized it, for he knew the power of an authoritative word as exemplified in the Roman military system. The rank of a centurion was not a high one, yet those under him at once obeyed his instructions, and his faith discovered in Jesus One whose word could accomplish the miraculous. The Lord acknowledged his faith

# MATTHEW

as great, and beyond anything He had found in Israel: He spoke the needed word and the servant was healed. He also prophesied that many a Gentile from a distance would enter the kingdom with the fathers of Israel while those who had considered it theirs by prescriptive right would be cast into outer darkness.

The third case is that of Peter's mother-in-law. Here His touch instantly cured her; there is no record of His having spoken a word. It might be His touch and His word, as with the leper; or His word only, as with the centurion's servant; or His touch only: the result in each case was the same — instantaneous deliverance. There was no convalescence from the results of the fever; she at once arose and served others. Sin induces *a fevered state of mind and soul,* but His touch dispels it.

In verses 16 and 17 we have first, a summary of His many works of power and mercy at eventide; and second, the quotation from Isaiah 53, which reveals to us the way and spirit in which He did these things. The words quoted have been used erroneously by some as though they meant that on the cross He bore our sicknesses, and thus the believer never ought to be ill. The right application is found here. He did not relieve men without feeling their sorrows and sicknesses. He bore in His spirit the weight of the very evils that He dismissed by His power.

The incidents recorded in verses 18-22 show us that not only our deliverance but our discipleship also must be at the call of His authoritative word. A certain scribe volunteered to follow without having received His call. The Lord at once showed him what would be involved in following such a One as Himself, for He was the homeless Son of Man. But conversely, His call is sufficient. It was one who was already a disciple who wished to put an earthly duty in the first place. The call and claim of the Master must be absolutely supreme. He had disciples who owned His claim and followed Him, as verse 23 shows, and they gave Him a place to lay His head in their ship. Yet, even so, following Him led them into trouble.

This brings us to the fourth of these striking cases—the storm on the lake; typical of how *the power of the devil lashes into fury the unrestful sea of humanity.* It was all nothing to Him and He peacefully slept. But at the cry of the disciples He arose and asserted His command of these mighty forces of nature. As a man commands his hound, and the obedient dog lies down at his feet, so did wind and sea lie down at the word of their Maker.

Arrived at the other side He was confronted by two men who were dominated by demonic servants of the devil. One of these was a special stronghold held by a whole legion of demons, as Mark and Luke show us; though evidently there were two, and thus a sufficient witness was borne to *His power over the enemy.* The demons knew Him, and also knew that they had no power to resist His word: hence they asked permission to enter the herd of unclean swine, that would never have been there had Israel been walking according to the law. As far as the record goes, Jesus spoke but one word—"Go!" In result the men were delivered and the swine destroyed.

Thus far we have considered the power of the Lord: before leaving the chapter let us notice the response on the side of men. There is a striking contrast between the "great faith" of the centurion and the "little faith" of the disciples in the storm. Great faith was marked by two things seen in verse 8. He said, "*I am not worthy*," condemning himself, and thus ruling himself out of the question. He also said, "*Speak the word only*," in addressing the Lord. *He had no opinion of himself, but he had a great opinion of Him*—so great that he was prepared to accredit His word without any support from without. Some folk want to have the word of the Lord supported by feelings, or by reason, or by experience; but great faith is produced by discovering in Jesus so great a Person that His naked word is enough.

With the disciples it was just the opposite. They were thinking altogether of themselves. It was, "*Save US: WE perish*." When Jesus calmed the storm they were astounded, saying, "What manner of man is this?" Yes, what manner indeed? Had they really known Him, they would have been surprised if He had not asserted His power. The fact was, *they had big thoughts of themselves and but little thoughts of Him;* and this is little faith. So they marvelled as He acted; whereas in the case of the centurion Jesus marvelled at his faith. In spite of their little faith, however, they loved and followed Him.

At the beginning of the chapter we see *defective faith* on the part of the leper. He clearly saw the power of Jesus, yet hardly apprehended His willingness. At the end of the chapter we see men with *no faith at all*. It did not weigh with them that demons had been dispossessed, for a spiritual deliverance meant little to them. What mattered to them was the loss of their pigs. Jesus they did not understand, but pigs they did understand! Apt figure of men of the world who have an eye for any material gain, but no heart for Christ. They evidently got nothing, but all the others did. Do not miss the delightful fact that defective faith and little faith got the blessing just as really and fully as great faith. The blessing is not according to the quality or quantity of faith, but according to His heart of grace.

## Chapter 9

THE GERGESENE PEOPLE not desiring His presence, He again crossed the sea, and was at once met by further cases of human need. In chapter 9 we are shown how He wrought deliverance for the man sick of the palsy, the diseased woman, the daughter of Jairus, the two blind men, and the dumb man possessed with a demon—again a five-fold exhibition of the power of the kingdom that had drawn near in His presence.

# MATTHEW

In the first of these cases the Lord plainly stated the connection that existed between the miracle He wrought for the body and the corresponding spiritual blessing; the one easily seen, the other unseen. In response to the faith of the men who brought the paralytic, the Lord went straight to the root of the mischief and pronounced forgiveness of sins. When this was challenged, He proved His power to forgive by His power to transform the man's bodily condition. His critics could neither forgive the sins nor cure the palsy. He could do both. The crowd saw it and glorified God.

In verses 9-17 we get the incident concerning Matthew himself. The transaction recorded in verse 9 may almost be called a miracle by any who are aware of the binding power exerted on the human mind by money. Matthew was actually seated in his tax office, engaged in the congenial task of receiving the cash, when he heard two words from the lips of Jesus— "Follow Me." The "ME" became so great in his eyes that the money was displaced, and its charm broken — a wonderful thing indeed! He arose and followed Jesus.

It was in *his* house that Jesus sat at meat with publicans and sinners and His disciples; so now he was disbursing money instead of receiving it. The other evangelists tell us this, though Matthew, with becoming modesty, does not mention it. The whole proceeding outraged the Pharisees, but this gave occasion for the concise statement as to His mission. The Pharisees had overlooked the word of the Lord through Hosea, that He preferred the exercise of mercy to the offering of ceremonial sacrifices—a word which many a modern Pharisee overlooks—and they were ignorant of His mission to the spiritually sick, in calling sinners to repentance. Had He come to call "the righteous," the Pharisees no doubt would have come forward in crowds; only to be rejected to a man, since "the righteous" according to the Divine standard do not exist.

The question raised by John's disciples led to a declaration which supplemented this. Having called sinners to repentance He attached them to Himself as "the children of the bridechamber," and led them into a position of liberty, as contrasted with legal observances. In the coming days of His absence there would be another kind of fasting. But there could be no real mixture between that which He newly brought and the old law system. The new wine of the kingdom must be contained in new skins. If the attempt is made to restrain the expansive grace of the kingdom within legal forms, the result is disastrous. The grace is lost and the forms are ruined.

Even while He spake these things other incidents supervened, which in some measure serve as an illustration of His words. On His way to raise the daughter of Jairus, there intervened the aggressive faith of the diseased woman. She was one of the sick ones who needed the Physician. Her action of faith held up the programme, but what was that to the One who delights in mercy and not sacrifice? Her faith was acknowledged, and she was instantly whole. Then when the programme was resumed, and the house of

# MATTHEW

Jairus reached, the prescribed, usual course of affairs was brushed aside by Jesus. The bottles of Jewish custom were quickly broken by the power of His grace. He said, *"Give place,"* and everything had indeed to give place to the power of life which He wielded: and the dead child was restored.

The cry of the two blind men (verse 27) had in it the accents of faith. They recognized Him as the promised Son of David. He recognized their faith, and challenged it. They responded and affiirmed their belief in His power. Hence, in this case, He granted their prayer, *according to their faith*. He knew their faith was real; and we know it to have been so, for at once their eyes were opened. Let us each ask ourselves, if my requests are to be answered according to *my* faith; *what shall I get?*

Sin has reduced man to helplessness; it has rendered him spiritually diseased and dead and blind; but it has also rendered him dumb towards God. Bound by the devil, he cannot speak. When the man, in verse 32, was brought to Jesus the demonic power which lay at the root was dealt with. The cause being reached, the effect at once disappeared. The man spoke, and the crowd marvelled. They had never before seen or heard of such deliverances as were wrought by the power of the kingdom in grace. Only the Pharisees were insensible to this; and not only insensible but wholly evil, for unable to deny the power, they wilfully evaded its force by attributing it to the devil himself.

The chapter closes with the wonderful fact that their wicked rejection of His grace did not shut up His bowels of compassion. He went on preaching the gospel of the kingdom, and showing its power in miracles of healing in all the cities and villages; and the sight of the needy multitudes only moved Him to deep compassion—the compassion of the heart of God. The crowd had no shepherd, and there was a great harvest yet to be reaped. He prepared to send forth labourers to the work.

## CHAPTER 10

AT THE CLOSE of the previous chapter the Lord told His disciples to pray for the sending forth of labourers. This chapter opens with His calling the twelve and commissioning them to go forth. They themselves were to be the answer to their prayer! Not infrequently this is the case. When we pray for this or that to be done in the Lord's service, often His answer to us would be in effect, "Then you are the ones to do it." Now for any commission to be effective, there must be the people selected, the power conferred, and the right procedure indicated.

This chapter is occupied with just these three things. In verses 2-4, we get the names of the twelve chosen disciples; and in verse 1 we read how Jesus conferred the necessary power upon them. This power was effective in two spheres, the spiritual and the physical. Unclean spirits had to obey them, and all kinds of bodily evils disappeared at their word. From verse 5 to the end of the chapter we have the record of the instructions He gave, so that they might proceed rightly on their mission.

The first item of instruction concerned *the sphere of their service* — neither Gentiles nor Samaritans, but the lost sheep of Israel only. This at once reveals decisively that the gospel today does not go forth under this commission. In the service of a false theory verse 6 has been wrested into meaning that they were to go to Israelites scattered amongst the nations. The word "lost" however means spiritually lost. If Jeremiah 50 be turned to, and verses 6 and 17 consulted, it will be seen that Israel is both "lost" and "scattered." They are lost because caused to go astray by their shepherds—spiritually lost. They are scattered by the action of the kings of Assyria and Babylon — geographically scattered. This distinction in the use of the two words seems to be observed through Scripture. The disciples never went outside the land while Christ was on earth, but they did preach to the spiritually lost Jews that were around them.

In verse 7 *their message* is summed up in seven words. It agrees exactly with that preached by John the Baptist (3: 2), and by the Lord Himself (4: 17), save that here the word, "Repent," is omitted. It was a very simple message, hardly allowing of much amplification or variety. They could not preach things not yet accomplished; but the predicted King was present in His own land, and hence the kingdom was nigh them. That they announced It was the glad tidings of the kingdom, and they were to support what they said by showing the power of the kingdom in bringing healing and deliverance gratuitously.

Moreover they were to discard all the ordinary provision of a prudent traveller, and so be manifestly dependent upon their Master for all their needs; and in entering any place they were to seek out the "worthy," that is, those who feared the Lord, and who manifested their reception of the Master by the reception of His servants. They were to render testimony against those who did not receive Him, and who consequently refused them and their words; and the responsibility of such would be far greater than that of Sodom and Gomorrah.

Next He plainly warned them that they were going to meet with opposition, rejection and persecution, and they are instructed as to their attitude in the presence of these things. This occupies verses 16-39. In going forth amongst men they would be as sheep in the midst of wolves; that is, they would be as their Master in *position*, and they were to be like Him also in *character*—wise and harmless. When accused before rulers they were to rest in God as their Father, and not concern themselves in preparing their defence, since in the hour of their need the Spirit of their Father would speak in and through them. Martyrdom in some cases would lie before them, and in all cases they would have to face hatred of a type that would override all natural affection. For those not martyred endurance to the end would mean salvation.

# MATTHEW

What "the end" signifies is shown in the next verse (23)—the coming of the Son of man. In chapter 24: 3, 6, 13, 14, we again have the Lord speaking of "the end," with a similar significance, for there it is "the end of the age." This mission then, which the Lord was inaugurating, is to extend to His second coming, and barely be completed even then. As verse 6 had indicated, the cities of Israel were the field to be covered while they were persecuted, and their endurance would be crowned by salvation at His coming. As we look back it looks as if there has been some failure in these predictions. How can we account for it?

The explanation evidently is that this testimony to the nearness of the kingdom has been suspended and will be resumed at the time of the end. The disciples are viewed as representative men, and what is said applied to them at that moment and will apply to others who will be in a similar position at the end of the age. The kingdom, as presented at that moment in Christ in person, was rejected, and consequently the testimony was *withdrawn*, as we see in chapter 16: 20. It will be *resumed* when the outgathering of the church is completed; and barely carried to its finish when the Son of Man comes to receive and establish the kingdom, as had been predicted in Daniel 7.

Meanwhile the disciple must expect to be treated as his Master, and yet he need have no fear. He will be denounced and maligned and even killed by men; but in verses 26-33, the Lord mentions three sources of encouragement. First, *light* shall shine upon everything, and all the malignings of men be dispersed. The disciple's business is to let the light shine now in his testimony. Second, there is the intimate *care* of God, descending to the minutest detail. Third, there is the *reward* of being publicly confessed by the Lord before the Father in heaven. Nothing but faith will enable any of us to appreciate and welcome the light, to rely upon the care, and to value the praise of God more than the praise of men.

Verse 28 is worthy of special note, for it very definitely teaches that the soul is not subject to death, as is the body. God can destroy both soul and body in hell; but the word for "destroy" is different from the word for "kill," and is one meaning to cause to perish, or to ruin, and has in it no thought of annihilation. The exact words, "the immortality of the soul" do not occur in Scripture, but here are words of our Lord which assert that solemn fact. The words of verse 34 may seem at first sight to clash with such statements as we have in Luke 1: 79; 2: 14; or Acts 10: 36. But there is no real discrepancy. God approached men in Christ with a message of peace, but He was rejected. At this point in Matthew's Gospel His rejection is coming into view, and hence He declares the solemn fact that the immediate effect of His approach is going to be strife and warfare. Peace on earth will be established by Him at His second advent, and this the angels foresaw and celebrated when first He came. Peace is indeed the *ultimate* thing, but the cross was the *immediate* thing; and if He was about to take

# MATTHEW

up the cross then His disciples must be prepared for a sword, and for the losing of their lives for His sake. That loss however was going to mean ultimate gain.

The closing verses show that the reception of the unpopular disciples would be in effect the reception of their unpopular Master, and even of God Himself. Any service thus rendered, even so small a thing as the giving of a cup of cold water, will not fail of a reward in the day to come.

## CHAPTER 11

THE SENDING OUT of the twelve did not mean that the Lord suspended His personal labours, as the first verse shows; and all this activity stirred up John in his prison. We can well imagine that he expected the great Personage, whom he had announced, to do something on his behalf; yet here He was, delivering all kinds of unworthy folk from their diseases and troubles, and apparently neglecting His forerunner. Tested thus, John's faith wavered a little. The Lord's answer to John took the form of further testimony to His own gracious activities, showing that He was indeed fulfilling the prophecy of Isaiah 61: 1; and happy was he who was not stumbled by His humiliation and the absence of the outward glory that will characterize His second advent.

Then Jesus bore witness to John. No oscillating reed nor man of luxury was he; but more than a prophet, even the messenger predicted by Malachi, who should prepare the way of the Lord. Moreover John was the "Elijah" of the first advent, and he marked the end of an epoch. The dispensation of law and prophets ran up to him, and from his day onward the kingdom of heaven was open, if there was the "violence" or vigour of faith to gain an entrance. When the kingdom arrives visibly, there will not be the same need for such vigour of faith. All this showed how great a man John was, nevertheless the least inside the kingdom would have a position greater than this great man, who prepared the way but did not live to enter himself. John's moral greatness was unsurpassed, though many of much less moral weight would be greater as to outward position.

From speaking of John, his greatness and the position he had been given as regards his ministry, the Lord passed to deal with the indifference of the people. They had listened to the forceful preaching of John, and now had heard the Lord and seen His works of power; yet neither one nor the other had really affected them.

They were like petulant children who would not be persuaded to join in the play. There had been a note of severity in John's ministry, but they showed no sign of lamenting in repentance: Jesus had come full of grace and of the joy of deliverance, yet they manifested no real signs of gladness. Instead they discovered ways of discrediting both.

# MATTHEW

The taunt they flung at John was a bare-faced lie, whilst their cry against the Lord had in it some element of truth, for He was in the highest sense "a Friend of publicans and sinners." They meant it however in the lowest possible sense; for when an adversary throws out accusations in order to discredit, he usually finds half a truth more serviceable than a downright falsehood. So long as we walk in obedience with a good conscience, we need not fear the mud which adversaries love to sling. John, amongst the greatest of prophets, and the Son of Man Himself had to endure it. Those who were the children of wisdom were not taken in by these slanders. They justified wisdom, and thereby condemned the adversaries. The same fact was stated in other words when Jesus said, "Ye believe not, because ye are not of My sheep . . . My sheep hear My voice" (John 10: 26, 27).

At this point we find the Lord accepting the fact that the cities of Galilee, where most of His mighty works had been done, had definitely refused Him. There had been rendered to them such a testimony as Tyre and Sidon, and the land of Sodom, had never had. Now, the greater the privilege, the greater the responsibility, and the severer the judgment, when the privilege is despised and the responsibility broken. A sad fate lay in store for Chorazin, Bethsaida and Capernaum. Their inhabitants at that time have to face the day of judgment, and the very cities themselves have been so obliterated, that their sites have been a matter of argument until today. They had rejected "Jesus Christ, the Son of David, the Son of Abraham" (1: 1), and consequently the kingdom as vested in Him.

But at that moment of crisis Jesus reposed upon *the purpose* of the Father and upon *the perfection of His ways* — the ways by which His purpose is to be reached. The people whose indifference the Lord had been deploring were just "the wise and prudent" according to worldly standards; but then there were the "babes," and to these, not those, the Father had revealed the things of all importance at that moment. This was the way that He was pleased to take, and Jesus accepted it with thanksgiving. This ever has been God's way, and is God's way today, as we see in 1 Corinthians 1: 21-31. God's purpose will not fail. The kingdom as presented in Christ was about to be rejected: God will establish the kingdom in another way altogether, even while we wait for the establishment of it in manifested power and glory. There will be found those who come under the yoke of the Son, and thus they will enjoy the rest of the kingdom in their souls.

The purpose of God is that all things shall rest in the hands of the Son. To this end all things have already been delivered to Him. In the day to come we shall see Him dispose of all things in mighty, discriminating judgment: today He is dispensing the knowledge of the Father. The Son is so truly God, that there are in Him unfathomable depths, known only to the Father. The Father is beyond all human knowledge, but the Son knows Him, and has come forth as His great Revealer. It is as the Revealer of the Father that He says, "Come unto Me . . . and I will give you rest." He was

# MATTHEW

at rest in the knowledge of the Father, of His love, His purpose, His ways; and into that rest He conducts those who come to Him.

His invitation was specially addressed to "all ye that labour and are heavy laden," that is, those who were sincerely and piously attempting to keep the law, which was as Peter said, "a yoke ... which neither our fathers nor we were able to bear" (Acts 15: The 10). more sincere, the more heavy laden they must have been, beneath that yoke. So the Lord's words were addressed to "wisdom's children," to the "babes;" in other words, to the godly remnant in the midst of the unbelieving mass of the people. They might now exchange the burdensome yoke of the law for the light and easy yoke of Christ. They would learn of Him things that the law could never teach them.

And moreover He would teach them in a new way. He exemplified the things that He taught. Meekness and lowliness of heart is needed if the subject place is to be taken and maintained; and these things were perfectly seen in Him. He was the Son, "yet learned He obedience" and that obedience having been carried unto death, He has "become the Author of eternal Salvation unto all them that obey Him" (Heb. 5: 8, 9). In our Gospel we see the obedient One calling us into obedience to Himself, an obedience which is not burdensome and which leads into rest. "Rest for your souls" was proposed as the result of a faithful walk in the "old paths" of the law (see Jer. 6: 16), but that rest was never attained by men. The only way to reach it was that made known by the Son, who had come to reveal the Father. The Father must be known if His purpose was to be achieved.

## CHAPTER 12

FROM THE HEIGHTS reached in the last chapter, we descend into the depths of human folly and blindness as displayed by the Pharisees. In this chapter we see Him very definitely rejected by the leaders of the Jews, and not merely by the cities of Galilee. In the first two instances the contention raged round the sabbath. The Lord defended the action of His disciples on at least four grounds (ver. 3-8).

When David, God's anointed king, was in rejection, his needs took precedence over a matter of tabernacle order, and his followers were associated with him in this. David's greater Son was now refused, so should not the needs of His disciples be met, even if it infringed their sabbath regulations? But, second, the temple had taken precedence over the sabbath, for the priests had always worked on the sabbaths; and Jesus claimed to be greater than the temple. God was indeed in Christ in infinitely fuller measure than He ever had been in the temple. Third, there was that word about mercy in Hosea 6, to which previously He had referred; that applied in this case. And, fourth, Jesus claimed that as Son of Man He was Lord of the sabbath: in other words, the sabbath had no binding power over Him. He was its Master, and He could dispose of it as He saw fit.

In the second case the Lord answered their quibble by an appeal to their own practice. They had no compunction in setting to work on the sabbath in order to show mercy to a sheep. Who were they then to object to His showing mercy to a man on the sabbath? The Lord promptly showed that mercy; yet such was the obdurate hardness of their hearts, that His mercy only stirred within them thoughts of murder. They decided from that moment upon His death.

In the presence of this, Jesus began to withdraw the witness that they were preparing to quench in death; charging those to whom He still extended mercy that they should not make Him known. Matthew quotes the beautiful prophecy from Isaiah 42, showing how it was fulfilled in Him. Some of it has yet to be fulfilled at His second advent, for He has not yet sent forth judgment unto victory. But He did meet the bitter hatred and rejection that confronted Him at His first advent without strife or cry or the crushing of His foes. Nothing is more worthless than a bruised reed, and nothing more repulsive to the nostrils than smoking flax. The Pharisees were like both these, but He will not break and quench them till the time of judgment arrives. Meanwhile in His Name the Gentiles are learning to trust.

In Isaiah 32 the advents are not distinguished, as is so often the case in Old Testament scripture, but now we can see clearly how both are involved. At this time Jesus came as the vessel of mercy, and not to exercise judgment. Rejected by the leaders of His people, He would turn to the Gentiles and let mercy flow out to them. This is plainly intimated here.

Is not this of immense interest to us, seeing we are amongst the Gentiles who have trusted in His Name?

On the part of the Pharisees we have seen hatred rising to the point of murder; and we have seen on the part of Jesus such meekness and lowliness of heart as led Him to suspend all action in judgment and accept their evil without strife or protest. Matthew now records the case of a man rendered both blind and dumb by a demon. Jesus gave him sight and speech by casting out the demon, and the people, greatly wondering, began to think of Him as the true Son of David. Seeing this, the Pharisees were aroused to desperate measures, and they repeated yet more boldly the blasphemous assertion that the power He wielded was Satan's. Their earlier blasphemy (see 9: 34), passed unanswered, but this time the Lord accepted their challenge.

In the first place, He met them on the ground of reason. Their accusation involved an absurdity, for if Satan cast out Satan he would destroy his own kingdom. It also involved an aspersion on their own sons, who professed to cast out demons. But secondly, He gave them the true explanation: He was here in manhood acting by the Spirit of God, and thus He had bound Satan, the strong man, and now was taking from beneath his

# MATTHEW

power those who had been but his "goods." This was another plain proof that the kingdom was in their very midst.

It also brought things to a very plain issue, that not to be definitely with Christ and gathering with Him, was to be against Him and scattering. This led the Lord to unmask the real nature of their sin, which was beyond the pale of forgiveness, in spite of the fact that all manner of sin may be forgiven. In the Son of Man God was presented to them objectively: they might speak against Him, and yet be brought by the work of the Spirit to repentance, and so be forgiven. But to blaspheme the Holy Spirit, by whom alone is repentance and faith wrought in the soul, is to put oneself in a hopeless position. It is to thrust from one both repentance and faith, to bolt and bar the only door that leads into salvation.

The sad fact was that these Pharisees were utterly corrupt trees, a generation of vipers, and their evil words had been just the expression of the evil of their hearts. In verses 33-37, the Lord unmasked their hearts in this way, and declared they would be judged by their words. If men will have to render account of even *idle* words in the day of judgment, what will *evil* words such as these merit? In that day by their words they would be utterly condemned.

By their request, recorded in verse 38, the Pharisees revealed that they were morally blind and insensible as well as corrupt and evil. Ignoring, whether ignorantly or wilfully, all the signs that had been given, they asked for a sign. We noticed five signs in chapter 8 and five in chapter 9, besides those recorded in our chapter. Being evil and adulterous they *could not perceive* the plainest sign, so no sign should be given but the greatest of all—His own death and resurrection, which had been typified in the remarkable history of Jonah. The generation which was refusing the Lord had been in the presence of signs, more than all others before them. Jonah and his preaching had been a sign to the Ninevites, and at an earlier date Solomon and his wisdom had been a sign to the queen of the south, and striking results had been achieved. Yet Jesus was rejected.

And yet Jesus stands infinitely above all of them. In our chapter He speaks of Himself as "greater than the temple," "greater than Jonas," "greater than Solomon." Also, it is to be observed that He pointed out how both Jonah and Solomon had been signs *to Gentiles*. Though servants of God in Israel, their fame went out northward to Nineveh and southward to Sheba respectively. These Gentiles had ears to hear and hearts to appreciate, yet the Pharisaic Jews surrounding our Lord were blind and bitterly opposed, to the extent of committing this unpardonable sin.

What would be the end of that unbelieving generation? The Lord tells us in verses 43-45. The evil spirit of idolatry, which had swayed them in their earlier history, had indeed departed from them. Christ, the Revealer of the true God, should have occupied the house; but Him they were rejecting. The end of this would be the return of that evil spirit with seven others worse than himself. Under Antichrist in the last days this word of our Lord will be fulfilled. The unbelieving race of Jews will worship the image of the beast, and be enslaved by Satanic powers of awful potency. When judgment falls, the apostate Jews on whom it will fall, will be worse than all that have preceded them. We believe that the same thing will be true of Gentile races also.

The chapter closes with the significant incident concerning the mother and brethren of Jesus. As a matter of fact they came in a wrong spirit, as is seen by consulting Mark 3: 21 and 31. That, however, is not the point here. The Lord took occasion by their intervention to disclaim a merely natural relationship, and to show that what was going to count henceforth was relationship of a spiritual nature. In this figurative way He set aside for the time the old link formed by His having come as the Son of Abraham, the Son of David, and showed that the link now to be recognized was that formed by obedience to the will of God. The Jews as a people had rejected Him, and He now disowns them. He owns His disciples as being in true relation with Him, for feeble though they were, they had begun to do the will of His Father in heaven.

## Chapter 13

This chapter opens with the fact that He proceeded to suit His actions to His words. He left the narrow confines of the house, and went forth to the open air and the sea—the sea being symbolic of the nations. There He began to teach the multitude from a boat, using the parabolic method. This chapter contains seven parables. We will begin by noticing the expression He used in verse 52, "things new and old," for this will help us as to the drift of the parables. Old things are mentioned, the kingdom of heaven for instance, which was predicted in Daniel, but new things predominate. We will point out four new things before looking at the parables in any detail. First, He adopted *a new method of teaching*—the parabolic. The new method struck the disciples, as verse 10 shows. Second, He indicated in the first parable *a new method of Divine working*. Instead of looking for fruit as the result of God's husbandry through law and prophets, He was going to sow the Word to produce fruit. Third, He makes known developments which give *a new meaning* to the term, "kingdom of heaven." Fourth, He utters *new revelations*, opening His mouth to utter things, "kept secret from the foundation of the world," as verse 35 says.

The first parable stands by itself, and except we understand it we shall not understand the others. The great work now was to be the sowing of the "word of the kingdom" in the hearts of men. This does not accord any special place to the Jew. In verse 19, Jesus said, "When *any one* heareth," so that opened the door to each hearer of the word, whoever he might be. What was needed was to hear with understanding. Militating against that

# MATTHEW

are the activities of the devil, the fickleness of the flesh, and the cares and riches of the world. But the word is received by some, and fruit produced in varying measures. This method of Divine working is still in vogue. It characterizes the day in which we live. Christianity is based not upon what it finds in man but upon what it produces by the power of God.

The disciples were puzzled by the change to a parable. Their enquiry elicited from the Lord the fact that He adopted this way of teaching so that the mysteries or secrets, of the kingdom of heaven might be hidden from the unbelieving mass and only revealed to those who believed. Those who unbelievingly had rejected the Lord had closed their eyes to the truth. Now He spoke in parables so that they might be left in their unbelief. Thus Isaiah's prophecy was to be fulfilled in them. The same prophecy is quoted by John in his Gospel—12: 40. It is quoted also by Paul for a third and last time in the closing chapter of Acts. It was just the working of the government of God. For believers the parables are very instructive, and, as verse 17 says, they helped to bring to the knowledge of the disciples things desired but never seen by prophets and righteous men in earlier days.

Even the disciples however needed the explanation which the Lord furnished, in order to understand the parable of the sower; and, this given to them, Jesus proceeded to utter three more parables in the ears of the multitude. Only when the crowd had been dismissed and He had retired into a house with His disciples did He furnish the explanation of the second parable. It is evident therefore that the first four were uttered in public, and deal with the outer manifestations of the kingdom; whereas the last three were spoken privately, and deal with its inner and more hidden reality.

The first parable, as we have indicated, gives us the key to all the rest; showing us that the kingdom is to be established as the result of the sowing of "the word of the kingdom," and not as the fruit of obedience to the existing law of Moses. This fact established, all the other parables tell us what the kingdom of heaven *is like*, and each of these six similitudes presents features which could not have been foreseen in the light of Old Testament scripture. There the kingdom in its glory had been foreseen, but here we find it is to assume a new character, in which it will exist before the glory arrives.

The second parable, that of the wheat and tares, shows that while the kingdom exists through the sowing of good seed by the Son of Man, the devil will also be a sower and his children will be found amongst the children of the kingdom. It sets forth the fact that until the hour of judgment arrives, when the Son of Man shall purge all the evil out of His kingdom, there is going to be, in one word, *mixture*. In this parable, "the field is the world" (38), be it remembered; so there is no thought here of the church being a place where the children of the wicked one must needs be tolerated. "The kingdom" indicates a sphere wider than "the church," and there is no possibility of disentangling things in the world till the Lord comes. Then by angelic service at the end of the age the evil will be consigned to the burning.

The wheat is to be gathered into the barn. In His explanation the Lord goes further, and speaks of the righteous shining forth *as the sun* in their Father's kingdom. By using this figure the Lord put the saints in a heavenly position, so we are not surprised when later we find the heavenly calling fully revealed. It is interesting to notice the Lord speaking in this parable of "the kingdom of heaven," "the kingdom of the Son of Man," and "the kingdom of your Father;" showing that the kingdom is one however it may be designated. It has however different departments—if we may so speak—and hence may be viewed in different ways.

The third parable, that of the mustard seed, shows that the kingdom is to be marked by *development*. It will grow and become imposing before men's eyes, but become a shelter for agents of evil—for in the first parable, when explaining "the fowls," the Lord said, "then cometh the wicked one;" and we know how Satan works through human agents.

The fourth parable, comprised in just one verse (33), shows that, as we might expect from what we have just seen, the kingdom will be gradually *permeated by corruption*. In Scripture leaven is used consistently as a figure of what is corrupting. This is the one place where some are wishful to make it mean what is good. But that is because they have a system of interpretation which demands such a meaning. The gospel, they think, is going to permeate the world with good. This sudden violation of the meaning of leaven should have warned them that their thoughts which demand it are wrong.

Here, then, the Lord is teaching us that the kingdom as viewed by man will be in such a form that it is marked by mixture, by development into an imposing institution in the earth, where agents of evil will find a home, and consequently there will be a process of permeation by the evil. He spoke as a prophet indeed, for just what He predicted has come to pass in that sphere on earth, where professedly the rule of Heaven is owned.

But in the privacy of the house the Lord added to His disciples three further parables. Here we have the kingdom from the Divine standpoint, and if our eyes are anointed we too shall see in it what God sees. First, we shall see that there is something of *hidden value*. The "field" here is still the world, and the Lord has bought it, with a view to securing the hidden treasure in it. This buying must be distinguished from redeeming, for evil men may go so far as "denying the Lord that *bought* them" (2 Peter 2: 1). They were bought but not redeemed, or they would not go on to "swift destruction." The kingdom is established that the hidden treasure in the world may be secured.

Again there is the parable of the one pearl of great price. In the kingdom as it exists today, there is to be found and purchased this object, marked in the Divine eye by *unique perfection*. Here doubtless we have in figure that

# MATTHEW

which the Lord is going to speak of in chapter 16, as "My church." True He has bought the field, but also He has bought the pearl, and in both cases He represents Himself as selling all He has to do so. He yielded up everything to achieve His object, in the spirit of 2 Corinthians 8: 9. We cannot purchase Christ by the selling of our worthless all. It is what He has done for us. It is what He will gain through the kingdom of heaven in its present mysterious form.

Lastly it is like the drag-net gathering fish out of the sea of nations. All kinds are gathered, but we see *discriminate selection* exercised. There is a similarity between this and the parable of the wheat and tares, inasmuch as in both cases there is a disentanglement accomplished by angels at the end of the age. The wicked are severed from the just and cast into the furnace of fire. But there is also a distinct difference, for in the former parable the wicked are in the world as the result of Satan's sowing; whereas here "the word of the kingdom" goes out among the nations like a net, and people of all kinds profess to receive it. At the end of the age discrimination will be made; the true elect of God will be gathered in, and the evil rejected.

How important that we should ever keep before us what the kingdom is like from the Divine standpoint. It has taken on this peculiar character as a result of the rejection of the true Son of David, and His consequent absence in the heavens. In spite of the mixture and corruption which will mark it outwardly, there is to be this inward work of God which will result in His obtaining the hidden treasure, the pearl of great price, and all the good fish which the net encloses. Have we understood all these things? The disciples felt that they had; yet later when they had received the Spirit, they may have discovered how very little they had done so. We too realize doubtless how little we have done so, for the kingdom in its present form is not understood as easily as it will be when it is unveiled in public display. Things predominate which are wholly new from an Old Testament standpoint: hence we read, "things new and old," not "old and new." The emphasis lies on "new."

This chapter closes with Jesus back in His own district, and there at that time they were quite unbelieving. They did not see in Him Emmanuel, or even the Son of Abraham, the Son of David; to them He was just the son of the carpenter, with whose relations they were so very familiar. Their unbelieving familiarity caused them to stumble at Him. His power was unabated, but their unbelief imposed a restraint upon its exercise, just as the unbelief of Joash, the king of Israel, imposed a limit upon his victories (see 2 Kings 13: 14-19).

## Chapter 14

AT THAT TIME, says the opening verse, Herod "heard of the fame of Jesus." Just when He had no fame at Nazareth His fame reached the ears of that godless man, and as it appears, touched his hardened conscience. It is remarkable that he should have thought it was John risen from the dead, since to a later Herod we have Paul saying, "Why should it be thought a thing incredible with you, that God should raise the dead?" (Acts 26: 8). That which they could not believe when it had happened was conjured up by a guilty conscience.

This leads Matthew to tell us the story of John's martyrdom, which had happened not long before. John's faithful witness had stirred up the anger of Herod and the revenge of Herodias, and the Lord's forerunner died as the result of a godless oath. Herod outraged the law of God in order to preserve the credit of his own word. Such was the man that ruled many of the Jews—a chastisement surely for their abounding sin.

Now John had always faithfully pointed to Jesus, and the people acknowledged that though he did no miracle, "all things that John spake of this Man were true" (John 10: 41). As the fruit of John's happy fidelity to Jesus, his disciples knew what to do, when he was so suddenly removed. They were granted his body, so having buried it, they "went and told Jesus." John was the burning and shining lamp whereas Jesus was the light, that coming into the world, shines for all men. The lamp was extinguished, so they turned to the great light, and found consolation there.

Hearing it, Jesus departed to a desert place. Mark shows us that just at this time His disciples had returned to Him from their mission. A period of solitude and quiet was suitable at this juncture for the Master, for His disciples, and for John's sad followers; if, as is likely, they accompanied Him.

The multitudes however still went after Him, and He met their needs. As ever He was moved with compassion. The indifference of Nazareth and the wickedness of Herod produced no change in Him. Let us meditate long and deeply on the unchanging compassions of the heart of Christ. Blessed be His Name!

It was not the Lord but His disciples, who suggested that the crowds should be dismissed to fend for themselves. It was His compassion that detained them and bade His disciples give them to eat. This tested the disciples, and brought to light how little they realized the power of their Master. They had to discover that His way was to use the tiny resources that were already in their hands, and multiply them until they were more than sufficient. The prophet indicated that Jehovah would find His rest in Zion, and that then His word would be, "I will abundantly bless her provision: I will satisfy her poor with bread" (Psa. 132: 15). Jehovah was now amongst His people in the person of Jesus, and though there was no rest for Him in Zion at that time, yet He proved what He could do with these five thousand men, beside women and children. He was dispensing the bounty of heaven, hence He looked up to heaven as He blessed.

# MATTHEW

At this point let us recall the situation, as presented in this Gospel. He had been definitely rejected by the nation, their leaders going so far as to commit the unpardonable sin in attributing His works of power to the devil. Consequently He had symbolically broken His links with them. This we saw in chapters 11 and 12. Then in chapter 13 He spoke the parables which reveal new developments as to the kingdom of heaven; and at the end of that chapter we find that the people of His own country saw nothing in Him beyond the son of the carpenter. We opened chapter 14 to find Herod slaying His forerunner, so that His refusal on all hands could hardly be more complete. Yet before we close the chapter we see a display of two great facts: first, He is *more than sufficient* when in the presence of human need, whether the wants of the multitude or the weakness of the disciples. Second, He is *more than supreme* when confronted with powers wielded by the adversary. He not only walked Himself upon the stormy waters, but He enabled a feeble disciple to do the same.

During the night He had been in prayer upon the mountain, and the disciples had been toiling against contrary circumstances. Towards morning He drew near to them, walking upon the waves. In the earlier episode on the lake (chap. 8) He had shown Himself able to quell the storm, since His power was above all the power of the devil. Now He shows Himself in absolute supremacy. The storm was simply nothing to Him. It was distressing to the disciples, but here was the One of whom it had been said, "Thy way is in the sea, and Thy path in the great waters, and Thy footsteps are not known" (Psa. 77: 19). His presence brought good cheer to them even while the storm still raged; and when He joined the boat the wind ceased.

But the Lord brought with Him more than good cheer, and Peter it was who discovered it: He can conform others to Himself. It involved for Peter stepping "out of the ship," and this could only be done when he had the authoritative word, "Come," which authenticated the fact that it was the Lord Himself who drew near. Assured that it was Himself, on the strength of His word, Peter stepped forth and walked on the sea. We may see here an allegory of what was shortly to come to pass. The Jewish system, which consisted so largely of "the law of commandments contained in ordinances," (Eph. 2: 15), was like a ship, quite suited to men who are "after the flesh." As the result of His coming, the disciples were to step out of that "ship" into a path of pure faith. Hence when Paul bade farewell to the Ephesian elders, he did not commend them to a code of laws nor to an institution or organization, but to "God and the word of His grace." Hence too the call to go "outside the camp" in Hebrews 13. Peter was "out of the ship," with Christ as his Object and His word as his authority. The Christian position is outside the camp with God and the word of His grace.

Yet Peter's faith was small, and, his mind turning from his Master to the violent wind, he was afraid and he began to sink. But still, he had faith, for in the emergency he at once called upon his Lord, and so was sustained, and by both together the ship was reached, when at once the wind ceased, and the land was reached, as John's Gospel shows us. Peter was quite illogical in his fears, for it is no more possible for us to walk on smooth water than on rough, but we are all like him when little faith possesses our hearts. Faith which is fully centred in Christ is strong, whilst that which is occupied with circumstances is weak.

We sometimes hear rather too much of Peter's failure, and not enough of what the power of Christ enabled him to do, though his faith was small. After all, he did not sink. He only *began* to sink and then, sustained by a power not his own, he reached his Lord and returned with Him to the boat. No other man has done a thing like that, and his momentary failure only made it so manifest that the power that sustained him was that of his Lord that all the rest worshipped Him as the Son of God. They got a great glimpse of His glory, and when arrived at the land of Gennesaret tribute was paid by the people to His grace as well as His power. The diseased flocked to His presence, and their faith was not misplaced, for *as many as touched Him* were made *perfectly whole*. True Divine healing means 100 per cent. cure in 100 per cent. of the cases! A perfectly wonderful state of things!

## CHAPTER 15

INTO THIS LOVELY scene intruded scribes and Pharisees from Jerusalem with their complaint and question as to the non-compliance of the disciples with the tradition of the elders as to the washing of hands. Just imagine the scene. The Son of God dispensing healing on every hand in the fulness of Divine grace, and these men, utterly blind to all that was happening, breaking in with their point of order. Blinded by legal technicalities, they could not perceive Divine grace working in power. Such a frame of mind might seem incredible did we not see the same feature displayed today by the Pharisaic mind, which still occupies itself with points of this kind, based upon tradition and common usage and not on the plain and definite word of God.

The Lord's reply to these men emphasizes the difference between "the commandment of God," and "your tradition" (v. 3). These traditions of the elders were explanations, amplifications and inferences drawn from the law by venerated teachers of old time. They dominated the minds of the Pharisees and quite beclouded the law of God; so much so that they transgressed the law to keep their tradition. The Lord charged them with this, and gave an illustration of it as regards the fifth commandment. Their tradition as regards gifts, professedly devoted to God, completely nullified that commandment. The "pious" and "orthodox" Jew of today has his mind filled with the Talmud, which is built up from these traditions, and it is like a veil, shrouding from his mind the true word of God.

# MATTHEW

Let us take care lest we fall into a similar snare. We may thankfully avail ourselves of the teachings of God's servants, but using them rightly we shall be led back to the fountain-head, even Scripture itself. It would not be difficult to turn the teachings of the best of God's servants into a kind of Talmud. Then we should have them as a sort of smoke screen, hiding from us the pure Word of God, just as the Talmud blinds the Jewish mind to the real force of the Old Testament.

This kind of thing, pushed as it was by the Pharisees to its extreme limits, stirred our Lord to a strong exposure of its evil. They were hypocrites, and He told them so plainly. They came under Isaiah's scathing denunciation, for this type of religious wickedness is always to be found with men who have hearts far from God and yet honour Him with their lips, whilst putting their own precepts and commandments in the place of His word. All such nominal worship is empty and in vain, yet it is not difficult for a true believer to get entangled in such things today.

Having exposed the Pharisees to their faces, the Lord turned to the people to warn them as to the error which lay at the root of this hypocrisy—the assumption that defilement is imposed upon men from without, rather than generated within: that it is physical rather than spiritual. The defiling thing is what comes out of a man's mouth, expressing what is in his heart. The heart of man is the fountain-head of defilement. Solemn fact! The Pharisees of course were offended at such teaching, which cut at the root of all their ceremonial observances, but that only showed that they were no plants of God's planting. Their end was to be rooted up. They were blind themselves and misleading others who were blind also. God would deal with them in His government, and the disciples were to leave them alone and not retaliate.

But what the Lord had just said sounded strange even to the disciples; so Peter asked for an explanation, treating it as a parable. This called forth a rebuke—though a gentle one—from the Lord. The fact was that none, not even the best of them, saw much beyond the letter of the law with its offerings and ceremonial regulations, and hence they had very little sense of its convicting power. They were concerned as to what went into their mouths, in order that they might be ceremonially clean. The law, if spiritually understood, concerns itself with the state of the heart, as the Lord had showed in His sermon on the mount. The evil things of verse 19 proceed out of the heart, and it is significant that evil thoughts head the list, for that is where they all begin. Thus the Lord exposed the evil which is in the heart of man.

He proceeded, in the case of the woman of Canaan, to reveal the goodness which is in the heart of God. Divine grace was ready to flow out freely without respect of persons, so that Gentile as well as Jew might receive it; one thing only was needful on the part of the recipient—honesty of heart. Now the woman addressed Jesus as the Son of David in presenting her plea for mercy. She came as though she were one of the people of Israel, thinking perhaps that by so doing she stood a better chance of being heard. There was a measure of insincerity in this, and hence "He answered her not a word."

But though there was insincerity there was also such earnest persistence of faith that the disciples intervened because of her cries, and this led to the Lord's words in verse 24, which cast some light on her mistake. She now presented her plea simply on the ground of her need, saying, "Lord help me;" and this led to yet more searching words from the Lord. His mission was to the house of Israel, who were spiritually lost, yet after all they were in the place of children, whereas the Gentiles were in the place of the dogs, unclean and outside the realm of God's dealings. Here was a test indeed! Would she throw away the last shred of pretence and humbly take her true place?

She did so in very striking fashion. Her reply, in verse 27, was saying in effect, "I am indeed but a Gentile, yet amongst men there is a sufficient surplus for the dogs to feed, and I am sure the heart of God is not more straitened than the heart of man." In this reply Jesus instantly detected great faith, and acknowledged it, giving her all her desire. Thus for the second time did He discover great faith and point it out. In both cases—the centurion in chapter 8, and here—it was a Gentile that displayed it; and in both cases it was allied with the condemnation of self. "I am not worthy," said the centurion: "I am but a dog," in effect said the woman here. It is ever thus: high thoughts of self go with little faith, and low thoughts of self with great faith. Let us search and see if the explanation of the smallness of our faith lies just here.

The heart of God was indeed larger than the woman imagined. She, though a dog, obtained a large crumb from the table; but presently the whole feast would be sent to the dogs, for this is the force of Paul's announcement in Acts 28: 28. Still, much had to transpire before that announcement could be made, and in our Gospel we see the beginnings of the wonderful transition. In the remainder of our chapter we see further striking manifestations of the heart of God. The mercy that blessed a Gentile woman was equally at the disposal of the afflicted multitudes of Israel. The multitude had but to bring their needy ones and "cast them down at Jesus' feet" for them to be healed in such a way that their minds were directed to the God of Israel, and they glorified Him.

This display of power, exercised in Divine mercy, was so attractive that the multitudes long outstayed their available food supplies, and in their need Jesus again manifested the compassion of the heart of God. There was a recurrence of the situation recorded in only the previous chapter, and yet apparently the disciples had no expectation that the Lord would act just as He had done before. In them we can see our own lack of faith exemplified. It is comparatively easy to remember how the Lord has acted

# MATTHEW

in days that are past; it is another thing to count on His acting today, in the assurance that He is ever the same. Still, lack of faith on our side is no insuperable barrier to action on His side. He again took their small resources and multiplied them into more than a sufficiency. Again there was food for all, and an overplus. Such is the compassion of the heart of God.

## CHAPTER 16

THE PHARISEES NOW renewed their attack, combining with their ancient foes, the Sadducees, for this purpose. The "sign from heaven" was merely a catch, being just the kind of thing that the Sadducees, with their materialistic notions, would never accept. In reply the Lord pointed out that they were quite good judges of material things seen in the face of the sky, but quite blind to the "signs of the times," which need spiritual discernment for their apprehension. Being "wicked and adulterous" they had no spiritual perception, and hence such signs as God gives were no use to them. As He had said before (12: 39), there remained "the sign of the Prophet Jonas," namely, His own death and resurrection. With that word He left them. When that great sign took place they used all their craft and their money in an effort to nullify it; as we see in the last chapter of this Gospel.

From these men the Lord turned to His disciples with words of warning. They were to beware of their "leaven." This warning the disciples took in a material sense at first, their misunderstanding being helped on by their omission to take bread. Yet they should not have had any thought on that score in the light of the feeding of the five thousand and the four thousand. At last they understood that by "leaven" the Lord meant "doctrine." It is evident therefore that though the true disciple could never be either Pharisee or Sadducee, he may be leavened by their doctrines—by either or by both.

The leaven of the Pharisee was that type of religious hypocrisy that lays all the stress on things outward and ceremonial. The leaven of the Sadducee was pride of intellect which elevates human reason into the place of sole judge, and waves aside God's revelation and faith. How much Christendom is leavened by both these things is sadly apparent today. Ritualism is rampant on the one hand, and rationalism, or "modernism," on the other, and not infrequently both are blended and the rationalistic ritualist is the product. The Lord's warning against them is supplemented by the Apostle Paul in Colossians 2. In verse 8 of that chapter we find his warning against rationalism, and in verses 16, 18, 20-22, against ritualism in various forms, and we are shown how these things divert us from Christ and prevent us from "holding the Head."

It is significant that in our chapter the Lord's warning against both comes just before the record of His visit to Caeserea Philippi, and of the

# MATTHEW

question He raised with His disciples there. In this place He was at the extreme northward limit of the land, and as far away from the haunts of these men as possible. Who was He? That was the supreme question. The answers given by the people were various and confused, and they were not sufficiently interested to make sober enquiry. But appealing more directly to His disciples Peter was able, as taught of God, to give a clear reply, which brought to light the Rock on which the church was to be built. Colossians 2 show us how destructive is the leaven, both of the Pharisee and the Sadducee, upon the church's position and faith. In Matthew 16 we see how the Lord warned His disciples against both, before making the first announcement of the church that He was going to build.

Simon Peter was a blessed man. From God Himself in heaven, whom Jesus spoke of as "My Father," there had reached him a revelation which never could have come to him from man. His eyes had been opened to see in Jesus the Christ. That was His official position as God's Anointed One. But who was this Anointed One? Peter discerned that He was "the Son of the living God." This was truly a striking confession. God is the living God, infinitely above the power of death. Jesus is the Son in the eternal Godhead, equally above all the power of death. This thing had evidently come to Peter as in a flash by Divine revelation. He was not yet established in the full understanding of it, as we see half a dozen verses lower down. Yet he saw it was so, and he confessed it.

Do we confess this too? And do we really understand its significance? If we do, we have indeed found an impregnable Rock, and like Peter we are blessed indeed.

In His word to Peter, recorded in verse 18, the Lord confirmed to him the name that He had given him at their first meeting, as recorded in John 1: 42, and also disclosed something more of its significance. The *meaning* of "Peter" is "stone," but what is its *significance*? This—that it connected him with the church which Christ, the Son of the living God, was about to build. Thus in Christ Himself lay the "Rock," on which the church is founded. Peter was no rock. Indeed he seems to have been the most impulsive and easily moved of the disciples—see Galatians 2: 11-13. He was only a stone, and there is no excuse for the error of confounding him and the Rock, for in His use of words the Lord signalized the distinction, saying, "Thou art *Petros*, and upon this *petra* I will build My church."

The building of the church was still in the future, for the Rock was not fully disclosed until the Son of the living God had proved His triumph through death and resurrection, and gone up on high. Then began Christ's *ecclesia*, or, "called-out company;" and here was found one of the stones that was then to be built up upon the Rock. In his First Epistle Peter shows us that this is not something confined exclusively to himself, for all who come to the Living Stone are living stones to be built also on that foundation.

# MATTHEW

In this great pronouncement the Lord spoke of His church as being His own handiwork, against which all adverse wisdom and power could not prevail. What is done in the power of Divine life nothing can touch. Other scriptures speak of the church as the community professing allegiance to Christ, brought into being through the labours of those who take the place of servants of God. On that community failure was stamped from the outset, and it merges into the kingdom of heaven, of which we learned so much in chapter 13, and which the Lord mentions in verse 19 of our chapter. The keys of that kingdom were given to Peter—not the keys of the church.

All who profess allegiance to the King are in the kingdom of heaven, and Peter was given a special administrative place in connection with that. We see him in the act of "loosing" as regards Jews in Acts 2: 37-40, and as regards Gentiles in Acts 10: 44-48; and in the act of "binding" in Acts 8: 20-23. And in these cases clearly his acts were ratified in heaven. But Simon the sorcerer, though he had been baptized as a professed subject of the kingdom, had never been built by the Lord into His church.

The kingdom of heaven had been revealed in Old Testament scripture, though its present mysterious form had not. On the other hand nothing had been said as to the church, and this word of Jesus was a preliminary disclosure of it. Having made the announcement He at once withdrew the testimony which His disciples had been giving as to His being the Christ, come on earth to confirm the promises made unto the fathers (Rom. 15: 8). His rejection was certain and His death impending. Only thus would there be laid the proper basis for the fulfilment of the promises to Israel, or the blessing of Gentiles so that they might glorify God for His mercy in bringing them into the church. Hence from this point Jesus turned the minds of His disciples to His death and resurrection—the grand climax of His earthly story. Christ in resurrection glory, rather than Christ in earthly glory, was the goal before them.

Here Peter displays his frailty and un-rock-like character, and comes under rebuke. It is striking how in these few verses we see him Divinely illuminated, then administratively privileged and then speaking in a way which reminded our Lord of Satan and fallen men. Such was Peter, and we are no better than he. His mind and the minds of the other disciples were set upon blessings to be realized upon earth. The Lord knew this and proceeded to tell them how all would be altered for them by His death: they too would have death borne in upon them and lose their lives in this world.

This saying of our Lord (verse 25) occurs no less than six times in the four Gospels, allowing for slight variations in the wording: twice in this Gospel, twice in Luke, and once in both Mark and John. The six occurences cover, we believe, four different occasions. So it was evidently a saying often upon the lips of Jesus; and this testifies to its great importance. It cuts across the grain with every one of us, and yet it puts in a nutshell a great principle of spiritual life which persists all through the period of His rejection and absence from the world. Only when He comes again will saints enjoy life on earth in any full and proper sense. To go in for gaining the world now is to lose the soul.

Having shown His disciples what lay before Himself, and before them in the more immediate future, He went on to speak of His coming in glory. He will then take the kingdom from His Father and the time of reward will have arrived, and some of them were to have the privilege of seeing the kingdom in miniature as a sample of what was coming. This was an expression of His thoughtful grace towards them, lest they should be utterly discouraged by what He had just been telling them.

## Chapter 17

THE TRANSFIGURATION, WITH which this chapter opens, furnished a view of the kingdom, inasmuch as Jesus Himself, shining as the sun, was the central figure, and with Him in heavenly conditions were Moses and Elias, whilst three disciples in earthly conditions had a share in it. The "bright cloud" which overshadowed them was evidently the reappearance of that which once dwelt on the tabernacle, and out of it spoke the voice of God the Father, declaring Jesus to be the Son, the beloved Object and delight of His heart. Peter had been speaking in his impetuous way, showing that he had as yet no adequate sense of the exclusive and supreme glory of his Master. Not Peter but Christ is the One to whom we are to listen. Our ears are to be filled with His voice, and our eyes with His presence, so that, like the disciples when the vision faded, we too see "no man, save Jesus only."

Though Peter at the moment had but small understanding of what it all signified he apprehended it later when the Spirit was given, as we see when we turn to his Second Epistle. He realized then that it was the confirmation of the prophetic word as to "the power and coming of our Lord Jesus Christ," for they were "eyewitnesses of His majesty" (1: 16-19). Not until the Son of Man was risen from the dead, and consequently the Holy Ghost was given, would the full significance of the transfiguration be understood. Hence the Lord's charge to the three disciples recorded in verse 9 of our chapter. The vision did however awaken questions in the minds of the disciples as to the prophecy concerning the coming of Elias; and the Lord's answer showed that as regards His first coming, that prophecy had found its fulfilment in John the Baptist who had been slain, and He took the opportunity of again predicting His own death.

On the top of the high mountain the disciples had been in the place of heavenly peace and communion; they descended with Jesus to the foot where all was distress and failure—distress on the part of the afflicted boy and his father; failure to meet the situation on the part of the disciples. The advent of Jesus altered everything in a moment, just as His approaching advent in glory will completely retrieve the situation which will then exist, meeting not only the power of the devil in the world but also all the failures of His saints.

The situation retrieved, the disciples invited the Lord to explain their failure, and thus they stood before His judgment seat, as we all shall in the day of His advent. His explanation of their failure in a general way was, "Because of your unbelief," but He added that the demon involved in this case was of a special "kind" which could only be dealt with if there was "prayer and fasting." As is so often the case with our failures the reason was not simple but compound. Three things were involved. First, absence of faith—little or no *confidence in God*. Second, absence of prayer—*dependence upon God*. Third, absence of fasting—*separation to God*, even from things quite right in themselves under ordinary circumstances. In these words we believe the Lord exposed the roots of all our failures in seeking to serve Him. We are defective in one or another or all of these three things. Let us enquire, searching our hearts and lives, and see if it be not so.

For the third time while in Galilee Jesus forewarned His disciples as to His death, adding the fact of His resurrection. Matthew's comment is, "They were exceeding sorry," which shows that they were more impressed by the tidings of His death than His resurrection. That is something which lies outside man's natural experience and they failed to apprehend it. The incident which closes this chapter shows that Peter only thought of his Master as a good Jew, who paid all His dues, and was anxious that all others should see Him in this light. When he would have spoken of it, Jesus anticipated him with a question which showed that such as Peter were children of the kingdom, and hence in due course they would be free from this tribute for the service of the temple. Still the moment had not quite come for this, and no occasion of stumbling was to be given, so by a remarkable miracle the Lord provided the exact sum needed for two payments, and in wonderful grace He associated Peter with Himself. The coin was to be handed over "for Me and thee." This was surely a token of the way in which saints as children of the kingdom were presently to be associated with Himself.

CHAPTER 18

THE DISCIPLES' QUESTION, "Who is the greatest in the kingdom of heaven?" showed that the kingdom was filling their thoughts just at that moment. The answer made it abundantly clear that the only way of entrance into the kingdom was by becoming small, not great. As the result of conversion a person humbles himself and becomes like a little child. Apart from this one is not in the kingdom at all. Then as we enter, so we progress; consequently the humblest is the greatest in the kingdom. The disciples needed to have their ideas on this matter revolutionized, and so all too frequently do we. It is evident that here the Lord speaks of the kingdom not as the

# MATTHEW

sphere of profession out of which evil will have to be cast, as in chapter 13, but as a sphere marked by vital reality.

To answer the question Jesus had called a little child and set him in the midst as an object lesson. He proceeds to show that one such child, if presented in His name, becomes a person of great importance. To receive him is equivalent to receiving the Lord Himself. In verses 2-5 the "little child" is in question; in verse 6 it is "one of these little ones *which believe in Me*." To offend one of these merits the severest judgment, and this leads the Lord to set His disciples in the light of eternal things. There is such a thing as "everlasting fire," and any sacrifice is better than incurring that.

Down to verse 14 we are still occupied with the little child. They are not to be despised for three reasons. First, they are the continual objects of angelic ministry, and are represented before the face of the Father in heaven. Second, they are objects of the Saviour's saving grace. Third, the Father's will is toward them in blessing; He does not desire that one should perish. Sweet words of comfort these for those who have lost their little ones in early life, giving ample assurance of their blessing. The comparison of verse 11 with Luke 19:10 is instructive. There a grown-up man was in question, who had had plenty of time to go astray; so the word "seek" is found. Here, where the little child is in question, it is omitted. The tendency to go astray is there in each, as verses 12 and 13 indicate, but the wandering is not put to account in the same way till years of responsibility are reached.

Verses 1-14, then, deal with the "little child" and the *kingdom:* verses 15-20 with the "brother" and the *church*. In chapter 16: 18, 19, we had the church and the kingdom, and both reappear here. If it be a question of the little child our tendency is to ignore and despise him. If our brother be in question there is a sad tendency for disagreements and occasions of trespass to occur, and these are now contemplated in the Lord's teaching. We have definite instructions as to the procedure to be followed, the ignoring of which has produced untold mischief. If a brother has injured me, my first step is to see him *alone*, and point out his wrongdoing. If I do this in the right spirit, I shall very likely gain him and get things rectified. Alternately, of course, I may find that my thoughts needed rectifying, for things were not as they seemed.

But he may not hear me, and then I am to approach him again with one or two brethren as witnesses, so that his wrong may be brought home to him in a more definite and impartial way. Only if he still remain obdurate is the church to be informed so that the voice of all may be heard by him. If he go so far as to disregard the voice of the church, then I am to treat him as one with whom all fellowship is impossible.

It will be noticed that the Lord does not go on to say what the church should do; doubtless because trespasses are of many kinds and varying degrees of gravity, so that no instruction would apply to all cases. Verse 18

# MATTHEW

does however imply that there would be cases where the church would have to "bind" the wrongdoer, and again others where their action would have to be in the nature of "loosing." Here we find that what had previously been said to Peter alone is now said to the church. To carry this out rightly would mean much dependence on God and prayer to God. Moreover even in the earliest days and under most favourable circumstances it would hardly ever be possible to get the whole church together in one place. Hence in verses 19 and 20 the Lord brings things down to the smallest possible plurality, showing that the potency of prayer and of church action does not depend upon *numbers* but upon *His Name*. In the case of the little child and the kingdom the important point was "in My Name." In the case of the brother and the church again "in [or, to] My Name" is the decisive thing. The whole weight of authority lies there.

Verse 20 is sometimes quoted as though it described a certain basis of fellowship, true at all times for those in the fellowship. But the Lord spoke not of being gathered simply, but of being "gathered *together;*" that is, He spoke of an actual meeting. His Name is of such value that, if only two or three are gathered together to it, He is there in the midst, and this gives power to their requests and authority to their acts. He is spiritually present, not visibly: a wonderful and gracious provision this for days when the church cannot be got together as a whole, owing to its broken and divided state. We may be very thankful for it, but let us beware how we use it.

There has been such a tendency to make this gathering together to His Name just a matter of a certain church position, eliminating from it all thought of moral condition. Then we may be tempted to argue this or that must be ratified in heaven, or granted by heaven, because we acted or asked in His Name. We should be much wiser if we trod more softly, and when we saw no signs of heaven either ratifying or granting, we humbled ourselves and searched our hearts and ways to discover wherein we had missed a true gathering together in His Name; whether all the time we really had ourselves before us, and our moral state was wrong.

In verse 21, we find Peter raising the other side of the matter. What about the offended rather than the offending party? The reply of Jesus came to this—the spirit of forgiveness towards my brother is to be practically unlimited.

Thereupon He spoke the parable as to the king and his servants, with which the chapter closes. The general bearing of this parable is very plain; the only point we notice is that it refers to God's *governmental* dealings with those who take the place of being His servants, as is made plain when we reach verse 35, which gives the Lord's own application of it. There is entirely another basis for eternal forgiveness, but governmental forgiveness does very often hinge upon the believer manifesting a forgiving spirit. If we treat our brethren ill, we shall find ourselves sooner or later in the hands of the "tormentors" and have a sorrowful time. And if any of us are witnesses

# MATTHEW

of one brother ill-treating another we shall be wise if, instead of taking the law into our own hands and attacking the wrongdoer, we imitate the servants of the parable and tell our Lord all that was done, leaving Him to deal with the offender in His holy government.

## Chapter 19

JESUS NOW APPROACHED Judaea again and the Pharisees returned to the attack. They raised a question regarding marriage and divorce, hoping to entrap Him. This they utterly failed to do for they were pitting themselves against Divine wisdom. A complete answer lay in referring them to what God had ordained at the beginning. Man was not to undo what God had done. This raised in their minds a question as to why divorce had been permitted in the law given through Moses. The answer was that it had been permitted because of the hardness of men's hearts. God knew that well, and hence He did not set the standard too high. The law set forth God's minimum requirement for life in this world. Hence to fail only once at any time was to incur the sentence of death. Only one thing can dissolve the tie according to God, and that is the virtual breaking of the bond by either of the parties.

It is only when we come to Christ that we get the full thoughts of God—God's maximum in every respect.

The Lord's teaching as to divorce was new and surprising even to His disciples, and prompted their remark recorded in verse 10. This in its turn led Him to declare that marriage is the normal thing for man, and the unmarried state the exceptional, as is also inferred by Paul's words in 1 Corinthians 7: 7. If "it is given" to a man, then "it is good not to marry;" but normally, "Marriage is honourable in all" (Heb. 13: 4).

Following this, the Lord gave to children their true place. The disciples manifested the spirit of the world when they treated them as of no importance, so much so that the bringing of them was an intrusion. Thus they showed that they had not as yet learned the lesson that He taught in the verses that open chapter 18. The Lord on the contrary laid His hands on them in blessing and uttered the memorable words, "Forbid them not, to come unto Me; for of such is the kingdom of heaven."

Next comes the case of the rich young man who claimed to have kept the law, as regards the commandments relating to one's duty towards one's neighbour. The Lord did not deny his claim, so apparently he had been blameless as far as outward observance was concerned. He was much mistaken however in thinking that by doing some good thing he could have eternal life. Coming on that ground, Jesus at once tested him, and under the test he utterly failed. "What lack I yet?" was his question, and the answer was designed to show him that he lacked the *faith* which discerned the glory of Jesus, and which consequently would have moved him to give up everything in order to follow Him. He approached Jesus as "Good Master," and the Lord would not accept the epithet "good," unless it were given Him as the fruit of acknowledging His Deity. "There is none good but one—God," so that if Jesus was not *God* He was not *good*. If the young man had recognized the Deity of the One who said to him, "Follow Me," his "great possessions" would have been as nothing to him, and he would gladly have followed Jesus. Have we each so recognized the glory of Jesus as to be lifted clean out of the love of mere earthly things?

The Lord now pointed out to His disciples how tenacious a hold earthly riches have on the human heart. The rich enter the kingdom of God with great difficulty. Among the Jews wealth was regarded as a sign of God's favour; hence this saying also overturned the thoughts of the disciples and greatly astonished them. They felt that nobody could be saved if the rich had such difficulty. This led to an even stronger statement. Salvation is a thing not merely difficult or improbable to man, but *impossible*. Only if the power of God be brought in, is it possible.

We may summarize verses 10-26 by saying that the Lord shed His light upon marriage, children and possessions: three things that occupy so much of our lives in this world, and in each case the light He shed overturned the thoughts which previously the disciples had entertained—see, verses 10, 13, 25.

Peter seized upon the Lord's words, desiring a definite pronouncement as to what reward was offered to those who like himself had followed the Lord. The reply made it plain that there is to come "the regeneration;" that is, a wholly new order of things, when the Son of Man should be no longer rejected but be seated on the throne of His glory, and that then the disciples should also be enthroned and vested with powers of administration over the twelve tribes of Israel. In that age the saints are going to judge the world, and here is indicated the place of special prominence reserved for the Apostles. It is also indicated that all who have given up earthly relationships and joys for His Name will receive a hundredfold together with everlasting life. The life which the rich young man desired, and missed by not following Christ, shall be theirs.

The last verse of the chapter adds a word of warning. Many who are first in this world will be last there, and vice versa; for God's thoughts are not as ours.

## Chapter 20

THIS CHAPTER OPENS with the parable of the householder and his labourers, which in verse 16 brings us back with fresh conviction to just that point. The parable also has direct reference to Peter's question, which asked for a definite promise of reward, since it contrasts the difference of treatment meted out by the householder between those who served him as the result of a bargain, and those who did so without any bargain, but with simple trust that he would give them "whatsoever is right." We can all well understand the feelings of those earliest workers, and the complaint they lodged of unfair treatment since they had borne the burden and heat of the day. What workman is there who would not be inclined to reason just as they did? But the "goodman of the house" placed great value on that *confidence* in the rightness of his mind and *faith* in his word, which characterized the later comers. He had a right to do what he willed with his own money, and so highly did he rate faith that he gave to the last just what he did to the first. And in distributing the money he began with the last. Thus the last were first and the first last.

Here then is a lesson that we all take a long time to learn. The Lord will not undervalue work, but He will value even more highly the simple faith in Himself—His rightness, His wisdom, His word—which will go on serving Him, even though late in the day, without much thought as to reward, or any attempt at a bargain. The faith and love which would move any to serve Him thus is sweeter to Him than the actual work they may be able to accomplish. We shall profit if we read, mark, learn and inwardly digest this parable.

Jesus was now on His way to Jerusalem for the last time, and He once more pressed upon His disciples His approaching death and resurrection. As far as the record of this Gospel is concerned, this is the fourth time He did so since His great prediction as to building His Church, in chapter 16. Here there is a wealth of detail in few words. He predicts His betrayal by Judas, His condemnation by the Sanhedrim, His being delivered by them to Pilate and his soldiers, the mocking, the scourging, the crucifixion, and finally His resurrection—all in the compass of two verses.

Yet the minds of the disciples were still filled with anticipation of the speedy establishment of the kingdom; so much so that James and John were brought by their mother with a request for places of prominence in it. Jesus answered by a question which indicated that honour in the coming kingdom will be proportionate to the measure in which one may have been identified with Him in His sufferings and rejection. At the same time He indicated that rewards in the kingdom were to be given according to the Father's award. The Son of Man Himself is going to receive the kingdom from the hands of the Father, as had been indicated in Psalm 8, and Daniel 7, so the saints too will receive their place in the kingdom at the Father's hand. The recollection of this will help us to understand the Lord saying of reward, it "is not mine to give."

This is the only case, as far as we remember, where a parent came to the Lord with a request for a child and met with a refusal. But then here the mother was asking for a prominent place as a reward: in all the other cases the request was for blessing from His hands. That was never denied. There was evidently a spirit of competition amongst the disciples, for the ten felt

# MATTHEW

that the two had stolen a march on them and were indignant. This led to one more beautiful lesson as to the humility that befits the kingdom. Even today we are very slow to recognize that the principles that prevail in the Divine kingdom are the opposite of those that prevail in the kingdoms of men. In the world greatness is expressed in dominion and authority: the great one is in a position to lord it over his fellows. Amongst the saints greatness expresses itself in ministry and service. The word for minister in verse 26 is "deacon," and that for servant in verse 27 is "bondman;" the word which Paul uses for Timothy and himself in the opening verse of the Epistle to the Philippians. Paul was pre-eminently a bondman of Jesus Christ, and he will not be found small when measured by the standard prevailing in the kingdom of heaven.

On the other hand there were in Paul's day men who aimed at dominion and authority by bringing believers into bondage, by devouring them, taking from them, exalting themselves and smiting others on the face. But such were false apostles and deceitful workers—see 2 Corinthians 11: 13-20. There are people about in our day who assert their dominion in the same fashion, and we do well to beware of them. The Lord sets Himself before us as the Son of Man who came not to be served but to serve, though to be served was His right. Daniel 7: 9-14 shows this in a twofold way, for Jesus may be identified with the "Ancient of Days" as well as the Son of Man. As Ancient of Days "thousand thousands ministered unto Him" before He descended amongst us. As Son of Man "all people, nations, and languages" shall "serve Him." Yet between came the time of His humiliation when He devoted Himself to service; which went to the extreme point of giving His life a ransom for many. Thus for the fifth time since chapter 16 the Lord set His death before the minds of His disciples; and this time He spoke of its *redeeming* virtue. Thank God! that we are amongst "the many."

The closing scenes of the Gospel begin with the incident concerning the two blind men as He departed from Jericho. Both Mark and Luke mention only one of them, whose name was Bartimaeus, but evidently there actually were two. The same feature is seen in the accounts of the casting out of the legion of demons, for at the end of chapter 8 Matthew tells us of two men, where Mark and Luke mention one only. In both cases there were two witnesses of the power and grace of Jesus, and Matthew mentions it since it would be specially impressive to Jewish readers, accustomed to the stipulation of their law as to the validity of the witness of two, whilst one only might be disregarded.

The Son of David was now for the last time approaching His capital city. These men had sufficient faith to recognize Him and they received from Him the physical eyesight that they desired. With opened eyes they became His followers. This was symbolic surely of the spiritual need of the masses of Israel. If only their eyes had been really open they would have seen their

# MATTHEW

Messiah in Jesus in the day of their visitation. The situation today is similar. People often complain of want of light. What they really want is the spiritual eyesight—that is, *faith*—which would enable them to see the light, that has shone so brightly in Him.

## CHAPTER 21

THIS CHAPTER OPENS with the Lord presenting Himself to Jerusalem according to the prophecy of Zechariah. The Lord had spoken through the prophet, and now some five centuries later the ass and her colt were standing ready exactly at the right time, under the charge of someone who would immediately respond to the need of the Lord. Once more the Lord was plainly authenticated before them as their Messiah and King. He had been born of the Virgin in Bethlehem, brought out of Egypt, and had risen as the great Light in Galilee, as the prophets had said. Now, when the sixty-nine weeks of Daniel 9 were completed, as King He entered His city. Alas! the people overlooked the fact that He was to be *meek*, and the salvation He was to bring must be compatible with that, and not based upon victorious power. Consequently they stumbled at that stumbling-stone.

Yet for a brief moment it looked as if they might receive Him. The example of the disciples was infectious, and the multitude did Him honour, saluting Him as the Son of David, and as the One who was to come in the name of the Lord. But the reality of their faith was soon tested, for entering the city the question was raised, "Who is this?" The answer of the multitude displayed no real faith at all. They said, "This is Jesus the prophet of Nazareth of Galilee." Quite true, of course, as far as it went; but it went no further than what was obvious even to those who had no faith. A good many prophets had entered before this, and Jerusalem had slain them.

Jesus had just presented Himself to them as King, so, having arrived in the city, He went straight to the temple, the very centre of their religion, and asserted His kingly power in cleansing it. He had done this at the very beginning of His ministry, as recorded in John 2; He did it again at the end. The trafficking and money-changing in the temple had doubtless sprung out of the kindly arrangements of the law, which Deuteronomy 14: 24-26 records. Ungodly men had taken advantage of this provision to turn the temple precincts into a den of thieves. God intended His temple to be the house where men drew near to Him with their requests. Its custodians had turned it into a place where men were swindled, and so the name of God was maligned. To defile or corrupt the temple of God is a sin of tremendous gravity. 1 Corinthians 3: 17 shows this, in its application to God's present temple.

Having driven out these evil men, Jesus dispensed mercy to the very people they would have kept outside. The blind and lame were forbidden to approach in Leviticus 21: 18, and 2 Samuel 5: 6-8 records David's sentence against them: he said, they "shall not come into the house." The

# MATTHEW

great Son of David had now arrived in Zion, and He reverses David's action. The kind of folk that were "hated of David's soul" were loved and blessed that day. The sordid money-changers had misrepresented the God whose house it was, and caused men to blaspheme His name: in healing the needy, Jesus rightly represented the very heart of God, and in result there was praise. Even the children were found crying, "Hosanna to the Son of David!" They had caught up the cry from the older folk.

The religious leaders themselves witnessed His wonderful works of power and grace, and to their sore displeasure they heard the children's cry. Jesus vindicated them in their simplicity, quoting the verse from Psalm 8 as finding a fulfilment in them. The Psalm says, "ordained strength," whereas He gave an application of it in saying, "perfected praise;" but in either case the thought is that God accomplishes what He desires, and receives the praise He looks for, through small and weak things. Thus it is made manifest that the strength and the praise is of and from Himself. Thus it was here. When the leaders were not only silent but opposed, God took care to have suitable praise through the lips of the babes.

For the moment however the city and temple were in the custody of these unbelieving men; so He left them and it, and went out to Bethany for the night—the place where was found at least one household that believed in Him and loved Him. Returning next morning He uttered His sentence against the fig tree that bore nothing but leaves. All outward show but no fruit; and on that tree no fruit was to grow for ever. It was utterly condemned. Immediately it withered away! The occurrence was so obviously miraculous that it compelled the attention and the comment of the disciples.

The Lord's reply turned their thoughts from the fig tree to "this mountain." The fig tree was symbolic of Israel, more particularly that part of the nation which had returned from the captivity and were now in the land. Judged nationally there was nothing in them for God and they were condemned; and since they were picked samples of the human race the fruitless tree set forth the fact that Adam's race, as men in the flesh, is condemned and there will never be found in them any fruit for God. Jerusalem and its temple crowned "this mountain," which symbolized, we believe, the whole Jewish system. If they had faith they might anticipate what God was going to do in removing the mountain so that it might be submerged in the sea of the nations. The Epistle to the Hebrews shows how the Jewish system was set aside, and "this mountain" was finally cast into the sea when Jerusalem was destroyed in A.D. 70.

What is needed is *faith*. Hebrews emphasizes this, for in that Epistle there occurs the great chapter on faith. Israel's system was after all but a shadow of good things to come and not the very image of the things. It needed faith to discern this and many who believed in Christ had not got clear of the shadows even when Hebrews was written. The man of faith it is

## MATTHEW

who penetrates to the realities which Christ has introduced, and such may pray in the confidence of receiving what they ask.

The religious leaders felt that the arrival of Jesus in Jerusalem and His wonderful actions were a challenge to their authority, so they determined to act aggressively and challenge His. By doing this they started a controversy, the record of which continues to the end of chapter 22. It produced three striking parables from the lips of the Lord, followed by three crafty questions from Pharisees and Herodians, from Sadducees, and from a lawyer, respectively; and then crowned by the Lord's own great question which reduced all His adversaries to silence.

In demanding that He produce His authority, the chief priests assumed that they had competency to assess its value when produced. The Lord's answer was virtually this, that if they would prove their competency by pronouncing on the far lesser question of John's authority, He would then submit His authority to their scrutiny. This at once plunged them into difficulty. If they endorsed John's baptism as coming from heaven, they condemned themselves for they had not believed him. If they rejected it as merely of men, they would lose popularity with the people who held him to be a prophet. That popularity was very dear to them, for "they loved the praise of men" (John 12: 43). They *would* not say John's baptism was valid, and they *dared* not say it was invalid, so they took the ground of ignorance, saying, "We cannot tell." Thus they destroyed their own competency to adjudicate and lost any possible ground of protest when Jesus refused to reveal His authority. The power of God that He wielded gave Him ample authority apart from anything else. But they had refused it and attributed it to the energy of the devil, as we saw earlier in the Gospel.

The Lord now took the initiative with His parables. As we consider them we shall see that the first concerns their response as under the law; the second their response as tested by the presence of the Son upon earth; the third is prophetic and looks on to the response which would be accorded to the Gospel. The Divine order is observed—the Law, the Messiah, the Gospel.

Jesus opened the first with the words, "What think ye?" since He submitted the short parable to their judgment and allowed them to condemn themselves. The parable as to two sons in Luke 15 is somewhat lengthy, whereas here we have a parable of two sons which is very short, yet in both the same two classes are portrayed—the religious leaders on the one hand, the publicans and sinners on the other. Here however we find their responsibility under the law, whereas in Luke 15 it is their reception according to the grace of the Gospel.

In several Old Testament passages the figure of a vineyard sets forth Israel under the law; so the words, "Go work today in My vineyard," most aptly express Jehovah's command. These words are often quoted as though they urged Christians to serve their Lord in the Gospel, but that is

# MATTHEW

not their meaning, if read in their context. The figure which would apply to us is that of labour in "the harvest" and not "the vineyard," as we see in chapter 9: 38, John 4: 35-38, and elsewhere. The great word under the law was, "This DO," for it set men to work; but by the works of the law no flesh has been justified.

This fact may be seen in the parable, for neither of the two sons was marked by full obedience. One made fair profession in words but totally disobeyed. The other flagrantly refused at first, but then was brought to repentance, and obedience as the fruit of that. Just so the chief priests and elders were deceiving themselves by their religious profession, while publicans and harlots repented and entered the kingdom. In verse 32 the Lord definitely connects the matter with John's ministry. He came at the close of the age of law, calling those who had failed under it to repentance. Thus the Lord Himself connected the parable with law and not the Gospel.

The parable of the householder and his vineyard follows. It is still the vineyard, we notice; and "the vineyard of the Lord of Hosts is the house of Israel" (Isa. 5: 7). Now we have not only their failure under the law but their ill-treatment of all the prophets by whom God had addressed their consciences, and then finally the mission of the Son, who came as the supreme test. The "husbandmen" of the parable evidently represent the responsible leaders of Israel, who now not merely repeated their failure to produce any fruit for the benefit of the "householder," but crowned their wickedness by slaying the Son. They desired the whole inheritance for themselves. Thus the Lord summed up the indictment against Israel under these three heads: no fruit for God; ill-treatment of His servants the prophets; the rejection and murder of the Son.

Having propounded the parable He again said, in effect, "What think ye?"—submitting to their judgment what fate the husbandmen deserved. His opponents, though so acute as to things concerning their own interests, were obtuse and very blind to everything of a spiritual nature. Hence they entirely failed to discern the drift of the parable, and gave an answer which foretold the righteous doom which would come upon their own heads. They would find themselves in two words, *dispossessed* and *destroyed*.

The Lord accepted as correct the verdict they had passed upon themselves, quoting Psalm 118: 22, 23, in corroboration. He was the stone which they, the builders, were rejecting. He in no way fitted into the building which they designed and they refused Him. A day is coming when He will be brought forth to be the foundation and set the lines of the building that God has in view; and this wonderful event will involve the destruction of wicked men and their false building.

In verse 43 and the beginning of verse 44 we get the present effects of His rejection. He becomes a stone of stumbling to the leaders of Israel and the mass of the nation, and in consequence they are broken as a people. This finally came to pass when Jerusalem was destroyed. God's kingdom had

## MATTHEW

been established in their midst through Moses, and now this was definitely taken from them, and it was to be given in another form to a "nation" that would produce its proper fruits. The prophets of old had denounced the sin of the people, and announced that God would raise up another nation to supplant them, as we see in such scriptures as Deuteronomy 32: 21; Isaiah 55: 5; 65: 1; 66: 8. That nation will be "born at once" at the beginning of the millenial age; that is, they will be born again, and so have the nature that delights in the will of God, and enables them to bring forth fruit. We Christians anticipate this, as we see in 1 Peter 2: 9. Redeemed and born again, we have been called out of darkness into God's marvellous light, and so are enabled as "an holy nation" to show forth the virtues of the One who has called us. This surely is bringing forth fruit which gratifies Him.

The latter part of verse 44 refers to what will happen to the unbelieving at the beginning of the millenium. The Lord's words look like a reference to Daniel 2: 34, 35, and set forth the pulverizing effect of the Second Advent upon men, whether Jew or Gentile. So the teaching of these two verses comprises the national breaking of Israel as a consequence of their rejection of Christ, the substitution for them of a new "nation", and the final destruction of all adversaries when the Lord Jesus shall be revealed in flaming fire.

Having heard these things it dawned upon the darkened minds of the chief priests and Pharisees that He was speaking of them, and that unwittingly they had been condemning themselves. What a shock it must have given them! In their defeat they thought of murder, and were only restrained for the moment by fear of popular opinion. In verse 26 we saw fear of the people putting its restraint upon their *tongues*. In verse 46 it lays a restraining hand upon their *actions*.

### CHAPTER 22

BUT THE LORD calmly pursued what He had to say to them, so in the opening of this chapter we have the parable of the marriage of the king's son, which predicts the Gospel day which was about to dawn. There is no question, "What think ye?" about this parable, for it travels beyond men's thoughts altogether. It is also distinguished from the other two parables by beginning, "The kingdom of heaven is like," or, more literally, "has become like." Men come under Heaven's jurisdiction by the reception of the Gospel invitation, when the breakdown is complete as figured in the other parables. We are now again going to hear something new, just as we did in chapter 13.

In this parable the king does not demand anything from anybody. He *gives* instead of *demanding*. He too has a "Son" in whose honour He makes a marriage feast, sending forth His servants to call men in. How aptly the

# MATTHEW

call sets forth the Gospel message: "I have prepared . . . all things are ready: come unto the marriage." *Prepared* through the sacrifice of Christ. *Ready*, since His is a finished work. Hence it is not now "Go, work," but *"Come."*

In the first place the invitation went to "them that were bidden," a number of specially privileged folk. We see the fulfilment of this in the early chapters of Acts. For a short time the Gospel went out only to the Jew, but the mass of them made light of it, occupied with worldly gain, while some actively opposed, persecuting and slaying some of the early messengers, as seen in the case of Stephen. This first stage ended with the destruction of Jerusalem, as foretold in verse 7.

Then the invitation is widened out as we see in verses 9 and 10. In the parable of Luke 14 we find one servant, representing doubtless the Holy Spirit; here many servants are in question, representing the human instruments that the Spirit may use. They go into the highways, bidding all, as many as they meet, whether bad or good. The Spirit can *"compel"* men to come in, as in Luke 14: the servants are instructed to *invite* any and all they run up against. Not all will respond, but by this means the feast will have its full complement of guests. The Gospel preacher has not to embarrass himself with questions as to God's electing grace. He has simply to pass on the word to all he meets; gathering in all who respond, for God will touch the hearts of men.

The second part of the parable, verses 11-14, shows that, as always when human service is referred to, what is unreal may enter and remain for a time. By not accepting the wedding garment the man had declined to honour the king's son. When the king came in he was detected and consigned to his true place in outer darkness. The Divine presence will unmask all that is unreal and disentangle everything. We saw this in chapter 13, and shall see it again in chapter 25.

That the Pharisees were now getting desperate is seen in the fact that they were driven to an alliance with the Herodians, whom they abominated. Their question as to the tribute was cleverly framed so as to bring Him into disrepute with either Caesar or the populace. They began with what they intended to be flattery, but which was a sober statement of truth. He *was* true. He *did* teach the way of God in truth. He *was* wholly above regarding the person of men. Asking for the tribute money, He showed them that it was evidently Caesar's, for it had his image upon it. If Caesar's it must be rendered to him; but then He set them in the presence of God. Were they rendering to God the things that were His? This great answer not only amazed them but also so smote their consciences that they went away. Jesus had stated a great principle of action applicable to all of us so long as we are under the jurisdiction of any kind of Caesar. We must render to Caesar all his rights, but the things that are God's are far higher and wider than all that is his.

# MATTHEW

The question propounded by the Sadducees was cleverly designed with the twofold object of embarrassing Jesus and of ridiculing belief in resurrection, which to their minds only meant a restoration to life under ordinary conditions in this world. Doubtless they felt sure that in result Jesus would be discomfited and themselves confirmed in their unbelief. But the Lord's reply showed that resurrection introduces into another world where different conditions prevail, and He quoted Exodus 3: 6, as showing that in the days of Moses the Patriarchs were living in that other world, though not yet raised from the dead. The fact that their spirits were there guaranteed that eventually they would be there in risen bodies.

In those days the priests were mainly of the Sadducee persuasion, and the Lord did not spare them in the directness of His rebuke. "Ye do err," was His plain word, and He indicated the source of their error; they knew neither the Scriptures, that they professed to expound, nor the power of the God, whom they professed to serve. This twofold error underlies all modern religious unbelief. First, the Scriptures are frequently misquoted and always misunderstood. Second, in their minds God is so stripped of His power and glory that endless difficulties are created. Let His power be admitted and difficulties cease to exist.

The Lord's answer astonished all who heard it. Evidently it was quite new to them, even to the Pharisees, who had never been able to silence the Sadducees like this. Hearing it, the Pharisees came together, and one of them put to the Lord his question about the law, raising a point that they had doubtless often discussed amongst themselves. He was thinking of the ten Commandments in Exodus 20, but the Lord turned him to Deuteronomy 6: 5, and added Leviticus 19: 18. The demand of the law is summed up in one word—*love*. First, love to God; second, love to one's neighbour. When Paul tells us, "Love is the fulfilling of the law" (Rom. 13: 10), he is only stating in other words what Jesus said here (verse 40).

The three parables had brought them face to face with the grace of the Gospel; the three questions had been so answered as to impress upon them love, as the supreme demand of the law. To that love they were strangers. Yet being still gathered together Jesus propounded to them His great question, "What think ye of Christ? whose Son is He?" They knew He was to be the Son of David, but why David should call him his Lord, in Psalm 110, they did not know. The only possible solution of that problem has been given in the first chapter of our Gospel. "Jesus Christ, the Son of David" is "Emmanuel, which being interpreted is, God with us." If faith once seizes that, the whole position is as clear as sunlight. If that be refused, as with these poor Pharisees, all is gloom. They were in darkness. Not a word could they answer, and their discomfiture was so complete that they dared not question Him more.

However though they were done with Him, the Lord had not finished with them. The time had now come to unmask these hypocrites in the presence of the multitudes, who were under their influence.

# MATTHEW

## Chapter 23

THIS CHAPTER RECORDS his burning words. In a few days the multitude, influenced by these men, would be shouting for His death. Their responsibility and guilt was greatly increased by this warning the Lord gave them as to the true character of their leaders.

He began by according to them the place they claimed as the exponents of the law of Moses. Therefore the people were to keep and do the law as they heard it from their lips. Yet they were to carefully avoid taking them as examples. Their lives contradicted the law they proclaimed. They legislated for others without the smallest conscience as to their own obedience. This the Lord stated in verse 4, and it is a very common offence with professional religionists, who love directing other people while having an easy time themselves.

Then, in verses 5-12, He exposed their love of notice and pre-eminence. All was for the eye of men. At feasts—the social circle—in synagogues—the religious circle—in markets—the business circle—they wanted the chief place as Rabbis and Masters. The disciple of Christ is to be the exact opposite of all this, so let us take it deeply to heart. The abasement of such men is only a matter of time. They were supposed to be signposts into the kingdom but really they were obstructions. They did not enter themselves and hindered others.

Moreover, they used their position to rob the poor and defenceless widow, covering up this enormity with the parade of long prayers, consequently they should receive severer judgment. Long prayers may impress the crowd, but they did not impress the Lord! Let us remember this and avoid them ourselves. We venture to affirm that no one marked by deep desire and really conscious of the presence of God, can wander about in a maze of words. As Ecclesiastes 5: 2 indicates, *his words must be few.*

Great zeal for the making of proselytes is characteristic of the Pharisaic mind, and the Lord's words in verse 15 expose a remarkable feature of mere proselytism. It reproduces with added emphasis the character of the proselytizers in those who are proselytized. The Pharisees were children of hell, and their converts were the same in a twofold way. This is why there is always a tendency for evil men and seducers to wax worse and worse, until all is ripe for judgment.

In verses 16-22, the Lord condemns their fanciful teachings. The distinctions they draw between the temple and the gold of the temple, between the altar and the gift upon it, might make the unthinking regard them with awe as possessing very superior minds; in reality their distinctions were purely imaginary and only a proof of their own blindness and folly. So with other matters; much punctiliousness over small things; much negligence as to great things—whether positively, as to what they observed, as in verse 23, or negatively, as to what they refused, as in verse 24. Blind they were indeed, and that type of blindness is all too common today.

Verses 25-28, expose another pernicious characteristic; they only concerned themselves about external cleanliness, so as to appear well in the eyes of men. They had no concern for the inside which was open to the eye of God. They were most careful as to possible defilement acquired by contact from without; yet most careless as to defilement which they themselves generated from within. In result they became centres of defilement, and far from acquiring it *from* others they diffused it *to* others. This is a most subtle evil, from any suspicion of which we may well pray to be preserved.

Lastly, verses 29-33, the Lord charged them with being the murderers of God's prophets. They built tombs for the earlier prophets, since the sting of their words was no longer felt, but they were truly the children of those that had killed them; and, true to the principle of verse 15, they would prove themselves twofold more the children of murder; filling up the sins of their fathers, and ending up without a doubt in the damnation of hell.

This passage furnishes us with the most terrible denunciation from the lips of Jesus, of which we have any record. He never said such things to any poor publican or sinner. These hot words were reserved for religious hypocrites. He was full of grace and truth. Grace with truth He extended to the confessed sinners. The searchlight of truth, without mention of grace, was reserved for the hypocrites.

So it came to pass that the blood of a long line of martyrs was going to lie at the door of that generation; and now for the last time Jerusalem was having the opportunity of trusting under the wings of Jehovah, who was amongst them in the person of Jesus. Often He would have thus sheltered them as the Psalms bear witness, and often would Jesus have gathered them during His sojourn amongst them; but they would not. Consequently the beautiful house in Jerusalem, once owned as Jehovah's was now disowned. It was just their house and desolate; and He who would have filled it was going from them, to be unseen till they should say, "Blessed is He that cometh in the name of the Lord." They will not say this, as Psalm 118 shows, until that day arrives "which the Lord hath made," when "the stone which the builders refused is become the head stone of the corner."

## CHAPTER 24

ALL THAT WE have been reading, from chapter 21: 23, had taken place in the temple precincts. Now, chapter 24: 1, Jesus departed, and the disciples desired to call His attention to some of its splendid buildings, only to draw from Him the prediction that it was to be razed to its foundations. This started their enquiries as to the time of the fulfilment of His saying,

## MATTHEW

which they connected with the end of the age. The first words of His reply show that His predictions are to forewarn and forearm us, and not merely to minister to our curiosity, or even our thirst for accurate knowledge. We are to take heed to ourselves.

False Christs are foretold together with wars and rumours, but these things do not indicate the end. There are to be famines, pestilences, earthquakes, as well as wars, but these are only the beginning of sorrows. Coupled with these things there shall be the persecution and martyrdom of disciples, the apostasy of some who have professed discipleship, the rising up of false prophets, the abounding of iniquity, and backsliding in heart of many professors. In an hour like that the real ones will be marked by endurance to the end when salvation will reach them. Moreover, all the time God will maintain His own witness among all the nations, and when this is completed the end shall come.

Three times in these verses does the Lord speak of "the end," and in each case He refers to the end of the age, as to which the disciples had enquired. To His true disciples, marked by endurance, the end will bring salvation. He emphasizes this first, before saying that it will bring judgment for His foes. Let it be noted that it is "*this* Gospel of the kingdom" which must be fully preached before the end comes; that is, the Gospel which the Lord Himself had preached—see 4: 23; 9: 35—announcing the kingdom as at their doors. The Gospel which we preach today—see, 1 Corinthians 15: 1-14—could not in the nature of things be declared before Christ had died.

At the time of the end the abomination of desolation, spoken of in Daniel 12: 11, is to be found in the holy place, and Jerusalem is in question, as verse 16 shows. Evidently there again will be a temple with its holy place at the time of the end, to be desecrated by this supremely abominable idolatry. At this time will be fulfilled the prophecy of chapter 12: 43-45: the evil spirit of idolatry will enter into the people with seven-fold force, and the mass of them will accept this abomination standing in the holy place—most probably "the image of the beast," spoken of in Revelation 13: 14, 15. Because of this crowning iniquity desolation will fall upon them in the government of God. Now the setting up of this abomination is to be the signal to the godly that the predicted great tribulation is begun, and that their safety lies in flight from Jerusalem and Judaea, where the furnace of affliction will be at its hottest. The Lord was speaking to His disciples, who at that moment were just godly Israelites surrounding their Messiah on earth, though presently they were to be built into the foundation of the church that was to be. Hence at that moment they represented, not the church, but the godly remnant of Israel, still carefully observing the law of the sabbath (verse 20), and many of them located in Judaea. Instant flight was to be their course. This agrees with what is set forth symbolically in Revelation 12: 6.

# MATTHEW

The great tribulation is wholly unprecedented and never to be equalled, let alone surpassed. This the Lord states in verse 21; and the reason of it is, that as the book of Revelation shows, it will be a time of infliction of wrath from heaven—the outpouring of the vials of judgment. It will not be merely a case of men afflicting men, or a nation scourging other nations, as we see so strikingly today, but of God scourging the nations as He settles His accounts with them. Wrath from God is "revealed from heaven" (Rom. 1: 18), though not yet executed, and as far as the nations are concerned it will fall at this time. Nations as such are only found in this world; they do not exist beyond the grave, though the men composing them do.

There will be elect souls on earth during the tribulation and for their sake it will be cut short, as verse 22 tells us: as it says in Romans 9: 28, the Lord will make "a short work . . . upon the earth," and this in order that a remnant may be saved. Today God is dispensing mercy through the Gospel, and He has made a very lengthy work of it, extending to nineteen centuries: when He dispenses wrath He will make swift work, cutting it short in righteousness. A brief three and a half years will cover it, as other scriptures show. Thus the goodness of God will be manifested both in mercy and in wrath.

At that time the devil will know very well that the coming of Christ is about to take place; hence he will aim at confusing the issue by raising up imposters and endowing them with supernatural powers, hoping to deceive the elect who are looking for Him. Verse 24 plainly indicates that not all miraculous signs are of God. There are two kinds—the Divine and the devilish. In the Divine kind there is a manifestation of the Divine character in grace and power; the devilish kind may often be more flashy and startling and attractive to unconverted men. People today, who have an itching desire for the miraculous should have great care lest they be deceived.

The coming of the true Christ of God will be marked by the greatest possible publicity, like the lightning. No one will need to penetrate to a remote desert or a secret chamber in order to see Him. Just as the vultures are found wherever the carcase is, so will He fall in judgment wherever men are found rotting in the putridity and pestilence of sin.

The tribulation will be followed by the breaking up and the overturning of existing powers both in heaven and on earth, and then the Son of Man will be manifested in His glory. Twice previously the Lord had spoken of "the sign of the prophet Jonas" (12: 39, 40; 16: 4) which was the Son of Man three days in the grave. Here, we have the sign of the Son of Man in heaven—The sign that at last God is about to assert His rights in this rebellious earth, and enforce them by the Man of His purpose and choice. Two great signs are these! Who shall say which of them is greater? Both are equally great in their season, and command our worshipful adoration.

# MATTHEW

Having appeared in His glory, He will gather together His elect, those for whose sake the tribulation days have been shortened. This gathering will be accomplished by angelic ministration and signalized by the great sound of a trumpet; it will be the fulfilment of the feast of trumpets (Lev. 23: 24, 25), just as the Passover has been fulfilled in the death of Christ, and Pentecost in the gift of the Spirit and formation of the church. This gathering of the elect is in view of millennial blessedness; there is no mention of any rapture to heaven, or even of resurrection, for it is the gathering together of living people on earth. In chapter 16 the Lord had revealed that He was going to build His church, but its heavenly calling and destiny had not been revealed, so the church must not be read into verse 31.

With verse 32 we commence a series of parables and parabolic sayings. The fig tree is a parable of the Jew; and when we see a reviving of national life with that people we are to know that summer time is at hand, but until all things are fulfilled and that moment comes "this generation" shall not pass away. The Lord has spoken a number of times of this generation—see 11: 16; 12: 39, 45; 16: 4. It is a very ancient and persistent generation, for Moses denounced it in Deuteronomy 32: 5 and 20—"children in whom is no faith." The unbelieving generation will meet its doom when Jesus comes, but not before. They will go, and the words of Christ will abide.

The exact time of His advent is a secret known only to the Father, who has reserved all times and seasons under His own authority (see Acts 1: 7); and because this is so it will come as a complete surprise to the heedless world. It will be just as in the days of Noah; men engrossed in their pleasures till the judgment falls upon them. Then an eternal separation for both men and women will take place. Zephaniah 3: 11-13, will be fulfilled; the transgressors will be taken away in judgment; the afflicted and poor people who trust in the name of the Lord will be left for millennial blessings, and these are "the remnant of Israel."

Arrived at verse 42, we again see how the Lord brought these prophetic realities to bear upon the conduct of His disciples. Since they did not know the hour, they were to be marked by watchfulness and faithful service. The servant to whom rule is entrusted must fulfil his responsibility. Doing so, he will be blessed and rewarded. On the other hand it is possible for men to take the place of servants and yet be evil. Such will ignore their responsibilities and maltreat their fellow-servants, saying in their hearts, "My Lord delayeth His coming." That is always the thought of the world. They listen to the prophecy and then say, "The vision that he seeth is for many days to come, and he prophesieth of the times that are far off" (Ezek. 12: 27). The true servant maintains himself in readiness for his Lord's approach and diligently cares for His interests while he waits.

Verses 50-51 show that the "evil servant" contemplated is not a man grievously failing and yet true at bottom, but a man who is entirely false.

His Lord will judge him and appoint him his portion with the hypocrites because he is a hypocrite. He is banished under judgment to his own company. When the hypocrite is unmasked and judged there is weeping and gnashing of teeth indeed.

## Chapter 25

THE PARABLE OF the ten virgins opens this chapter. This world presents a very tangled scene in every direction. The coming of the Lord is going to produce a thorough disentanglement. We have already seen this in the parables of the wheat and the tares, and that of the net cast into the sea, in chapter 13, and again in the verses we have just considered at the close of chapter 24. The same great fact meets us again in this fresh similitude of the kingdom of heaven. The Lord had already mentioned the church in an anticipatory way, but He does not here say, "Then shall the church be likened . . . " but, "the kingdom of heaven," which is wider than the church, though including it. Hence the "ten virgins" do not represent the church *distinctively*, though it is included within their scope.

Hence we are surely right in applying the parable to saints of the present moment—*to ourselves*. The virgins "went forth" to meet the bridegroom, and we have been *called out* of the world to wait for the Lord. There *did* supervene a period of forgetfulness and slumber in the church's history. A stirring cry as to the Bridegroom's coming *has been* sounded forth, a cry which has said, "*Go ye out* to meet Him;" that is, revert to your original position as a called out people. So long as there was slumber there was little or no discernible difference between the true and the false, but directly they awoke and reverted to their original place the difference became manifest, and those who had no oil were revealed. The oil represents the Holy Spirit, and "if any man have not the Spirit if Christ, he is none of His" (Rom. 8. 9).

This parable has been pressed into service to support the idea that only devoted, wide-awake believers will meet the Lord when He comes, and that believers of lesser merit will be penalized. We believe this to be a mistake. The point all through this passage is the way in which the coming of the Lord will make complete separation between those who really are His and those who are not. In this parable we see the separation made between real and spurious in the sphere of profession, and the seal of the Spirit is only possessed by those truly Christ's. The shutting of the door sealed the rejection of the false. The foolish do not represent backsliders who once knew the Lord and were known of Him. The word is not "I once knew you, but now disown you," but rather, "I know you not." Now the Lord knows those who are His, but these were strangers to Him.

In verse 13 the Lord applies this parable to His disciples, and to us. We know not the time of the coming of the Son of Man, and we are to watch.

# MATTHEW

Thus again and again does He bring His prophetic teaching to bear upon our characters and behaviour. He does not give us light as to what is coming just to inform our minds and satisfy our desires for us. So having exhorted us to watchfulness He proceeds to show in the rest of this chapter how His coming is going to affect us as servants, and indeed how it will affect the world. The disentanglement it is to produce will be complete.

The parable of the servants and the talents is brought in to reinforce the exhortation to watch, given in verse 13; and it shows how the coming of the Son of Man will test all who take the place of being His servants, and lead to the casting out of all that is unreal. It is a thought calculated to sober us all, that during the time of His absence the Lord has committed His "goods" to His people. His interests have been placed in our hands, and we cannot avoid the point of the parable by saying, "I have no special gift and therefore it does not apply to me."

The master delivered his goods to his servants, "every man" of them, and he had the discrimination which enabled him to appraise the capacity of each, and so he apportioned to each "according to his several ability." We may distinguish therefore between *the gifts* that may be bestowed upon us and *the abilities* that we may possess, always remembering that the Lord adjusts the relation between the two things. Our abilities would cover our natural powers as well as our spiritual, and if these are not very large five talents, or even two, might be only a burden to us. If that be so, the Lord knows it and He only gives us one. We might connect this with the gifts spoken of in Romans 12: 6-15, which are of such a character as to cover all the people of God. Whether the gift bestowed be large or small, the great thing is to use it with diligence.

Equal diligence was shown by the servants who received the five talents and the two. Each succeeded in doubling that which was entrusted to him, and when their Lord returned they both shared equally in his approbation and reward. Again in this parable, be it noted, the contrast does not lie between the more or less faithfulness and diligence, which may mark true servants, but between servants who were true, though their measure of ability differed, and the one that was no true servant at all. He that had received the one talent hid it in the earth instead of using it in his master's interest; and this he did because he had no real knowledge of his lord. He claimed to know that he was a hard man, exacting more than his due, one to be afraid of. His lord took him up on the ground of the knowledge that he claimed to have, and showed that his plea only aggravated his guilt, for had he been a hard man the more reason there would have been for diligent use of the talent entrusted.

In reality the lord was anything but a hard man as witnessed by his treatment of the servants who were good and faithful. The fact of the matter was that this servant had no true knowledge of his lord, no true link with

## MATTHEW

him. In result he lost all that had been entrusted to him, and he was ejected into outer darkness to weeping and gnashing of teeth, as was the false servant portrayed at the end of the previous chapter. In the similar parable recorded in Luke 19, the distinction is drawn between the different servants with their degrees of zeal and faithfulness, and they are rewarded accordingly. The servant with one pound suffers loss but he is not ejected into outer darkness. It is worthy of note that in both cases the failure is seen with the man who is entrusted with the least. If we probe our own hearts, we shall recognize that when we are only capable of *small* things our tendency is to do *nothing*. The Lord will assuredly honour the servant who, though of small ability, does the small things with zeal and fidelity.

The closing paragraph of this chapter (verses 31-46) is not introduced as a parable. The parables began with verse 32 of chapter 24, and now that they are completed, verse 31 picks up the thread of the prophetic recital from 24: 31. When He comes, the Son of Man will not only gather together His elect, but He will summon the nations before Him, so that there may be a complete disentanglement right through the earth of the good and the evil. All the nations are to be assembled before Him, and the scene is one that takes place on the earth. In the final assize, when earth and heaven are fled away, predicted in Revelation 20, no nations appear: it is just "the dead, small and great," for in death all national distinctions disappear.

Other scriptures inform us as to the warrior judgments to be executed by Christ in person, when at Armageddon the mighty armies of the various kings of the earth will be destroyed. These judgments however will still leave multitudes of non-combatants, and all these must pass before the scrutiny of the Son of Man, for only He can discriminate and disentangle with unerring wisdom. He will do this as a shepherd divides the sheep from the goats; and the issues depending on His judgment will be eternal, just as they will be in the judgment of the great white throne. Also here, as there, men will be judged according to their works.

The true state of every heart is known to God altogether apart from works; yet when public judgment is instituted it is always according to works, since they indicate plainly and infallibly what that state is, and thus the rightness of the Divine judgments is manifest to all beholders. These messengers, whom the King owns as "My brethren," had gone forth as His representatives, and the treatment they received had varied according to the view taken of the Son of Man whom they represented. Those who believed in Him identified themselves with His messengers, and ministered to them in their rejection and afflictions: those who did not believe in Him paid them no attention at all. Those who had faith declared it by their works. Those who had no faith equally declared it by their works.

Take note of the fact that the King does not charge the condemned ones with persecuting and imprisoning His servants, but only with ignoring them—treating them with neglect. It fits in with the great question of

# MATTHEW

Hebrews 2, "How shall we escape if we *neglect* so great salvation?" In that day it will be seen that if men treat Christ with neglect, by neglecting His servants, they came under eternal condemnation.

Who are "these My brethren"? If we consider the whole prophetic discourse, of which this is the concluding part, the answer is not difficult. In the opening of His discourse the Lord addressed His disciples personally and told them how they would be hated, afflicted and betrayed, but that the end would only come when "this gospel of the kingdom" should have been preached for a witness to all nations, and that those who endured to the end should be saved. He spoke as though the disciples before Him would be there at the end because He viewed them in a representative capacity. The "brethren" at the end of the discourse are the disciples of the *last* days, who were represented by the disciples of the *first* days, to whom the Lord was speaking. Now though these were a little later baptised by the Spirit into the one body, which is the church, as recorded in Acts 2, they were at that moment simply a remnant of Israel who had discovered the Messiah in Jesus, and attached themselves to Him. They represented a similar remnant of Israel who in the last days will have their eyes opened and pick up the broken thread of "this gospel of the kingdom"—broken when Christ was rejected on earth, and picked up and renewed just before He returns to earth to reign.

In the closing paragraph of chapter 25 the end is come. The Son of Man is King, the disciples who endured to the end are saved, the nations are judged, the disentanglement of the good and the evil is complete, the result of the judgment is eternal. Three times the word *eternal* occurs. The punishment of the wicked and the fire into which they go are eternal: the life into which the righteous pass is eternal. The antithesis to life is not cessation of existence, as it would be if life merely signified existence as the result of the vital spark remaining in us: it is punishment, because eternal life signifies the whole realm of blessed and eternal verities in which the righteous will move for ever. The point here is not that the life is *in them*, but that they pass *into it*. On that happy note the Lord's prophetic discourse ended.

## CHAPTER 26

THIS CHAPTER BRINGS us back to the history of the last few days of the Lord's life on earth. The opening verses give us a peep into the palace of the high priest, and we find it to be full of craft and counsels of murder. In verses 6-13, we turn from this most atrocious wickedness in high places to behold an action of love and devotion in a humble home, where some of the godly remnant dwelt. From John 12 we gather that the woman was Mary of Bethany. She evidently anointed both His head and His feet, but Matthew, emphasizing His kingly character, mentions that His head was

# MATTHEW

anointed, as befits a king: John emphasizing His Deity, tells us that His feet were anointed, though a great servant like John the Baptist was not worthy to unbind His sandals.

The disciples were entirely out of sympathy with this act of devotion, regarding it as mere waste. Their complaint was instigated by Judas Iscariot, as John's Gospel shows us, yet it revealed them as thinking first of money and then of the poor, while ignorant and mystified as to His approaching death. The woman thought neither of money nor of the poor. Christ filled her vision, and He knew how to interpret her action. Very probably she acted more from instinct than from intelligence; but she was conscious that death now threatened the Object of her affection and worship, and the Lord accepted what she did as for His burial. Not only did He approve but He ordained that her devoted act should be held in continual remembrance wherever the gospel is preached. And so it has been.

The woman's devotion stands in the strongest possible contrast with the hatred of the religious leaders, related in the preceding paragraph, and the treachery of Judas, related in the paragraph that follows. Violence reached its climax in the leaders—they would slay Him at once without scruple. Corruption reached its climax in Judas, who having companied with Jesus for three years was desirous of making the paltry profit of thirty pieces of silver by His betrayal. A bond-slave in Israel was estimated as being worth thirty shekels of silver, as Exodus 21: 32 shows.

Then again, if the second paragraph of our chapter (verses 6-13) shows us the devotion of a disciple to her Lord, the fourth paragraph (verse 17 and onwards) shows us the solicitude of the Lord for His disciples, and how He counted on their remembrance of Him during the approaching time of His absence.

The passover was eaten in the place of the Lord's choosing, and as it proceeded He identified the traitor and warned him of his doom. The going of the Son of Man by betrayal into death had been predicted in the Holy Writings, but this did not in any degree lessen the gravity of the traitor's act. The fact that God is omniscient and can foretell men's acts does not relieve them of responsibility for what they do. By his act Judas revealed his true self. Jesus was about to reveal Himself fully by His death.

As the Passover meal drew to its close Jesus instituted His supper as the memorial of His body given and His blood shed for us for the remission of sins. In the wording of verses 26-29 there is nothing that definitely states that the institution is to be observed until He comes again: for that we have to turn to 1 Corinthians 11. The fact is inferred in verse 29, for the cup speaks of blessing and joy, and of that the Lord will drink in a new way when the kingdom comes: meanwhile the cup is for us and not for Him. Today He is marked by patience: in the day of the kingdom He will enter into blessing and joy in an altogether new way. Meanwhile we have the memorial of His death, for in it His body and blood are presented to us not

# MATTHEW

conjointly as though He were a living Man on earth, but separately: this bread, His body, and that cup, His blood, poured forth; thus symbolizing His death.

On their way to the Mount of Olives Jesus foretold how His death would mean their scattering, as the Scripture had said, but He pointed them to His resurrection and appointed a meeting place in Galilee, where He would regather them. Peter, however, filled with self-confidence, resisted the warning to his own undoing, and also to his missing the fact and import of the resurrection. All the disciples were marked by the same thing, though not to the same degree.

They were very soon put to the test in Gethsemane. There Jesus entered in spirit into the sorrow of the death that was before Him, but wholly in communion with His Father. His very perfection caused Him to shrink from all that was involved in suffering and death as the judgment of God, yet He accepted that cup from the Father's hand. Further, it was a tribute to the perfection of His manhood that He should desire sympathy from the chosen disciples, but the prophetic word was fulfilled—"I looked for some to take pity, but there was none; and for comforters, but I found none" (Psa. 69: 20). Peter and the others, who were so sure that they never would deny Him, could not watch with Him one hour. Their flesh was too weak, but as yet they knew it not. Neither did they know that the treachery of Judas was coming to fruition, and the crisis was upon them.

Yet so it was; and in the rest of this chapter we see the amazing contrast between the Christ of God and all others who in any way came into contact with Him. All display their own peculiar deformities: His is the one serene figure in the centre of the picture.

First there comes Judas, the traitor; masking his treachery with such hypocrisy that nineteen centuries after the event "the traitor's kiss" remains a proverbial expression of disgust. In the language of Psalm 41: 9, here was "Mine own familiar friend, in whom I trusted, which did eat of My bread," and he had "lifted up his heel against Me." Hence Jesus addressed him as "Friend," but asked him the searching question, "wherefore art thou come?" He had come to betray his Master so that he might gain thirty paltry pieces of silver.

The sickening hypocrisy of the false disciple is followed by the fleshly zeal of a true one, whom we know to be Peter from John's Gospel. The self-confident man sleeps when he should be awake, and he smites when he should be quiet, and when his action would have been to his Master's discredit, had it not been disallowed. A time is coming when "the saints" will be "joyful in glory," when "the high praises of God" will be "in their mouth, and a two-edged sword in their hand, to execute vengeance" (Psa. 149: 5-7); but that is at the time of the second Advent and not the first. Peter's action was entirely out of place and inviting a sword-stroke upon himself. It was also entirely out of harmony with his Master's attitude,

# MATTHEW

who had irresistible might at His disposal and yet suffered Himself to be led as a lamb to the slaughter, as the Scripture had indicated.

When God would blot out from under heaven the cities of the plain He sent but *two angels* to deliver the blow. If *twelve legions* had been launched at the rebellious world what would have happened? The prayer that would have launched them was not uttered, and Peter's blow, that was struck as much for himself as for his Master, was simply ridiculous. When we are content to suffer as Christians we are spiritually victorious; when we take the sword we lose the spiritual battle and ultimately perish by the sword. One of the main reasons why the Reformation of four centuries ago was so badly arrested and defaced was that its chief promoters flew to the sword in its defence, and thereby turned it into a national and political movement rather than a spiritual one.

Next we see the Lord calmly dealing with the rough mob who, led by Judas, had come to arrest Him. He showed them the unsuitability and even folly of their doings. Yet in the presence of this mob the fortitude of all the disciples collapsed, and they forsook their Master and fled. Such are even the best of men!

The mob deliver Him to the leaders of Israel, and these men who claimed to represent God, had thrown away any pretence of seeking righteousness. We are not told that they were *misled* into accepting false evidence, nor that they were *tempted* into receiving it because it was thrust upon them. No, it says, they "*sought* false witness against Jesus, to put Him to death." They SOUGHT it. Has there ever, we wonder, been another trial upon this earth where the judges started by hunting for liars, that they might condemn the accused? Thus it was here; and in the presence of it Jesus held His peace. Judgment being utterly divorced from righteousness, He met them with a dignity that was Divine, and He only spoke to affirm His Christhood, His Sonship, and to affirm His coming glory as the Son of Man.

On this they condemned Him, but the high priest broke the law by rending his clothes as he condemned Him, thereby only condemning himself. This was the signal for a pandemonium of insults, in the midst of which stood the serene figure of our Saviour and our Lord. The calm brightness of His presence helps us to see the dark degradation in which they were sunk.

Lastly, in this chapter, Peter reaps what he had sown by his self-confidence. We read of his following afar off in verse 58, now we find him amongst the enemies of his Lord and unable to stand. He proves himself to be weak just where he had appeared to be strong, inasmuch as impetuosity is not the same thing as courage. Fleshly energy had impelled him into a position where he never ought to have been, and he fell. We cannot throw stones at him. Rather let us pray that if we find ourselves in a similar

# MATTHEW

case we may be granted repentance similar to that recorded in the last verse—a repentance that started directly the fall had been consummated.

## Chapter 27

THE CLOSING SCENES of the Lord's life are told by Matthew in a way that emphasizes the excessive guilt of the leaders of Israel. This feature has been noticeable all through, and we specially see it in chapter 23. The opening verses of this chapter show us that though His official condemnation had to come from Pilate, yet the animus that hounded Him to His death was found with them.

The sequence of the story is broken by a parenthetical paragraph giving us the miserable end of Judas. It looks as if he had expected the Lord to evade His adversaries and pass from their midst as He had done aforetime, but now seeing Him condemned and submitting to their hands he was filled with remorse and horror at what he had done. His was not the genuine "repentance to salvation not to be repented of," for that goes hand in hand with faith. Now faith was what he lacked, for had he possessed it he would have turned to his Master as did Peter, who also had grievously failed. His eyes were opened to his sin and he confessed it, while also confessing the innocence of Jesus, yet he flung himself out of life and into a suicide's grave. The very man who was instrumental in handing the Saviour over to His foes had to confess His innocence. God so ordained it; and this is very striking.

The very name, Judas, has become a byword for iniquity, but Annas and Caiaphas were worse than he. Verse 4 shows this. Judas *betrayed* innocent blood and they *condemned* it. He at least had *some feeling* of remorse for what he had done—sufficient to drive him to self-destruction. They had *no feeling* whatever. What was innocent blood to them? They had no compunction in shedding it, nor had they any fear of the God who requites evil. They were prepared to "murder the innocent," saying in their hearts, "Thou wilt not require it" (Psa. 10: 8, 13). Had they the smallest fear of God they would never have said, "His blood be on us, and on our children," as recorded in our chapter.

Judas never profited by his thirty pieces of silver. Seduced and ultimately possessed by the devil, he threw away everything for nothing. That is always the end of the story when silly little men attempt to drive a bargain with the giant spirit of evil. The silver was now again in the hands of the priests and became the occasion for them to crown their other sins with supreme hypocrisy. With legal scrupulosity they could not put it in the treasury because it was the price of blood. But who made it such? Why, they themselves! So they fulfilled the scripture by buying the potter's field. Their act became public, and thus the field acquired its name. The irony of Divine governmental judgment can be discerned in the name, for that land

# MATTHEW

has been a field of blood and a burial place for strangers ever since that day; and will be yet in larger measure, and until the day when at last the Redeemer shall come to Zion.

The religious authorities had now handed Jesus over to the civil governor, and verses 11-26 relate what transpired before him. When examined by Pilate before the multitude Jesus only uttered two words, "Thou sayest," the equivalent of one English word, "Yes," He confessed that He indeed was the King of the Jews, which was the specific charge laid at His door in the presence of the Roman power. The three Synoptic Gospels agree on this point. John records other questions raised by Pilate and answered by the Lord in the comparative privacy of the judgment hall, and three times he records Pilate *going out* from thence to the people. As far as the public examination was concerned Jesus "answered nothing," for there was really nothing to answer; as Pilate very soon perceived, though he marvelled greatly. He was well versed in the subtle ways of the Jews and his acute legal mind soon discerned that envy was at the bottom of the prosecution. On the other hand he feared the people and wished to stand well with them.

Hence Pilate had a strangely disturbed mind. To condemn Jesus he must violate his judicial sense as well as his wife's dream and intuition. He was evidently agitated as the subterfuge failed, by which he hoped to extricate himself from the dilemma. The accusing multitude was agitated by the cunning priests and elders. The only serene figure in the terrible scene is that of the Prisoner Himself. We see Pilate virtually abdicating as to his judicial function in the case and throwing the responsibility on the people. He did not really absolve himself of course, but it did lead to the people putting themselves under full responsibility for the blood of their Messiah. In verse 25 we find the explanation of the sorrows that fell upon the people, and that have continued to dog the footsteps of their children to this day. They have yet to face the great tribulation before the account is settled according to the government of God.

Barabbas was released and Jesus condemned to be crucified, and next (verses 27-37) we see Jesus in the hands of the Roman soldiers. Here we see vulgar mockery, brutality, and at last the act of crucifixion. To complete His humiliation they numbered Him amongst the transgressors by placing a thief on either hand. There was no justice, no mercy, no ordinary compassion whether He was in the hands of the *religious*, the *civil* or the *military* authorities. Jew and Gentile alike condemned themselves in condemning Him.

Verses 39-44 show us how all classes united in reviling Him as He was dying on the cross. Deep-dyed criminals have had to listen to stern words when they have been condemned to death, but we have not heard of even the most atrocious and depraved being mocked in their death agonies. Yet this is what happened when He who was the embodiment of all perfection, Divine as well as human, was on the cross. There was no difference, save

# MATTHEW

in the type of language used. "They that passed by" were the *ordinary folk* on business bent. "The chief priests . . . with the scribes and elders" were the *upper classes*. "The thieves also . . . cast the same in His teeth." They represented the lowest, *the criminal class;* but they only followed the fashion in their crude and vulgar way. He was the Son of God and the King of Israel: He could have displayed His might then as easily as He will display it in judgment very shortly. Then He was displaying Divine love by remaining where men had put Him with wicked hands, and bearing the judgment of sin Himself.

Matthew does not develop this in a doctrinal way, but he does pass on to record the solemn three hours of darkness, about the end of which time the holy Sufferer uttered with a loud voice the cry that had been written by the Spirit of prophecy in the opening words of Psalm 22, a thousand years before. The answer to the cry is supplied in the third verse of the Psalm, "Thou art holy, O Thou that inhabitest the praises of Israel." A holy God can only dwell in the praises of sinful people if atonement be wrought by the bearing of sin's judgment. The forsaking was the inevitable result of the One who knew no sin being made sin for us. The onlookers knew nothing of this: indeed they did not seem able to distinguish between God and Elijah.

After this there was, as verse 50 records, a last loud cry, and then the yielding up of His spirit. The actual words of that last cry are given us partly in John and partly in Luke. It was loud, showing that His strength was not impaired, and so the yielding up of His spirit was His own deliberate act. His death was supernatural and it was at once followed by supernatural signs, indicating its significance and power.

The first of these acts of God touched the veil of the temple, which typified His flesh, as Hebrews 10 tells us. Under the law "the way into the holiest of all was not yet made manifest" (Heb. 9: 8); but now it is made manifest, for the death of Christ is the basis of our approach to God. The second act touched the material creation, for the earth quaked, the rocks were rent, and graves opened. The third touched the bodies of sleeping saints, and after His arising they arose and appeared to many in Jerusalem. A threefold witness was thus rendered in most striking manner. The first concerned the presence of God, but it took place in the type of the veil, which was seen by the eyes of the priests alone. The second in the realm of nature must have been felt by everybody. The third, doubtless, was for the eyes of true saints alone. In addition to these signs the sun had previously been darkened. There was ample witness to the wonder of that hour, yet we do not read of any being impressed save the centurion on duty and those with him. In his heart was wrought the conviction that here was the Son of God—the very thing that His own people denied, and still deny.

As is often the case, when the men fail in courage and devotion the women supply the lack. The disciples had disappeared but many women lingered round the scene though standing afar off. One man, however, came forward and had the courage to identify himself with the dead Christ, begging His body from Pilate, and he an unexpected one. He was a disciple of Jesus but hitherto a secret one, as we are told in John's Gospel. Here was the rich man with the new tomb, who so acted that Isaiah 53: 9 was fulfilled. We know of nothing that Joseph of Arimathaea did save this one thing. God never fails to have a servant of His will who shall fulfil His Word. Joseph was born into the world to fulfil that one brief prophetic statement and so, though men would have appointed His grave with the wicked, He was with the rich in His death.

The women who were witnesses of His death and His burial were marked by devotion but not by intelligence. It was His bitter enemies who remembered that He had predicted that He would rise from the dead. Their hatred sharpened their memories and their wits, and led to their deputation to Pilate with a request for special precautions to be taken. His achievements in life they repudiated, regarding them as the first error. They dreaded lest His resurrection should be established, realizing that it would have far more potent effects. It would to their minds be the last error and worse than the first. It would inevitably vindicate Him and condemn them, as they saw very well.

As with Joseph so with these men Pilate was in an acquiescent mood. Their request was granted: the watch of soldiers was set, but it does seem as if there was a touch of irony in his words, "Make it as sure as ye can." They did all they could, and in result accomplished nothing save putting the fact of His resurrection beyond all reasonable doubt when once He was risen, and their elaborate arrangements were all brushed aside. God turned their wisdom into folly and made their scheme serve His own purpose and overthrow their own.

## CHAPTER 28

VERSE 1 OF this chapter tells us that the two Marys who had watched His burial were back at the sepulchre immediately the sabbath day had ended. They came "as it was the dusk of the next day after the sabbath" (New Trans.). The day according to Jewish reckoning ended at sunset, and their devotion was such that directly the sabbath was over they were on the move and visited the grave. It is not easy to piece together the details given us by the four Evangelists to form a connected narrative, but it would appear that the two Marys made this special visit and then returned at daybreak with Salome and possibly others, bearing spices for embalming. Mark and Luke tell us about this, and we should judge that verse 5 of our chapter refers to this second occasion, so that what is recorded in verses 2-4, took place between the two visits. Be that as it may, it is clear that by sunrise on the first day of the week Christ was risen.

# MATTHEW

An earthquake signalized His death, and a great earthquake, though apparently a very local one, for it was connected with the descent of the angel of the Lord, heralded His resurrection. The authorities of earth had sealed the tomb but a vastly higher authority broke the seal and flung back the stone door. At his presence the guards trembled and were smitten into death-like unconsciousness. The sealed tomb was the challenge of daring men. God accepted their challenge, broke their power, and reduced their representatives to nothingness. The Lord Jesus had been raised by the power of God, and the tomb was opened that men might see that without a doubt He was not there. The angel not only rolled back the stone but sat upon it, placing himself as a seal upon it in its new position, that no one might roll it back until an ample number of witnesses had seen the empty tomb.

Matthew tells us of one angel sitting on the stone. Mark tells us of one sitting on the right side, but inside the tomb. Luke and John both speak of two angels. Yet they all show us that though the women feared in the presence of the angels they were not smitten as were the soldiers. They were seeking the crucified Jesus, so "Fear not ye," was the word for them. His resurrection was announced and they were invited to see the spot where His body had lain, and where, as we gather from John's account, the linen wrappings lay all in their place and undisturbed, but out of which the sacred body had gone. One had only to see the place where He lay to be convinced that the body had not been abstracted or stolen. A supernatural act had taken place; and they were to go as messengers to the disciples, telling them to meet Him in Galilee.

Though filled with the conflicting emotions of fear and joy, the women received the angel's word with faith and consequently they set out in obedience. The obedience of faith was quickly rewarded by an appearance of the risen Lord Himself, and this brought them to His feet as worshippers, and sent them on their way as messengers of the Lord and not merely of the angel. On the occasion of the last supper the Lord had appointed Galilee as the meeting place, and He confirmed it to them.

The parenthetical paragraph, verses 11-15, furnishes us with a striking contrast. We pass from the bright scene of resurrection with joy, faith, worship and testimony, to the dense darkness of unbelief with hatred, plotting, bribery and corruption, resulting in a lie of so flagrant a kind that its falsity was carried on its face. If they were asleep how could they know what had transpired? Money and the love of it lay at the root of this particular evil. The soldiers were bribed, and we should suppose that the pursuading of the governor would be achieved in the same way. Anything to stop the truth as to the resurrection coming out! They realized how it would wreck their cause while establishing His, and the devil, who moved them, realized it far more keenly than they did. They only gave thirty silver coins to Judas to encompass His death, but they gave *large money* to the soldiers, endeavouring to suppress the fact of His resurrection.

# MATTHEW

The Gospel closes with the disciples meeting their risen Lord in Galilee, and with the commission He gave them there. No mention is made of the various appearances in Jerusalem or the ascension from Bethany. While pointing forward to the establishment of the church, this Gospel has in the main traced for us the transition from the presentation of the kingdom as connected with the Messiah upon earth as foretold by the prophets, to the kingdom of heaven in its present form: that is, in a mysterious form while the King is hidden in the heavens. Jerusalem was the place where they were to receive the Spirit and be baptized into the body, the church, not many days hence: Galilee was the district where was found the great majority of the godly remnant of Israel who, receiving Him, entered the kingdom whilst the mass of the people missed it.

So the Lord resumed links in resurrection with that remnant, the eleven disciples being the most prominent members of it; and though we do not hear of His being caught up into heaven yet He commissions them as though He were speaking from heaven, for all power was His, in heaven as much as on earth. The time had not yet come to reveal fully the Christian enterprise of gathering out of the nations a people for His name: the terms here are more general. They were to go and make disciples and baptize them, and this is a commission which can be taken up by the believing remnant of Israel after the church is gone. As Israel were baptized to Moses their leader, so the disciple is to be baptized to the risen Christ as coming under His authority, and the baptism is to be in the name of God as He has been fully revealed. It is not plural but singular—not *names* but *name*—for though revealed in three Persons, the Godhead is one.

The closing word is, "I am with you all the days, until the completion of the age," so that in this closing word we have "all" no less than four times. Our exalted Lord wields *all power* in both spheres, so that nothing is beyond His reach. If anything adverse happens to His servants it must be by His permission. *All nations* are to be the scope of their service, and not in the midst of Israel only as heretofore. Those baptized from the nations are to be taught to observe *all the Lord's commands* and instructions, for the servants are to be marked by obedience, and to bring those that they reach into obedience also. Then *all the days* to the finish they can count on the support and spiritual presence of their Master.

Such is the commission with which the Gospel ends. As we travel on into the Acts and pass through the Epistles we find coming to light developments which furnish us with the full gospel commission of today; yet we do not lose the light and benefit of what the Lord says here. We still go to all nations, baptizing in the Name. We still have to teach all the Lord's word. All power is still His. His presence will be with us all the days till the end of the age, no matter what may betide.

# MARK

## Chapter 1

THE WRITER OF this Gospel was that "John, whose surname was Mark," (Acts 15: 37), who failed in his service when with Paul and Barnabas on their first missionary journey, and who afterwards became a bone of contention between them. He first failed himself, and then became the occasion of further failure with others greater than himself. This was a sorry beginning to his story, but eventually he was so truly restored that he became serviceable to the Lord in the exalted work of writing the Gospel which presents the Lord Jesus as the perfect Servant of Jehovah, the true Prophet of the Lord.

He entitles his book, "Gospel" or "Glad Tidings" of "Jesus Christ, the Son of God," so from the very outset we are not allowed to forget who this perfect Servant is. He is the Son of God, and this fact is further enforced by the quotations from Malachi and Isaiah in verses 2 and 3, where the One whose way was to be prepared is seen to be Divine, even Jehovah Himself. The mission of the messenger, the one crying in the wilderness, is the very beginning of His glad tidings.

That messenger was John the Baptist, and in verses 4 to 8 we get a brief summary of his mission and testimony. The baptism that he preached signified repentance, for the remission of sins, and those who submitted to it came confessing their sins. They had to acknowledge they were all wrong. Very fittingly therefore John kept himself severely apart from the society that he had to condemn. In his clothes, in his food, and in his location, going out into the wilderness, he took a separate place.

Moses had *given* the law. Elijah had accused the people of their departure from it, and had *recalled* them to a fresh allegiance to it. John, though he came in the spirit and power of Elijah, did not urge them to keep it, but rather to *honestly confess* that they had utterly broken it. This prepared them for his further message concerning the infinitely greater One who was just to come, who would baptise with the Holy Ghost. His baptism would be far greater than John's, just as personally HE was far above him. He who can thus pour forth the Holy Spirit cannot be less than God Himself.

The beginning of the Glad Tidings in the work of John being thus described, we are introduced next to the baptism of Jesus. This is condensed into verses 9 to 11. Here, as all through this Gospel, the utmost brevity and conciseness characterises the record. Jesus comes from Nazareth, the humble and despised place in Galilee, and submits to John's baptism; not because He had anything to confess, but because He would identify Himself with these souls who in repentance were making a move in the right direction. It was just then, ere He came forth in His public ministry, that Heaven's approbation of the perfect Servant was manifested, lest any should misinterpret His lowly baptism. The Spirit descended upon Him as a dove, and the Father's voice was heard declaring His Person and His perfection. The Servant of the Lord is Himself sealed with the Spirit; the dove being emblematic of purity and peace. Having become Man, He must receive the Spirit Himself; presently in His risen estate He will shed forth that Spirit as a baptism upon others. In that Spirit He went forth empowered to serve. It is also to be noticed that for the first time there was a clear revelation of the Godhead, as Father, Son and Holy Spirit.

The first action of the Spirit in His case comes before us in verses 12 and 13. Coming forth to serve the will of God, He must be tested, and the Spirit thrusts Him forth to this. Here for the first time we find the word "immediately" which occurs so often in this Gospel, though it is sometimes rendered as "anon," "forthwith," "straightway." If service be rendered rightly it must be characterised by prompt obedience, hence we see our Lord as One who never lost a moment in His path of service.

He must be tested before He publicly serves, and the test takes place at once. When the first man appeared he was soon tested by the devil and he fell. The second Man has now appeared and He too shall be tested by the same devil. Only instead of being in a beautiful garden He is in the wilderness into which the first man had turned his garden. He was with beasts who were wild because of Adam's sin. He was tested for forty days, the full period of probation, and He emerged as Victor, for holy angels ministered to Him at the close.

No details as to the various temptations are given to us here; only the fact of it, the conditions under which it took place and the result. The Servant of the Lord is fully tested, and His perfection is made manifest. He is ready to serve. So in verse 14 John is dismissed from the story. The beginning of the Glad Tidings is over, and we plunge without further explanation into a brief record of His marvellous service.

His message is described as "the Gospel of the kingdom of God," and a very brief summary of its terms is found in verse 15. The kingdom of God had been spoken of in the Old Testament, notably in Daniel. In chapter 9 of that book a certain time had been set for the coming of Messiah and the fulfilment of the prophecy. The time was fulfilled, and in Himself the kingdom was near to them. He called upon men to repent and to believe this. With this proclamation He came into Galilee. For the moment He was alone in this service.

But He was not alone for long. Here and there His message was received and from the ranks of those who believed He began to call some who should be more closely associated with Him in His service, and in their turn become "fishers of men." He Himself was the great Fisher of men, as is revealed by the two incidents recorded in verses 16 to 20. He knew whom He would call to His service. Seeing the sons of Zebedee He called them "straightway," and it is said of the sons of Jonas that when He called them "straightway they forsook their nets and followed Him." As the great

# MARK

Servant of God, He was prompt in issuing His call: as under-servants they were prompt to obey.

It is worthy of note that all four who were called were men of diligence in their work. Peter and Andrew were engaged in their fishing. James and John were not lolling about during their time of leisure. They were mending the nets.

In verse 16, "*He* walked," but in verse 21, "*they* went." The men whom He had called were now with Him, listening to His words and seeing His works of power. Entering Capernaum, He taught "straightway" on the sabbath, and *authority* marked His utterances. The scribes were mere retailers of the thoughts and opinions of others, falling back on the authority of great Rabbis of earlier times, so it was this note of authority which astonished the people. It was so distinct that they at once detected it. He was indeed that Prophet with the words of Jehovah in His mouth, of whom Moses had spoken in Deuteronomy 18: 18, 19.

And not only had He authority but also *power*—real dynamic force. This was manifested on the same occasion in His treatment of the man with an unclean spirit. Controlled by the demon, the man recognised Him as the Holy One of God yet thought of Him as One bent upon destruction. Thus challenged, the Lord revealed Himself to be the Deliverer and not the destroyer. It is the devil who is the destroyer, and hence the demon, who was his servant, did as much as he could in that line by tearing the poor man before he came out of him. He could not retain his grip upon his victim in the presence of the power of the Lord.

Again the people were filled with amazement. They now saw "authority" expressed in His work, as before they had felt it in His word. Their question therefore was two-fold: what *thing?* and what *new doctrine?* These two things must ever be kept together in the service of God. Word must be supported by work. When it is not thus, or when, even worse, our works contradict our words, our service is feeble or vain.

In His case both were perfect. His teaching was full of authority, and with equal authority He commanded obedience even from demons; hence His fame spread abroad with a promptness which was in keeping with the promptitude of His wonderful service for God in regard to man.

We have not yet finished with the activities of this wonderful day in Capernaum, for verse 29 tells us that having left the synagogue they entered into the house of Simon and Andrew. This they did "forthwith,"—that same characteristic word, indicating promptness. There was no waste of time with our blessed Master, nor was there waste of time with His new followers, for they present to Him "anon"—the same word—the case of need in that house. Human need, the fruit of human sin met Him at every turn. It was as evident in the house of those who had become His followers as it had been in the synagogue, the local centre of their religious observances.

# MARK

Demoniac power was manifest in the religious circle, and disease in the domestic circle. He was more than equal to both. The demon left the man completely and at once. The fever left the woman with similar promptness, and no period of convalescence was necessary before she resumed her ordinary household duties. No wonder that very soon "all the city was gathered together at the door."

The picture presented in verses 32 to 34 is very beautiful. "At even, when the sun did set," the work of the day being over, the multitudes gathered bringing a great concourse of needy folk, and He dispensed the mercy of His healing power in all directions. He would permit no testimony to Himself to be uttered by the powers of darkness. The mercy and might displayed were sufficient witness to who it was that was serving amongst men. In his Gospel John tells us that there were many other things that Jesus did, which have not been put on record. Here some are indicated without details being given.

The story, as given to us by Mark, moves rapidly forward. Till late in the evening the work of mercy went on, and then long before day He rose up and sought solitude for prayer. We have just noted the authority and power of God's perfect Servant. Here we see His *dependence* upon God, without which there can be no true service. The Servant must hang upon the Master, and though He who serves is "Son," HE does not dispense with this feature: rather He is the highest expression of it in perfect obedience. We read that He learned obedience "by the things that He suffered" (Heb. 5: 8); and this word doubtless covers all His pathway here and not merely the closing scenes of suffering of a more physical sort.

What a voice this has for all who serve, no matter how small our service! His day was so full of activity that He took a large part of the night for prayer: *and He was the Son of God.* Much of our powerlessness is occasioned by our lack in the matter of solitary prayer.

The next four verses (36-39) show us the *devotedness* of God's Servant. Simon and others appear to have regarded His retirement as unaccountable diffidence, or perhaps as a waste of valuable time. All were seeking for Him, and He seemed to be missing this tide of popularity. But popularity was by no means His object. He had come forth in service to preach the Divine message, and so regardless of popular feeling He went on with His service through the towns of Galilee. He devoted Himself to the mission with which He had been entrusted.

And now, in the closing verses of this first chapter, we have a lovely picture of the *compassion* of this perfect Servant of God. He is approached by a leper, in body about as loathsome a specimen of humanity as can be. The poor fellow had some faith, but it was defective. He was confident of His power, but had doubts as to His grace. We should have been moved with disgust, considerably tinged with indignation at the aspersion cast

# MARK

upon our kindly feelings. He was moved with compassion. *Moved* with it, mark you! Not only did He view this miserable specimen with compassionate love but He acted. The deep fountain of Divine love within Him rose up and overflowed. With His hand He touched him and with His lips He spoke, and the man was healed.

There was no actual need that He should touch him, for the Lord cured many a desperate case at a distance. No Jew would have dreamt of touching him and thus contracting defilement, but the Lord did so. He was beyond all possibility of defilement, and His touch was one of sympathy as well as of power. It confirmed His word, "I will," and removed all doubt of His willingness from the man's mind for ever.

Again we see how our Lord did not court popular enthusiasm and notoriety. His instruction to the man was that he should allow the testimony to his cure to flow in the channel indicated by Moses. He however, filled with delight did the very thing he had been told not to do, and as a consequence for some days the Lord had to shun the cities and dwell in desert places. Very few things stir up human interest and excitement more than miraculous healing, but He was seeking spiritual results. There are modern healing movements which create considerable excitement in spite of the fact that their so-called "healings" are very unlike our Lord's. The actors in these movements most certainly do not retreat from the blaze of publicity, but rather delight in it.

## CHAPTER 2

THIS CHAPTER OPENS with another work of power that took place in a private house, when after some time He was again in Capernaum. This time faith of a very robust type comes into view, and that, remarkably enough, on the part of friends and not on the part of the sufferer. The Lord was again preaching the Word. That was His *main* service; the healing work was *incidental*.

The four friends had faith of the sort that laughs at impossibilities, and says, "It shall be done," and Jesus saw it. He dealt instantly with the *spiritual* side of things, granting forgiveness of sins to the paralysed man. This was but blasphemy to the reasoning scribes who were present. They were right enough in their thought that no one but God can forgive sins, but they were wholly wrong in not discerning that God was present amongst them and speaking in the Son of Man. The Son of Man was on earth, and on earth He has authority to forgive sins.

The forgiveness of sins however is not something which is visible to the eyes of men; it must be accepted by faith in the Word of God. The instantaneous healing of a bad case of bodily infirmity is visible to the eyes of men, and the Lord proceeded to perform this miracle. They could no more release the man from the grip of his disease than they could forgive his sins. Jesus could do both with equal ease. He did both, appealing to the miracle in the body as proof of the miracle as to the soul. Thus He puts things in their right order. The spiritual miracle was primary, the bodily was only secondary.

Here again the miracle was instantaneous and complete. The man who had been utterly helpless suddenly arose, picked up his bed and walked forth before them all in a fashion that elicited glory to God from all lips. The Lord commanded and the man had but to obey, for the enabling went with the command.

This incident which emphasises the spiritual object of our Lord's service is followed by the call of Levi, afterwards known to us as Matthew the publican. The call of this man to follow the Master exemplifies the mighty *attraction* of His word. It was one thing to call lowly fishermen from their nets and toil: it was another to call a man of means from the congenial task of scooping in the cash. But He did it with two words. "Follow Me," fell upon Levi's ears with such power that he "arose and followed Him." God grant that we may feel the power of those two words in our hearts!

What a wonderful glimpse we have been granted of the Servant of the Lord, His promptitude, His authority, His power, His dependence, His devotedness, His compassion, His refusal of the popular and superficial in favour of the spiritual and the abiding; and lastly, His mighty attractiveness.

Having risen up to follow the Lord, Levi soon declared his discipleship in a practical fashion. He entertained his new-found Master in his house, together with a large number of publicans and sinners, displaying thus something of the Master's spirit. He exchanged his "sitting at the receipt of custom," for the dispensing of bounty, so that others might sit at his board. He began to fulfil the word, "He hath dispersed, he hath given to the poor," (Psa. 112: 9), and that evidently without having been told to do so. He began showing hospitality to his own set in order that they too might meet the One who had won his heart.

In this he is an excellent pattern for ourselves. He began to expend himself for others. He did the thing which most readily came to his hand. He gathered to meet the Lord those who were needy, and who knew it, rather than those who were religiously self-satisfied. He had discovered that Jesus was a Giver, who was seeking for such as should be receivers.

All this was observed by the self-satisfied Scribes and Pharisees, who voiced their objection in the form of a question to His disciples. Why did He consort with such low-down and degraded folk? The disciples had no need to answer, for He took up the challenge Himself. His answer was complete and satisfying and has become almost a proverbial saying. The sick need the doctor, and sinners need the Saviour. Not the righteous but the sinners He came to call.

# MARK

The Scribes and Pharisees may have been well versed in the law but they had no understanding of grace. Now He was the Servant of the grace of God, and Levi had caught a glimpse of this. Have we? Far more than Levi we ought to have done so, inasmuch as we live in the moment when the day of grace has reached its noontide. Yet it is possible for us to feel a bit hurt with God because He is so good to folk that we would like to denounce, as Jonah did in the case of the Ninevites, and as the Pharisees did with the sinners. The great Servant of the grace of God is at the disposal of *all that need Him*.

The next incident—verses 18 to 22—discloses the objectors again at work. Then they complained of the Master to the disciples: now it is of the disciples to the Master. They evidently lacked courage to come face to face. This oblique method of fault-finding is very common: let us forsake it. In neither case did the disciples have to answer. When the Pharisees maintained the exclusiveness of law, He met them by asserting the expansiveness of grace, and He silenced them. Now they wish to put upon the disciples the bondage of law, and He most effectively asserts the liberty of grace.

The parable or figure that He used plainly inferred that He Himself was the Bridegroom—the central Person of importance. His presence governed everything, and ensured a wonderful fulness of supply. Presently He would be absent and then fasting would be appropriate enough. Let us take note of this, for we live in the day when fasting is a fitting thing. The Bridegroom has long been absent, and we are waiting for Him. At the moment when the Lord spoke the disciples were in the position of a godly remnant in Israel receiving the Messiah when He came. After Pentecost they were baptised into one body, and were built into the foundations of that city which is called "the Bride, the Lamb's wife" (Rev. 21: 9). Then they had the place of the Bride rather than that of the children of the bridechamber; and that position is ours today. This only makes it yet more clear that not feasting but fasting is fitting for us. Fasting is abstaining from lawful things in order to be more wholly for God, and not merely abstinence from food for a certain time.

The Pharisees were all for maintaining the law intact. The danger for the disciples, as after events proved, was not so much that as attempting a mixture of Judaism with the grace which the Lord Jesus brought. The law system was like a worn-out garment, or an old wine skin. He was bringing in that which was like a strong piece of new cloth, or new wine with its powers of expansion. In the Acts we can see how the old outward forms of the law gave way before the expansive power of the Gospel.

Indeed we see it in the very next incident with which chapter 2 closes. Again the Pharisees come, complaining of the disciples to the Master. The offence now was that they did not exactly fit their activities into the "old bottle" of certain regulations concerning the sabbath. The Pharisees pushed their sabbath-keeping so far that they condemned even rubbing ears of corn in the hand, as though it were working a mill. They contended for a very rigid interpretation of the law in these minor matters. They were the people who kept the law with meticulous care, whilst they considered the disciples to be slack.

The Lord met their complaint and defended His disciples by reminding them of two things. First, they should have known the Scriptures, which recorded the way in which David had once fed himself and his followers in an emergency. That which ordinarily was not lawful was permitted in a day when things were out of course in Israel because of the rejection of the rightful king. 1 Samuel 21 tells us about it. Once again things were out of course and the rightful King about to be refused. In both cases needs connected with the Lord's Anointed must be held to override details connected with the ceremonial demands of the law.

Second, the sabbath was instituted for man's benefit, and not the reverse. Hence man takes precedence of the sabbath; and the Son of man, who holds dominion over all men, according to Psalm 8, must be Lord of the sabbath, and hence competent to dispose of it according to His will. Who were the Pharisees to challenge His right to do this? — even though He had come amongst men in the form of a Servant.

The Lord of the sabbath was amongst men and He was being refused. Under these circumstances the solicitude of these sticklers for the ceremonial law was out of place. Their "bottles" were worn out, and unable to contain the expansive grace and authority of the Lord. The sabbath "bottle" breaks before their very eyes.

CHAPTER 3

THE PHARISEES HOWEVER were by no means convinced, and they re-opened the whole question a little later when on another sabbath He came into contact with human need in one of their synagogues. The conflict raged around the man with a withered hand. They watched Jesus anticipating that they would be furnished with a point of attack. He accepted the challenge which lay unspoken in their hearts by saying to the man, "Stand forth" (v. 3), thus making him very prominent, and ensuring that the challenge should be realised by everyone present.

Another point concerning the sabbath is now raised. Is the law intended of God to prohibit good as well as evil? Does the sabbath render unlawful an act of mercy?

The question, "Is it lawful to do good . . . or to do evil?" may be connected with James 4: 17. If we know the good and yet omit it, it is sin. Should the perfect Servant of God, who knew the good, and moreover had full power to execute it, withhold His hand from doing it because it happened to be the sabbath day? Impossible!

# MARK

In this striking way did the holy Servant of God vindicate His ministry of mercy in the presence of those who would have tied His hands by rigid interpretations of the law of God. It is important that we should learn the lesson taught by all this, in case we should fall into a like error. The "law of Christ" is very different in character and spirit from "the law of Moses," yet it may be misused in similar fashion. If the light and easy yoke of Christ is so twisted as to become burdensome, and also a positive hindrance to the outflow of grace and blessing, it becomes a more grievous perversion than anything we see in these verses.

The hearts of the Pharisees were hard. They were tender enough about the technicalities of the law, but hard as to any concern for human need, or any sense of their own sin. Jesus saw the dreadful state they were in and was grieved, but He did not withhold blessing. He cured the man, and left them to their sin. They were outraged because He had broken through one of their precious legal points. They went forth themselves to outrage one of the major counts of the law by plotting murder. Such is Phariseeism!

Faced by this murderous hatred, the Lord withdrew Himself and His disciples. We see Him withdrawing Himself from the blaze of popularity at the end of chapter 1. He did not court favour, nor did He desire to stir up strife. Here we find the perfect Servant acting in just the way that is enjoined upon the under servants in 2 Timothy 2: 24.

But such was His attractiveness that men pressed upon Him even as He withdrew. Multitudes thronged about Him, and His grace and power were manifested in many directions, and unclean spirits recognized in Him the Master whom they had to obey, though He did not accept their testimony. He blessed men and delivered them, yet He did not seek anything from them. First He had a small boat on the lake into which He could retire from the throng; and then He went up into a mountain, where He called to Him only those that He desired, and of them He chose twelve who were to be apostles.

So not only did He answer the hatred of the religious leaders by retiring from them, but also by calling the twelve who in due time should go forth as an extension of His matchless service. He prepared thus to widen out the service and testimony. The chosen twelve were to be with Him, and then, when their period of instruction and preparation was complete, He would send them forth. The period of their training lasts until verse 6 of chapter 6. In verse 7 of that chapter we begin the account of their actual sending forth.

This being "with Him" is of immense importance to the one called to service. It is as necessary for us as it was for them. They had His presence and company upon earth. We have not that, but we have His Spirit given to us and His written Word. Thus we may be enabled prayerfully to maintain contact with Him, and gain that spiritual education which alone fits us to intelligently serve Him. The twelve were first chosen, then educated, then sent forth with power conferred upon them. This is the divine order, and we see these things set forth in verses 14 and 15.

Having called and chosen the twelve upon the mountain, He returned to the haunts of men and was in an house. At once the multitudes came together. The attraction He exerted was irresistible, and the demands upon Him such that there was no leisure for meals. So the first thing to be witnessed by the twelve when they began to be with Him was this strong tide of interest and the apparent popularity of their Master.

They soon however saw another side of things, and firstly that He was totally misunderstood by those who were nearest to Him according to the flesh. The *"friends"* were of course His relations, and they were filled doubtless with well-meaning concern for Him. They could not understand such incessant labours and felt they ought to lay a restraining hand upon Him as though He were out of His mind. Light upon this extraordinary attitude on their part is cast by John 7: 5. At this point in His service His brethren did not believe in Him, and apparently even His mother had as yet but a dim conception of what He was really doing.

But secondly, there were *enemies*, who were becoming even more bitter and unscrupulous. In verse 6 of our chapter we saw Pharisees making friends with their antagonists the Herodians in order to plot His death. Now we find scribes making a journey from Jerusalem in order to oppose and denounce Him. This they do in the most reckless way, attributing His works of mercy to the power of the devil. It was not just vulgar abuse, but something deliberate and crafty. They could not deny what He did, but they attempted to blacken His character. They looked His miracles of mercy full in the face, and then deliberately and officially pronounced them to be the works of the devil. This was the character of their blasphemy, and it is well to be quite clear about it in view of the Lord's words in verse 29.

But first of all He called them to Him and answered them by an appeal to reason. Their blasphemous objection involved an absurdity. They suggested in effect that Satan was engaged in casting out Satan, that his kingdom and house was divided against itself. That, if it were true, would mean the end of the whole Satanic business. Satan is far too astute to act in that way.

We must admit, alas! that we Christians have not been too astute to act in that way. Christendom is full of division of that suicidal kind, and it is Satan himself who, without a doubt, is the instigator of it. Had it not been that the power of the Lord Jesus on high has remained unaltered, and that the Holy Ghost abides, dwelling in the true church of God, the public confession of Christianity would long since have perished. That the faith has not perished from the earth is a tribute not to the wisdom of men but to the power of God.

Having exposed the foolish unreasonableness of their words, the Lord proceeded to give the true explanation of what had been happening. He was the One stronger than the strong man, and He was now occupied in spoiling his goods, by setting free many who had been captivated by him. Satan was bound in the presence of the Lord.

Thirdly, He plainly warned these wretched men as to the enormity of the sin they had committed. The perfect Servant had been delivering men from Satan's grip in the energy of the Holy Ghost. In order to avoid admitting this they denounced the action of the Holy Ghost as the action of Satan. This was sheer blasphemy; the blind blasphemy of men who shut their eyes to the truth. They put themselves beyond forgiveness with nothing but eternal damnation ahead. They had reached that fearful state of hardened hatred and blindness which once characterized Pharaoh in Egypt, and which at a later date marked the northern kingdom of Israel, when the word of the Lord was, "Ephraim is joined to idols: let him alone" (Hosea 4: 17). God would leave these Jerusalem scribes alone, and that meant no forgiveness but damnation.

This then was the unpardonable sin. Understanding what it really is, we can easily see that the folk of tender conscience, who today are troubled because they fear they may have committed it, are the last people who really have done so.

The chapter closes with the arrival of the friends of which verse 21 has told us. The Lord's words as to His mother and His brethren have seemed to some unnecessarily harsh. There certainly was in them a note of severity, which was occasioned by their attitude. The Lord was seizing the opportunity to give needed instruction to His disciples. They had seen Him in the midst of much labour, and apparently popular; and also the centre of blasphemous opposition. Now they are to have an impressive demonstration of the fact that the relationships that God recognizes and honours are those which have a *spiritual* basis.

Of old, in Israel, relationships in the flesh counted for much. Now they are to be set on one side in favour of the spiritual. And the basis of what is spiritual lies in *obedience* to the will of God: and for us today the will of God lies enshrined in the Holy Scriptures. Obedience is the great thing. It lies at the foundation of all true service, and must mark us if we would be in relation with the one true and perfect Servant. Let us never forget that!

CHAPTER 4

THE PREVIOUS CHAPTER ends with the Lord's solemn declaration that the relationships He was now going to recognize were those that had a spiritual basis in obedience to the will of God. This statement of His must necessarily have raised in the minds of the disciples some questions as to *how* they might know what the will of God is. As we open this chapter we find the answer. It is *by His word*, which conveys to us tidings of what He is, and of what He has done for us. Out of these things His will for us springs.

# MARK

There were still great multitudes waiting upon Him, so that He taught them out of a ship; but it was at this point that He commenced speaking in parables. The reason for this is given in verses 11 and 12. The leaders of the people had already rejected Him, as the last chapter has made manifest, and the people themselves were in the main unmoved, save by curiosity and the love of the sensational, and of "the loaves and fishes." As time went on they would veer round, and support the leaders in their murderous hostility. The Lord knew this, so He began to cast His teaching in such a form as should reserve it for those who had ears to hear. He speaks in verse 11 of "them that are without."

This shows that already a breach was becoming manifest, and those "within" could be distinguished from those "without." Those within could see and hear with perception and understanding, and so the "mystery" or "secret" of the kingdom of God became plain to them. The rest were blind and deaf, and the way of conversion and forgiveness was being closed to them. If people *will not* hear, a time comes when they *cannot*. The people wanted a Messiah who should bring them worldly prosperity and glory. They had no use, as events proved, for a Messiah who brought them the kingdom of God in the mysterious form of conversion and forgiveness of sins.

We have the kingdom of God today in just this mysterious form, and we enter it by conversion and forgiveness, for thus it is that the authority of God is established in our hearts. We are still waiting for the kingdom in its displayed glory and power.

The first parable of this chapter is that of the sower, the seed, and its effects. Having uttered it He closed with the solemn words, "He that hath ears to hear, let him hear." The possession of hearing ears, or their absence, would indicate at once whether a man belonged to the "within" or to the "without." The mass of His listeners evidently thought it was a pretty story and pleasant to the ear, but left it at that, showing they were *without*. Some others, along with the disciples, were not content with this. They wanted to arrive at its inner meaning, and pushed their enquiries further. They belonged to the *within*.

The Lord's word in verse 13 shows that this parable of the sower must be understood or His other parables will not be intelligible to us. It holds the key which unlocks the whole series. The Lord Jesus, when He came, brought in the first place a supreme test to Israel. Would they receive the well-beloved Son, and render to God the fruit that was due under the cultivation of the law? It was becoming evident that they would not. Well then, a second thing should be inaugurated. Instead of *demanding* anything from them He would *sow* the Word, which in due season, in some cases at least, would *produce* the fruit that was desired. This the parable indicates, and unless we grasp its significance we shall not understand that which subsequently He has to say to us.

# MARK

The Lord Himself was the Sower, without a doubt; and the Word was the Divine testimony that He disseminated, for the "so great salvation ... at the first began to be spoken by the Lord, and was confirmed unto us by them that heard Him" (Heb. 2: 3). In John's Gospel we discover that Jesus *is* the Word. Here He *sows* the word. Who could sow it like He who was it? But even when *He* sowed the word, not every grain that He sowed fructified. In only one case out of the four was fruit produced.

It is equally certain that the parable applies in its principles to all those under-sowers who have gone forth with the word as sent by Him, from that day to this. Every sower of the seed therefore must expect to meet with all these varieties of experience, as indicated in the parable. The imperfect servants of today cannot expect better things than those which marked the sowing of the perfect Servant in His day. The seed was the same in each case. All the difference lay in the state of the ground on which the seed fell.

In the case of the wayside hearers the word got no entrance at all. Their hearts were like the footpath well trodden down. There was not even a surface impression made, and Satan by his many agents completely removed the word. Their case was one of complete *indifference*.

The stony ground hearers are the impressionable yet superficial folk. They respond to the word at once with gladness, but are quite insensible as to its real implications. It was said of true converts that they "received the word in much affliction, with joy of the Holy Ghost" (1 Thess. 1: 6). This affliction, which preceded their gladness, was the result of their being awakened to their sin under the convicting power of the word. The stony ground hearer skips over the affliction, because *insensible* of his real need, and lands himself into a merely superficial gladness, which fades in the presence of testing; and he fades with it.

The thorny ground hearers are the *preoccupied* people. The world fills their thoughts. If poor, they are swamped in its cares: if rich, in its riches and the pleasures that riches bring. If neither poor nor rich, there are the lusts of other things. They have climbed out of poverty, and they lust for more of the good things of the world that seem to be coming within their reach. Engrossed by the world, the word is choked.

The good ground hearers are such as not only hear the word but receive it and bring forth fruit. The ground has come under the action of plough and harrow. Thus it has been *prepared*. Even so, however, all good ground is not equally fertile. There may not be the same amount of fruit; but fruit there is.

There was great instruction for the disciples in all this, and for us also. Presently He was going to send them forth to preach, and then they too would become sowers. They must know that it was the word they had to sow, and also what to expect when they sowed it. Then they would not be unduly affected when much of the seed sown appeared to be lost; or when, some result appearing, it faded away after a time; or even when, fruit appearing, there was not as much fruit as they had hoped for. If we know what is being aimed at on the one hand, and what to expect on the other, we are greatly fortified and strengthened in our service.

We must remember that this parable applies just as much to the sowing of the seed of the word in the hearts of saints as in the hearts of sinners. So let us meditate upon it with hearts very much exercised as to HOW *we ourselves receive the word that we may hear*, as well as to how others may receive the word that we present to them.

In verses 21 and 22 there follows the brief parable of the candle, and then in verse 23 another warning word as to having ears to hear. At first sight the transition from seed sown in the field to a candle lit in a house may seem incongruous and disconnected, but, if indeed we have ears to hear, we shall soon see that in their spiritual significance both parables are congruous and connected. When the word of God is received into an exercised and prepared heart it brings forth *fruit* that God appreciates, and also *light* that is to be seen and appreciated of men.

No candle is lit in order to be hid under a bushel or a bed. It is to shed its beams abroad from the candlestick. The second part of verse 22 is rather striking in the New Translation, "nor does any secret thing take place but that it should come to light." The work of God in the heart by His word does take place *secretly*, and the eye of God discerns the fruit as it begins to appear. But in due season the secret thing that has taken place *must* come to *light*. Every true conversion is like the lighting of a fresh candle.

The bushel may symbolize the business of life, and the bed the ease and pleasure of life. Neither must be permitted to hide the light, just as the cares and the riches and the "other things" should not be permitted to choke the seed that is sown. Have we ears to hear this? Are we letting the light of our little candle to shine? There is nothing hidden which shall not be made manifest, so it is quite certain that if a light has been lit it is bound to shine out. If nothing is manifested, it is because there is nothing to manifest.

This parable is followed by the warning as to what we hear. The dealings of God in His government of men enter into this matter. As we measure things out, so things will be measured out to us. If we really do hear the word in such a way as to enter into possession of it, we shall gain more. If we do not, we shall begin to lose even that which we had. In Luke 8: 18, we get similar sayings connected with "how" we hear. Here they stand connected with "what" we hear.

*How* we hear is emphasized in the parable of the sower, but *what* we hear is at least of equal importance. Not a few have had taken from them even that which they had by lending their ears to error. They heard, and heard very attentively, but, alas! what they heard was not the truth, and it perverted them. If through our ears error is sown in our hearts, it will bring forth its disastrous crop, and the government of God will permit it, and not prevent it.

Verses 26 to 29 are occupied with the parable concerning God's secret work. A man sows the seed, and when the harvest is ripe he gets again to work, putting in the sickle to reap. But as to the actual growth of the seed from its earliest stages to the full fruition, he can do nothing. For many a week he sleeps and rises, night and day, and the processes of nature, which God has ordained, silently do the work though he does not understand them. "He knoweth not how," is true today. Men have pushed their investigations very far, but the real *how* of the wonderful processes, carried on in God's great workshop of nature, still eludes them.

So it is in what we may term God's spiritual workshop, and it is just as well for us to remember it. Some of us are very anxious to analyze and describe the exact processes of the Spirit's work in souls. These hidden things sometimes exert a great fascination over our minds, and we wish to master the whole process. It cannot be done. It is our happy privilege to sow the seed, and also in due season to put in the sickle and reap. The workings of the word in the hearts of men are secretly accomplished by the Holy Spirit. His work of course is perfect.

Imperfection always marks the work of men. If permitted, as we are, to have a hand in the work of God, we bring imperfection into that which we do. The next parable, occupying verses 30 to 32, shows this. The kingdom of God today exists vitally and really in the souls of those who by conversion have come under God's authority and control. But it may also be viewed as a more external thing, to be found wherever men profess to acknowledge Him. The one is the kingdom as established by the Spirit. The other the kingdom as established by men. This latter has become a great and imposing thing in the earth, extending its protection to many "fowls of the air;" and what they signify we have just seen—in verses 4 and 15—agents of Satan.

This closing parable of the series was full of warning for the disciples, as the others were full of instruction. They were with Him and being educated before being sent forth on their mission. We have seen at least seven things:—

1. That the present work of the disciple is in its nature, *sowing*.

2. That what is to be sown is, *the word*.

3. That the results of the sowing are to be classified under four heads; in only *one* case is there *fruit*, and that *in varying degrees*.

4. That the word produces *light* as well as fruit, and that light is to be *manifested* publicly.

5. That the disciple is himself a hearer of the word as well as a sower of the word, and in that connection must take care *what* he hears.

6. That the working of the word in souls is *God's work* and not ours. Our work is the sowing and the reaping.

7. That as man's work does enter into the present work of extending the kingdom of God, evil will gain an entrance. The kingdom, viewed as man's handiwork, will result in something *imposing* yet *corrupt*. This is the solemn warning, which we have to take to heart.

There were many other parables spoken by the Lord, yet not put on record for us. The others, spoken to the disciples and expounded to them, were doubtless very important for them in their peculiar circumstances, but not of the same importance for us. Those that were of importance for us are recorded in Matthew 13.

With verse 34 His teachings end, and from verse 35 to the end of chapter 5 we resume the record of His wonderful acts. The disciples needed to observe closely what He did and His way of acting, as well as to hear the teachings of His lips. And so do we.

The crowd, who had listened to these sayings of His but without understanding them, was now dismissed, and they crossed to the other side of the lake. It was evening and He was in the stern, sleeping on a cushion. The lake was noted for the sudden and violent storms that disturbed it, and one of special violence arose, threatening to swamp the boat. Satan is "the prince of the power of the air," and therefore we believe that his power lay behind the raging forces of nature. At once therefore the disciples were confronted with a test and a challenge. Who was this Person who lay asleep in the stern?

Could Satan wield the forces of nature in such a way as to sink a boat in which was reposing the Son of God? But the Son of God is found in Manhood, and He sleeps! Well, what does that matter?—seeing He is the Son of God. The action of the adversary, raising the storm while He slept, was indeed a challenge. As yet, however, the disciples realized these things very dimly, if at all. Hence they were filled with fear as the resources of their seamanship were exhausted: and they roused Him with an unbelieving cry, which cast a slur upon His kindness and love, though showing some faith in His power.

He arose at once in the majesty of His power. He rebuked the wind, which was the more direct instrument of Satan. He told the sea to be quiet and still, and it obeyed. Like a boisterous hound which lies down humbly at its master's voice, so the sea lay down at His feet. He was the complete Master of the situation.

Having thus rebuked the forces of nature, and the power that lay behind them, He turned to administer gentle rebuke to His disciples. Faith is *spiritual sight*, and as yet their eyes were hardly opened to discern who He was. Had they but realized a little of His proper glory they would not have been so fearful. And having witnessed this display of His power they were still fearful, and still questioning as to what manner of man He was. A Man who can command winds and sea, and they do His will, is obviously no ordinary Man. But, who is He?—that is the question.

No disciple can go forth to serve Him until that question is answered and thoroughly settled in his soul. Hence before He sends them forth there must be further exhibitions of His power and grace before their eyes, as recorded for us in chapter 5.

We too, in our day, must be fully assured who He is, before we attempt to serve Him. The question, What manner of Man is this? is a very insistent one. Until we can answer it very rightly and very clearly we must be still.

## Chapter 5

THE CONVICTION, AS to "what manner of Man" the Lord Jesus is, once having been reached by faith, it carries with it the assurance that He must be equal to meeting every emergency. Yet, even so, it is well for the disciple to actually see Him dealing with men, and with the troubles that have come upon them by reason of sin, in His delivering mercy. In this chapter we see the Lord displaying His power, and thereby educating His disciples still further. That education may be ours also as we go over the record.

While crossing the lake, the power of Satan had been at work hidden behind the fury of the tempest: on arriving at the other side it became very manifest in the man with an unclean spirit. Defeated in his more secret workings, the adversary now gives an open challenge without loss of time, for the man met Him immediately He landed. It was a kind of test case. The devil had turned the wretched man into a fortress that he hoped to hold at all costs; and into the fortress he had flung a whole legion of demons. If ever a man was held in hopeless captivity to the powers of darkness, it was he. In his story we see mirrored the plight into which humanity has sunk under Satan's power.

He "had his dwelling among the tombs:" and men today live in a world that is more and more becoming a vast graveyard as generation after generation passes into death. Then, "no man could bind him," for fetters and chains had often been tried to no purpose. He was beyond restraint. So today there are not lacking movements and methods intended to curb the bad propensities of men, to restrain their more violent actions, and reduce the world to pleasantness and order. But all in vain.

Then, with the demoniac another thing was tried. Could not his nature be changed? It is stated however, "neither could any man tame him;" so that idea proved useless. Thus it has always been: there is no more power in men to *change* their natures than there is to *curb* and *repress* them, so that they do not act. "The carnal mind ... is not subject to the law of God, neither indeed can be" (Rom. 8: 7), so it cannot be restrained. Again, "That which is born of the flesh is flesh" (John 3: 6), no matter what attempts may be made to improve it. So it can not be altered or changed.

"Always, night and day, he was in the mountains and in the tombs,"— utterly restless—"crying,"—utterly miserable—"cutting himself with stones,"—damaging himself in his madness. What a picture!

And we must add, what a *characteristic* picture of man under the power of Satan. This was an exceptional case, it is true. Satan's grip on the majority is of a gentler sort, and the symptoms are much less pronounced; still they are there. The cry of humanity may be heard, as men damage themselves by their sins.

When the man spoke, the words were framed by his lips, but the intelligence behind them was that of the demons who controlled him. *They knew* what manner of Man the Lord was, even if others did not. On the other hand they did *not* know the manner of His service. There will indeed be an hour when the Lord will consign these demons along with Satan their master into torment, but that was not His work at that moment. Much less was it the manner of His service at that time in regard to men. To the demoniac Jesus came, bringing not torment but *deliverance*.

The Lord had bidden the demons to come out, and they knew that they could not resist. They were in the presence of Omnipotence, and they must do as they were told. They had even to ask permission to enter into the swine that were feeding not far away. The swine, being unclean animals according to the law, ought not to have been there. The spirits being unclean also, there was an affinity between them and the swine, an affinity with fatal results for the animals. The demons had led the man toward self-destruction, using the sharp stones: with the swine the impulse was immediate and complete. The man was delivered: the swine were destroyed.

The result, as regards the man himself, was delightful. His restless wanderings were over, for he was "sitting." Formerly he "ware no clothes," as Luke tells us, now he is "clothed." His delusions had ceased, for he is "in his right mind." The gospel application of all this is very evident.

The result, as regards the people of those parts was very tragic however. They displayed a mind that was anything but right, though no demons had entered into them. They had no understanding or appreciation of Christ. On the other hand they did appreciate and understand pigs. If the presence of Jesus meant no pigs, even if it also meant no raging demoniac, then they would rather not have it. They began to pray Him to depart out of their coasts.

The Lord yielded to their desire and left. The tragedy of this was very great, though they did not realise it at the time. It was succeeded by the even greater tragedy of the Son of God being cast right out of this world; and we have now had nineteen centuries filled with every kind of evil as the result of that. The departure of the Lord created a fresh situation for the man just delivered from the demons. He naturally desired the presence of his Deliverer, but was instructed that for the present he must be content to abide in the place of His absence and there witness for Him, particularly to his own friends.

Our position today is very similar. Presently we shall be with Him, but for the present it is ours to witness for Him in the place where He is not. We too may tell our friends what great things the Lord has done for us.

Having recrossed the lake, the Lord was immediately confronted with further cases of human need. On His way to the house of Jairus, where lay his little daughter at the point of death, He was intercepted by the woman with an issue of blood. Her disease was of twelve years' standing and utterly beyond all the skill of physicians. Hers was a hopeless case, just as much as the case of the demoniac. He was in helpless captivity to a great crowd of demons, she to an incurable disease.

Again we can see an analogy to the spiritual state of mankind, and particularly to the efforts of an awakened soul as depicted in Romans 7. There are many struggles and much earnest striving, but in result, "nothing bettered but rather grew worse" would describe the case delineated there, until the soul comes to the end of its searchings, and having "spent all," has "heard of Jesus." Then ceasing all efforts at self-improvement and coming to Jesus, He proves Himself to be the great Deliverer.

In the case of the man we can hardly speak of faith at all, for he was completely dominated by the demons. In the case of the woman we can only speak of a faith that was defective. She was confident of His power, a power so great that even His clothes would impart it; yet she doubted His accessibility. The thronging crowds impeded her, and she did not realise how completely He—the perfect Servant—was at the disposal of all who needed Him. Yet the cure she needed was hers in spite of everything. The access she needed was made possible, and the blessing was brought to her. Satisfied with the blessing she would have slunk away.

But this it was not to be. She too was to bear witness to that which His power had wrought, and thereby she was to receive a further blessing for herself. The Lord's dealings with her are full of spiritual instruction.

The perfect knowledge of Jesus comes to light. He knew that virtue had gone out of Him, and that the touch had fallen on His clothes. He asked the question, but He knew the answer; for He looked round to see "her" that had done it.

His question also brought to light the fact that many had been touching Him in various ways, yet no other touch had drawn any virtue from Him. Why was this? Because, of all the touches, hers was the only one that sprang out of a consciousness of need, and faith. When these two things are present the touch is always effective.

A good many of us would be like the woman, and wish to obtain the blessing without any public acknowledgment of the Blesser. This must not be. It is due to Him that we confess the truth and make known His saving grace. Directly virtue has gone out from Him for our deliverance, the time of witness-bearing has come for us. Just as the man was to go home to his friends, the woman had to kneel at His feet in public. Both bore witness to Him; and, be it noted, in the opposite way to what we might have expected. Most men would find the witness at home the more difficult: most women the witness in public. But the man had to speak at home, and the woman in the presence of the crowd. She spoke however not *to* the crowd, but *to Him*.

As the fruit of her confession the woman herself received a further blessing. She got definite assurance from His word, that her cure was thorough and complete. A few minutes before she had "*felt* in her body that she was healed," and then she confessed, "*knowing* what was *done in her.*" This was very good, but it was not quite enough. Had the Lord permitted her to go away simply possessed of these nice "feelings," and this "knowledge" of what had been "done in her," she would have been open to many a doubt and fear in the days to come. Every small feeling of indisposition would have raised anxiety as to whether her old malady might not recur. As it was, she got His *definite word*, "Be whole of thy plague." That settled it. *His word* was far more reliable than *her feelings*.

So it is with us. Something is indeed done in us by the Spirit of God at conversion, and we know it, and our feelings may be happy: yet, even so, there is no solid basis on which assurance can rest in *feelings*, or in what has been done *in* us. The solid basis for assurance is found in *the Word of the Lord*. Not a few today lack assurance just because they have made the mistake which the woman was on the point of making. They have never properly confessed Christ, and owned their indebtedness to Him. If they will rectify this mistake as the woman did, they will get the assurance of His Word.

At the very moment of the woman's deliverance the case of Jairus' daughter took on a darker hue. Tidings of her death arrived, and those who sent the message assumed that though disease might disappear before the power of Jesus, death lay outside His domain. We have seen Him triumph over demons and disease, even when the victims were beyond all human help. Death is the most hopeless thing of all. Can He triumph over that? He can, and He did.

The way that He sustained the faltering faith of the ruler is very beautiful. Jairus had been quite confident as to His ability to heal; but now, what about death?—that was the great test to his faith, as also of the power of

Jesus. "Be not afraid, only believe," was the word. Faith in Christ will remove the fear of death for us as well as for him.

Death was but a sleep to Jesus, yet the professional mourners mocked Him in their unbelief. So He removed them, and in the presence of the parents and those of His disciples who were with Him, He restored the child to life. Thus for the third time in this chapter is deliverance brought to one who is beyond all human hope.

But the beginning of verse 43 is in sharp contrast to verses 19 and 33. There is to be *no testimony* this time; accounted for, we suppose, by the contemptuous unbelief that had just been manifested. At the same time there was the most careful consideration for the needs of the child in the way of food, just as there had been for the spiritual need of Jairus a little before. He thought both of *her body* and of *his faith*.

## Chapter 6

AFTER THESE THINGS, leaving the lakeside He went into the district where His early life had been spent. Teaching in the synagogue, His words astonished them. They quite clearly recognized the wisdom of His teachings and the might of His acts, and yet all this wrought no conviction or faith in their hearts. They knew Him, and those related to Him according to the flesh, and this but blinded their eyes as to who He really was. They were not insulting in their expression of unbelief, as were the mourners in the house of Jairus; but it was rank unbelief nevertheless, so great that He marvelled at it.

The view that they had of Jesus was just that of the modern Unitarian. They were altogether convinced of His humanity, for they were so well acquainted with its origins as far as His flesh was concerned. They saw it so clearly that it blinded them to anything beyond, and they were offended in Him. The Unitarian sees His humanity, but nothing beyond. We see His humanity no less clearly than the Unitarian, but beyond it we see His deity. It does not trouble us that we cannot grasp intellectually how both can be found in Him. Knowing that our minds are finite, we do not expect to explain that into which infinity enters. If we could grasp and explain, we should know that what we thus comprehend is not Divine.

As a result of this unbelief, "He could there do no mighty work," save that He healed a few sick folk, who, evidently, did have faith in Him. This emphasizes what we have just noted in connection with verse 43 of chapter 5. As, in the presence of ribald unbelief, the Lord withdrew any testimony to Himself, so, in the presence of His unbelieving fellow-countrymen, He did no mighty works.

Now we might feel inclined to think that His action should have been just the opposite. But it does seem in Scripture that when unbelief rises to the height of *mockery*, the testimony *stops*—see, Jeremiah 15: 17; Acts

13: 41; 17: 32—18: 1. Also it is evident that though "Jesus of Nazareth" was "approved of God . . . by miracles and wonders and signs" (Acts 2: 22), yet the main object was not to convince stubborn unbelief, but to encourage and confirm weak faith. We are shown in John 2: 23-25, that when His miracles did produce intellectual conviction in certain men, He Himself put no trust in the conviction so produced. Hence He did no great works in the Nazareth district. He "could" not do them. He was limited by moral considerations, not by physical ones. Miracles were *not suitable* to the occasion, according to God's ways: and He was the Servant of God's will.

What *was* suitable was the faithful rendering of a clear testimony; hence "He went round about the villages, teaching." A great display of miracles might have produced a revulsion of feeling and intellectual conviction, which would not have been worth having. The steady teaching of the Word meant sowing the seed, and there would be some worth-while fruit from that, as we have seen.

This brings us to verse 7 of this chapter, where we read of the twelve being sent forth on their first mission. Their period of training was now over. They had listened to His instructions, as given in chapter 4, and witnessed His power, as displayed in chapter 5. They had also had this striking illustration of the place that miracles should occupy, and of the fact that though there were times when they might be unsuitable, the teaching and preaching of the Word of God was *always in season*.

Miracles and signs of a genuine sort are not in evidence today; but the Word of God abides. Let us be thankful that the Word *is* always in season, and *let us be diligent in sowing it*.

The sending forth of the twelve was the inauguration of an extension of the Lord's ministry and service. Hitherto all had been in His own hands, with the disciples as onlookers; now they are to act on His behalf. He was absolutely sufficient in Himself; they are not sufficient, and hence they are to go forth two and two. There is help and courage in companionship, for just where one is weak another may be strong, and He who sent them knew exactly how to couple them together. Companionship is specially helpful where pioneering work is being done; and so in the Acts we see Paul acting on this instruction of the Lord. Service is an individual matter, it is true, but even today we do well to esteem rightly fellowship in serving. "We are God's *fellow-workmen*" (1 Cor. 3: 9. N. Tr.).

Before they left, they had power or authority given to them over all the power of Satan. They also had instructions to strip themselves of even the ordinary necessaries, carried by the traveller of those days. Further, they were given their message. As their Master had preached repentance in view of the kingdom (see 1: 15), so were they to preach it.

Those who serve today do not hold their commission from Christ on earth, but Christ in heaven; and this introduces certain modifications. Our message centres in the death, resurrection and glory of Christ, whereas theirs in the very nature of things could not do so. They discarded travelling necessities, inasmuch as they represented the Messiah on earth, who had nothing, but who was well able to sustain them. We are followers of a Christ who has gone on high, and His power is usually exercised in freeing His servants from dependence on props of a spiritual nature rather than from those of a material sort. We may certainly, however, take great comfort from the thought that He does not send His servants forth without giving them power for the service before them. If we are to cast out demons He will give us power to do it. And if our service is not that but something else, then power for the something else will be ours.

They—and we too—are to be marked by utmost simplicity: no running about from house to house in search for something better. They represented Him. He acted by proxy through them; and hence to refuse them was to refuse Him. His saying in verse 11 as to Sodom and Gomorrah is similar to what He said of Himself in Matthew 11: 21-24. Those who serve Him today are not apostles, still in a lesser degree the same thing doubtless holds good. God's message is not the less His message because it comes through feeble lips.

Their service, whether in preaching, casting out demons or in healing, was so effective that *His* Name—not theirs—was spread abroad, and even Herod heard His fame. This miserable king had so bad a conscience that he at once assumed that John the Baptist, his victim, had come to life. Others considered Christ to be Elijah, or one of the old prophets. No one knew, for no one thought of God as able to do some new thing.

At this point Mark digresses a little to tell us, in verses 17-28, how John had been murdered at the behest of a vindictive woman. Evil man though he was, Herod possessed a conscience that spoke, and we see the masterly craft by which the devil captured him. The trap was set by means of a young woman with pretty face and form, an older woman attractive and revengeful, and a foolish vanity which made the unhappy king think much more of his oath than of God's law. Thus the vain and lustful man was manouevred into the act of murder, with ultimate damnation for himself. His uneasy conscience only provoked superstitious fears.

In verse 29, Mark merely records that John's disciples gave his mutilated body burial. He does not add as Matthew does that they "went and told Jesus" (14: 12). He passes on to record the return of the disciples from their journeyings, telling their Master of all that they had done and taught. It was then that the Lord withdrew them into a desert place, that apart from the crowd and the busy service they might spend quiet time in His presence. It is instructive to notice that the passage in Matthew makes it pretty certain that the distressed disciples of John also arrived just at that time.

Let us never forget that a period of rest in the presence of the Lord, apart from men, is necessary after a period of busy service. The disciples of

# MARK

John came from their sad service heavy-hearted and distressed. The twelve came from triumphant encounters with the power of demons and disease, probably flushed with success. Both needed the quiet of the presence of the Lord, which avails equally to lift up the drooping heart and check undue elation of spirit.

However, the period of quiet was but brief, for the people sought after Him in their crowds, and He would not say them nay. The heart of the great Servant comes out most beautifully in verse 34, where we are told He was "moved with compassion." The sight of them, "as sheep not having a shepherd," only induced *compassion* in Him, not—as so often with us, alas!—feelings of annoyance or contempt. And He was *moved* by the compassion He felt; that is the wonder of it.

His compassion moved Him in two directions. First, to minister to them as to spiritual things. Second, to minister to them carnal things. Notice the order: the spiritual came first. "He began to teach them many things," though what He said is not recorded; then when the evening was come He relieved their hunger. Let us learn from this how to act. If men have bodily needs it is good that we should meet them according to our ability; but let us always keep the Word of God in the first place. The needs of the body must never take precedence over the needs of the soul, in our service.

In feeding the five thousand, the Lord first of all tested His disciples. How much had they taken in as to His sufficiency? Very little apparently, for in answer to His word, "Give ye them to eat," they *only* think of human resources and of money. Now any resources of a human sort that were present were by no means ignored. They were very insignificant, but they were appropriated by Jesus that in them His power might be displayed. He might have turned stones into bread, or indeed produced bread from nothing; but His way was to utilize the five loaves and two fishes.

His work has been carried on in just this way throughout the present epoch. His servants possess certain small things, which He is pleased to use. And further, He dispensed His bounty in an orderly manner, the people being seated in hundreds and fifties, and He employed His disciples in the work. The feet and hands that conveyed the food to the people were theirs. Today the feet and hands of His servants are used, their minds and lips are placed at His disposal, so that the bread of life may reach the needy. But the power that produces results is *wholly His*. The very feebleness of the means used makes this manifest.

As the perfect Servant He was careful to connect all that He did with heaven. Before the miracle took place He looked up to heaven and rendered thanks. Thereby the thoughts of the crowd were directed to God as the Source of all, rather than to Himself the Servant of God on earth. A word to ourselves, containing a similar principle, is found in 1 Peter 4: 11. The servant who ministers spiritual food is to do so as from God, that God may be glorified in it and not himself.

# MARK

We may also extract encouragement from the fact that when the great crowd was fed, far more remained than the little with which they started. The Divine resources are inexhaustible, and the Servant who relies upon his Master will never run out of supplies. In this respect there is a very happy resemblance between the loaves and fishes placed in the hands of the disciples and the Bible placed in the hands of disciples today.

The feeding of the multitude accomplished, the Lord at once dispatched His disciples to the other side of the lake and gave Himself to prayer. He not only connected all with heaven by thanksgiving in the presence of the people, but He ever maintained touch for Himself as the Servant of the Divine will. From John 6 we learn that at this point the people were enthusiastic and would have made Him a king by force. The disciples might have been entrapped by this, but He was not.

The crossing of the lake furnished the disciples with a fresh demonstration of who their Master was. The contrary wind hindered their progress, and they toiled forward slowly. He again proved Himself supremely above both wind and wave, walking upon the water, and able to pass them by. His word calmed their fears, and His presence in their boat ended the storm. In spite of all this, the real significance of it eluded them. Their hearts were not yet ready to take it in. Nevertheless the people generally had learned to recognize the Lord and His power. Abundance of need was presented to Him, and He met it with abundance of grace.

## Chapter 7

As we commence this chapter the opposition of the religious leaders again comes to light. The disciples, filled with labour—as verse 31 of the previous chapter has told us—were not observing certain traditional washings, and this roused the Pharisees, who were the great sticklers for the tradition of the elders. The Lord accepted the challenge on behalf of the disciples, and answered by a searching exposure of the whole Pharisaic position. They were hypocrites, and He told them so.

The essence of their hypocrisy lay in the profession of worship, consisting in outward ceremonials, when inwardly their hearts were utterly estranged. *Nothing counts with God if the heart be not right.*

Then, in carrying out their ceremonials they brushed aside the commandment of God in favour of their own tradition. The Lord not merely asserted this, but proved it by giving an instance of the way in which they set aside the fifth commandment by their rules concerning "Corban;" that is, things devoted to the service of God. Under cover of "Corban" many a Jew divested himself of all his rightful duties towards his poor old parents. And he did the thing with an air of sanctity, for did it not appear more pious to devote things to God rather than to one's parents?

# MARK

The things that came under "Corban" were not things that God *demanded;* had it been so His demand must have prevailed. There were things that *might be* dedicated, if so desired; whereas the obligation to support parents was a distinct *command.* Pharisaic tradition permitted a man to use a permissive enactment in order to avoid complying with a distinct command. They might try to support their tradition with sophistry which appeared pious, but the Lord charged them with nullifying the Word of God. The *written words* of Exodus 20: 12 were to Jesus *"the Word of God."* There is no support here for that religious fastidiousness which declines to attach the designation "Word of God" to the written Scriptures.

We believe we should be right in saying that all human tradition in the things of God ultimately sets the Word of God at naught. The originators of the tradition probably have no such thought, but the master spirit of evil, lying behind the business, has *just that intention.*

Having unmasked the Pharisees as men whose hearts were far from God, and who dared to make of no effect the Word of God, the Lord called the people and publicly proclaimed the truth which cuts at the root of all religious pretension. Man is not defiled by physical contact with external things, but *is himself the seat of what defiles.* A hard saying this, and only they who have ears to hear will receive it.

The disciples had to ask Him privately concerning it, and in verses 18 to 23 we have the explanation. Man is corrupt in his nature. What comes from his very heart defiles him. Out of his heart proceed evil thoughts which develop into every kind of evil action. This is the most tremendous indictment of human nature ever uttered. No wonder the Pharisaic heart was far from God; but what a terrible thing that men with hearts like this should profess to draw near and worship Him.

These searching words of our Lord cut at the root of all human pride, and show the worthlessness of all human movements, whether religious or political, which deal merely with externals and leave the heart of man untouched.

His disciples as yet hardly understood these things, and experience will show us that professing Christians are very slow to accept and understand them today; but we shall not get very far except we do understand them. However, it is one thing to expose the heart of man: something more is needed—the heart of God must be expressed. This the Lord proceeded to do, as the rest of the chapter shows.

To the very borders of the land which harboured so much of hypocrisy He went, and there came in contact with a poor Gentile woman in desperate need. His fame had reached her ears and she would not be denied. Yet the Lord tested her by His little parable about the children's bread and the dogs. Her answer, "Yes, Lord: yet the dogs under the table eat of the children's crumbs," was happily free of hypocrisy. She said in effect, "Yes, Lord: it is true that I am no child of the kingdom but a poor Gentile dog without any claim; but I am confident that there is enough power with God and enough goodness in His heart, to feed a poor dog like me."

Now this was *faith*. Matthew indeed tells us that the Lord called it "great faith," and it delighted Him. It also brought her all that her heart desired. Her daughter was delivered. How great the contrast between the heart of God and the heart of man! The one full of benevolence and grace: the other full of every kind of evil. How happy for us when instead of harbouring hypocrisy we are marked by honesty and faith.

In verse 31 He again returns to the neighbourhood of the lake, there to meet a man who was deaf and dumb—a condition that was strikingly symbolic of the state in which the mass of the Jews were found. The poor Gentile woman had had ears to hear, and consequently found her tongue to utter words of faith, but they were deaf and had nothing to say.

In healing this man the Lord performed certain actions, which doubtless have symbolic meanings. He took him aside from the crowds, that He might deal with him in privacy. His fingers, symbolic of Divine action, touch his ears. That which came from His mouth touched the mouth of the dumb man. Thus the work was done, and the deaf and dumb both heard and spoke. If any ears are opened to hear the voice of the Lord, it is the fruit of Divine action which takes place in secret. And if any tongue can utter the praise of God or the Word of God, it is because that which comes from His mouth has been brought into contact with ours.

Nothing is said as to the faith of the man. What he felt he was unable to express, and others brought him to Jesus. He was met, however, in full and unstinted grace. Once more it was a case of the goodness of the heart of God being manifested by Jesus.

Evidently the people in some measure were conscious of this, and in their amazement they confessed, "He hath done all things well!" Coming where it does, this word is all the more striking. The early part of the chapter reveals man in his true character, and we find his heart to be a fountain whence proceeds nothing but evil — he has done all things *ill!* The perfect Servant reveals the goodness of the heart of God. He has done all things *well*.

With this verdict we too have abundant cause to agree.

## Chapter 8

WHEN THE FIVE thousand were fed, as recorded in chapter 6, the disciples took the initiative by calling their Master's attention to the needy condition of the crowd. On this second occasion the Lord took the initiative, and drew His disciples' attention to their need, expressing His compassion and concern on their behalf. As on the first occasion so again now the disciples have simply *man* before them, and think only of his powers which are wholly unequal to the situation. They had not yet learned to measure the difficulty by the power of their Lord.

Hence the instruction which was conveyed by the feeding of a huge crowd with earthly resources of the tiniest order, was repeated. There were slight differences, both as to the number of the people and the number of the loaves and fishes used, but in all the essentials this miracle was a repetition of the other, as once more He fulfilled Psalm 132: 15, and displayed *the power of God* before their eyes.

Having fed the multitude, He dismissed them Himself, and immediately after departed with His disciples to the other side of the lake, just as on the previous occasion. On His arrival certain Pharisees came with aggressive intent requesting a sign from heaven. He had as a matter of fact just been giving very striking signs from heaven in the presence of thousands of witnesses. The Pharisees had no intention of following Him, and hence had not been present so as to see the sign for themselves, still there was ample witness to it if they cared to listen. The fact was of course that on the one hand they had no desire to witness any sign that would authenticate Him and His mission, and on the other hand they had no ability to see and recognize the sign even when it was plainly before their eyes. Their utter unbelief grieved Him to the heart.

In verse 34 of the previous chapter, when He was confronted with human weakness and disability of a bodily sort, He sighed: here confronted with blindness of a spiritual sort, He sighed *deeply* in His spirit. Spiritual incapacity is a far more serious matter than bodily incapacity. They were blind leaders of a blind generation and groping about for a sign. No sign would be given to them, for to blind men signs are useless. This was the occasion when, as recorded at the beginning of Matthew 16, the Lord told them they could discern the face of the sky, but not the signs of the times.

Let us not dismiss this matter as being something which only concerns the Pharisee: in principle it also concerns ourselves. How often has the true believer been troubled and disheartened, thinking God has not spoken, or acted, or answered, when really He has, only we have not had eyes to see. We may have continued beseeching Him for more *light*, when all the time all that was wanted was a few *windows* in our house!

The motive actuating these Pharisees was wholly wrong, since their object was to tempt Him. So the Lord abruptly left them and departed again to the other side of the lake, which He had left but a short time before, and the disciples were without bread. Thus for the third time they were face to face with the problem raised in the feeding of the five thousand and the four thousand, only on a very small scale.

Alas! the disciples no more met the problem in the strength of faith when it was on the small scale than when it was on the great scale. They too had not so far had eyes to see the power and glory of their Master, as displayed twice in His multiplication of the loaves and fishes. True faith has penetrating vision. They should have discerned who He was, and then they would have looked not to their paltry loaves or fishes but to Him, and every difficulty would have vanished. In the small crises that mark our own lives are we any better than they were?

The Lord's charge about the leaven of the Pharisees and of Herod is not explained to us here, as it is in Matthew, but we must note its significance. He referred to the doctrine of the two factions, which worked like leaven in those who came under the influence of the one and the other. That of the Pharisees was hypocristy. That of the Herodians was utter worldliness. In Matthew we read of the leaven of the Sadducees, and this was intellectual pride which led them into rationalistic unbelief. Nothing does more effectually blind the mind and understanding than leaven of these three kinds.

The blind man of Bethsaida, of whom we read in verses 22 to 26, exactly illustrates the condition of the disciples at that time. When the blind man was brought to the Lord, He took him by the hand and led him out of the town, thus separating him from the haunts of men, just as previously He had turned His back upon the Pharisees and those with them (verse 13). Outside the town the Lord dealt with him, performing His work in two parts — the only time, as far as we remember, that He acted thus. As the result of the first touch he saw, "men as trees, walking." He saw, but things were badly out of focus. He knew that the objects he saw were men, but they looked much bigger than they were.

Thus it was with the disciples — *man* was too great in their eyes. Even as they looked at the Lord Himself it would seem that His humanity eclipsed His Deity in their eyes. They needed, like the blind man, a second touch before they saw all things clearly. The presence of the Son of God amongst them in flesh and blood was the first touch that reached them, and as a result they began to see. When He had died and risen again and was ascended to glory, He laid His second touch upon them in shedding forth His Spirit, as recorded in Acts 2. Then they saw all things clearly. We may well earnestly pray that our spiritual vision may not be near-sighted and out of focus, lest the great trees, we think we see, turn out to be merely feeble little men strutting about. Such a state is possible for us, as 2 Peter 1: 9 shows; and there is no excuse for us, since the Spirit has been given.

The blind man, when cured, was not to go into the town nor testify to any in the town; moreover the Lord Himself now withdrew with His disciples to Caesarea Philippi, the most northerly town within the confines of the land, and very near the Gentile border. Clearly He was beginning to withdraw Himself and the testimony to His Messiahship from the blind people and their yet more blinded leaders. Here He raised the question with His disciples as to who He was. The people hazarded differing guesses, but all imagined Him to be some old prophet revived, just a *man*, and none had sufficient interest to really find out.

Then Jesus challenged His disciples. Peter became the spokesman and answered confessing His Messiahship, but this only produced a rejoinder which probably astonished them greatly, and may astonish us as we read it today. He charged them to be silent as to His Messiahship, and began to teach them as to His approaching rejection and death and resurrection. Any testimony that had been rendered to Him as the Messiah on earth was now formally withdrawn. From this point He accepted His death as inevitable, and began to turn the thoughts of His disciples to that which was impending as the result of it. This was the orderly progress of things on the human side; and it does not contradict nor clash with the divine side—that He knew from the outset that which was before Him.

Moreover, the disciples were as yet hardly fit to bear further testimony, had it been needed. Peter indeed had some measure of spiritual sight, for he had just confessed Him as the Christ; yet the intimation of His approaching rejection and death raised a vehement remonstrance from this very man. In this Peter's mind was being swayed by Satan, and the Lord rebuked this spirit of evil who was behind Peter's words. Peter's mind was set on "the things that be of *men*," and so he answered very aptly to the man of whom we have just read, who saw men as trees walking. Though he recognized the Christ in Jesus, he still had men before him, and in this the other disciples were no better than he. So how could he go forth as an effectual witness to the Christ whom he recognized? No wonder, after all, that at this point He charged His disciples that they should tell no man of Him.

We may pause here, each to face the fact that we cannot effectually go forth in testimony unless we really know the One of whom we testify, and also know and understand the situation that exists, in the face of which the testimony has to be rendered.

In the closing verses of our chapter the Lord begins to instruct His disciples in the presence of the people as to consequences that would follow from His rejection and death. They imagined themselves to be following a Messiah who was to be received and glorified on earth; and the fact was, He was about to die and rise again and be for the present glorified in heaven. This entailed an immense change in their outward prospects. It meant the denying of self, the taking up of the cross, the losing of life in this world, the bearing of shame as identified with Christ and His words, in the midst of an evil generation.

The force of "deny himself" is hardly expressed by "self-denial," which is the denying oneself *of something*. What the Lord speaks of is not that but the denial, or the saying of "no," *to oneself*. Also, "take up his cross" does not mean bearing trials and troubles merely. The man who in those days took up his cross was being led to execution. He was a man who had

# MARK

to accept death at the hands of the world. To say "no" to oneself is to accept death *internally*, on one's own spirit: to take up one's cross is to accept death *externally* at the hands of the world. That is what discipleship must mean, since we follow the Christ who died, rejected of the world.

This thought is expanded in verses 35-37. The true disciple of Christ is not aspiring to gain the whole world; he is ready rather to lose the world, and his own life in it, for the sake of the Lord and His Gospel. The perfect Servant, whom Mark depicts, gave His life that there might be a Gospel to preach. Those who follow Him, and are His servants, must be prepared to give up their lives in preaching the Gospel. If they should be ashamed of Him now, He would be ashamed of them in the day of His glory.

## Chapter 9

THESE WORDS, IF they at all realized their import, must have come to the disciples as a great blow. Hence the Lord, in His tender consideration for them, proceeded to give them very ample assurance as to the reality of the glory that is to come. They had expected God's kingdom to come with power and glory in their lifetime, and that illusion being dispelled, they might easily jump to the conclusion that it was not coming at all. Hence the three disciples, who seemed to be leaders among them, were taken aside to the high mountain that they might be witnesses of His transfiguration. There they saw the kingdom of God come with power—not in its fulness but in sample form. They were granted a private view of it in advance.

In the first chapter of his second Epistle Peter shows us the effect that this wonderful scene had upon him. He was an eye-witness of the majesty of Christ, and thereby he knew that His power and the promise of His coming was no cunningly devised fable, but a glorious fact, and so the prophetic word was made "more sure," or "confirmed." He knew, and we may know, that not one jot or tittle, of that which has been foretold concerning the glory of Christ's coming kingdom, will fail.

The transfiguration scene itself was a prophecy. Christ is to be the shining Centre of the kingdom glory, as He was on the mountain top. Saints will be with Him in heavenly conditions, just as Moses and Elijah were: some of them buried and called forth by God, like Moses; some raptured to heaven without dying, like Elijah. In the kingdom too there will be saints on earth below, enjoying earthly blessedness in the light of the heavenly glory, just as the three disciples were conscious of blessedness during the brief vision. It was "after six days," and only six were present, so all was on a small and incomplete scale; still the essentials were there.

Peter, ready to speak as ever, blurted out what he intended to be a compliment, but which in reality was far otherwise. The scene of glory could not then be prolonged upon earth, nor could the Christ—nor even

Moses and Elijah—be confined to earthly tabernacles. But more serious than this mistake was the thought that Jesus was only *the first amongst the greatest of men.* He is not the first amongst the great, but "the beloved Son," of the Father, *perfectly unique, immeasurably beyond all comparison.* No other may be mentioned in the same breath with Him. He stands alone. This the Father's voice declared, adding that He is the One who is to be heard.

The Father's voice has been heard very rarely by men. He spoke at Christ's baptism, and now again at His transfiguration, this time adding, "Hear Him." Since then His voice has never been heard by men in intelligible fashion. The Son is the Spokesman of the Godhead, and it is to Him that we have to listen. God once spoke through the prophets, Moses and Elijah: He now has spoken in His beloved Son. This shuts Peter out, as well as Moses and Elijah, which is significant when we remember what the Romish system makes of Peter and his supposed authority. In this incident Peter again showed that as yet he was just like the man whose eyes were out of focus, so that he saw men as trees walking.

No sooner had the Father's voice thus exalted His beloved Son than the whole vision was gone, and only Jesus was left with the three disciples. Saints disappear, but Jesus remains. The words, "They saw no man any more, save Jesus only," are very significant. If any of us approximate to that in our spiritual experience, we shall no longer be like a man who sees men as trees walking, but be like the man after the second touch, seeing all things clearly. Jesus will fill the picture as far as we are concerned, and man be eclipsed.

All this was made known to the disciples, as verse 9 shows, in view of the time when His death and resurrection should be accomplished. Only then would they really understand it all, illuminated by the Holy Spirit, and be able to effectually use it in testimony. At that moment they did not even understand what rising from among the dead really signified, as the next verse shows. The rising *of* the dead would not have puzzled them in any special way: it was this rising *"out of,"* or *"from among,"* the dead — which first took place in Christ—that raised such questions. The first resurrection of the saints, the resurrection of life, is of the same order. Are there not many, calling themselves Christians, who are full of questions as to it today?

The disciples' question as to Elijah, and his predicted coming, was naturally raised in their minds by the transfiguration scene. The Lord used it to again turn their thoughts to His death. In regard to this first advent of His, the part of Elijah had been played by John the Baptist; and his murder was symptomatic of what was to happen to the greater One, of whom he was the forerunner.

The scene on the high mountain soon came to an end but not so the scenes of human sin and misery and suffering which filled the plains below.

# MARK

From the heights to the depths they had to come, to find the rest of the disciples defeated and anxious in the absence of their Master. Immediately He appeared the crowds were amazed, and all eyes turned from the distracted disciples to the calm and all-sufficient Master. A moment before the scribes had been heckling the disciples, now He questions the scribes, invites the confidence of the troubled father, and displays His sufficiency.

Happy is the saint who is able to bring something of the grace and power of Christ into this troubled world! But even so, we shall have to wait for His coming and kingdom to see fully accomplished what this scene foreshadows. Only then will He transform the whole world, and turn the defeat and disquietude of His tried and distracted people into *the calm of His presence* and into a *complete and manifested victory*.

There had been a singular manifestation of the glory of God in the peaceful scene upon the mountain-top, whilst at the foot of the mountain the dark power of Satan had been displayed, with all the distraction that it brings. The boy demon-possessed, the father disappointed and distracted, the disciples defeated and dejected, the scribes not at all averse to making capital out of the incident. The Lord walks into the midst and all is changed.

In the first place, He puts His finger upon the spot where the root of the failure lay. They were a faithless generation. The root was *unbelief*. This applied to His disciples, as well as to the rest. If their faith had fully laid hold of who He was, they would not have been baffled by this test, any more than when confronted by the matter of feeding the multitudes. They were still like the man of chapter 8, before he saw all things clearly.

But now the Master Himself is in the midst, and the word is, "Bring him unto ME." However, the first result of the boy being brought was disappointing, for the demon flung him down in a terrible fit. Yet this was made to serve the purpose of the Lord, for on the one hand it made the more manifest the terrible plight of the boy the very moment before he was delivered, and on the other it served to bring out the feelings and thoughts of the anguished father. His cry, "If Thou canst do anything, have compassion on us, and help us," revealed his lack of faith as to His power, whilst he was not too sure of His kindness.

The reply of Jesus was, "The 'if thou couldst' is [if thou couldst] believe" (N. Trans.). That is, He said in effect, "There is no 'if' on My side, the only 'if' that enters into this matter is on your side. It is not 'if I can do anything,' but 'if you can believe.' " This put the whole thing in the true light, and in a flash the man saw it. Seeing it, he believed, whilst confessing his former unbelief.

Having evoked faith in the man, the Lord acted. The object before Him was not to create a sensation amongst the people; had it been, He would have waited for the crowd to collect. His object evidently was to confirm the faith of the father, and of any others who had eyes to see. The demon had to obey, though he wrought his worst before relinquishing his prey. This display of demonic power, after all, only gave an opportunity for a more complete display of Divine power. Not only was the boy completely delivered but also delivered for ever, since the demon was commanded to enter him no more.

Having thus manifested the power and kindness of God, the perfect Servant did not court popularity amongst the crowds but retired to a certain house. There His disciples in quietness enquired as to the reason of their failure, and got His answer. Again and again we ought to be asking their question, as we find ourselves weak in the presence of the foe; and as we do so we shall doubtless get just the answer they got, as recorded in verse 29. The Lord had already declared how unbelief lay at the root of their powerlessness: now He specifies two further things. Not only is faith needed, but also prayer and fasting.

Faith indicates a spirit of confidence in God: prayer—dependence on God: fasting—separation to God, in the form of abstinence from lawful things. These are the things which lead to power in the service of God. Their opposites—unbelief, self-confidence, self-indulgence, are the things that lead to weakness and failure. These words of our Lord play like a searchlight upon our many failures in serving Him. Let us consider our ways in the light of them.

In verses 30 and 31 we again see the Lord withdrawing Himself from publicity, and instructing His disciples as to His approaching death and resurrection. We first saw this in verses 30 and 31 of the previous chapter. It was the next great event in the Divine programme, and He now began to keep it steadily before the minds of His disciples, though at the moment they failed to take it in. Their minds were still filled with expectations of the coming of a visible kingdom, so they were unable to entertain any idea that controverted that.

The idea that Christ's kingdom would immediately appear appealed to them because they expected to have a large place of honour in it. They conceived of it in a carnal way, and it awakened carnal desires in their hearts. Hence on the journey to Capernaum they fell to discussing who of them was to be greatest. The Lord's question was sufficient to convict them of their folly, as was evidenced by their abashed silence; yet He knew it all, for He proceeded to answer them though they made no confession.

His answer appears to be two-fold. First, the only way that leads to real greatness is one that goes to the bottom as servant to all. This being so, we can see how the Lord Jesus is pre-eminent even apart from His Deity. In manhood He has taken the lowest place, and become Servant to all in a way that is infinitely beyond the service of all others. The one most like Him is likely to be first.

In the second place, He showed that the personality of the servant is of small significance: what does count is the Name in which He comes. We have that beautiful and touching scene in which He first set a small child in their midst, and then took him up in His arms, in order to enforce His point. That child was an insignificant scrap of humanity, yet to receive one such in His Name was to receive the Lord Himself, and also the Father who sent Him. The reception of a thousand such in any other name or on any other ground would signify but little. The fact is that the Master Himself is so supremely great that the relative position of His little servants is not worth disputing about.

This teaching seems to have come as an illumination to John, and caused his conscience to prick him as to their attitude towards a zealous man who acted in His Name, though not following the twelve. Why he did not follow, we are not told; but we must remember that it was not open to anyone to attach themselves to the twelve just as they chose: the Lord's own choice decided that matter. Whatever it was, the Lord's reply again laid all the emphasis on the value of His Name. Acting in His Name, the man was clearly for Christ and not against Him.

As a matter of fact this unofficial individual had been doing the very thing which the disciples had just failed to do—he had cast out a demon. Office is one thing: power is quite another. They should go together, in so far as office is instituted in Christianity. But very frequently they have not done so. And in these later days when offices have been unscriptually instituted, we again and again see some simple and unofficial person doing the thing which the official has no power to do. The power lies in *the Name* not the *office*.

Verse 41 shows that the smallest gift in the Name, and for Christ's sake, is of value in the sight of God and will meet with reward at His hands. Verse 42 gives us the converse of this: to be a snare to the feeblest of those who are Christ's is to merit and to get severe judgment. The losing of life in this world is a small thing compared with loss in the world to come.

This leads to the very solemn passage with which this chapter closes. Some of His hearers might have thought the Lord's word about the millstone a bit extreme. He adds yet stronger words, which have hell-fire itself in view. His thoughts at this point evidently broadened out beyond His disciples to men generally, and He shows that any loss in this world is very small compared with the loss of all that is life in the next, and being cast into the fire of Gehenna. Hand and foot and eye are very valuable members of our bodies, and not to be lightly parted with; but life in the coming age is beyond all price, and hell-fire an awful reality.

The Valley of Hinnom, the refuse dump outside Jerusalem, where fires always burned and maggots continually did their work, was known as Gehenna; and this word on the Lord's lips became a terribly apt figure of the abode of the lost. Verily hell will be the great refuse heap of eternity, where all that is incorrigibly evil will be segregated from the good, and lie for ever under the judgment of God. This terrible fact reaches us from the lips of Him who loved sinful men and wept over them.

The first statement of verse 49 sprang out of what the Lord had just been saying. Fire searches and consumes and disinfects. Salt not only seasons but preserves. Fire symbolizes the judgment of God, which all must face in one way or another. The believer must face it in the way indicated by 1 Corinthians 3: 13, and by it he will be "salted," since it will mean the preserving of all that is good. The ungodly will be subjected to it in their persons, and it will salt them; that is, they will be preserved *in* it and not destroyed *by* it.

The latter part of the verse is an allusion to Leviticus 2: 13. Salt has been described as symbolizing that "power of holy grace, which binds the soul to God and inwardly preserves it from evil." We cannot present our bodies a living sacrifice to God if that holy grace is absent. It is indeed good, and nothing would compensate for its absence. We are to have in ourselves this holy grace which would judge and separate us from all that is evil. If each is concerned to have it *in oneself*, there will not be difficulty in having peace *amongst ourselves*.

## Chapter 10

THE OPENING OF this chapter brings us near to the closing scenes of the Lord's life. He was on the farther side of Jordan but near the borders of Judaea, and the Pharisees appeared, opposing Him by tempting Him. By raising questions as to marriage and divorce, they expected to entangle Him in some contradiction of the things that Moses had commanded, and so find a point of attack. The Lord did not contradict Moses, but He went behind him to God's original thought in the creation of man and woman. The Pharisees were great sticklers for the law of Moses, but He showed them that in this instance the law did not enforce God's original thought. It is important to notice this, for it supplies us with one reason why the law is not made the rule of life for the Christian.

The law fell below the height of God's thought, but Christ did not: He fully maintained it. Verse 9 lifts the whole matter of marriage from the level of man and human expediency to the level of God and His action. It is a divine institution and not a human arrangement, and therefore is not to be tampered with by men. If God joins, man is not to put asunder.

This verse states a great principle which is true universally. The converse also would be true—man is not to join what God has put asunder. It is a sad fact that ever since sin came in man has been consumed with a desire to undo what God has done. It is so in natural things, and many of the ills we suffer come from our tampering with things given of God, even in matters of food, etc., and generally upsetting the balance of things which He established. It certainly is so in things spiritual. Many a difficulty and much needless soul trouble springs from misunderstanding as to things which God has joined together in His Word, or things which He has sundered.

Having set marriage before them in the right light, the Lord deals, in verses 13—16, with children. As to these, the disciples share the ordinary thoughts of the world, which fall far below the thoughts of God. The disciples judged them to be too insignificant for the Master's attention, but He thought far otherwise. He received them gladly, took them up in His arms, put His hands upon them and blessed them. He also showed that the only way of entrance into the kingdom of God is by having the spirit and mind of the little child. If anyone approaches that kingdom as a *significant somebody* he finds the entrance barred. If he comes as an *insignificant nobody* he may enter.

Then, verses 17—27, we get the Lord's teaching in regard to possessions. It is striking how marriage, children and possessions follow one another in this chapter, for so much of our lives in this world is occupied with these three things. All three are perverted and abused in the hands of sinful men; and all three are put in their right place in the teachings of our Lord.

The one who came running to Jesus exhibited many commendable features. Matthew tells us he was young, and Luke that he was a ruler. He was earnest and reverent and recognized in Him a great Rabbi, who could direct men to eternal life. He took it for granted that the life was to be obtained by human doings, according to the law. Evidently he had no idea of the Deity of Jesus, and hence the Lord's words in verse 18. He repudiated goodness apart from His being God, saying in effect, "If I am not God, I am not good."

As the young man asked his question with the law in his mind, the Lord referred him to the law, particularly to the commandments dealing with man's duty to his neighbour. He could claim to have observed these, at least as regards his acts, and Jesus beholding him loved him. This shows that his claim to correct observance of these things which the law enjoined was a true one. He was an exceptionally fine character, with features which in themselves were pleasing to God. The Lord did not belittle these pleasing features. He admitted them, and looked upon him with eyes of love.

Yet He tested him. One thing he lacked, and that was the God-given faith, which would have seized who Jesus was, and led him to take up the cross and follow Him; the faith which would have made treasure in heaven preferable to treasure on earth. He expected the Lord to direct him to some *work of the law* by which life should be reached; instead he was directed to a *work of faith*. Sad at heart he went away. He did not possess the faith, so it was impossible for him to show his faith by his works. The same test comes to us. How have we answered to it?

# MARK

This is a tremendous question. How slow we all are to give up law-keeping for Christ and earth for heaven! No wonder the Lord speaks of the difficulty with which the rich enter the kingdom. Verse 23 speaks of them "that have riches," and verse 24 of "them that trust in riches." The fact is, of course, that it is very difficult to have them without trusting in them. We naturally cling to riches and earth. Christ offers the Cross and heaven.

The disciples, accustomed to regard riches as a sign of God's favour, were very astonished at these words; they felt that they cut the ground away completely from under our feet. So, indeed, they do. "Who then can be saved?" is a momentous question. Verse 27 gives a definite answer. Salvation is impossible with men, though possible with God. In other words it was as though the Lord said, "If it is a question of what man can do, *nobody* can be saved: but if a question of what God can do, *anybody* can be saved."

We emphasize that word. Salvation with men is not improbable, but IMPOSSIBLE. The door, as regards our own efforts is barred against us. God has opened another door however, but that is by death and resurrection, to which the Lord was now turning the thoughts of His disciples.

Though death and resurrection were before the mind of the Lord, earthly glory was still before the mind of Peter, and he betrayed it by his remark recorded in verse 28. He referred of course to the test which the Lord had just presented to the rich young ruler. Peter felt that, though the ruler had failed before the test, he and his fellow-disciples had not: indeed, he actually added, as Matthew records, "What shall we have therefore?" His mind, enquiring and impetuous, wished to anticipate the good things to come. The Lord's answer indicated that in the present age there should be great gain, though with persecutions, and in the coming age eternal life.

This saying of our Lord is illustrated by Paul's life of service, as seen in such scriptures as, Acts 16: 15; 18: 3; 21: 8; Romans 16: 3, 4, 23; 1 Corinthians 16: 17; Philippians 4: 18; Philemon 22. Houses were at his disposal in many a city, and many counted it an honour to fulfil the part of brother, sister, mother or child toward him. Persecutions certainly were his. Eternal life in the world to come lies before him. Such is the lot of those who follow and serve this perfect Servant of God.

Verse 31 was evidently uttered as a warning and corrective to Peter. Forwardness here may not mean the first place there. All depends upon the motive underlying the service. If Peter wished to drive a bargain—so much following for so much reward—that alone would show defective motive. Still it does not say that *all* that are first shall be last, and *all* last first. Paul went ahead of all in his day, and who can challenge the purity of his motive, or the reality of his devotion to his Lord?

# MARK

The thing that Peter and the rest greatly needed was to realize and understand the fast approaching death and resurrection of their Master. There is nothing that we today, nineteen centuries after the event, more deeply need to realise and understand. Not only is it the basis of all our blessing but it imparts its own character to all Christian life and service. No intelligent service can be rendered save in the light of it.

Verses 32 to 34 give us the fourth occasion on which the Lord instructed His disciples in regard to it; and the request of James and John, recorded in verse 37, furnished the Lord with a fifth occasion. Their minds were still filled with expectations concerning a glorious kingdom on earth, and they wished to advance their own interests in that kingdom. Now the Lord Jesus was here as the perfect Servant of the will of God, and this involved for Him the cup of suffering and the baptism of death. Places of honour in the coming kingdom will be apportioned to those who have served this wonderful Servant, according to the measure in which they had accepted suffering and death on His behalf. Yet, even so, He does not apportion these places of distinction. All that is at the discretion of the Father, for He remains true to the place of Servant which He has taken. Except we remain true to the place in which we are set, the place of identification with our rejected Lord, we cannot expect any place of special recognition in the glory of the kingdom.

This unblushing place-hunting on the part of James and John might incline us to blame them above the rest, were it not for verse 41, which shows that the same selfish desires were entertained by all, and that they objected, not because of the request the two had made, but because they had been forestalled in the way the two made it. Their annoyance however only gave further occasion for the display of the perfect grace of their Lord.

How easy it was, and is, for the disciples of Jesus to accept and adopt the standards and customs of the world that surrounds them, to take for granted that, because everybody seems to be doing it, it is the right thing to do. Again and again our Lord would say to us, "But so shall it not be among you." The nations have their great men, who exercise their authority in a lordly way. Amongst disciples of the Lord greatness is manifested in an entirely different way. There true greatness is displayed in taking the lowly place of service to others—serving the Lord in serving them.

The Son of Man Himself is the shining example of service of this kind. Who so great as He in His original estate? Then "thousand thousands ministered unto Him" (Dan. 7: 10). Who took so lowly a place, ministering to others? Who carried service to such a length as "to give His life a ransom for many"? For this reason alone, apart from other considerations, the place of pre-eminence must be His. They, who follow Him most closely in lowly service in this day, will be chiefest in that day.

In verse 45, the Lord not only brings His death before His disciples for the fifth time, but He explains its significance. Previously He had emphasized the fact of His death, so that the minds of the disciples might no longer be obsessed by expectations of a coming visible kingdom. Now the meaning of the fact appears. He would die to pay the *ransom price* for many. Here then we have a plain statement as to the substitutionary and atoning character of His death from His own lips. It is "many" here, for the actual, realized effect of His ransoming death is the point. In 1 Timothy 2: 6, where the bearing and scope of it is in question, the word is "all."

These dealings with His disciples took place "in the way going up to Jerusalem" (verse 32). In verse 46 they arrive in Jericho, and the closing scenes of His life begin. Bartimaeus, the blind beggar, furnished Him with a striking opportunity of setting forth the mercy of God. Mercy was what the blind man craved, though the people, who did not understand mercy of a divine sort, would have silenced him. Mercy however he got, and it went beyond his thoughts, for it not only gave him *sight* but enlisted him as a *follower* of the One who extended the mercy. The faith of Bartimaeus was shown in that he addressed Jesus as the Son of David though others spoke of Him only as Jesus of Nazareth. His may only have been little faith, for he did not rise to the height of calling Him Son of God; yet little faith receives an abundant answer as surely as great faith does. Let us be thankful for that.

## Chapter 11

JESUS NOW DREW near to Jerusalem. His disciples were in His train, not only those who had spent three years in His company but Bartimaeus also, who had spent perhaps three hours. Bethany was the home of some who loved Him, and there He found the colt of an ass, so that He might enter the city as Zechariah had predicted. The Lord had need of that colt, and He knew who the owner was and that His need would meet with a ready response. He was the Servant of the will of God, and He knew where to lay His hand upon all that was necessary to fulfil His service, whether the ass in the chapter, or the guestchamber in chapter 14, or as on other occasions.

He entered as the prophet said He would, "just," "lowly," and "having salvation." There was a burst of temporary enthusiasm, but men had no lasting desire for what was just, and holiness made no appeal to them. Moreover the salvation they desired was one of a merely outward sort: they would be glad to be free from the tyranny of Rome, but had no desire to be released from the bondage of sin. Their Hosannas had in view the kingdom of David which they hoped was coming, and hence their cries soon died away. The Lord made straight for the heart of things by entering the temple. As regards Israel's dealings with their God, this was the centre of all; and here their state religiously was most manifest. Everything came under His survey, for He "looked round about upon all things."

# MARK

The incident as to the fig tree transpired the following morning. The fig tree is symbolic of Israel, and more particularly of the remnant of the nation which had been restored to the land of their fathers, and amongst who Christ had come. Luke 13: 6-9 shows this. The whole nation had been the Lord's vineyard, and the restored remnant were like a fig tree planted in that vineyard. The King having entered, according to the prophetic word, the supreme moment of testing had come. There was nothing but leaves. Even though it was not the time of figs, there should have been plenty of immature figs, the promise of future fruitfulness. The fig tree was worthless, and should bring forth no fruit for ever.

Following this, verses 15—19, we have the Lord's action in cleansing the temple. God's thought in establishing His house at Jerusalem was that it might be a place of prayer for all nations. If any man, no matter what race he belonged to, was feeling after God, he might come to that house and get into touch with Him. The Jews had turned it into a den of thieves. This was the appalling spectacle that met His holy eye when He inspected the house the evening before.

The Jews would doubtless have furnished good reasons for permitting these abominations. Did not the strangers need to change their varied monies? Were not the doves a necessity for the very poorest who could afford no larger sacrifice? But the whole thing had been debased into a money-making concern. The man who came from afar seeking God might easily be repelled when he got to the house by the rascality of those who were connected with it. A terrible state of affairs! The custodians of the house were a pack of thieves, and the Lord told them so. This roused the scribes and priests to fury, and they determined upon His death.

Exactly similar evils have long ago been manifested in Christendom. This is a terrible thing to say, but truth demands that it should be said. Again religion has been turned into a money-making concern, so much so that the would-be seeker after God has often been utterly repelled. This thing may be seen in its most extravagant forms in the great Romish system, but it may be seen elsewhere in a modified way. It is the error of Balaam, and many run after it "greedily," as Jude 11 tells us. Let us see that we carefully avoid it. The house of God on earth today is formed of saints—not dead stones but "living" ones—but we have to learn how we are to behave ourselves in it, and Paul's first letter to Timothy give us the needed instructions. In that letter such words as these are prominent: "Not covetous," "Not greedy of filthy lucre," "Destitute of the truth, supposing that gain is godliness . . . But godliness with contentment is great gain." If such words as these govern us, we shall be preserved from this snare.

Coming into the city the following morning the fig tree, to which the Lord had spoken, was seen to be dried up from the roots. The blight that had fallen upon it worked in a way that was contrary to nature, which would have been from the top downwards. This fact proclaimed it to be an act of God, and Peter was struck by it, and called attention to it, thus inviting the Lord to remark upon the occurrence. His comment appears to be twofold, since the word, "For," which begins verse 23 seems to be of doubtful authority.

The first thing is, "Have faith in God." Their tendency was to have faith in things visible, in the Mosaic system, in the temple, in themselves as a people, or in their priests and leaders. We have exactly the same tendency, and may easily pin our faith to systems, or to movements, or to gifted leaders. So we need to learn just the same lesson, which is that all such things fail, but that God remains. He is faithful, and He remains as the Object of faith when a curse falls upon our cherished little fig tree. Literally the word is, "Have the faith of God," it is as though the Lord says to us, "Hold on to the faithfulness of God no matter what may wither up and disappear."

But this led to the further word as to prayer, in which emphasis is again laid upon faith. "Whosoever shall say . . . and shall not doubt in his heart, but shall believe . . . he shall have whatsoever he saith." The *whosoever* and the *whatsoever* make this a very sweeping statement; so sweeping as almost to take our breath away. But this is connected with the prayer contemplated in the next verse, where we have, "*What things soever* ye desire . . . believe . . . and ye shall have them." In both these verses everything evidently hinges on the believing.

Now belief is faith, and faith is not just a human product, a kind of make-believe or imagination. Verse 24, for instance is not that if only I can work myself up to imagine I receive my request, I do receive it. My prayers according to verse 24, and my words, according to verse 23, must be the product of genuine faith; and faith is the spiritual faculty in me which receives the divine Word. Faith is the eye of the soul, which receives and appreciates Divine light. If my prayer is based on intelligent faith, I shall believe that I receive, and I shall actually receive the desired thing. And so also with what I may say, as in verse 23.

Cases which illustrate the 23rd verse might be cited from present-day missionary service. Not a few times in heathen lands have the servants of the Lord been confronted with sad cases of demon possession challenging the power of the Gospel. With full faith in the Gospel's power they have both prayed and spoken. What they said came to pass, and the demon had to depart.

Verses 25 and 26 introduce a further qualifying factor. Faith puts us into right relations with God, but our relations with our fellows must also be right, if we are to pray and speak effectually. As those who are the subjects of mercy, who have been so greatly forgiven, we must be filled with the spirit of mercy and forgiveness ourselves. If not, we shall come under the government of God.

# MARK

Being again in Jerusalem and walking in the temple, the chief priests and other temple authorities came up challenging the authority by which He had acted in cleansing the building the day before. The Lord answered them by asking them to pronounce upon a preliminary question as to the validity or otherwise of John's baptism and ministry. They demanded the credentials of the great Master, but what about the credentials of the humble forerunner? It would be time enough to undertake the consideration of the greater problem when they had settled the lesser problem. Let them decide as to John.

They were betrayed by the way they handled this matter. They had no thought of deciding it on its merits; the only thing that weighed with them was expediency, and as to that they were impaled upon the horns of a dilemma. A decision either way would land them in a difficulty. They were sharp enough to see this, and hence they decided to plead ignorance. But this plea was fatal to their demand that the Lord should submit His credentials to their scrutiny. They proclaimed their incompetence in the easier matter, and so could not press their demand in the more difficult.

"From heaven or of men?" this was the question as to John. It is also the question as to the Lord Himself. In our day we may go further and say it is the question as to the Bible. John was but a man, yet his ministry was *from* heaven. The Lord Jesus was truly here by means of the Virgin, yet He was *from* heaven, and so also His matchless ministry. The Bible is a Book given us *by* men, yet it is not *of* men, for those who wrote were "moved by the Holy Ghost" (2 Peter 1: 21).

Once we have in our souls a divinely given conviction that both the Living Word and the written Word are from heaven, their authority is well established in our hearts.

## Chapter 12

As we closed chapter 11 we heard the leaders of the Jews plead ignorance. Whether John's baptism was from heaven or of men they could not tell, and much less could they understand the work and service of the Lord. We open this chapter to see it plainly demonstrated that He perfectly knew and understood them. He knew their motives, their thoughts and the end to which they were heading. He revealed His knowledge of them in a striking parable.

The first verse speaks of "parables," and Matthew's Gospel shows us that at this point He uttered three. Mark only records the middle one of the three—the one that foretold what these Jewish leaders were going to do, and what the results would be for them. In this parable the "husbandmen" represented the responsible leaders of Israel, and a summary is furnished of the way in which through the centuries they had refused all God's demands.

# MARK

In speaking of a vineyard the Lord Jesus was continuing a figure which had been used in the Old Testament—Psalm 80; Isaiah 5; and elsewhere. In the Psalm the vine is clearly identified with Israel, and out of it is to come a "Branch" who is, "the Son of Man whom Thou madest strong for Thyself." In Isaiah it is very manifest that God was not getting out of His vineyard what He was entitled to expect. Now we find the story carried a good deal forward. The owner of the vineyard had done his part in providing all that was needful and the responsibility as to the fruit lay with the husbandmen to whom the vineyard was entrusted. They failed in their responsibility, and then proceeded to deny the rights of the owner and maltreat his representatives. Last of all they were tested by the advent of the owner's son. So the leaders of Israel had maltreated the prophets, and slain some of them. And now the Son had appeared, who is the Branch of whom the Psalm speaks. This was the supreme test.

The position of the Jew as under the law is portrayed in this parable. Consequently the question was whether they could produce that which God demanded. They had not done so. Not only was there an absence of fruit, but there was the presence of positive hatred for God and those who represented Him; and this hatred reached its climax when the Son appeared. The responsible leaders were moved by envy, and they wished to monopolize the inheritance for themselves, and so they were prepared to slay Him. A day or two before they had determined upon His death, as verse 18 of the last chapter told us. Now the Lord discovers to them that He knew their evil thoughts.

And He showed them also what would be the terrible consequences for themselves. They would be dispossessed and destroyed. This was historically fulfilled at the destruction of Jerusalem, and will doubtless have a further and final fulfilment in the last days. The One whom they rejected will become the dominant Head of all that God is building for eternity. When that prediction is fulfilled it will indeed be a wonder in the eyes of Israel.

The statement that the lord of the vineyard "will give the vineyard unto others," is an intimation of what comes more fully to light in John 15. Others will become branches in the true Vine, and will bring forth fruit: only they will no longer be under the law in doing so, nor will they be selected from amongst the Jews only. The Lord's words were a warning that their rejection of Him would mean their setting aside by God, and the gathering in of others, till ultimately the One they rejected would dominate everything. They saw that the parable pronounced judgment against them.

Not daring for the moment to lay hands on Him, they commenced a verbal offensive against Him, endeavouring to catch Him in His words. First came the Pharisees jointly with the Herodians. Their question as to the tribute money was skilfully designed to make Him an offender one way or the other—either against the national feelings of the Jew or the Roman.

His answer however reduced them to impotence. He made them admit their servitude to Cæsar by an appeal to their coinage. Their lips, not His, pronounced it to be Cæsar's image. Then He not only gave the answer to their question which was perfectly obvious in the light of their own admission, but also used it as an introduction to the far more weighty matter of God's claims upon them. No wonder they marvelled at Him.

We may notice how, in verse 14, these opponents paid tribute to His perfect truth. In a way far beyond anything they realized—in the most absolute sense—He was the truth and taught the truth, wholly undeflected by man and his little world. Of no other servant of God could this be said. Even Paul was influenced by human considerations, as Acts 21:20-26 shows. Jesus alone is the perfect Servant of God, and He was so poor that He had to ask for a "penny" to be brought to Him.

Next came the Sadducees, asking Him to unravel the matrimonial tangle which they propounded. He did this and convicted them of their folly; but before doing so He revealed its underlying causes. They did not know the Scriptures—that was ignorance. They did not know the power of God —that was unbelief. Their unbelieving error was upheld on these twin pillars. Modern unbelief of the Sadduceean type is supported by just the same two pillars. They continually misquote, misinterpret, or otherwise mangle Scripture, and they conceive of God as though He were anything but Almighty—as just a man, though of larger powers than ourselves.

The Lord proved the resurrection of the dead by quoting the Old Testament. The fact of it lies implicit in Exodus 3:6. God was still the God of Abraham, Isaac and Jacob hundreds of years after their death. Though dead to men, they lived to Him, and that meant they must rise again. There the fact lay in the Scripture, and in denying it the Sadducee only convicted himself of ignorance.

Since the fact was there in Scripture the Lord, true to His Servant character, appealed to the Scripture and did not assert the fact dogmatically on His own authority. What He did state dogmatically is in verse 25, where he makes clear the state or condition into which resurrection will introduce us, thus going beyond what the Old Testament taught. The resurrection world differs from this world. Earthly relationships cease in those heavenly conditions. We are not *to be* angels, but we are to be "*as* the angels which are in heaven." Immortality and incorruptibility will be ours.

The plain fact was therefore that the Sadducees had conjured up a difficulty in their ignorance which had no existence in fact. Their discomfiture was complete.

One of the scribes who was listening perceived this, and he ventured to propound a question that they often debated amongst themselves, concerning the relative importance of the various commandments. The Lord's answer brushed aside all their elaborate arguments and quibbles as to one or other of the ten commandments by going straight to the word contained in Deuteronomy 6: 4, 5. Here was a commandment which brought within its scope all the other commandments. God demanded that He should be absolutely supreme in the affections of His creatures; if only He were so, all other things would fall into their right place. Here is the great master-commandment which governs everything.

In this commandment there lay an element of great encouragement. Why should God care about possessing the undivided love of His creature? Faith would answer this question by saying—Because He Himself is love. Being love, and loving His creature, even though lost in his sins, He cannot be satisfied without the love of His creature. Israel could not "steadfastly look to the end" of the law. Had they been able to do so, that is what they would have seen.

For the second commandment the Lord referred the man to Leviticus 19: 18, another unexpected passage. But this commandment evidently springs out of the first. No one can have ability and inclination to treat his neighbour rightly except he first is right in his relations with his God. But love is the essence of this second commandment no less than of the first. To love one's neighbour as oneself is the limit under the law. Only under grace is it possible to go a step beyond this, as for instance Aquila and Priscilla did, as recorded in Romans 16: 4. However, "Love is the fulfilling of the law" (Rom. 13: 10), and this is said in connection with this second commandment.

The scribe felt the force of this answer, as verses 32 and 33 show. The series of questions began with the confession, "Master, we know that Thou . . . teachest the way of God in truth." This was said by the Pharisees and Herodians in the spirit of hypocrisy. It ended with the scribe saying in all sincerity, "Well, Master, Thou hast said the truth." The man saw that the love which would lead to the fulfilling of these two great commandments is of far more importance than offering all the sacrifices which the law enjoined. The sacrifices had their place but they were only a means to an end. Love is "the end of the commandment," as 1 Timothy 1: 5 tells us. The end is greater than the means. Thus the scribe approved of the answer that had been given to him.

The Lord's rejoinder in verse 34 is very striking. He pronounced the man as "not far from the kingdom of God," and this showed two things. First, that anyone who gets away from what is outward and ceremonial, to realize the importance of what is inward and vital before God, is not far from blessing. Second, that important as such a realization is, it does not of itself suffice for entrance into the kingdom. Something further is needed, even the spirit of a little child, as we saw when considering chapter 10. The scribe was near the kingdom but not yet in it. This reply, we judge, staggered the man, as well as the other listeners, and because of this no one cared to ask further questions. Such a man as this, well versed in the law of God, they took to be in the kingdom as a matter of course. The Lord's words challenged their thoughts. Yet, in seeing that God aims at, and values, that which is moral and spiritual beyond what is ceremonial and fleshly he had travelled a long way towards the kingdom. Romans 14: 17 enforces the same thing as regards ourselves, at least in principle. Have we fully recognized it?

His opponents having finished with their questions the Lord propounds to them His great question, arising out of Psalm 110. The scribes were quite clear that the Messiah was to be the Son of David; yet here is David speaking of Him as his Lord. Amongst men, and in those days, a father never addressed his son in such terms, but the reverse: the son called his father, lord. How could the Christ then be Son of David? Were the scribes wrong in what they asserted? Or could they explain it?

They could not explain it. They were silent. The explanation was exceedingly simple, but face to face with the Christ, and unwilling to admit His claims, they wilfully shut their eyes to it. He was the Son of David, and David called Him Lord by the Holy Ghost, so there was no mistake. The explanation is that it was the Son of God who became the Son of David according to the flesh, as is so plainly stated in Romans 1: 3. When once the Deity of the Christ is fully acknowledged all is plain. These verses throw a good deal of light upon the statement in 1 Corinthians 12: 3, that, "No man can say that Jesus is the Lord, but by the Holy Ghost."

The Lord had now answered all the questions of His adversaries, and asked them a question which they could not answer. Had they been able to answer it, they would have been put into possession of the key to the whole situation. The mass of the people were still glad to listen to Him but the scribes were blind, and in verses 38—40 the Lord warns the people against them. Those who were being blindly led are warned against their blind leaders. The real motives and objects of the scribes are unmasked. The Word of God from His lips pierces between soul and spirit in an unerring way.

Their characteristic sin was self-seeking in the things of God. Whether in the market-place — the business centre, the synagogue — the religious centre, or in feasts—the social circle, they must have the commanding place, and to this end they wore their distinctive dress. Having gained the leading position they used it to feather their own nests financially at the expense of widows, the most defenceless class in the community. The acquisition of power and money was the end and object of their religion. They followed "the way of Balaam the son of Bosor, who loved the wages of unrighteousness" (2 Peter 2: 15); and there are all too many in our day who still tread that evil way, the end of which is "greater damnation," or "severer judgment." The adjective, you notice, is not "longer" as though differences might exist in the *duration* of punishment; though there will be differences as regards its *severity*.

The adversaries had provoked this discussion with their questions, but the last word was with the Lord. The closing words must have fallen from His lips with the force of a sledge-hammer. He calmly took to Himself the office of Judge of all the earth and pronounced their doom. Had He not been the Son of God this had been folly and worse.

But the same Son of God sat over against the treasury and beheld the gifts of the crowd, and lo! He can with equal certainty appraise the value of their gifts. A poor widow approaches—possibly one who had suffered from the swindling of rapacious scribes — and casts in her little all. Two of the smallest coins were left to her, and she threw them both in. According to human thoughts her gift was absurd and contemptible in its smallness; its presence would not be noticed, and its absence would not be felt. In the Divine estimation it was more valuable than all the other gifts put together. God's arithmetic in this matter is not ours.

With God the motive is everything. Here was a woman who instead of blaming God because of the misdemeanors of the scribes, who claimed to represent Him, devoted her all to the service of God. This delighted the heart of our Lord.

He called His disciples to Him, as verse 43 tells us, and pointed the woman out, proclaiming the virtue of her act. This is particularly striking if we notice how chapter 13 opens, for His disciples were anxious to point out to Him the greatness and beauty of the Temple buildings. *They* pointed to *costly stones* wrought by men's busy hands. *He* pointed to the *moral beauty* of a poor widow's act. He told them that their great buildings would all crash into ruin. It is the widow's act that will be remembered in eternity.

And yet the widow gave her two mites to the temple chest that received contributions for the upkeep of the temple fabric! The Lord had already turned His back on the temple and now was pronouncing its doom. She did not know this; but in spite of being a little behind the times in her intelligence, her gift was accepted and valued according to the devoted heart that prompted it. What a comfort this fact is!

God was before her in her gift, and God abides even when temples are destroyed. Things material—upon which we may set our hearts—disappear, but God remains.

## CHAPTER 13

THE LORD'S PREDICTION that the Temple should be utterly destroyed led to His prophetic discourse. The disciples did not question the fulfilment of His words, they only wished to know the time of fulfilment and, true to their Jewish instincts, what the sign of it would be. His answer to their questions is very instructive.

In the first place, He fixed no dates: any answer He gave as to the time was of an indirect sort. In the second place, He went beyond the immediate scope of their questions to the larger issues of the last days and His own advent in glory. This feature is seen in many Old Testament prophecies, which were given in view of some impending event of history, and which definitely applied to that event, and yet were so worded as to apply with yet greater fulness to events that are to transpire in the last days. In the case before us, there was *a* fulfilment in the destruction wrought by the Romans in A.D. 70, which comes out more clearly in Luke's account of this discourse, and yet *the* fulfilment is connected with the coming of the Lord. This feature of prophecy is alluded to in the saying,"No prophecy of the Scripture is of any private interpretation" (2 Peter 1: 20).

In the third place, He brought the full weight of His prophecy to bear upon the consciences and hearts of His hearers. If their question was prompted by a considerable measure of curiosity, He lifted the whole matter to a much higher plane by His opening words, "Take heed lest any man deceive you." The course of things that prophecy reveals runs counter to all that men naturally would expect. The attractiveness of the false prophets lies in the fact that they ever predict things which fall in with men's desires and seem eminently reasonable. We must be on our watch, for false prophets abound today in the pulpits of Christendom.

The first warning, in verse 6, concerns those who come, impersonating the Christ. The central point of the conflict is always here. The devil knows that if he can deceive men as to Him, he can deceive them in everything else. If we are wrong as to the centre we are bound to be wrong to the far circumference. To be rooted in our knowledge of the true Christ renders us proof against the seductions of the false ones.

Next we are warned not to expect easy times as to world conditions. Wars and turmoil amongst the nations, and disturbances in the face of nature are to be expected. These things must not be interpreted as indicating the great climax, for they are but the preliminary throes. Moreover the disciples of the Lord must expect to be confronted with special difficulties. They will be subjected to opposition and persecution, and their nearest relations will turn against them, and hatred from men generally must be their portion. Against this however the Lord sets the fact that these adverse circumstances shall turn to occasions of testimony, and that they would have special support and special wisdom, as to their utterances, from the Holy Ghost.

Some have deduced from verse 10, reading it in conjunction with Matthew 24: 14, that the Lord cannot be coming for His saints until the Gospel has been carried to all the nations of today. But we have to bear in mind that the disciples, whom the Lord was addressing, were at that moment the God-fearing remnant in Israel, and had not yet been baptized into one body, the church: and also that the "Gospel" in this verse is a general term that would cover not only the Message that is being preached today, but also that "Gospel of the kingdom" of which Matthew speaks, and which will be carried forth by the God-fearing remnant, which will be raised up after the church is gone.

Verse 14 does give us the sign for which the disciples asked. Daniel speaks of "the abomination that maketh desolate" (12: 11), and this is alluded to in our verse, for the word "desolation," we are told "is an active word," having the force of "causing desolation."

There is to be the public establishment of an idol in the sanctuary in Jerusalem—such as we have predicted in Revelation 13: 14, 15—an insult to God of a most flagrant kind. That sign will indicate two things: first, that the time of special affliction, of which Daniel 12: 1 speaks, has begun: second, that the end of the age, and the intervention of Christ in His glory, is very near. The remainder of the Lord's discourse is occupied with these two things. Verses 15—23 deal with the former; verses 24—27 deal with the latter.

The language of verse 19 shows that the Lord had the great tribulation in view, and the earlier verses show that its centre and most intense fury is found in Judaea. Verses 15 and 16 would indicate that it will set in with great suddenness. Instant flight will be the only way of escape for those who fear God. Its ferocity will be such that if it were permitted to run a lengthy course it would mean extermination. For the elect's sake it will not be permitted to continue, but will be cut short by the advent of Christ. From Daniel 9: 27 we gather that the tribulation will commence, when the head of the revived Roman empire causes "the sacrifice and the oblation to cease," in the midst of the last seven years. This being so, there will be only three and a half years to run before the Lord Jesus puts an end to it by His glorious appearing.

By the tribulation the devil will seek to crush and *exterminate* the elect. But this is not all, as verses 21 and 22 show. There will be at that time a special number of false Christs and prophets appearing, by whom he hopes to *seduce* the elect. He would accomplish it, "if it were possible." Thank God, it is not possible. The true saints will know that the real Christ is not going to hide Himself in some corner, so that men have to say, "Lo, here is Christ; or, lo, He is there." He will shine forth in His glory at His coming, and every eye shall see Him.

The tribulation will come to its end in final convulsions that will affect even the heavens, as verses 24 and 25 show. Sun, moon and stars are sometimes used in Scripture as symbols of supreme power, derived power and subordinate power respectively; and "powers that are in heaven" are in view, as the latter part of verse 25 shows. Still this discourse of the Lord is

# MARK

not marked by a large use of symbols, as the book of Revelation is, so we think that literal convulsions affecting the heavenly bodies must not be excluded, especially as we know there was a literal darkening of the sun when Jesus died. The darkening of that day will serve to throw into greater relief the brightness of His shining forth, when He comes in the clouds with great power and glory.

The glorious appearing of the Son of Man will be followed by the gathering together of "His elect." These were mentioned in verse 20, and they are those who "endure unto the end" (verse 13), and they shall be saved by the appearing of Christ. These elect are the God-fearing remnant of Israel in the last days; for the Lord was addressing His disciples who at that moment were the God-fearing remnant in the midst of Israel, and they would without a doubt have understood His words in that sense. These elect ones will be found in all parts of the earth, and the instruments used in their gathering together will be angels: gathered together, they will become the redeemed Israel who will enter upon the millennial reign. All this must be differentiated from the coming of the Lord for His saints as predicted in 1 Thessalonians 4, when the Lord Himself will descend from heaven and our gathering together will be unto Him.

The allusion to the fig tree in verse 28 is a parable, and therefore we must expect to find in it a meaning deeper than that which is connected with a simile or an illustration. The fig tree doubtless represents Israel, as we saw in reading chapter 11, and therefore the budding of her branches sets forth the beginning of national revival with that people. The "summer" represents the age of millennial blessedness for the earth. When real national revival sets in for Israel then indeed the appearing of Christ and the millennial age is very near.

The word "generation" in verse 30 is evidently used in a moral sense and not in a literal, meaning people of a certain type and character, just as the Lord used the word in verse 19 of chapter 9, and in Luke 11: 29. The unbelieving generation will not pass until the second advent, nor indeed will the generation of those that seek the Lord. The coming of the Lord will mean the passing away of the evil generation, and at the same time the full establishment of all His words, which are firmer and more durable than all created things.

Verse 32 has presented much difficulty to many minds because of the words, "neither the Son." We may not be able to explain them fully, but we may at least say two things. First, that in this Gospel the Lord is presented as the great Prophet of God, and that this was a matter reserved by the Father and not given to Him as a Prophet to reveal. Second, that if Matthew 20: 23, and John 5: 30, be read and compared with our verse, we shall see that the three passages run on parallel lines, as to giving, knowing and doing, respectively. In Matthew we get the actual words, "Not mine to *give*." We might summarize Mark as "Not Mine to *know*," and John as

# MARK

"Not Mine to *do*." Unbelief has made great use of the word used in Philippians 2: 7, "made Himself of no reputation," or more literally, "emptied Himself," building upon it the theory that He divested Himself of knowledge so as to become a Jew with the notions of His time; and thus they are enabled—so they think—to impute error to Him on many points. He did empty Himself, for Scripture says He did so. The three passages we have mentioned give us a proper idea of what was involved in it, and lead us to bless His Name for His gracious stoop. The theory of unbelief would rob Him of His glory, and us of any regard for His words—words which, He has just told us, will never pass away.

The five verses which close this chapter contain a very solemn appeal, which should come home to all of us. In verse 33 we get for the fourth time the words, "Take . . . heed." The Lord opened His discourse with these words, and He closed with them, and twice between (verses 9 and 23) He uttered them. The prophetic revelations He gave are all made to bear upon our consciences and lives: He forewarns us that we may be forearmed. Knowing the infallibility of His words, but not knowing when the time is, we are to "watch," that is, be keenly awake and observant, and also to pray, for we are no match for the powers of darkness, and so we must maintain dependence upon God. We are left to do our appointed work in a spirit of expectancy, anticipating the coming of the Son of Man.

The threefold repetition of the word, "Watch," in these five verses is very striking. We must lay great emphasis on it in our minds, and the more so in that our lot is cast in the late days of this dispensation when His coming cannot be far distant. It is very easy to succumb to the lure of the world, when our minds become drowsy and unalert. A great and important word is this word—WATCH. And the last verse of our chapter shows that it certainly is intended to apply to us.

## Chapter 14

As we open this chapter, we come back to historical details, and reach the closing moments of our Lord's life. Verses 1—11 provide us with a very striking introduction to the last scenes. In verses 1 and 2, crafty *hatred* rises to its climax. In verses 10 and 11, the supreme exhibition of heartless *treachery* is briefly recorded. The verses between tell a story of devoted *love* on the part of an insignificant woman—its beauty enhanced by the story standing between the record of such hatred and such treachery.

The hatred of the chief priests and scribes was equalled by their craft, yet they were but tools in the hands of Satan. They said, "Not on the feast," yet it was on the feast: and again, "Lest there be an uproar of the people," yet there was an uproar of the people, only it was in their favour and against the Christ of God. They little knew the power of the devil to whom they had sold themselves.

# MARK

The woman of Bethany — Mary, as we know from John 12—may not herself have fully understood the import and value of her act. She was moved probably by spiritual instinct, realizing the murderous hatred that was surrounding the One she loved. She brought her very precious ointment and expended it upon Him. Her action was misunderstood by "some" —Matthew tells us that these were disciples, and John adds that Judas the traitor was the originator of the censure—who were thinking about money and the poor, particularly about the former. The Lord vindicated her, and that was enough. He accepted her act and valued it according to His understanding of its significance and not according to her intelligence, even though she was, as we suppose, the most intelligent of the disciples. We may see in this a sweet forecast of the gracious way in which He will review the acts of His saints at the Judgment Seat.

His verdict was, "She hath done what she could," which was very high praise. Moreover He ordained that her act should be her memorial wherever the Gospel is preached. Her name is known and her act remembered by millions today—nineteen centuries after—with all honour, just as also Judas is known in dishonour, and his name has become a synonym for baseness and treachery.

These opening verses show us then that as the moment of crisis approached everybody came out in their true light. The hatred and the treachery of the opponents became blacker: the love of the true was kindled, though none expressed it as did Mary of Bethany. In verse 12, however, we pass to the preparation for the Last Supper, during the course of which the Lord gave far more impressive witness to the strength of His love for His own. There was some testimony to their love for Him, but it was nothing in the presence of His love for them.

The Lord Jesus had no home of His own, but He knew well how to put His hand on all that was needed for the service of God. The owner of the guest-chamber was doubtless someone who knew and reverenced Him. The disciples knew the sufficiency of their Master. They attempted nothing on their own initiative, but simply looked to Him for direction, and acted on it. Hence the One who had not where to lay His head had no lack of suitable accommodation for the last meeting with His own.

For many centuries the Passover had been celebrated, and those who ate it knew that it commemorated Israel's deliverance from Egypt; few, if any, realized that it looked forward to the death of the Messiah. Now for the last time it was to be eaten before it was fulfilled. What filled the minds of the disciples we know not, but evidently the mind of the Lord was centred on His death, and to it He turned their thoughts in announcing that His betrayer was amongst them, and that a woe rested upon him. Then He instituted His own Supper.

Brevity characterizes Mark's record all through, but nowhere is it more pronounced than in his account of the institution of this. The essentials however are all here: the bread and its meaning, the cup and its significance and application, which causes it to be designated by Paul, "the cup of blessing which we bless." For the Lord Himself the fruit of the vine, and what it symbolized, earthly joy, was all past: no more would He touch it until in the kingdom of God He would taste it in a new way altogether. All earthly hopes and joys on the old basis were closed for Him.

The lesson that we have to learn is in keeping with this fact. God may in His gracious providences permit us to enjoy on earth many things that are happy and pleasant, yet all our proper joys as Christians are not of an earthly order but of a heavenly.

From the upper chamber, where He had instituted His supper, the Lord led forth His disciples to Gethsemane. A hymn or psalm was sung—Psalms 115-118 being the usual portion, it is said. It was for the disciples just the customary thing, no doubt; but what must it have been for the Lord? To sing, as He went forth to fulfil the Passover type by becoming the sacrifice; and Psalm 118, towards the end, speaks of binding "the sacrifice with cords, even unto the horns of the altar." He went forth to suffering and death, bound by the cords of His love; and the disciples to failure, defeat and scattering.

He warned them of what was before them, referring them to the prophecy of Zechariah, which foretold the smiting of Jehovah's Shepherd and the scattering of the sheep. But the prophet proceeded to say, "and I will turn mine hand upon the little ones," and this answers to verse 28 of our chapter. Those who were His sheep nationally were scattered, but the "little ones," elsewhere called by Zechariah "the poor of the flock," were regathered on a new basis, when once the Shepherd was risen from the dead. Hence He was to meet them not in Jerusalem but in Galilee.

Peter, filled with self-confidence, asserted that he would not stumble though all the others might do so, and this in the face of the most explicit declaration by the Lord, foretelling his fall. The others did not wish to be outdone by Peter and so committed themselves to a similar assertion. What accounted for it was the unholy rivalry that existed amongst them, as to who should be the greatest. Mark makes this manifest with especial clearness, as may be seen if we compare, 9: 33, 34; 10: 35-37, and 41. Peter no doubt felt that now had come the opportunity in which he might demonstrate once and for all that he was head and shoulders above the rest. And the rest were not willing for him thus to forge ahead; they had to keep up with him. Peter's fall seemed to come very suddenly, but all this shows us that the secret roots of it went back a long way into the past.

Peter's bold words were soon to be tested, and first of all in Gethsemane which was reached immediately after. He and his two companions were only asked to watch for an hour. This they could not do; though only to Peter, who had been so particularly boastful, did the Lord address His gentle words of remonstrance, using his old name of Simon. This was appropriate, for he was not true at that moment to his new name, but rather displaying the characteristics of the old nature that was still in him. Their Master was "sore amazed" and "very heavy," and "exceeding sorrowful unto death," and yet they slept, not once merely but thrice.

Against the dark background of their failure, however, the perfection of their Master only shone the more brightly. The reality of His Manhood comes before us very strikingly in verses 33 and 34, and the perfection of it too. Being God, He knew in infinite fulness all that would be involved in dying as the Sin-bearer. Being perfect Man, He possessed every proper human sensibility untarnished—our sensibilities have been blunted by sin, but in Him was no sin. Hence He felt everything in infinite measure, and fervently desired that the hour might pass from Him. And yet again, having taken the Servant's place, He was perfect in His devotion to the will of the Father, and so though desiring that the cup might be taken from Him, He added, "Nevertheless not what I will, but what Thou wilt."

We may summarize it all by saying, that being *perfect God* He had infinite capacity for knowing and feeling all that the approaching hour of death meant for Him. As *perfect Man* He entered fully into the sorrow of that hour, and could do no other than pray for that cup to be taken from Him. As *perfect Servant* He presented Himself to the sacrifice in wholehearted subjection to His Father's will.

Three times did our Lord thus commune with His Father, and then He returned to face the betrayer with his band of sinful men. We may remember that three times was He tempted of Satan in the wilderness at the outset, and it seems certain, though not mentioned here, that the power of Satan was also present in Gethsemane, for when going forth from the upper chamber He had said, "The prince of this world cometh, and hath nothing in Me" (John 14: 30). This also helps to account for the extraordinary somnolence of the disciples. The power of darkness was too great for them, as it ever is for us, except we are actively supported by Divine power. Let us take note that not only does the power of Satan sometimes rouse believers to wrongful actions, it sometimes *just sends them to sleep*.

In saying to Peter, "The spirit truly is ready," the Lord evidently acknowledged that there was in His disciples that which He could appreciate and recognize. Yet "the flesh is weak," and Satan just then was terribly active, so that nothing but watchfulness and prayer would have met the situation. Let us take the word home to ourselves. As the end of the age approaches Satan's activities are to become more rather than less, and we need to be awake with every spiritual faculty alert, and also to be filled with the spirit of prayerful dependence upon God.

Verses 42—52, occupy us with His arrest by the rabble sent by the chief priests under the leadership of Judas. They were, of course, not Roman soldiers but servants of the temple and of the ruling classes amongst the Jews. What a story it is! The multitude with their violence, expressed in their swords and staves: Judas with the basest treachery, betraying the Lord with a kiss: Peter springing to sudden and carnal activity: all the disciples forsaking Him and fleeing: an unnamed young man attempting to follow, but ending only in flight with shame added to his panic—violence, treachery, false and mistaken activity, fear and shame. Again we say, What a story! And such are we when brought face to face with the power of darkness, and out of communion with God.

As to Peter, this was step number three on his downward road. First came his entanglement in the ruinous competition for the first place amongst the disciples, which worked out into self-confidence and self-assertion. Second, his lack of watchfulness and prayer, which led to his sleeping when he should have been awake. Third, his carnal anger and violence, followed by abject flight. The fourth step, which brought things to a climax we have at the end of the chapter.

As to the Lord Jesus, all was calmness in perfect submission to the will of God, as expressed in the prophetic Scriptures. His light shone as ever without the smallest flicker.

"Faithful amidst unfaithfulness,
'Mid darkness only light."

Verses 53-65, summarize for us the proceedings before the Jewish religious authorities. All were assembled to sit in judgment upon Him, and so the thing as far as they were concerned was not done in a corner. This shows strikingly what depth of feeling had been aroused. A crowded council, and it was at the dead of night! The fire burned in the courtyard, and we are permitted to see Peter creeping in amongst the foes of his Lord for the sake of a little warmth.

There was no thought of an impartial trial. His judges were unblushingly seeking such witness as would enable them to pronounce on Him the sentence of death. However the power of God was at work behind the scenes, and every attempt to fasten on Him the trumped-up charges came to nothing. Many efforts were made; a sample of them is given us in verse 58, and we recognize a distortion of His utterance which is recorded in John 2: 19. Accusation after accusation broke down by the perjurors falling into confusion and contradicting one another. It seems as though God enveloped their ordinarily acute minds in a fog of confusion.

Driven to desperation, the high priest stood up to examine Him, but to his first question Jesus answered nothing—evidently for the sufficient reason that there was as yet nothing to answer. When challenged as to whether He was the Christ, the Son of God, He at once answered, saying, "I am." Both question and answer lacked nothing in definiteness. There stood the Christ, the Son of God, by His own plain confession; and not only this but He asserted that as Son of Man He would have all power in

# MARK

His hand, and that He would come again in glory from heaven. On this confession He was condemned to death.

The prophet Micah had predicted that "the Judge of Israel" should be made subject to human judgment. This came to pass: yet it is most striking that when the great Judge *was* brought into human judgment every attempt to convict Him upon *human* evidence failed: *all human witnesses fell into confusion*. They condemned Him on the ground of the witness He bore to Himself; and even in doing this they broke the law themselves. It was written: "He that is the high priest among his brethren . . . shall not . . . rend his clothes" (Lev. 21: 10). This the high priest ignored, so agitated was he in the presence of his Victim, so transported with anger and hatred.

The storm of hatred burst upon the Lord as soon as they had discovered a pretext upon which to condemn Him; but in their buffetings and spittings they were but unconsciously fulfilling the Scriptures. The mock trial before the Sanhedrin ended in scenes of disorder, just as confusion had been stamped upon their earlier proceedings—confusion made the more conspicuous by His serene presence in their midst. The only word He uttered as far as Mark's account is concerned, is recorded in verse 62.

Verses 66-72, give us in a parenthesis the climax of Peter's failure: the earlier steps which led to it we have already noticed. He was now warming himself in company with those who served the adversaries of his Lord, and three times he denied Him. Satan was behind the testing, as Luke 22: 31 shows us, and this accounts for the skilful way in which the remarks of the different servants drove him into a corner. The first asserted that he had been "with" Jesus. The second that he was "one of them," evidently meaning one of His disciples. The third reaffirmed this, and claimed that he had proof of it in his dialect, and this one apparently was kinsman to Malchus, whose ear Peter had cut off, as John records.

As Peter saw the net of evidence with its fine meshes closing in around him, his denials became more violent: first, a pretence that he did not understand; second, a flat denial; third, an avowal that he did not even know the Lord, accompanied with curses and swearing. They were unwilling to accept his protestations of "unfaith," but they must have been convinced by the sad "works" he produced, that Jesus was to him quite unknown. We have to contemplate the warning with which Peter furnishes us, and see to it that we have *faith* which expresses itself in the appropriate *works*.

But if Satan was at work in regard to Peter so also was the Lord, according to Luke 22: 32. He had prayed for him, and His action brought back to Peter's fevered mind the very words of warning that He had uttered. The remembrance of them smote his conscience and moved him to tears; and in that work in his heart and conscience lay the beginnings of his recovery. When any saint is permitted so to fail, that his sin becomes

# MARK

public and a scandal, we may be sure that it has roots of a secret sort which go back into the past. We may be sure also that the journey back to full recovery is not taken all in a moment.

## Chapter 15

THE FIRST VERSE of this chapter picks up the thread from verse 65 of chapter 14. The Romans had taken away the power of capital punishment from the Jews and vested it wholly in Caesar's representative; hence the religious leaders knew they must present Him before Pilate and demand the death sentence upon some ground which appeared adequate to him. Verse 3 tells us that they "accused Him of many things," but we are not told by Mark what those things were. We are struck however by the way in which one phrase occurs over and over again in the earlier part of the chapter—"The King of the Jews" (verses 2, 9, 12, 18, 26). Luke tells us definitely that they said He was "forbidding to give tribute to Caesar, saying that He Himself is Christ a King." Mark's brief account infers this, though not stating it.

Once more, before Pilate, the Lord confessed who He was. Challenged as to being the King of the Jews He simply answered, "Thou sayest it," the equivalent of "Yes." For the rest He again answered nothing, for the reason that in all the wild charges of the chief priests there was nothing to answer. It is worthy of note that Mark only records two utterances of our Lord before His judges. Before the Jewish hierarchy He confessed Himself to be the Christ, Son of God and Son of Man: before the Roman governor He confessed Himself to be the King of the Jews. No evidence prevailed against Him; He was condemned because of who He was, and He could not deny Himself.

Moreover Pilate had sufficient knowledge to discern what lay at the root of all the accusations, "he knew that the chief priests had delivered Him for envy." This led to his ineffectual attempt to divert the thoughts of the multitude to Jesus, when it was a question of the prisoner to be released. The influence of the priests with the people was too much for him however, and hence, desirous of pleasing the crowd, Pilate outraged what sense of justice he had. He released Barabbas, the rebel and murderer, and, scourging Jesus, delivered Him to be crucified.

The voice of the people prevailed over the better judgment of the representative of Caesar: in other words, autocracy on that occasion abdicated in favour of democracy, and the popular vote determined it. An old Latin proverb states that the voice of the people is the voice of God. The facts of the crucifixion flatly deny that proverb. Here the voice of the people was the voice of the devil.

Verses 16-32 give us in a very graphic way the terrible circumstances surrounding the crucifixion. All classes combined against the Lord. Pilate

# MARK

already had scourged Him. The Roman soldiers mocked Him in ways that were cruel as well as contemptuous. The ordinary people—just passers-by —railed at Him. The priests mocked Him with sarcasm. The two crucified thieves—representatives of the criminal classes, the very scum of humanity — reviled Him. High-born and low-born, Jew and Gentile, were all involved. Yet in result they were all helping to fulfil the Scriptures, though doubtless unconsciously to themselves.

This is particularly striking if we take the case of the Roman soldiers— men who were unaware of the existence of the Scriptures. Verse 28 takes note that the crucifixion of the thieves on either side was a fulfilment of Isaiah 53: 12, but many other things they did also fulfilled the Word. For instance, His visage was to be "marred more than any man," according to Isaiah 52: 14, and there was fulfilment of this in the crown of thorns and the smitings. The Judge of Israel was to be smitten "with a rod upon the cheek," according to Micah 5: 1; this the soldiers did, as verse 19 of our chapter shows. Verse 24 records the fulfilment by them of Psalm 22: 18. "They gave Me also gall . . . and . . . vinegar," says Psalm 69: 21, and this also the soldiers did, though the fulfilment is not recorded here but in Matthew. We think we are right in saying that at least 24 prophecies were fulfilled in the 24 hour day when Jesus died.

All men in that hour were displaying themselves in their darkest hue, and in these verses we do not read of one thing that He said. It was just as the prophet had said, "As a sheep before her shearers is dumb, so He openeth not His mouth." It was man's hour, and the power of darkness was at its zenith. The perfection of the holy Servant of the Lord is seen in His suffering in silence all that He endured from the hands of men.

That which the Lord Jesus suffered at the hands of men was very great, yet it falls into comparative insignificance when we turn to consider what He endured at the hands of God as the Victim, when made sin for us. Yet all this far greater matter is compressed by Mark into two verses—33 and 34; whereas his account of the lesser matter covers 52 verses (14: 53-15: 32). The fact is, of course, that the lesser could be described, whilst the greater could not be. The darkness which descended at midday hid from men's eyes even the externals of that scene.

All that can be related historically is that for three hours God put the hush of night upon the land and thus blinded men's eyes, and that at the end of the hours Jesus uttered the cry of anguish, which had been written as prophecy a thousand years before, in Psalm 22: 1. The holy Sin-bearer was forsaken, for God must judge sin and irrevocably banish it from His presence. That utter and eternal banishment *we deserved*, and it will fall upon all who die in their sins. *He endured it to the full*, but since He possessed the holiness, the eternity, the infinitude of full Deity, He could emerge from it at the close of the three hours. Yet the cry, that came from

# MARK

His lips as He did so, showed that He felt the full horror of it. And He had a capacity to feel that was *infinite*.

That which He suffered at the hands of men is not to be thought of lightly. Hebrews 12: 2, says, "Who . . . endured the cross, despising the shame," but we must note the difference between *shame* and *suffering*. Many a man of great physical courage would feel the shame more than suffering. He felt the suffering but He despised the shame, inasmuch as He was infinitely above it, and He knew that He was, "glorious in the eyes of the Lord" (Isaiah 49: 5). We believe that we may say that never was He more glorious in the eyes of the Lord than when He was suffering under the judgment of God as the Sin-bearer. Such was the paradox of Divine holiness and love!

The effect of that cry upon the onlookers is given to us in verses 35 and 36. They would hardly have seen a reference to Elijah in His words if they had not been Jews: but then, how dense and ignorant not to have recognized the cry to God which lay enshrined in their own Scriptures.

The fact of His actual death is given by Mark in the briefest possible fashion. He breathed out His spirit into the hands of God directly after He had cried with a loud voice. What He said is recorded in Luke and John. Here we are simply told the way He said it. There was no gradual failing of strength so that His last words were in a feeble whisper. At one moment a loud voice and the next moment He was dead! His death was so manifestly supernatural as to greatly impress the centurion who was on duty and watching. Whatever may have been, in his own mind, the exact significance of his words, he must have at least felt that he was a witness of the supernatural. We endorse his words and say, "Truly this Man was the Son of God," in the fullest sense.

The truth of these words was also borne witness to by the rending of the veil of the temple. This great happening appears to have synchronized with His death. It was the Divine hand that rent it, for any human hand would have had to rend it from the bottom to the top. The elaborate typical system instituted in Israel, in connection with sacrifices and temple, all looked forward to the death of Christ; and, that death accomplished, the Divine hand tore the veil as a sign that the day of the type was over, and the way into the holiest was made manifest.

In every emergency God has in reserve some servant who will come forward and carry out His will. Stones *would* cry out, or be raised up to become men, if God needed them in an emergency; but they *never do*, because God is *never* in an emergency like that. He always has a man in reserve, and Joseph was the man on this occasion. This timid and secret disciple was suddenly filled with courage, and boldly faced Pilate. He was the man born into the world to fulfil in its season the prophetic word of Isaiah 53: 9, — "with the rich in His death." Having fulfilled it, he drops completely out of the record.

# MARK

He missed the opportunity of being identified with Christ in His life, but he did identify himself with Him when He was dead. This is remarkable, for it exactly reversed the procedure of the disciples. They identified themselves with Him during His life, and failed miserably when He died. The apparent defeat of Jesus had the effect of emboldening Joseph. It stirred the smouldering embers of his faith into a sudden blaze. He "waited for the kingdom of God," and we may be sure that in the day of the kingdom the faith and the works of Joseph will not be forgotten by God. His kind of faith is just the sort we need today—the sort that blazes up when defeat seems sure.

Joseph's action had the effect incidentally of bringing before Pilate the supernatural character of Christ's death. No man could take His life from Him; He laid it down by Himself, and that at the suitable moment when all was accomplished. The two thieves, as we know, lingered on for hours after, and their death had to be hastened by cruel means. Pilate marvelled, but the fact being corroborated, he yielded to the request. Thus the will of God was done, and from that moment the sacred body was out of the hands of the unbelievers. Hands of love and faith performed the offices and laid Him in the tomb. Devoted women too had stood as witnesses when even the disciples had disappeared, and they saw where He had been laid.

## Chapter 16

Love and faith were clearly there, but as yet their faith was dull and unintelligent as to His resurrection. Even the devoted women were full of thoughts as to the embalming of His body, as the opening verses of this chapter show. But this dullness of theirs only enhances the clearness of the proofs that ultimately overwhelmed them with the conviction of His resurrection. At the rising of the sun on the first day of the week they were at the sepulchre only to find that the great stone blocking its entrance had been rolled away. They entered to find no sacred body, but an angel, in appearance like unto a young man.

Matthew and Mark speak of an angel: Luke and John speak of two. This presents no difficulty of course, since angels appear and disappear at will. The angel who appeared as "a young man . . . clothed in a long white garment" to the affrighted women had appeared a little before to the keepers as one with a countenance "like lightning, and his raiment white as snow," so that a kind of paralysis fell upon them. He was one thing to the world and quite another to disciples. He knew how to discriminate, and that these women were seeking Jesus, though they thought Him to be still in death. Ignorant they were, yet they loved Him; and that made all the difference.

# MARK

The angelic testimony however did not accomplish much for the moment. It impressed the women right enough, but mainly in the way of fear and trembling and amazement. It did not produce that calm assurance of faith which opens the mouth in testimony to others. They could not yet take up the words, "I believed, therefore have I spoken" (Psalm 116: 10; 2 Corinthians 4: 13). Presently they would share in this "spirit of faith," which was possessed by both Paul and the Psalmist, but that would be when they came into touch with the risen Christ for themselves.

Scripture clearly indicates that angels have a ministry to perform *on behalf of* saints—as witness, Hebrews 1: 14. Their ministry *to* saints is infrequent, and usually alarming to those who receive it, as was the case here. However their message was very definite. "He is not here," was the negative part of it, and that the women could verify for themselves. The positive word was, "He is risen." That they could not verify, for the moment, and hence it does not seem to have very deeply impressed them.

There follows, in verses 9-14, a brief summary of the three striking appearances of the risen Lord, accounts of which in more detail are given to us in the other Gospels.

First comes that to Mary Magdalene, which is given us so fully in John's Gospel. She was the first to actually see the Lord in resurrection: Mark puts this fact beyond doubt. This is significant as showing that the Lord thought in the first place of the one whose heart was perhaps more devastated by the loss of Him than any other. In other words, love had the first claim on His attention. In result, she did indeed believe, and therefore she was able to speak in the way of testimony to others. But, even so, her words had no appreciable effect. The others did indeed love the Lord, for they mourned and wept, and the very depth of their grief rendered them proof against any testimony which fell short of an actual sight of Himself.

Second, comes His appearance to the two going into the country, which is given to us in Luke with such detail. These had not denied Him like Peter, but they had so lost heart that they were drifting aimlessly away from Jerusalem, as if wishful now to turn their backs on a place filled for them with broken hopes and a most tragic loss and disappointment. Their sight of the risen Christ reversed their footsteps and brought them back to their brethren with the glad tidings. Even that however did not overcome their unbelieving dejection. It is just as well for us that it was so. Resurrection carries us outside the present order of things, and His resurrection is a fact of such immense import, that it must indeed be established by multiplied evidence of an unimpeachable sort.

Third, His appearance to the eleven. This may possibly *not* be one of the occasions that are given us in more detail in Luke and John, for it says, "as they sat at meat," or, more literally, "lay at table." Take the account in Luke for instance—He would hardly have asked, "Have ye here any meat?" if they had been reclining at a meal. The presence of food would

# MARK

have been too obvious. It may therefore have been an occasion not noticed in the other Gospels. On this occasion He brought home to them their unbelief as a matter of reproach, and yet notwithstanding He gave them a commission.

It is remarkable how the commissions, that are recorded in the four Gospels, differ the one from the other. That which is stated in Acts 1: 3, would prepare us for this. Many times during the forty days He appeared to them, speaking of things pertaining to the kingdom of God. During this time He evidently presented to them their commission from different points of view, and Mark gives us one of them. We may well wonder that, having had to upbraid them for their unbelief, He should send them forth to preach the Gospel so that others should believe. Yet, after all, the one who through hardness of heart has been stubborn in unbelief is, when thoroughly won himself, a valuable witness to others.

The scope of this Gospel commission is the largest possible. It is "all the world," and not merely the little land of Israel. Moreover it is to be preached to "every creature," and not to the Jew only. It is, in other words, for *everybody everywhere*. The blessing that the Gospel conveys is spiritual in nature, for it brings salvation, when faith is present and baptism is submitted to. We must not transpose the words, *baptized* and *saved*, and make it, "He that believeth and is saved shall be baptized."

In no scripture is baptism connected with justification or reconciliation, but there are other scriptures which connect baptism with salvation. This is because salvation is a word of large content, and includes within its scope the practical deliverance of the believer from the whole world system, whether Jewish or Gentile in character, wherein once he was embedded. His links with that world system are to be cut, and baptism sets forth the cutting of those links—in one word, *dissociation*. He who believes the Gospel, and accepts the cutting of his links with the world that held him, is a saved man. A man may say he believes, and even do so in reality, yet if he will not submit to the cutting of the old links, he cannot be spoken of as saved. The Lord knows them that are His of course, but that is another matter.

When it is a question of "damnation," (or "condemnation"), baptism is not mentioned. This is very significant. It shows the ground on which condemnation rests. Even if a man *is* baptized, if he does *not* believe, he will be condemned. The outward ordinance is plainly prescribed by the Lord, but it can only be administered as faith is professed; and profession, as we know only too well, is not synonymous with possession. Salvation is not effective apart from faith. Peter may tell us that, "Baptism doth also now save us" (1 Peter 3: 21), but note that it is "*us*," and the "us" are believers.

A good deal of controversy has raged around verses 17 and 18. The miraculous things mentioned are connected by some with the preachers of the Gospel, and it is asserted that they ought to be in full manifestation today. Two or three things may be helpfully noted.

In the first place, the things are to follow not them that *preach*, but them that *believe*.

In the second place, the Lord asserts that these signs *will follow*, apart from any previous conditions on the part of the preacher. There is no stipulation that he must experience a special "baptism of the Spirit," such as is often urged. If men believe, these signs shall follow; so says the Lord. All that could be deduced from their absence would be that no one has really believed.

In the third place, certain words do not appear in the statement, which some seem mentally to read into it. *It does not say*, that these signs will follow *all* that believe, in *all* places, and for *all* time. If it did we should be shut up to the conclusion that hardly anybody today has believed the Gospel: we have not even believed it ourselves!

These words of our Lord have of course been fulfilled. We can point to four things out of the five occurring, as recorded in the Book of Acts. The fifth thing, the drinking without harm of some deadly thing, we have no record of, yet we have not a shadow of doubt that it happened. He said it would, and we believe Him. His word is enough for us. He gives the signs according to His own pleasure, and as He sees they are needed.

The two verses that close our Gospel are exceedingly beautiful. We remember that it has set before us our Lord as the great Prophet, who has brought us the full Word of God, the perfect Servant, who has fully accomplished His will. All has been related with striking brevity, as becomes such a presentation of Himself. And now at the close, with the same brevity, the end of the wonderful story is set before us. The Lord having communicated to His disciples all that He desired, "He was received up into heaven, and sat on the right hand of God."

On *earth* He had been *cast out*, but He is *received up into heaven*. His works on earth had been *refused*, but now He takes His seat in a place which indicates administration and power *of an irresistible sort*. But it is put that He was "received up," and thus what is emphasized is, that both His reception and His session are due to *an act of God*. The perfect Servant may have been refused here, but by the act of God He takes the place of power, where nothing shall stay His hand carrying out the pleasure of the Lord.

The last verse indicates the direction in which His hand is moving during the present time. He is not as yet dealing with the rebel earth in righteous government: that He will do when the hour strikes for it, according to the purpose of God. Today His interests are centred in the going forth of the Gospel, as He had just indicated. His disciples did go forth, preaching without boundaries or limitations, but the power that gave efficacy to their words and labours was *His*, and not theirs. From His lofty seat on high He wrought with them, and gave the signs which He promised, as recorded in verses 17 and 18. He gave these signs to confirm the word, and that confirmation was specially needed at the outset of its proclamation.

Though the signs of verses 17 and 18 are but rarely seen today, signs do still follow the preaching, signs in the moral and spiritual realm—characters and lives that are wholly transformed. The perfect Servant at the right hand of God, *is working still*.

# LUKE

## Chapter 1

IN THE OPENING verses Luke avows the object before him in writing his Gospel; he wished to bring certainty to the mind of a certain Gentile convert. God had given him a perfect understanding of all things from the outset, so now he wrote them "in order," or "with method;" and we shall see as we proceed that he sometimes ignores historical order to present things in a method that is moral and spiritual. The understanding of that moral and spiritual order, together with having the facts clearly in writing, would bring certainty to Theophilus, as also it will to us. We see here how *certainty* is linked with *the Holy Writings*—the Word of God. If we had not the Holy Writings, we should have certainty of nothing.

The first and second chapters present us with facts concerning the birth of Christ, and with very interesting pictures of the godly remnant in Israel, out of whom, according to the flesh, He appeared. The first picture, verses 5-25, concerns the priest Zacharias and his wife. They were "righteous before God," from which we may deduce that they were a couple marked by faith, and consequently they were marked by obedience to the instructions of the law. Yet, when told by an angel that his elderly and barren wife should bear a son, he asked for a sign of some kind to be given in support of the bare Word of God. In this he proved himself to be an "unbelieving believer," though very true to type, for "the Jews require a sign" (1 Cor. 1: 22); and he suffered governmentally, inasmuch as the sign granted was the loss of his power of speech. The sign was quite appropriate however. The Psalmist said, "I believed, therefore have I spoken." Zacharias did not believe, and therefore he could not speak.

The angel's prediction concerning the son of Zacharias was that he should be great in the sight of the Lord, and be filled with the Holy Ghost, so that in the spirit and power of Elijah he might "make ready a people prepared for the Lord." In verses 6, 9, 11, 15, 16 and 17, "Lord" is the equivalent of the Old Testament "Jehovah," so the advent of the Messiah is to be the advent of Jehovah. There were to be people on earth who were prepared to receive Christ when He came. The Gospel starts then with a godly priest fulfilling the ritual of the law in the temple, and granted a promise that had to do with a people waiting for the Messiah to appear on earth. We ask special attention to this, for we think we shall see that this Gospel gives us the transition *from law to grace, and from earth to heaven*, so that it ends with tidings of grace for all nations, and with Christ ascending into the heavens to take up high-priestly service there. In chapter 1 the earthly priest was dumb. In the closing verses of the Gospel the men who are to be priests in the new dispensation of the Holy Spirit, were in the temple and anything but dumb—they were praising and blessing God.

In verses 26-38, we have the angel's announcement to Mary concerning the conception and birth of her Son. She was the chosen vessel for this great event. A few details of much importance must be briefly noted. In the first place, verse 31 makes it abundantly plain that He was truly a Man; "made of a woman," as Galatians 4: 4 says.

In the second place, verses 32 and 33 make it plain that He was far more than a mere Man. He was "great," in a way that no other man ever was, being Son of the Highest; and He is destined to be the looked-for King over the house of Jacob, and take up a kingdom that abides for ever. We observe that there is as yet no hint of anything outside those hopes as to the Messiah which could be based upon Old Testament prophecies. The Son of the Highest was coming to reign, and that reign might be immediate as far as this message was concerned.

A difficulty occurred to Mary's mind which she expressed in verse 34. The coming Child was to have David as His ancestor and yet be the Son of the Highest! She did not ask for a *sign*, since she accepted the angel's words, but she did ask for an *explanation*. How could this thing be? Mary's question and the angel's answer in verses 35-37, make quite plain in the third place the reality of the virgin birth and the wholly super-natural character of the Manhood of Jesus.

There was to be an action of the Holy Ghost, producing "that Holy Thing," and then the over-shadowing of the Power of the Highest—a process we believe—protecting "that Holy Thing," while as yet unborn. In result there was to be a suitable vessel of flesh and blood for the incarnation of the Son of God. He is Son of David truly, as is indicated at the end of verse 32, but Romans 1: 3 shows that it was *the Son of God* who *became* Son of David according to the flesh. In verse 35 of our chapter the article "the" is really absent—"called Son of God"—that is, it indicates character rather than the definite Person. When *the* Son of God became the Son of David through Mary, there was such a putting forth of the power of God as ensured that the "Holy Thing" born of Mary should be "Son of God" in character, and therefore the fit vessel for His incarnation. It was a miracle of the first order; but then, as the angel said, "with God nothing shall be impossible."

The faith of Mary, and her submission to the pleasure of God concerning her, comes out beautifully in verse 38. Verses 39-45 show the piety and prophetic spirit that characterized Elisabeth, for seeing Mary she at once recognized in her the mother "of my Lord." She was filled with the Holy Ghost, and recognized Jesus as her Lord even before He was born, an instructive illustration, this, of 1 Corinthians 12: 3.

This is followed by Mary's prophetic utterance in verses 46-55. It was called forth by her sense of the extraordinary mercy that had been shown to her in her humble circumstances. Though descended from David she was but the espoused wife of the humble carpenter of Nazareth. In the mercy shown to her she saw the pledge of the final exaltation of those who fear

# LUKE

God and the scattering of the proud and mighty of this world. She saw moreover that the coming of her Child was to be the fulfilment of the promise that had been made to Abraham—God's unconditional promise. She had no thought of Israel having deserved anything under the covenant of law. All depended upon the covenant of promise. The hungry were being filled and the rich dismissed empty. This is ever God's way.

We must not omit to notice that Mary spoke of "God my Saviour." Though the mother of our Saviour, she herself found her Saviour in God.

In due time the son was born to Zacharias and Elisabeth and at the time of his circumcision his father's mouth was opened. He wrote, "His name *is* John," showing that he now fully accepted the angel's word, and hence the name of his son was a settled question. At last he believed, though it was faith that follows sight, of the true Jewish type; consequently his mouth was opened. He praised God, and filled with the Holy Ghost he prophesied.

A striking thing about this prophecy is that, though it was provoked by the birth of his own son John, that child was only before his mind in a minor and secondary way. The great theme of his utterance was the yet unborn Christ of God. He held things in their right proportion. This was the fruit of his being filled with the Spirit, who always magnifies Christ. Had he spoken merely in the enthusiasm engendered by the birth of the unexpected son, he would have talked mainly or altogether about him and the exalted prophetic office to which he was called.

He spoke of the coming of Christ as though it had already materialized, and he celebrated the effects of His coming as though they had already been accomplished. This is a common feature of prophecy: it speaks of things as accomplished which historically are still in the future. For the moment the prophet is carried in his spirit outside all time considerations. In the imminent appearance of Christ, Zacharias saw the Lord God of Israel visiting His people in order to redeem them. The salvation that He would bring would deliver them from all their enemies and enable them to serve Him in freedom, and in holiness and righteousness all the days of their life. And all this would be in fulfilment of His promise and oath to Abraham. Notice how the Holy Spirit inspired him to refer to the unconditional promise to Abraham, just as Mary had done. Israel's blessing will be on that basis and not on the basis of the covenant of law.

In all this we observe as yet no clear distinction between the first and second comings of Christ. Verses 68-75, contemplate things which will only be brought to pass in any full sense at His second coming. True, redemption was wrought by Christ at His first coming, but it was redemption by blood, and not by power; and it is true of course that the holiness and righteousness in which a restored and delivered Israel will serve their God through the bright millennial day will be based upon the work of the cross. Still in these verses the two comings are regarded as one whole.

# LUKE

Verses 76 and 77 refer directly to John, who had just been born. He was to go before the face of Jehovah preparing His ways. He was to give knowledge of salvation to His people by the remission of their sins. This he did as verse 3 of chapter 3 records, in connection with his baptism. Notice that here "His people" acquires a rather new sense—not Israel nationally, but those who were the believing remnant in the midst of that people. All is on the ground of mercy even with John and his Elijah-like ministry. It is, "the remission of their sins on account of the bowels of mercy of our God" (New Trans.).

In verses 78 and 79 Zacharias returns to the coming of Christ, and all of course is on the ground of that same mercy, for the word "whereby," connects what follows with the mercy just mentioned. The "Dayspring from on high" is a peculiarly lovely description of Christ. Alternative words for "Dayspring" would be "Daydawn" or "Sunrising." His advent was indeed the dawning of a new day. Every earthly sunrising has been, to human eyes, from beneath upwards. This one was "from on high" that is, from above downwards. The Spirit of God moved Zacharias to announce by inspiration the dawning of a day that would be new, though the full wonder of it was as yet hidden from his eyes.

He saw however that it meant the bringing in of both light and peace for men; and here he does begin to speak of things that were blessedly accomplished in the first coming of Christ. When He came forth in His public ministry the light began to shine, and the way of peace was well and truly laid in His death and resurrection, and the feet of His disciples led into it immediately after. The prophecy of Zacharias closes on this strikingly beautiful note. In the first glimpse we have of him he is a troubled and fearful man. His last word recorded in Scripture is "peace." He had seen by faith the coming of the Saviour, like the dawning of a new day of blessing, and that made all the difference.

Verse 80 summarizes the whole of John's life up to the opening of his ministry. God dealt with him in secret in the deserts, educating him in view of his solemn preaching of repentance in the days to come.

## Chapter 2

THE OPENING VERSE of this chapter shows how God may use the great ones of the earth, all unconsciously to themselves, for the accomplishing of His designs. The case here is the more remarkable inasmuch as the decree of Augustus was not carried out immediately but delayed until Cyrenius was governor of Syria. Prophecy however had indicated Bethlehem as the birthplace of the Messiah, and the decree of the Emperor came just at the right time to send Joseph and Mary to Bethlehem, though subsequently the proceedings were stayed for a time. It was owing to this disturbed state of affairs, no doubt, that the inn was full, and the fact that the infant Christ was born in a stable was a testimony to the poverty of Joseph and Mary, for then as now inconveniences can always be obviated by money. It was symbolic however of the outside place as regards the world and its glory which Christ was to have from the outset.

Verses 8-20, are occupied with the episode in connection with the shepherds. This has become so well known in connection with hymns and carols that we are in danger perhaps of missing its full significance. Shepherds as a class, were not held in much esteem in those days, and these were the men who took night duty, unskilled in comparison with the men who cared for the sheep by day. To these exceedingly humble and unknown men the angels appeared. Heaven's secret concerning the arrival of the Saviour was disclosed to such nobodies as these!

The thing becomes even more remarkable when we compare this chapter with Matthew 2. There the scene is cast amongst the great ones in Jerusalem—Herod the king, his courtiers, chief priests and scribes—and they are completely ignorant of this marvellous event for months afterwards, and then they only hear of it through the wise men of the east arriving, men who were complete outsiders as regards the nation of Israel. The explanation is given to us in the words of the Psalmist, "The secret of the Lord is with them that fear Him" (25: 14). God respects no man's person, but He has respect to humility and integrity of heart before Himself; so He passed by the grandees in Jerusalem, and sent a deputation of angelic beings to wait on a small group of despised night watchmen that they might be initiated into the secret of Heaven's ways. These shepherds were a few of the godly remnant waiting for the Messiah, as their subsequent words and actions show us.

First came the message of the angel, and then the praise of the angels. The great joy of the message centred in the fact that it was as Saviour that He had come. They had had the Lawgiver and the prophets, but now had arrived the Saviour, and He was so great an One as Christ the Lord. This good news was for "all *the* people," — not "all people" as our A.V. has it. For the moment a wider circle than all Israel is not in view. The sign of this marvellous event was one that never could have been anticipated. Men might have expected to see a mighty warrior wrapped in garments of glory and seated on a throne. The sign was a Babe, wrapped in swaddling clothes, lying in a manger. But then the sign indicated the whole manner and spirit of His approach to men at this time.

The praise of the angels is compressed into fourteen words, recorded in verse 14—though few in number, words of deep meaning. They put on record the ultimate results that were to flow from the advent of the Babe. God is to be glorified in the highest seats of His power, the very place where the slightest slur cast upon His name would be most keenly perceived and felt. On earth, where since the fall warfare and strife had been incessant, peace is to be established. God is to find His good pleasure in men. "Good pleasure in men," is the rendering of the New Translation. From the moment that sin came in there was no pleasure for God in Adam or in his race: but now had appeared One who is of another order of humanity than Adam, owing to the Virgin birth, which has been so plainly stated in the first chapter. In Him the good pleasure of God rests in supreme measure, as also it will rest in men who are in Him as the fruit of His work. Wonderful results indeed!

To all this the shepherds gave the response of faith. They did not say, "Let us go . . . and see *if* this thing is come to pass," but "see this thing which *is* come to pass." They came with haste and saw the Babe with their own eyes; then they bore testimony to others. They could then say, "God has *said* it, and we have *seen* it." — the Divine testimony backed by personal experience. Such testimony is bound to have effect. Many wondered, and Mary herself kept these things, pondering them in her heart; for evidently she did not herself yet understand the full significance of it all. As for the shepherds, they caught the spirit of the angels, glorifying and praising God. So there was praise *on earth* as well as praise in *heaven* on this great occasion; and we venture to think that the praise of these humble men below had in it a note that was absent from the praise of the angels of His might above.

We are permitted to see in verses 21-24, that all things that the law enjoined were carried out in the case of the holy Child, and when presented to the Lord in the temple two aged saints, walking in the fear of the Lord, were there to greet Him as guided by the Spirit of God. We have just noted how the great men of Jerusalem were totally out of touch with God and knew nothing about Him: there were those in touch with God and they soon new, even though no angel appeared to them. The Holy Ghost was upon Simeon, and by the Spirit he not only *knew* that he should see Jehovah's Christ before he died but also he *came* into the temple at the exact moment that the child Jesus was there. So too with old Anna. Her visit was timed perfectly, so that she saw Him.

Reading verses 28-35, we can feel how affecting the scene must have been. The old man addressed God and then addressed Mary. He was ready to depart in peace having seen Jehovah's salvation in the holy Child. He actually went one step further than the angel, for he recognized that God's salvation had been prepared before the face of "all peoples" — the word is in the plural this time. Not only was Jesus to be the glory of Israel but also a light to lighten the Gentiles. It was revealed to him that grace was going to flow beyond the narrow borders of Israel.

It was revealed to him also that the Christ had come to be spoken against. Dimly perhaps he saw it, but there it was—the shadow of the cross when the sword should pierce through Mary's soul. This we learn from his words to her.

# LUKE

We may wonder perhaps that Simeon, having been permitted to live until he actually held the Saviour in his arms, should have been so ready to "depart in peace." We might have anticipated that he would have felt it a tantalizing thing to see the beginning of God's intervention in this way, and yet have to depart before the climax was reached. But evidently it was given to him as a prophet to foresee the rejection of Christ, and therefore he did not expect the immediate arrival of the glory, and was prepared to go.

He announced that the Child would put Israel to the test. Many who were high and lifted up would fall, and many who were low and despised would rise up; and as He would be spoken against and rejected, the thoughts of many hearts would come to light, as they came into contact with Him. In the presence of God all men are forced to come out in their true character, so this feature about Christ was an involuntary tribute to His deity. Moreover Mary herself should be pierced with sorrow as with a sword: a word that was fulfilled when she stood by the cross.

The very aged Anna completes this beautiful picture of the godly remnant in Israel. She served God continually, and when she had seen the Christ, she "spake of Him."

We may recapitulate at this point by summing up the features that marked these pious folk. The shepherds illustrate *the faith* that characterized them. They accepted at once the word that reached them through the angel, then their own eyes verified it, then they glorified and praised God.

Mary exemplified *the thoughtful and meditative spirit*, that waits upon God for understanding—verse 19.

Simeon was the man who was *waiting* for the Christ under the instruction and power of the Spirit of God. He was *satisfied* with Christ when he found Him, and *prophesied* concerning Him.

Anna was one who *served* God continually, and *witnessed* of the Christ, when she had found Him.

Lastly, there was great care exercised that every detail concerning the Christ should be carried out as the law of the Lord had ordained. Five times over it is stated that the law was observed—verses 22, 23, 24, 27, 39. This excellent feature, we presume must be credited to Joseph, the husband of Mary—this *careful obedience to the Word of God*.

We are now waiting for His second advent. How good it would be if in our cases these excellent features were strongly marked.

Verse 40 covers the first twelve years of our Lord's life. It conveys to us the fact that the ordinary development of mind and body, which is proper to mankind, marked Him; a testimony to His true Manhood.

This is reinforced too by the further glimpse we are given of Him at the age of twelve years. He was not teaching the learned men, but He was

## LUKE

hearing them and asking them questions in such a way as to astonish them as they questioned Him. Here again we see Him fulfilling perfectly that which is proper to a child of such an age, while displaying features that were supernatural. His reply to His mother also showed that He was conscious of His mission. Yet for many years to come He took the subject place in regard to Joseph and Mary, and thus displayed all human perfection proper to His years.

### CHAPTER 3

THE COMMENCEMENT OF John's ministry is very fully dated in the opening two verses. They show that things were entirely out of course, government was vested in the Gentiles, and even in Israel things were in confusion, for there were two high priests instead of one. Hence repentance was the dominant note in his preaching. Earlier prophets had reasoned with Israel and recalled them to the broken law. John no longer does this, but demands repentance. They were to acknowledge that they were hopelessly lost on the ground of the law, and take their place as dead men in the waters of his baptism. It was "the baptism of repentance for the remission of sins." If they listened to John and repented, they were morally prepared to receive the remission of sins through the One who was about to come. Thus the path before the Lord would be made straight.

Note how this quotation from Isaiah speaks of Jehovah coming, and how this coming of Jehovah is obviously fulfilled in Jesus. Verse 5 states the same truth as we had in verses 52 and 53 of chapter 1, and verse 34 of chapter 2, only putting it into language of a more figurative sort. Verse 6 shows that since He who was about to come was One no less than Jehovah, the salvation He would bring was not to be confined within the narrow boundaries of Israel, but go forth to "all flesh." Grace was about to come, and it would overflow in all directions. This grace is one of the special themes of the Gospel of Luke.

But John not only preached repentance in a general way, he also made it a very pointed and personal matter. Crowds flocked to him, and his baptism threatened to become a popular service, almost a fashionable recreation. Things work in just the same way today: any religious ordinance, such as baptism, very easily degenerates into a kind of popular festival. Evidently John was not in the least afraid of offending his audience and spoiling his own popularity. Nothing could be more vigorous than his words recorded in verses 7-9. He told the people what they were very plainly; he warned them of wrath ahead; he called for the genuine repentance which would bring forth fruits; he showed that no place of religious privilege would avail them, for God was about to judge the very roots of things. The axe was now about to cut, not in the way of lopping off branches but of smiting at the root so as to bring down the whole tree.

# LUKE

A very graphic figure, this; and fulfilled not in the execution of outward judgment, such as will mark the Second Advent, but in that moral judgment which was reached at the cross. The Second Advent will be characterized by the fire which will consume the dead tree: the First Advent led to the cross, where the judicial sentence of condemnation was promulgated against Adam and his race; or in other words, the tree was cut down.

John demanded deeds, not words, as the practical fruits of repentance, and this led to the people's question, recorded in verse 10. The publicans and the soldiers followed with similar questions. By his answers in each case John put his finger upon the particular sins that marked the different classes. Yet, though the answers varied, we can see that covetousness provoked all the wrongs that he dealt with. Of all the evil weeds that flourish in the human heart covetousness is about the most deep-seated and difficult to deal with: like the dandelion its roots penetrate to a great depth. True repentance leads to true conversion from the old way of sin, and John knew this.

Thus John prepared the way of the Lord, and not only so he also faithfully pointed to Him, and did not for one moment permit the people to think great things of himself. He proclaimed himself to be but the humblest servant of the great Person who was coming—so humble as to be unworthy to perform the very menial service of unlacing His sandal. The Coming One was so great that He would baptize men with the Holy Ghost and with fire: the former for blessing, and the latter for judgment, as the next verse makes abundantly plain. Here again we may notice that the two Advents are not as yet quite plainly distinguished. There was a baptism of the Spirit, recorded in Acts 2, as the result of the First Advent, but the baptism with fire, according to verse 17, awaits the Second Advent.

Luke records John's faithful ministry and then briefly dismisses him from the record in order to make way for Jesus. The imprisonment of John did not take place just at this juncture, but Luke deviates from the historical order to set the thing before us in a moral and spiritual way. The Elijah-like ministry of John disappears before the One who was to be the vessel of the grace of God; and who was baptized, and thus introduced to His ministry. We are not even told here that it was John who baptized Him, but we are told that He was praying when baptized, a thing not mentioned elsewhere. This Gospel evidently emphasizes the perfection of our Lord's humanity. Grace for man is vested in One who is the perfect Man, and the very first feature of perfection in man is that of dependence upon God. Prayer is an expression of that dependence, and we shall notice in this Gospel how many times it is put on record that Jesus prayed. This is the first instance.

On this praying and dependent Man the Holy Ghost descended in bodily shape like a dove, while the Father's voice declared Him to be the beloved Son, the Object of all the Divine delight. Thus at last the truth of

# LUKE

the Trinity became manifest. The Spirit became for a moment visible; the Father became audible; the Son was here in flesh and blood, and consequently not only visible and audible but tangible also. It is very wonderful that the heaven should be opened, and all its attention focused upon a praying Man on earth. But in that praying Man God was to be known, for it was pleasing that "in Him should all fulness dwell" (Col. 1: 19).

The Father's voice having thus owned Him as the beloved Son, Luke now introduces His genealogy through Mary to show how really He is also Man. Matthew traces His descent down from Abraham, the depository of promise, and David, the depository of royalty. Luke traces Him up to Adam and to God, for it is simply His Manhood that is the point, and that was through Mary, for Joseph was only supposed to be His father. He is truly a Man though the Son of God. He is the Second Man, the Lord from heaven, the One overflowing with the grace of God.

## CHAPTER 4

OUR CHAPTER OPENS with Him returning from His baptism, full of the Holy Ghost. But before beginning His service He must for forty days be tempted of the devil. To this testing the Spirit led Him, and here we see the glorious contrast between the Second Man and the first.

When the first man was created God pronounced all to be very good, but Satan came promptly on the scene, tempted man and ruined him. The Second Man has appeared, and the Father's voice has pronounced His excellence, so again Satan comes on the scene with promptness, but this time he meets Man, full of the Holy Ghost, who is impervious to his wiles. When the first man fell, he knew no pangs of hunger, for he dwelt in the fertile garden planted by his Creator's hand. The Second Man victoriously stood, though the garden had been turned into a wilderness and He was an hungered.

Luke evidently gives us the temptations in the moral order and not the historical. Matthew gives us the historical order, and shows us that the end of the temptation was when the Lord bade Satan get behind Him, as recorded in verse 8 of our chapter. The order here agrees with John's analysis of the world in chapter 2 of his first Epistle. The first temptation was evidently designed to appeal to the lust of the flesh, the second to the lust of the eyes, and the third to the pride of life. But no such lust or pride had any place in our Lord, and the three testings only served to reveal His perfection in its details.

The Lord Jesus had become truly a Man, and in answer to the first temptation He took man's proper place of complete *dependence* upon God. Just as man's natural life hangs upon his assimilation of bread, so his spiritual life hangs upon his assimilation of, and obedience to, the Word of God. In answer to the second temptation was seen His whole-hearted

# LUKE

*devotedness* to God. Power and glory and dominion in themselves were as nothing to Him; He was wholly set for the worship and service of God. He met the third temptation, in which He was urged to put God's faithfulness to the test, by His unswerving *confidence* in God. The great adversary found no point of attack in Him. He trusted God without testing Him.

The three features thus brought so prominently into display — dependence, devotedness, confidence — are those which mark the perfect Man. They are very distinctly seen in Psalm 16, which by the Spirit of prophecy sets forth Christ in His perfections as a Man.

Having been tested by Satan, and triumphed over him in the power of the Holy Ghost, the Lord Jesus returned to Galilee to begin His public ministry in the power of the same Spirit, and His first recorded utterance is in the synagogue at Nazareth, where he had been brought up. He read the opening words of Isaiah 61, stopping at the point where the prophecy passes from the first Advent to the second. "The day of vengeance of our God" has not yet come, but by stopping at the point He did, where in our Version only a comma appears, He was able to begin His sermon by saying, "This day is this scripture fulfilled in your ears." It presented Him as the One anointed by the Spirit of God, in whom was to be made known to men the fulness of the grace of God.

This presentation of Himself appears to be characteristic of Luke's Gospel. Though He was God in the fulness of His Person, yet He comes before us as the dependent Man full of the Holy Ghost, speaking and acting in the power of the Spirit, and flowing over with grace for men. What struck the hearers at Nazareth was, "the gracious words which proceeded out of His mouth." The law of Moses had often been rehearsed within the walls of the synagogue, but never before had grace been thus proclaimed there. But it was not enough to proclaim grace in the abstract: He proceeded to illustrate grace in order that the people might realize what it involved. He cited two instances from their own Scriptures where the kindness of God had been shown, and in both cases the recipients of the grace were sinners of the Gentiles. The Sidonian widow was in a hopeless plight—"without strength." The Syrian soldier was amongst the "enemies" of God and His people. Hence the two cases quite aptly illustrate Romans 5: 6-10, for the woman was saved and sustained, and the man was cleansed and reconciled.

This beautiful presentation of grace in its practical working did not suit the people of Nazareth. Gracious words were all very nice in the abstract, but the moment they realized that grace presupposes nothing but demerit in those who receive it, they rose up in proud rebellion and great fury, and would have slain Jesus had He not passed from their midst. The good things that grace brings were acceptable enough, but they did not want them on the ground of grace, since it assumed they were no better than Gentile sinners. The modern mind would probably approve of grace being offered in the slum, while regarding it as an affront if preached in the synagogue. The Jewish mind would not even hear of it being exercised in the slum!

Thus in a very definite way there was a rejection of grace the very first time it was proclaimed, and this not in Jerusalem among scribes and Pharisees but in the humbler parts of Galilee in the very place where He had been brought up. Their familiarity with Him acted as a veil upon their hearts.

In the light of all this the closing section of the chapter is very beautiful. When men offer a kindness in the spirit of grace and it is spurned with contumely and violence they are offended, and turn away with disgust. It was not so with Jesus. If it had been so, where should we have been? He withdrew Himself from Nazareth but passed to Capernaum and there He preached. His teaching astonished them, doubtless because of the new note of grace that characterized it, and then also because of the Divine authority with which it was clothed.

In the synagogue He came into conflict with the powers of darkness. The synagogue was a dead affair, hence men possessed by demons could be present undetected. But instantly the Lord appeared the demon revealed himself, and also showed that he knew who He was, even if the people themselves were in ignorance. Jesus was indeed the Holy One of God, but instead of accepting the demon's testimony He rebuked him and cast him out of his victim. Thus He proved the power of His word.

In verse 36 we have both authority and power, the latter word meaning dynamic force. In verse 32 the word is really authority. So we have the *grace* of His word in verse 22, followed by the *authority* of His word, and the *power* of His word. No wonder that folk were saying, "What a word is this!" And we, who have in this day received the Gospel of the grace of God, have equal cause for such an ejaculation. What wonders of spiritual regeneration are being wrought by the Gospel today!

From the synagogue He passed to the home of Simon in which disease was holding sway. It vanished at His word. And then at eventide came that marvellous display of the power of God in the fulness of grace. All kinds of diseases and miseries were brought into his presence, and there was deliverance for all. "He laid His hands on every one of them, and healed them." Thus He exemplified the grace of God, for it is exactly the character of grace to go out to all irrespective of merit or demerit. On God's side it is offered freely and for all. Verse 40 inspired the hymn,

"At even when the sun was set,"

and surely we all rejoice to sing that,

"Thy touch has still its ancient power,
No word from Thee can fruitless fall."

But beautiful as that hymn is, the reality spoken of in verse 40 is far more lovely. Such is the grace of our God.

# LUKE

And the grace that was displayed on that memorable evening was not exhausted by the display. He went forth elsewhere to preach the kingdom of God—a kingdom to be established not on the basis of the works of the law but on the basis which would be laid by grace as the fruit of His own work.

## Chapter 5

IN THE PREVIOUS chapter we saw the Lord Jesus coming forth in the power of the Spirit to announce the grace of God, and being confronted at once with man's rejection. We saw that nevertheless He pursued His way of grace unmoved by it. This chapter now presents us with a series of lovely pictures, illustrating what grace accomplishes in the case of those who receive it. Four men come before us — Peter, the leper, the paralytic, Levi —and a different feature marks each. They follow one another in an order which is moral, if not strictly chronological.

Both Matthew and Mark tell us how the Lord called the four fishermen to be His followers, but only Luke informs us as to the miraculous draught of fishes, which made so profound an impression upon Peter. The Lord had used his boat and would not be his debtor, but grace it was that poured so abundant a recompense back upon him. It was made the more striking by the fact that they had just been spending a laborious and wholly fruitless night. Now there was not merely abundance but super-abundance. Where futile labour had abounded, there rich results did much more abound. The only breakdown was in connection with their ability to conserve what grace gave.

Peter's boat went out twice into the lake, once by night, when fish might be expected, once by day when they would not be. The place was the same on both occasions, so were the men, and so was their equipment. What made the difference? One thing, and one thing only. *Christ had stepped into the boat.* Peter had his eyes opened to see this fact, and it evidently made the Saviour shine before him in a light that was Divine. Finding himself in the presence of God, even though it was God present in the fulness of grace, wrought in Peter's heart conviction of his own sinfulness.

Now this is the first thing that grace brings with it—conviction of sin. It produces it in deeper measure than ever did the law, and it attracts while producing it. Herein lies the wonderful contrast. The law of Moses, when given at Sinai, wrought conviction of unfitness on the part of the people, but it repelled them and sent them afar off from the burning mountain. Grace in the person of Jesus so convicted Peter that he confessed himself to be full of sin, and yet casting himself at Jesus' knees, he got as near to the Saviour as ever he could.

The next incident, fittingly enough, is about a man, not exactly full of sin, but full of leprosy, which is a type of sin. So full of leprosy was he that

# LUKE

he felt himself to be too repulsive an object to count with confidence upon the kindness of Jesus. He was confident of His power but rather dubious as to His grace. So he approached with the words, "If Thou wilt . . ." revealing himself to be wholly filled with leprosy and partly filled with doubt. The grace of the Lord instantly rose to its full height. All power was in His word, yet He put forth His hand and touched him, as if to wipe out of his mind for ever the last lingering doubt and set him perfectly at ease.

Now here we see that grace brings cleansing, a cleansing which the law did not bring though it made provision for the recognition by the priests of any cleansing which should be at any time effected by the power of God. Here was the power of God at work in the fulness of grace, and it was a lovely sight indeed! We do not wonder that great crowds came together to hear and be healed, as verse 15 records.

Do not miss verse 16. Jesus has taken the place of Man in dependence upon God, acting by the power of the Spirit. Grace has been freely flowing from Him, and He takes time for communion in prayer, withdrawn from the haunts of men, before further coming into contact with human need.

Next comes the case of the man smitten by paralysis and reduced to a state of utter helplessness. Nothing is said as to his faith, though striking and energetic faith was displayed by the men who brought him, and the Lord abundantly answered it. The Pharisees and doctors of the law, who were present, fill in a kind of dark background to the picture. They had plenty of needs and the power of the Lord was present to heal them, since grace brings its ample supplies freely and for all. They were present however to give and not to receive. What they gave was criticism, and it proved to be wrong! They flung out their criticisms and missed the blessing.

The man got the blessing—power was conferred upon him. This was just what he needed. The man full of sin not only needs cleansing from his sin but also power over his sin, and he needs that power in connection with forgiveness. Evidently in the case of this man his paralysis was the result of his sin, and the Lord dealt with the *root* of the trouble before addressing Himself to the *fruit*. This is the way that grace ever takes, for there is never anything superficial about its methods. The criticising Pharisees could no more deliver the man's body from the grip of paralysis than they could deliver his soul from the guilt of his sins. Jesus could do both: and He proved His power to accomplish the wonder of forgiveness, which was outside human observation, by performing the wonder of healing right before their eyes.

The Pharisees were quite right in believing that *no one save God can forgive*. But when they heard Him give absolution they denounced Him as a *blasphemer*. We deduce from it that *He is God*. We each have to face this crisp and clear-cut alternative, and happy for us it is if we have made the right decision. The healing the man received was given in God-like fashion.

# LUKE

He rose up a strong man, able to shoulder his couch at once and march off to his house. He did so glorifying God, and the beholders were moved in the same way. Grace, when displayed, does lead to the glory of God.

In the fourth place Levi comes upon the scene, and he illustrates the fact that grace supplies an Object for the heart. When Jesus called him he was occupied in the pleasant task of receiving money. His mind and heart was instantly diverted from his money and he began to follow the Lord, with the result that we next see him reversing the process, and dispersing by giving to the poor according to Psalm 112:9. Levi invited a great company of publicans and others to his feast, showing how at once his thoughts had been brought into concert with his newly found Lord, and that he had caught the spirit of grace. Yet Christ was the real Object of the feast, for it says "Levi *made Him* a great feast in his own house." The Pharisees were entirely out of sympathy with this spirit of grace, but their objections only served to bring forth the great saying, "I came not to call the righteous, but sinners to repentance."

All that we have been saying might be summarized in this:— Grace *produces conviction of sin,* and then *works cleansing from sin.* Then it *confers power,* and also *conforms the recipient to the likeness of the One in whom it is expressed.* Christ becoming Levi's Object, we can see how he began to catch the spirit of his Master.

From verse 33, and onwards into chapter 6, another thing begins to emerge pretty clearly; and that is that grace *conducts out of bondage and into liberty.* The Pharisees disliked grace and were very strong as to the fastings and prayers and other ceremonies prescribed by the law. The law generates bondage and grace brings liberty: this is taught very fully in the Epistle to the Galatians. The full truth expounded there could not be made known until the death and resurrection of Christ were accomplished and the Spirit had been given, still here we find the Lord beginning to speak of the things so soon to shine forth clearly. He uses parabolic or illustrative language, but His meaning is clear. Being the true Messiah, He was the "Bridegroom," and His presence with His disciples forbade their being under these restrictions.

Then, further, He was introducing that which was *new.* In Him the grace of God was beginning to shine out, and like a piece of new cloth it could not be treated as a patch to be put on the old garment of the law. The new will impose such a strain upon the old fabric that it will tear, and also there will be no suitability between the new and the old. They will prove to be wholly incongruous.

Again, changing the figure, grace with its expansiveness may be likened to the action of new wine; whereas the forms and ordinances of the law are marked by the rigidity of old bottles. If the attempt is made to confine the one within the other, disaster is certain. New vessels must be found capable of containing the new power.

# LUKE

In this striking way did the Lord indicate that the grace of God, which had arrived in Himself, would create its own new conditions, and that the "carnal ordinances" instituted in Israel under the law were only "imposed on them until the time of reformation" (Heb. 9: 10). But at the same time He indicated that men naturally prefer law to grace—the old wine suits them better than the new. One great reason for this is that by the very fact of giving the law to men it is supposed that they may be capable of keeping it; whereas grace is proffered upon the assured basis that man is a hopelessly lost creature.

## CHAPTER 6

AS WE OPEN this chapter, we see the Pharisees and scribes attempting to confine the actions of the disciples, and then also the gracious power of the Lord, within the limits of the Jewish sabbath, as they were accustomed to enforce it. This illustrates His teaching at the close of chapter 5, and in result the "bottle" of the Jewish sabbath burst, and grace flows forth in spite of them.

The words, "The second sabbath after the first," refer we believe to Leviticus 23: 9-14, and are intended to show us that the "wave-sheaf" had already been offered, and hence there was no objection to the action of the disciples except the Pharisees' own strict enforcement of the sabbath. The Lord's answer to their objection was twofold: first, His position; second, His Person.

His *position* was analagous to that of David when he went into the house of God and took the shewbread. David was God's anointed king and yet rejected, and it was not the mind of God that His anointed with his followers should starve in order to uphold small technicalities of the law. The whole system of Israel was out of course by the refusal of the king, and it was no time for concentrating upon the smaller details of the law. So here, the Pharisees were concerned about trivialities whilst rejecting the Christ.

Verse 5 emphasizes His *Person*. Man, as originally created, was made lord over the earthly creation. The Son of Man is Lord over a far wider sphere. He was not bound by the sabbath, the sabbath was at His disposal. Who then is this Son of Man? That was what the Pharisees did not know, but the Lord indicated His greatness by this claim which He made.

The incident concerning the man with the withered hand follows in verses 6-11. Here again the sabbath question came up, and the Pharisees would have pushed their technical objections to the length of forbidding the exercise of mercy on that day. Here we see, not the assertion of the Lord's position, nor of His Person, but of His *power*. He had power to heal in grace, and that power He exercised whether they liked it or not. He accepted their challenge, and making the man stand forth in the midst, He healed him in the most public way possible. The lords of the Philistines

# LUKE

attempted to tie the hands of Samson with "seven green withs," but they tried in vain. The lords of Israel were trying to make cords from the law of the sabbath, wherewith to tie the gracious hands of Jesus, and they also tried in vain.

Failing to do it, they were filled with madness, and they began to plot His death. In the face of their rising hatred Jesus retired into the solitude of communion with God. In the last chapter we saw Him retiring for prayer when multitudes thronged Him and success seemed to be His. He does just the same when dark clouds of opposition seem to surround Him. In all circumstances prayer was the resource of the perfect Man.

It is significant further that what followed this night of prayer was the selection of the twelve men who were to be sent forth as Apostles. Amongst the twelve was Judas Iscariot, and why he should have been included appears to us mysterious. The Lord chose him however, and thus his selection was right. No mistake was made after that night of prayer.

From verse 17 to the end of the chapter we get a record of the instruction which He gave to His disciples, and especially to these twelve men. We may give a general summary of His utterances by saying that He instructed them as to the character that would be produced in them by the grace of God that He was making known. The discourse much resembles the Sermon on the Mount of Matthew 5-7, but the occasion appears to have been different. No doubt the Lord again and again said very similar things to varying crowds of people.

On this occasion the Lord addressed His disciples personally. In Matthew He described a certain class, and says that *theirs* is the kingdom. Here He says, "*yours* is the kingdom," identifying that class with the disciples. His disciples were the poor, the hungry, the weepers, those hated and reproached. A description such as this shows that already He was treating His own rejection as a certainty, and the succeeding verses (24-26) show that He was dividing the people into two classes. There were those identified with Himself, sharing His sorrows, and those who were of the world and sharing its transient joys. Upon the head of the one class He called down a blessing: upon the head of the other a woe. This of course involved a tremendous paradox. The sad and rejected are the blessed: the glad and the popular are under judgment. But the one follow in the footsteps of the Son of Man and suffer for His sake: the other follow in the way of the false prophets.

Having thus pronounced a blessing upon His disciples, He gives them instructions which, if carried out, would mean that they reflected His own spirit of grace. He does not actually send them for the moment, but He instructs them in view of their going out to represent Him and to serve His interests. The spirit of grace is specially marked in verses 27-38. The love that can go forth and even embrace an enemy is not human but Divine; whereas any sinner can love the one who loves him. The disciple of Jesus is to be a lover, a blesser, a giver; and on the other hand he is not to be one who judges and condemns. This does not mean that a disciple is to have no powers of sound judgment and discrimination, but it does mean that he is not to be characterized by the censorious spirit that is quick to impute wrong motives and thus judge other people.

These instructions were exactly fitted to those who were called to follow Christ during His sojourn upon earth. The spirit of them equally applies to those called to follow Him during His absence in heaven. This is the day of grace, in which the Gospel of grace is being preached, and it is therefore of the utmost importance that we should be marked by the spirit of grace. How often, alas, has our conduct belied the cause with which we are identified. A great deal of gracious preaching can be totally nullified by a little ungracious practising on the part of the preacher or his friends. By the manifestation of love we prove ourselves to be the true children of God—the God who is "kind to the unthankful and to the evil."

It is not so easy to discern the sequence of the teaching contained in verses 39-49, but a sequence there undoubtedly is. These disciples were to be sent forth as apostles before long, so they must be *seeing* persons themselves. If they were to be seeing they must be *taught;* and for that they must take the humble place at the feet of their Master. They were not above Him: He was above them, and the goal set before them was to be like Him. He was perfection, and when their "college course" was completed they would be *as He is.*

That this might be so, a spirit of *self-judgment* is to be cultivated. Our natural tendency is to judge others and perceive their smallest faults. If we judge ourselves we may discover some very substantial faults. And faith fully judging ourselves we may be able eventually to help others.

From verse 43 the outward profession of discipleship is contemplated. The Lord may have had such an one as Judas specially in view, in speaking thus. Amongst those who took the place of being His disciples there might be found "an evil man," as well as "a good man." They are to be discerned by their fruits, seen in both speech and action. Nature is revealed in fruit. We cannot penetrate the secrets of nature either in a tree or in a man, but we can easily and correctly deduce the nature from the fruit.

This leads to the consideration that mere profession counts for nothing. Men may repeatedly call Jesus their Lord, but if there is no obedience to His word, there is no discipleship that He acknowledges. The kind of foundation that cannot be shaken under the testings is only laid by *obedience.* The mere hearing of His word apart from obedience may erect an edifice which looks like the real thing; but it means disaster in the day of testing.

Let us all bring ourselves under the searching power of this word. The truest believer needs to face it, and not one of us can escape it. It applies

# LUKE

to the whole circle of truth. Nothing is really and solidly ours until we yield to it the obedience of faith—not only the *assent* of faith, but the OBEDIENCE of faith. Then, and only then, we become established in it, in such a way that we are "founded upon a rock."

These words of our Lord uncover for us, without a doubt, the secret of many a tragic collapse as regards their testimony, on the part of true believers; as also collapse and abandonment of the profession of discipleship on the part of those who have taken it up without any reality.

*Reality* is that, which above all things, the Lord must have.

## Chapter 7

LUKE HAS JUST recorded the choice by the Lord of the twelve Apostles and also the instructions He gave them, particularly as to the gracious spirit that was to characterize them, and the reality that was to mark them. We find that He did not immediately dispatch them on their mission but retained them in His company, that they might further learn of Himself both by His words and His actions. The sending out to serve does not come till the beginning of the ninth chapter.

We have already noticed how this Gospel is characterized by the unfolding of grace. This chapter, we see, carries on this theme by showing very strikingly the extent to which grace reaches. The blessing goes out to *the Gentile*, to *the dead*, to *the degraded*. Moreover the way in which grace is received comes very clearly to light—by *repentance* and *faith*.

The first case recorded is that of the Gentile. The centurion showed that he accepted his place among the "aliens from the commonwealth of Israel, and strangers from the covenants of promise" (Eph. 2: 12), by sending the Jewish elders to intercede for him. The elders, true to their upbringing under the law, would have utterly spoiled grace by representing the centurion as worthy. His worthiness, according to them, consisted in his kindly attitude and acts towards themselves! This was quite typical of the Jewish mind. Instead of seeing how their own law condemned them, they treated it as a distinction conferred upon them, they became self-centred; they made themselves, and the treatment accorded to themselves, the criterion of others. Judged by their standards this Gentile was a *worthy* man.

The centurion himself, however, was under no illusion on the point. He confessed himself to be *unworthy*, and thus manifested the spirit of repentance. At the same time he manifested remarkable faith in the grace and power of the Lord. He held a minor position of authority in the military organization of Rome, yet his power was absolute in his own small circle. He discerned in the Lord One who wielded authority in a vastly greater domain, and he was confident that a word from Him would effect all that was needed. Our language should be similar to his. It is enough that He

## LUKE

should "say in a word," and we need nothing beside. The faith that simply takes Him at His word, without reasonings, feelings or experiences, is "great faith" according to our Lord. We see moreover how intimately faith and repentance are connected. They go hand in hand.

From this case we pass to that of the dead man, being carried out of Nain to the grave. Here faith is not visible at all: His compassions and His action fill the scene. Grace and authority are equally and harmoniously displayed. Divine compassion shone forth in the words, "Weep not," uttered to the sorrowing mother. His authority was displayed, in that the moment He touched the bier the whole funeral procession came to a standstill. Then His word of power brought the young man back to life.

Here is One who speaks, and the dead obey Him. "I say unto thee, Arise." Who is this "I"? We may well ask this question. The people evidently asked it, and they decided that God had raised up a great prophet in their midst, and tidings of these things reached as far as to John the Baptist in his prison. Now a question, as to who He was after all, was at that time uppermost in John's mind, so this incident as to John's messengers comes in very appropriately at this juncture.

Verses 19-35 seem to be a kind of parenthesis in which we are shown that the display of *power exercised in grace*, and not in outward pomp, is the proof of the presence of the Messiah. The messengers of John were permitted to see ample proofs of that gracious power. They saw Him doing what Isaiah 61: 1 had said He would do. That was ample proof of who He was.

Then, turning to the people when John's messengers were gone, He pointed out that John himself, His forerunner, had not been a mere nonentity, nor had he come in pomp and luxury. His whole mission had been strictly in keeping with the character of the One whom he announced, who was infinitely great and yet come in lowly grace. He designated John as a prophet so great that there was none greater than he. This of course at once showed that when the people spoke of Christ Himself as "a great prophet" they were falling far short of the truth concerning Him.

As far as John was concerned, though so great, the one that should be least in the coming kingdom of God would be greater than he — not morally, but in the position that would be his. Morally John was very great indeed, and his testimony of such importance that men's destiny was determined by their attitude towards it. The publicans and sinners accepted it, and, thus justifying God, were led ultimately to Christ. The Pharisees and lawyers rejected it, and in due course they rejected Christ. Verse 28 can only be understood as we distinguish between that moral greatness, which depends upon a man's character, and the greatness which springs from the position into which God may be pleased to call us, which varies in different dispensations.

# LUKE

The Lord now gives in a striking little parable the character of the unbelieving generation that surrounded Him. They were like petulant children who were agreeable to nothing; neither the gay nor the grave would they accept. So the Jews would not bow to the searching testimony of John, nor would they rejoice in the gracious ministry of Jesus. They denounced the one as being possessed by a demon, and falsely criticized the Other. Still there were those who discerned the Divine wisdom in both testimonies, and these were the true children of wisdom.

In the incident which closes this chapter we have all this most strikingly exemplified. Simon, the Pharisee, was amongst the critics, whom nothing pleased, though he invited Jesus to a meal in his house. The poor woman of the city was one of those who justified Jesus, and thereby she proved herself to be a true child of wisdom, and also she herself was justified.

The sorrow and contrition of the woman was nothing to the proud Pharisee. Satisfied with himself he was critical of Jesus, imputing to Him the feelings which he would have entertained toward such a person. As a result he felt sure that Jesus was no prophet at all. Verse 16 has shown us that the common people at least thought that He was a prophet, and a great one; Simon had not got as far as that. They had a glimmer of light; he was totally blind, for false religion is the most blinding thing on earth. However, the Lord quickly gave Simon a sample of the mighty prophetic powers that He possessed.

Simon only "spake within himself." He *thought* that Jesus had no discernment as to the woman. The Lord at once showed him that He knew his hypocrisy, and read his secret thoughts, by propounding to him the parable of the two debtors. One debtor was involved in liabilities ten times greater than the other; yet, since neither had any assets, both were equally bankrupt. And the creditor treated them alike; there was forgiving mercy for both. This parable was intended to bring home to Simon that though his sins might be fewer than the woman's, he too was utterly insolvent and he needed forgiving mercy just as she did.

Now debtors do not usually love their creditors, yet a sense of the grace that forgives does provoke love, and even Simon could judge rightly as to this. But then, the application was easy. Simon had studiously refrained from offering the Lord the most ordinary courtesies according to the customs of those days. Neither the water for His feet, nor the kiss of welcome, nor the oil for the head had been forthcoming. He had received the Lord in a way that amounted to offering Him an insult; yet the poor woman had made up for it all in abundant measure. He had no sense of guilt, and no love for the One who came in the grace of forgiveness: she had a true and deep repentance, coupled with faith in Jesus, and a fervent love for Him.

So we see how grace flows out to the degraded, and again we see how repentance and faith go hand in hand: they are like the obverse and reverse of a single coin. The grace that flowed out to this woman is the more striking inasmuch as it reached her in a purely spiritual way. She did not come with *bodily* ills and distresses to be cured; her ills were *spiritual;* her burden was that of her sins. Grace bestowed upon her an abundant forgiveness, and Simon was plainly told that such was the case.

But the Lord did not only speak of her forgiveness to the Pharisee, He also dealt with her personally as to it. What balm for her weary spirit must have been those four words, "Thy sins are forgiven." The saints of earlier days brought the appropriate sacrifice for each trespass or sin, and then knew that the particular sin was forgiven; they hardly knew such a complete absolution as the words of Jesus gave to her. The onlookers might well ask, "Who is this that forgiveth sins also?" God was here in the fulness of grace in the humbled Saviour.

Not only did He *forgive,* He gave the woman the assurance of *salvation,* and also declared that *her faith* had been the means of it. Apart from this word, she might have imagined that it had been procured by her sorrow or her tears. But no: faith it is that establishes the all-essential contact with the Saviour which brings salvation. She could indeed "Go in peace," for she not only had forgiveness, which covered all her past, but salvation, which meant a deliverance from the evil that had enslaved her. This is what grace accomplishes.

## CHAPTER 8

THE OPENING VERSES show the thorough and systematic way in which the Lord Jesus evangelized the cities and villages. He announced the kingdom of God, which involves God's authority being established and man's salvation secured through judgment. It was too early as yet for the Gospel of 1 Corinthians 15: 1-4 to be preached, though, now that we have that Gospel, we can still preach the kingdom of God in its present form. The twelve were with Him, and being trained under His eye. The other Gospels show us this, but only Luke tells us how certain women, who had experienced His delivering power, followed Him and ministered to Him of their goods. This comes in very fittingly after the story of the salvation of the sinful woman of the city.

In verses 4-15, we have the parable of the sower and its interpretation. This reveals to us *the agency* which Divine grace uses to accomplish its benign results—*the Word of God.* The *fruit* of which the parable speaks is not something which is natural to man: it is only produced by the Word, as that Word is received into prepared hearts. In our natural condition our hearts are marked by insensibility, like the hardened wayside, or they are shallow without conviction, or preoccupied with cares or pleasures. The heart prepared like the good ground is one that has been awakened and exercised by the Holy Spirit of God. When the heart is thus made "honest," the Word is retained and treasured, and ultimately fruit is produced.

Verse 16 adds the fact that *light* as well as fruit is produced by the true reception of the Word. Every real conversion means the lighting of a fresh candle in this dark world. Now just as cares and riches and pleasures choke the word, so may some "vessel," speaking of work and daily toil, or "bed," speaking of ease, hide the candle which has been lit. Every candle lit by the reception of the Word is to be conspicuously displayed for the benefit of others. Let us all take this home to ourselves, for the fact is that if the light be really there it cannot be altogether hid, as verse 17 indicates. If year after year nothing is manifested, only one conclusion can be drawn —*there is nothing to be manifested.*

All these considerations lead us to conclude how imperative it is that we hear the Word rightly. Hence, *how* we hear is of all importance. *What* we hear is of equal importance, and this is emphasized in Mark 4: 24. If we do not hear aright we lose that which we seem to have possessed. This is stated in verse 18, and it is illustrated above, in the case of the wayside, the stony ground and the thorny ground hearers.

Verses 19-21 add a further striking fact: *if the word be rightly received it brings the recipient into relationship with Christ Himself.* The Lord plainly shows here that the relationship He was going to acknowledge was not based upon flesh and blood, but upon spiritual realities—upon the hearing and the doing of the Word. This thought is amplified in the epistles: Paul speaking of "the hearing of faith," (Galatians 3: 2; Romans 10: 8-17); James of the works of faith, for "faith without works is dead" (James 2: 20). If we consult Matthew and Mark we shall probably conclude that this incident, as to the Lord's mother and brethren, did not take place exactly at this point, but Luke here again observes an order which is moral rather than historical. The Word received in faith produces fruit for God, light for men, and introduces into true relationship with Christ himself. There is a moral sequence in these things.

Now we come, verses 22-25, to the storm on the lake which was so miraculously calmed. Here again we believe we see a moral sequence. He had just pointed out that the relationship that He acknowledged had a spiritual basis, and the disciples were those who had entered into it. Now they have to discover that relationship with Him means *opposition and trouble in the world.* The water of the lake was lashed into rough waves by the power of the wind, just as Satan, who is "the prince of the power of the air," lashes men and nations into furious opposition against Christ and all that are connected with Him. The disciples came into that particular storm because of their identification with Him.

It was for the moment a terrifying experience, but one which afterwards must have yielded them much encouragement. It served as an opportunity for Him to display His complete mastery of wind and sea, and of the power that lay behind them. At the moment the faith of the disciples was small. They were thinking of their own safety, and had as yet but little understanding of who He was. When later the Spirit was given, and they saw all things clearly, they must have marvelled at their own obtuseness, that they had so little grasped the majesty of His action. If only they had grasped it, their hearts would have been calmed, equally with the waters of the lake.

On the lake the Lord triumphed over the power of Satan working upon the elements of nature: arrived in the country of the Gadarenes He was confronted by the same power, but much more directly exercised over man by means of demons. Opposition must be expected, but the power of His word was supreme. This man presented a very extreme case of demon possession. It had existed "long time;" it endowed him with super-human strength, so that no ordinary restraints held him; it drove him into deserts and the place of death—the tombs. Moreover he was enslaved not by one demon but by many. For some reason he had become like a fortress, strongly held for Satan by a whole legion of demons; so when Jesus met him there was a trial of strength indeed.

The cry of the demon-possessed man, in which he acknowledged Jesus as "Son of God most high," is strikingly in contrast with the exclamation of the disciples, "What manner of man is this!" The demons had no doubt as to who He was, and they knew that they had met their supreme Master, who could have banished them into "the deep," or "the abyss," with a single word. Instead He permitted them to enter into the swine. This meant deliverance for the man but disaster for the swine. Incidentally too, it must have meant degradation for the demons to change their residence from a man to a herd of pigs; and this new residence was lost to them in a few minutes as the pigs choked themselves in the lake. Satan would have drowned the great Master and His disciples in the lake but an hour or so before; actually it was the swine, of which he had taken possession by his agents, that were drowned.

Just as the wind and water had obeyed His word, so the demons had to obey. The man was completely delivered and his whole character changed. In the words, "sitting at the feet of Jesus, clothed, and in his right mind," we may see a beautiful picture of what grace accomplishes for men, who today have been held captive by Satan's power. We may also see in this delivered man another feature which stands good for us today. We too are not permitted as yet to be with our Deliverer: we have to go back to our friends and show what has been wrought in us. The more complete the change wrought, as in the case of this man, the more effective is such testimony.

The testimony was lost however on the Gadarene people, who had lost their swine. Pigs they did appreciate and grace they did not appreciate, so

# LUKE

they refused the Deliverer. Jesus accepted their refusal and returned to the other side of the lake to continue the display of His grace there.

The disciples had witnessed the triumph of their Lord over opposition both on the lake and in the Gadarene country, they were now to see further triumphs on the Capernaum side of the sea. The underworld of demons had owned His power as well as the elements of nature: now disease and death are to yield in His presence. It is worthy of note that the one who approached the Lord first was not the first to receive the blessing.

Jairus was a representative son of Israel; death was invading his house, and he appealed to the Lord, meeting with an immediate response. On the way Jesus was intercepted by this unnamed woman suffering from an incurable disease. Her touch of faith brought her instant healing. Though later in coming and irregular in her proceedings she was the first to experience the delivering grace of the Lord. We may trace here an analogy with the present ways of God. While still He is on the way to raise up to life and blessing the "daughter of Israel" others, and those mainly Gentiles, are giving the touch of faith and getting the blessing.

It was only *a touch*, and it was only *the hem* of His garment, yet the blessing was hers in full measure—thus illustrating the fact that the measure of our faith does not determine the measure of the blessing that grace bestows—for she was *perfectly healed*. We also see that a touch in itself brought nothing, for Peter's word of remonstrance showed that many had for various reasons been brought into contact with Him. Only the touch of faith counted. In other words, *faith* was the all-essential thing, and *that* we may exercise today, though the touch of faith can now only be given spiritually and not physically.

By His questions Jesus brought the woman to the point of confession. In accord with the spirit of the Gospel the faith of her heart had to be followed by the confession of her lips, and that brought her an accession of blessing, for she got the words, "Thy faith hath made thee whole; go in peace." Apart from that word her mind might have been overshadowed by the dread of the recurrence of her plague. Her faith, expressed in the touch, brought the healing; but her confession brought forth the word of assurance that set her mind at ease. How many there may be today who lack the full assurance of salvation because they have lacked courage to confess fully His Name.

At that moment came the news of the death of the damsel, and this furnished a fresh opportunity for the importance of faith to be emphasized. To men death is the dispeller of every hope; yet the word of Jesus was, "Fear not: believe only." To her parents and friends it was death, but it was only sleep to Him: yet the very unbelief of those who bewailed her enables us to see that she really was dead, as we speak. The mocking unbelievers were all put out and only a few who believed saw His work of power. At His word her spirit came again and she was restored to life.

# LUKE

The charge "that they should tell no man what was done" was entirely contrary to all human ideas. Men love notoriety, but not so the Lord. He wrought to make God known, and only faith understood His works, and was confirmed thereby.

## CHAPTER 9

THE DISCIPLES HAD now had full opportunity of learning their Master's spirit and methods and power; so they were sent forth, and verses 1-6 tell us how they were commissioned. "Then He *called* . . . and *gave* . . . He *sent* . . . He *said* . . . " The order of the four verbs is very instructive. His is the choice and not ours. But then He not only calls but also gives the authority and power adequate for the service to which He calls. Not until that power is given does He send. And then in sending He gives the specific instructions that are to control and guide them in their service. The instructions He gave them were exactly suited to men who were sent to support the testimony rendered by the Messiah, the Son of Man, present personally on the earth.

The testimony we are called upon to render today is not that, but rather to the Christ who is risen and glorified on high; still any service we can render is subject to just the same conditions. He must call and send. If He calls any of us He will give the power and grace that is needed for the work; and when sent we too must be careful to observe the instructions that He has left us.

The disciples went forth with the power of their Lord behind them, and the testimony thus being multiplied the attention of even an ungodly monarch like Herod was drawn to the Lord. The great question was, "Who is this?" The people asked it and indulged in speculations. Herod asked it with an uneasy mind, for he had already beheaded John. His wish to see Jesus was fulfilled, but hardly in the way he had anticipated—see 23: 8-11.

All details of the disciples' mission are passed over in silence. In verse 10 it is recorded that they returned and told their Master all that they had done, and He took them aside in private. Thus it will be for all of us when we reach Him at His coming. That will mean being manifested before His judgment seat; and it will be in the privacy and rest of His presence.

On this occasion there was very little rest for Him. Desert place though it was, the people flocked after Him, and He turned no one away. He received, He spoke of the kingdom of God, He healed and, when the evening drew on and they were hungry, He fed them.

The disciples were like ourselves: they had much to learn. In spite of having been sent forth as His messengers they had no adequate sense of His power and sufficiency, and hence they judged as to the difficult situation in the light of their own powers and resources instead of judging everything by Him. When He said to them, "Give ye them to eat," they thought

# LUKE

of their loaves and fishes—pitifully few and small. They might have said, "Lord, it is to Thee we look: we will gladly *give them all that Thou dost give to us.*"

How easily we can see what they might have said, and yet fail in just the same way as they did! We have to learn that if He commands, He enables. He did enable on this occasion, and the disciples were employed in dispensing His bounty. Thus they were instructed as to the fulness of supply that was in Him.

Before multiplying the loaves and fishes Jesus looked up to heaven, thus publicly connecting His action with God. In verse 18 we again find Him in private prayer, thus expressing the dependent place which He had taken in Manhood. The grace was the grace of God, though flowing to men in Him.

Having given His disciples this glimpse of His fulness, He warned them of His approaching rejection, and of its results as far as they were concerned. The people were still completely in the dark as to who He was, but Peter—and doubtless the other disciples too—knew that He was God's Christ, or Messiah. This confession of Peter's was met by the Lord's command to tell no man that thing. This injunction must have been a great surprise to them, as up to this point the joyful tidings that they had found the Messiah must have been the chief item of their testimony. Now however the moment had arrived for them to know that what lay before Him was not the earthly glory of the Messiah but death and resurrection. In breaking the news of this the Lord spoke of Himself as the Son of Man —a title with wider implications. The Messiah is to rule over Israel and the nations, according to Psalm 2: the Son of Man is to have all things under His feet, according to Psalm 8.

In speaking of Himself in this way, the Lord was beginning to lead their thoughts toward the new developments that were impending, though not as yet unfolding what the developments were. Still He did intimate very plainly to them that if death lay before Him, it would also lie before them. This surely is the significance of the words, "deny himself, and take up his cross daily." To deny oneself is to accept death inwardly—death lying upon the motions of one's own will. To take up one's cross daily is to accept death outwardly, for if the world saw a man carrying his cross it knew him to be under its sentence of death.

Verses 24-26 amplify this thought. There is life according to the reckoning of this world, made up of all the things that appeal to man's natural tastes. If we seek to save that life we only lose it. The path for the disciple is to lose that life for Christ's sake, and then we save life in the proper sense, that which is life indeed. The man of the world grasps at the life of this world and ends by losing himself; and that is loss of an irreparable and eternal kind. The disciple who loses the life of this world is no loser in the end. Verse 26 only speaks of the one who *is* ashamed. The converse however is true: the one who is *not* ashamed will be acknowledged by the Son of Man in the day of His glory.

The Lord knew that these words of His would fall as a blow upon the minds of the disciples, and therefore He at once ministered to them great encouragement, not by words so much as by giving them a sight of His glory. This was granted not to all but to the chosen three, and they could communicate it to the rest. In the transfiguration they saw the kingdom of God, since for that brief moment they were "eyewitnesses of His majesty" (2 Peter 1: 16). The expression the Lord used—"taste of death"—is worthy of note. It would cover not only actual dying but also the spiritual experience which He had indicated in verse 23. The same thing stands true for us in principle. It is only as we see the kingdom by faith that we are prepared to taste of death in that experimental way.

Once more we find Him praying, and it is only Luke who puts on record that the transfiguration took place as He prayed. It is a striking fact that it was the praying, dependent Man who shone forth in glory as the King. Long before this David had said, "He that ruleth over men must be just, ruling in fear of God" (2 Sam. 23: 3). Here we see the One who will take up the kingdom and hold it for God, ruling as the dependent Man. All the elements of the coming kingdom were there in sample form. The King Himself was manifested as the central Object. Moses and Elijah appeared from the unseen, heavenly world, representing heavenly saints who will appear with the King when He is manifested: Moses representing saints who have been raised from the dead, and Elijah those raptured to heaven without dying. Then Peter, James and John represented the saints who will be on earth, blessed in the light of His glory.

While the disciples were heavy with sleep the heavenly saints were conversing with their Lord concerning His approaching death, which is to provide the basis on which the glory must rest. Luke speaks of it as His "departure" or "exodus," for it meant His going out from the earthly order into which He had entered, and His entrance into their world by resurrection from among the dead. When the disciples did awake Peter's only thought was to perpetuate the earthly order, and keep his Master in it. He would have detained Moses and Elijah in it also, had he been permitted to make his three tabernacles. As yet he did not grasp the reality of the heavenly order of things just displayed before his eyes, and he had as yet no proper apprehension of the supreme glory of Jesus.

Hence at that moment there came the cloud—evidently the well-known cloud of the Divine presence—which overshadowed them with its brightness, and silenced them with fear. Then the Father's voice proclaimed the supreme glory of Jesus and marked Him out as the one and only Speaker to whom all are to listen. No Moses, no Elijah is for one moment to be

# LUKE

coupled with Him. Jesus is indeed to be "found alone." Though Peter did not at that moment understand the full significance of all this, and therefore "told no man in those days," he did afterwards, as his allusion to it in his second Epistle so plainly shows. It confirmed for him, and for us, the prophetic word, giving the assurance that in anticipating "the everlasting kingdom of our Lord and Saviour Jesus Christ" we are not following "cunningly devised fables" but resting in solid truth.

How great the contrast when the next day they came down from the hill! Above, all had been glory, the power and glory of Christ, with its accompanying order and peace. Below, all was under the power of Satan, with disorder and distraction. The nine disciples left at the foot of the hill had been tested by the child possessed by a particularly virulent demon, and had failed. The distracted father appealed to the Lord, though evidently with but little expectation that He could do anything. Jesus instantly acted for the child's deliverance, and "they were all amazed at the mighty power [majesty] of God." The majestic power He displayed amid the disorders at the foot of the hill was equal to the glory that had been displayed on its crest the day before.

Then once more, just when He had thus manifested His power, He spoke of His death. Said He, "Let these sayings sink down into your ears." What sayings? we may ask, for Luke has not recorded any particular sayings in connection with the casting out of the unclean spirit. The words refer perhaps to the saying on the holy mount, where His decease had been the theme. But that was the trouble with the disciples at that moment: they could not tear away their minds from expectations of an immediate kingdom on earth, so as to realize that He was about to die. The sad consequence of this is seen in verse 46.

By nature we are self-important creatures, loving prominence and greatness above all else; and the flesh in a disciple is no different from that in an unbeliever. Jesus countered the thought of their heart by the object lesson of the little child, and by words that indicated that true greatness is found where the littleness of a child is manifested, and where that "least" disciple is truly a representative of his Master. To receive an insignificant child is to receive the Divine Master, if the child comes "in My Name." The significance is in the Name, not in the child.

This episode evidently stirred John's conscience so that he mentioned a case that had occurred some time before. They had forbidden some zealous worker because "he followeth not with us." They had attached far too much importance to the "us" which, after all, is but a group of individuals each of which is of no importance in himself. All the importance, as the Lord has just shown them, lay in the Name. Now the one who had cast out the demons—the very thing they had just failed to do—had done so "in Thy Name." So he had *the power of the Name* and they had *the imagined importance of the "us."* The Lord dealt gently with John yet firmly. The man was not to be forbidden. He was for the Lord and not against Him.

Luke now groups together four further incidents in the close of the chapter. It seems that the Lord having displayed to the disciples the power of His grace and of God's kingdom, is now instructing them as to the spirit that befits them as those brought under both; and He also warns them of things which would be hindrances thereto.

The first hindrance is obviously *selfishness*. This may take an intensely *personal* form, as in verse 46. Or it may be *collective*, as in verse 49. Yet once more it may be *under cover of zeal for the Master's reputation*, and this is the most subtle form of all. The Samaritans were wholly wrong in their attitude. But He was going up to Jerusalem to die, while James and John wished to vindicate His importance—and incidentally their own—by bringing death upon others. Elijah had indeed acted thus when confronted by the violence of an apostate king, but the Son of Man is of another spirit. That was the trouble with the disciples; they did not as yet enter into the spirit of grace—the grace that characterized their Master.

The three incidents which briefly close the chapter show us that if we would be disciples indeed, and fit for the kingdom, we must beware of mere *natural energy*. An energy which is more than natural is needed if we would follow a rejected Christ. Also there must be no *half-heartedness* and no *indecision*. The claims of the kingdom must take precedence over all else.

## CHAPTER 10

THE DISCIPLES HAVING been instructed in this way, the Lord still further extended the scope of the witness that had to be rendered in connection with His presence on earth, by appointing and sending forth seventy other disciples, two and two before His face. This saying as to the greatness of the harvest and the fewness of the labourers, seems, according to Matthew 9: 37, 38, to have been uttered on another occasion. There, the prayer is answered by the sending forth of the twelve: here, by the sending forth of the seventy.

The instructions which the Lord gave to the seventy are similar to those given to the twelve. There was to be the same simplicity and absence of self-seeking, the same dependence upon Himself for the supply of their needs. They had however additional warnings which indicated increasing opposition from the people. They were told they were to be as lambs amongst wolves, a very striking simile. Yet, in spite of refusal, they were to make it very plain that the kingdom had come nigh to the people.

These seventy had not the distinguished place of the twelve, but nevertheless they fully represented the Lord, as verse 16 makes manifest. This verse establishes the same principle as verse 48 of the previous chapter,

# LUKE

only here the Lord carries the matter back to "Him that sent Me." Humble folk the seventy might be, yet much depended on the attitude of men towards their message. Capernaum and other cities of that day, having this testimony, would have greater responsibilities; and refusing it, would merit severer judgment than cities that had never had such testimony rendered to them.

No details are given as to what transpired during the service of the seventy, and one verse (9: 6) sufficed to sum up the earlier labours of the twelve. We note this because Luke was chosen of God to record the doings of the disciples in the Acts; but that was after the Holy Ghost was given. Before the Spirit was given their work had much less significance, and any light there was in it was eclipsed in the shining of the perfect light in their Master. In verse 17 we pass on to their return at the end of their mission.

They came back with joy, rejoicing mainly in what was more spectacular, the subjection of even demons through the Name of their Master. Now this was indeed a great thing, and a pledge of Satan's ultimate casting out of the heavens. The allusion in verse 18 is not, we believe, to the original fall of Satan but to his final dispossession, as predicted in Revelation 12: 7-9. The past tense is often used in prophetic utterances to describe future events. It is used in those verses in Revelation, as also in Isaiah 53: 3-9. So the Lord confirmed the authority which at that moment He had given them, exerted over all the power of the enemy, but at the same time He indicated something that went beyond all power exerted upon earth.

He said to them, "Your names are written in heaven." It is more than likely that at that moment they did not appreciate the wonder of that statement. Later on they must have done so, and we should appreciate it, since it applies also to us. The figure is a simple one. Our names are enrolled in the city or district, *where we are domiciled*. The Lord said to these men in effect, a heavenly citizenship is to be yours, and that is a greater cause of rejoicing than any power conferred on earth. Luke's Gospel specially gives us the transition from law to grace and from earth to heaven, and this verse is a distinct landmark on the way. It was the first intimation of the truth which comes fully to light in Philippians 3: 20, "Our conversation [commonwealth] is in heaven."

In that same hour—the hour of the rejoicing of the seventy — Jesus Himself rejoiced. He saw not only the coming fall of Satan, with the consequent overthrow of all his evil designs, but the Father's action towards the establishment of all His designs. At the basis of those bright designs lay this, that He Himself is to be perfectly revealed and known, and that "babes" rather than the wise and prudent of this world are to receive the revelation.

The Son had entered into Manhood that thus He might reveal the Father to men. And not only this, He is Himself the Heir of all things. The dependent Man on earth knew that all things had been delivered to Him of the

Father. Moreover, the very fact that He had become Man adds an element in His case which defies all human grasp. He became Man that the Father might be known: as Man He is the Heir of all things: yet let no man pretend to fathom the mystery that must surround so infinite a stoop. If we esteem ourselves to be wise and prudent we may attempt it to our own undoing. If we indeed are babes we shall accept the mystery with humble and subject minds, and rejoice rather in all that He has revealed to us of the Father and of the Father's designs.

Having thus rejoiced in His own mission, and in the grace that took up the insignificant "babes," the Lord turned to the disciples to show them the greatness of their present privilege. They were seeing things which had been the desire of the godly of past ages. They saw and heard things which had to do with the manifestation of the Father upon earth, and the doing of a work which would result in the calling of a people for heaven. All this was for the moment private to the disciples.

Publicly there was nothing but conflict. The question of the lawyer, recorded in verse 25, apparently so sincere, was really asked with an evil ulterior motive. He asked what he should do, and the Lord who knew the man's motive, took him up on the ground of his doing. It was the law that demanded doing from man: hence the Lord's question. In saying that the supreme demand of the law was for love; firstly towards God, and then towards one's neighbour, the man answered rightly. Jesus had simply to say, "This do, and thou shalt live;"—not, "have eternal life," but just, "live." There is no life for earth except the law be kept.

The lawyer set out to entrap the Lord, and now found himself entrapped by his own answer. Desirous of justifying himself, he enquired who was his neighbour; as though he would infer that, granted he had sufficiently attractive neighbours, he would find no difficulty in loving them. This enquiry was met by the parable concerning the Samaritan, and the lawyer was left to judge who was the neighbour. Again the man answered rightly in spite of the antipathy felt by the Jew for the Samaritan. Thus judging, he answered his own question, and was left under the obligation of acting as the Samaritan on the one hand, and loving the Samaritan as himself on the other.

The teaching of this parable however goes beyond the mere answering of the man's question. In the action of the Samaritan we can see a picture of the grace that marked the coming of the Lord Himself. Priest and Levite, representatives of the law system, passed by on the other side. The law was not instituted to help sinners, much less to save them, and had the half-dead man died on their hands, both priest and Levite would have been defiled, and for a time disqualified from the exercise of their office. Like the Samaritan, Jesus was the rejected One, and yet He was the Minister of grace and salvation. If in verse 20 we see the transition from earth to heaven intimated, in this parable we see intimated the transition from law to grace.

In the light of this it is also plain that the Lord Jesus was the best and truest Neighbour that man ever had—the perfect Neighbour, in fact. He was also God, perfectly revealed and known. In Him God and the Neighbour were united, and in hating and rejecting Him, men broke at once and hopelessly both counts of the law.

But not all rejected Him: some received Him. And so there follows, in the end of this chapter and the early part of chapter 11, very happy intimations of the ways in which such are put into touch with Him. There is the virtue of *His word*, there is *prayer*, and the coming gift of the *Holy Sprit*.

Mary had discovered the power of His word. It opened to her a door of entrance into the thoughts of God, so she sat at His feet and listened. It would seem that, in serving, Martha was only doing the duty that rightly belonged to her. Her trouble was in aiming at *much* serving: she wished to do the thing in very special style, and this "cumbered" or "distracted" her. Her distraction was such that she spoke in a way that was an aspersion not only on her sister but on the Lord. Mary, she thought, was neglecting her duty, and the Lord was indifferent to her neglect. Martha represents distraction and Mary, communion.

Martha's distraction was the result of having too much service on hand, a thing which itself is quite good. She became careful and troubled about many things, and missed the one thing that is needful. Mary had discovered that all she could do for the Lord was nothing compared with what He had to convey to her. To receive His word is the one thing needful, for out of that will flow all service that is acceptable to Him. It is the good part, that shall not be taken away.

We believe that much of the weakness which characterizes present-day Christians may be explained by this one word—*distraction*. So many things from all quarters, and often enough harmless in themselves, are presented to us that we are distracted from the one thing of importance. We may not always be careful and troubled about them; we may be merely fascinated and occupied with them. But the result is the same: the one thing is missed. Then we are losers indeed.

## Chapter 11

Once again we find the Lord in prayer, and this awakened in His disciples a desire to be taught to pray. As yet they did not possess the Spirit as we do today, and hence "praying in the Holy Ghost" (Jude 20), and the help and intercession of the Spirit, of which Romans 8: 26, 27, speaks, could not be known by them as we may know it. At this period the Lord was their "Comforter" and Guide from without: we have "another Comforter," who is within. In response, the Lord gave them the pattern prayer, and added to it an illustration to enforce the need for importunity. If a man will rise at the midnight hour at the earnest solicitation of a friend, we may well come with confidence to God.

The Lord had instructed His disciples to address God as Father and the assurances He gave in verse 10 fit in with this, as also the statements of verses 11-13. The Father in heaven is not to be conceived of as less interested and considerate than an earthly father. He will not give that which is useless or harmful in answer to requests for necessary food. Nor, we may add, will He give what is useless or harmful if we foolishly desire it and ask for it. Many an unanswered prayer is, no doubt, accounted for by this.

Man in his evil condition knows how to give good gifts to his children; the heavenly Father will give to those who ask Him the greatest of all gifts —the Holy Spirit. Here we see the Lord in His teaching leading on to the developments that were soon to come. The Holy Spirit was not given until Jesus was glorified, as we know from John 7: 39; but when He was given, He came upon a band of men and women who were continuing in prayer and supplication, as Acts 1: 14 records. We live in the day when the Spirit has been given; and so we may rejoice in the fruit of His presence, as well as in the power of the Word of God and of prayer.

In the next paragraph (14-28) we get the definite rejection of the grace displayed, and of the Lord Himself who displayed it; which leads the Lord to unfold the fearful result of this rejection and also to further emphasize the importance of obedience to the Word.

The dumb demon being cast out, the change in the man who had been his victim was impressive and undeniable. Many of the people however adopted the plan of vilifying what they could not deny. The remark about Beelzebub is not attributed to the Pharisees, as it is in Matthew. Doubtless they instigated it, but the common people supported them in it, as Luke records here. Others, shutting their eyes to the many signs already given, had the effrontery to demand a sign from heaven. In His reply, Jesus firstly showed that their accusation was wholly unreasonable: it involved the absurdity of Satan acting against himself. Secondly, He showed that, if true, their accusation would recoil on the head of their sons, if not on their own.

But thirdly, and this most important of all, He gave the true explanation of what He was doing. He had arrived on the scene stronger than Satan. Before His coming Satan had held his captives in an undisturbed peace. Now the stronger One was releasing these captives. His coming presented a test to all of them: they were either with Him or against Him. Not to be with Him was tantamount to being against Him, for there could be no neutrality. Men might appear to be gathering together, but if not *with Him* it would prove to be but scattering. This is a point we do well to note.

# LUKE

There is a great urge today for gathering men together in all kinds of associations and groups; but if not with Christ, central and dominant, it is a process of scattering, and will ultimately be manifested as such.

Verses 24-26 are evidently prophetic. At that moment the unclean spirit of their ancient idolatry had gone out of Israel, but though they were "swept and garnished" in an outward way, they were engaged in refusing the One sent of God to occupy the house. As a result the old unclean spirit would return with others worse than himself, and so their state be worse than at the beginning. This word of Jesus will be fulfilled when unbelieving Israel receives Antichrist in the last days.

Not all were refusing Him however. A woman of the company perceived something of His excellence, and pronounced His mother to be blessed. This He accepted, for the first word of His reply was, "Yea." Yet He indicated something more blessed still. The truest blessedness for us lies in the receiving and keeping of the Word of God. The spiritual link formed by the Word is more intimate and enduring than any link formed in the flesh. The Lord was leading the thoughts of His disciples to these spiritual verities, and the hearing of the Word is that good part, as we have just seen in the case of Mary.

The Lord now proceeded to speak of the insensibility that characterized the people of His day. They were asking for a sign as though no signs had been given to them. Only one sign remained for them, which He speaks of as "the sign of the prophet Jonas." Jonah preached to the Ninevites but he was also a sign to them, inasmuch as he appeared among them as one who had come up out of what looked like certain death. The Son of Man was about to go into actual death and come forth in resurrection, and that was the greatest of all signs: moreover He was displaying among them wisdom far greater than Solomon's and His preaching went far beyond that of Jonah. Why was it that the people were not moved?

It was not because there was no light shining. Men do not light a candle in order to hide it, as verse 33 says. The Lord had come into the world as the great Light and His beams were shining upon men. What was wrong was wrong, not with the light but with the eyes of men. This is emphasized in verses 34-36. The sun is the light of our bodies objectively: but our eyes are light to us subjectively. If the sun went out, there would be universal darkness, but if my eye went out, there would be absolute darkness for me. If my spiritual seeing faculty be evil, my mind is full of darkness: if single, all is light. In other words, the state of the one upon whom the light shines is of great importance. The state of the people was wrong, hence their insensibility to the light that shone in Christ.

But, if the people did not receive the light to their blessing, the Lord at least would turn the searchlight of truth on their state. He began with the Pharisees, and the rest of the chapter gives us His indictment of them. The Pharisee who invited Him was true to type; a critic, and obsessed with

# LUKE

ceremonial details. The hour had struck for the critic to be criticized and exposed. Nothing could be more trenchant than the Lord's words. As we read them we may form some conception of how men will be searched in the day of judgment.

Their *hypocrisy* is the point of verses 39-41. Ostentatious cleanliness where the eyes of men reach, filthiness where they do not. And further, rabid *self-seeking* lay under their apparent piety. They were full of "ravening" or "plunder." The word, "give," in verse 41, is in contrast with this. If only they became givers, rather than plundering other people, all things would be clean to them, inside as well as outside. Such a radical change as that would imply true conversion.

Verse 42 points out their *perverted judgment*. They specialized on things that were neither important nor costly and ignored things of utmost weight. Verse 43 shows that *love of notoriety* and the adulation of men consumed them. Hence they became unsuspected *centres of defilement* for others, as verse 44 indicates. They damaged others as well as themselves. A terrible indictment indeed, but one that sadly applies in varying measures at all times to those who are exponents of a merely outward and ceremonial religion.

At this point one of the doctors of the law protested that these words were also an insult to such as himself. This only led to the indictment being more closely pressed home against himself. These teachers of the law busied themselves with laying burdens on others. They legislated for others, and coolly *ignored the law for themselves.* Moreover they were marked by the rejection of God's word and of the prophets who brought it, though after the prophets had been killed they honoured them in building their tombs, thus hoping to gain the prestige of their names now that they were no longer tested by their words. A cunning device, that! But one not unknown even in our day. It is easy to laud to the skies a century after his death a man that would be fiercely opposed during his life of testimony. The Lord's words imply that what their fathers had done would be done again by the sons. The generation to whom He spoke were guilty not only of the blood of the former prophets, but of the Son of God Himself.

Finally, in verse 52 we find that just as the Pharisees defiled other people (verse 44) so the lawyers took away the key of knowledge, and so did Satan's work in hindering others from entering into the true knowledge of God. They *slew the prophets*, and *blocked the way of life.*

The Lord evidently uttered these tremendous denunciations with calmness of spirit. The best of men would have spoken differently. Hence to us comes the injunction, "Be ye angry, and sin not" (Eph. 4: 26). We easily sin in being angry against sin. He needed no such command. His opponents thought they had but to provoke Him further and He would easily succumb. He did no such thing as they anticipated, as the next chapter shows.

# LUKE

## Chapter 12

INSTEAD OF BEING provoked by the vehement opposition of the scribes and Pharisees, the Lord improved the occasion by calmly instructing His disciples in the presence of the enormous crowd, that the controversy had drawn together. He had just been turning the searchlight of truth on the religious leaders: He now turned the same light on the disciples and their path.

In the first place He warned them against the hypocrisy, which He had just been unmasking in the Pharisees. It is indeed a "leaven;" that is, a type of evil which, if unjudged, ferments and grows. The hypocrite aims at having things "covered" from God in the first place, and then from the eyes of his fellows. Everything however is coming into the light, so that in the long run hypocrisy is futile. Still, while it exists, it is absolutely fatal to the soul having to do with God in any way. Hence from a moral point of view the warning against it must come in the first place. For the disciple of Christ there must be *no covering* of anything from the eyes of the Lord.

In the second place He warned them against the fear of man—verses 4-11. He did not hide from them the fact that they were going to encounter rejection and persecution. If they were to be free of hypocrisy in a world which is so largely dominated by it, they could not expect to be popular. But, on the other hand, if they were to have nothing covered from the eyes of God, they would be able to stand forth with *no cowardice* in the presence of persecuting men. They who fear God much, fear men little.

The Lord did not merely exhort His disciples to have no fear of men, He also made known to them things which would prove great encouragements to that end. In verse 4 He addressed them as, "My friends." They knew that they were His disciples, His servants, but this must have set matters in a new and very cheering light. In the strength of His friendship they, and we, can face the world's enmity. Then, in verses 6 and 7, He set before them in a very touching way the care of God on their behalf. So intimate is it, that the very hairs of our head are not merely counted but numbered.

In verse 12 He assures them that in their moments of emergency they could count upon the special teaching of the Holy Ghost. They would have no need to prepare an elaborate defence when arraigned before the authorities. The hatred and opposition of men was to lie as a liability upon them: but what marvellous assets are these—the *friendship* of Christ, the *care* of God, the *teaching* of the Holy Ghost. And in addition to this, their confession of Christ before hostile men would be rewarded by His confession of them before holy angels.

At this point in His discourse the Lord was interrupted by a man who wished Him to interfere on his behalf in a matter of money. Had He been the social reformer or socialist, that some imagine Him to have been, here was the opportunity for Him to have laid down correct rules for the division of property. He did nothing of the kind: instead, He unmasked the covetousness which had led to man's request, and spoke the well-known parable concerning the rich fool. To reconstruct his barns, so as to conserve all the fruits given to him by the bounty of God, was just ordinary prudence. To lay all up *for himself*, and to neglect all the Divine riches for *the soul*, was the substance of his folly.

The rich fool was filled with covetousness, since he regarded all his goods as guaranteeing the fulfilment of his programme—"take thine ease, eat, drink, and be merry." This is precisely the programme of the average man of the world today—plenty of leisure, plenty to eat and drink, plenty of fun and amusement.

Now the believer is "rich toward God," as verse 32 makes very plain. So, when the Lord resumed His discourse to His disciples, in verse 22, He began to relieve their minds of all those cares which are so natural to us. Since we are enriched with the kingdom, *no covetousness* is to characterize us; and we are to be burdened with *no care*, since God's care on our behalf is all-sufficient. His words were, "Your Father knoweth." Thus He taught His disciples to know God as One who took a fatherly interest in them, and in all their needs as relating to this life.

But this He did, in order that they might be set free in spirit to pursue things that at the present moment lie outside this life. There is no contradiction between verses 31 and 32. The kingdom is given to us and yet we are to seek it. We must seek it because it is not yet in manifestation; consequently it is not found in the things of this life, but lies in the spiritual and moral realities connected with the souls of those who are brought under the Divine authority. Nevertheless the kingdom is to be a manifested reality in this world, and the title-deeds of it are already sure to the people of God. As our thoughts and our lives today are filled with the things of God and the service of God, we seek the kingdom of God.

Hence the lives of the disciples were to run on lines diametrically opposed to those of the votaries of this world. Instead of laying up goods for an easy time of pleasure, the disciple is to be one who is a giver, one who lays up treasure in heaven, one whose loins are girded for activity and service, and whose light of testimony is shining. He is, in fact, to be like a man waiting for the return of his master. We have already noticed the things which are *not* to characterize us: here we have the things which *are* to characterize us.

As servants we are to be waiting for our Lord, and not only waiting but "watching" (verse 37), "ready" (verse 40), and "doing" (verse 43)—doing that which is our allotted task. The time of reward will be when our Lord returns. Then the Lord will Himself undertake to minister to the full blessing of those who have watched for Him. This, which we find in verse 37, indicates a reward of a general sort. Verse 44 speaks of a reward of a more special sort to be given to those marked by faithful and diligent service in their Master's interests.

The Lord's discourse to His disciples extends to the end of verse 53. A few salient points are these:

(1) *Heaven* is again set before the disciples. In chapter 10, as we noticed, they are instructed that their citizenship is to be in the heavens. Now they are taught so to act that their treasure may be in heaven, and consequently their heart there too. They are to live on principles altogether opposed to those governing the rich fool.

(2) The Lord *assumes His rejection* all through, and speaks of it yet more plainly towards the end—verses 49-53. "Fire" is symbolic of that which searches and judges, and it had been already kindled by His rejection. By His "baptism" He indicated His death, and until that was accomplished He was "straitened," that is, narrowed up, or restrained. Only when expiation had been accomplished could love and righteousness flow forth in full power. But then, the fire being kindled and the baptism accomplished, all would be brought to an issue, and the line of demarcation clearly drawn. He would become the test, and division take place even in the most intimate circles. In the anticipation of all this, the Lord *assumes His absence*, and consequently speaks freely of His second coming.

(3) To Peter's question (verse 41) the Lord did not give a direct answer. He did not definitely limit His remarks to the small circle of His disciples, nor enlarge the circle to embrace the thousands of Israel who were standing round. Instead He rested the whole weight of His words upon the responsibility of His hearers. If men were in the place of His servants—no matter how they got there—they would be recompensed according to their works, whether they proved to be faithful or evil. The evil servant does not desire the presence of the Lord, and consequently in his mind he defers His coming. Being thus wrong in relation to the Master, he becomes wrong in his relations with his fellow-servants, and wrong in his personal life. When the Lord comes his portion will be with the unbelievers, inasmuch as he has proved himself to be only an unbeliever. Verses 47 and 48 clearly show that penalty as well as reward will be graduated with equity in keeping with the degree of responsibility.

(4) The marks of the true servant are that he devotes himself to his Master's interests while He is absent, and he waits for his reward until He returns. Three times in this discourse does the Lord refer to eating and drinking, as a figure of having a good time. The worldling has his good time of merriment (verse 19), which ends in death. The false servant has his good time when he begins "to eat and drink, and to be drunken" (verse 45), which ends in disaster at the coming of his Master. The worldling was not only merry; he was *drunk*, which is worse. As a matter of fact, when unconverted men take the place of being servants of God, they seem to fall

## LUKE

more easily under the intoxicating influence of seductive religious and philosophic notions than anyone else. The true servant waits for his Master, who will make him to sit down to eat and drink and be the Servant of his joy (verse 37). His good time will be then.

In verse 54 the Lord turned from His disciples to the people with words of warning. They were in a most critical position and did not know it. They were well able to read the signs of the weather, but unable to read the signs of the time. By their rejection of the Lord they were forcing Him into the part of their "adversary," that is, the opposing party in a law-suit. If they persisted in their attitude, and the case came before the Judge of all, they would find themselves altogether in the wrong and the penalty to the uttermost would come upon them. They would have to pay "the very last mite."

### Chapter 13

Just at that moment some of those present mentioned the case of certain unhappy men of Galilee, who had paid the extreme penalty under Pilate. They had the impression that they were sinners of the deepest dye. The Lord charged home upon His hearers that their own guilt was just as great, and that they too would perish, and He cited the further case of the eighteen slain by the fall of the tower at Siloam. In the popular view these were exceptional happenings indicating exceptional wickedness. The people listening to Him were committed to worse wickedness by failing to understand their opportunity; and, rejecting Him, they would not escape. Thus He warned them of the retribution coming upon them.

In the parable of the fig tree we have the ground of the retribution stated (verses 6-10). God had every right to expect fruit from the people; He sought it but found none. Then for one year there was to be *ministry to* the tree instead of *demand from* the tree. Jesus was amongst them, ministering to them the grace of God instead of pressing home the demands of the law. If there was no response to that, then the blow must fall. In all this His teaching flows on from the end of chapter 12: there is no real break between the chapters.

Now comes the beautiful incident, verses 10-17, in which is set forth figuratively what the grace will accomplish, where it is received. The poor woman, though bowed together and helpless, was one who waited upon the service of God in the synagogue. Her physical condition was an apt figure of the spiritual plight of many. They were full of spiritual infirmity, and the law they found to be an oppressive yoke, so much so that under its weight they were bowed together, unable to straighten themselves and look up.

This woman was a "daughter of Abraham," that is, a true child of faith —see Galatians 3: 7. Yet Satan had a hand in her sad state, taking advantage of her infirmity. Moreover the ruler of the synagogue would have used the ceremonial law to hinder her being healed. But the Lord brushed all this aside. By His Word, and by His personal touch, He wrought her immediate deliverance. Many there are who would say, "With me it was law, and infirmity, and hopeless bondage, and the power of Satan, until Christ intervened in the might of His grace: then what a change!" Deliverances such as these shame the adversaries and fill many with rejoicing. They are indeed, "glorious things that were done by Him."

At this point the Lord showed that even the introduction of the grace and power of the kingdom was not going to result in an absolutely perfect state of things. The parables of the mustard seed and the leaven, brought in here, indicate that, while there would be much growth and expansion in the outward form of the kingdom, it would be accompanied by undesirable elements, and even by corruption.

With verse 22 of our chapter a distinct break comes from an historical point of view. The Lord is now seen journeying up to Jerusalem, teaching in the cities and villages as He went. But though this is so, there does not seem to be any marked break in His teaching recorded. The question in verse 23, seems to have been prompted by curiosity, and in reply the Lord gave a word of instruction and warning which was much in keeping with what has gone just before. If the incoming of the grace of the kingdom was going to result in the mixed condition of things, pictured in the parables of the mustard seed and the leaven, then the narrow way of life must be sought with much sincerity and earnestness.

The word "Strive," in verse 24, does not signify *work* of any kind but *earnestness* of such intensity as to be almost an agony. It is as though He said, "Agonize to enter in at the narrow gate while the opportunity lasts." Many seek a wider entrance through things of a ceremonial sort, as indicated in verse 26. But only that which is personal and spiritual will avail. There is no real entrance save through the narrow way of repentance. So again here the Lord shows the futility of a merely outward religion. There must be inward reality.

The parables of verses 18-21 show there will be mixture in the kingdom in its present form; but verse 28 shows that in its coming form there will be none. Then the patriarchs will be in it and the mere ceremonialists thrust out. Verse 29 gives an intimation of the calling of the Gentiles that was impending, for grace was about to go out worldwide with mighty effects. Grace, as we saw much earlier in this Gospel, cannot be confined within Jewish limits or forms. Like new wine it will burst the bottles. The Jew was first historically, but in the presence of grace his ingrained legalism often hindered him, so that he came in last. The Gentile, not hindered thus, becomes the first when grace is in question.

The chapter closes on a very solemn note. Now it is not the Jew but Herod who comes up for judgment. Herod hid his animosity with the cunning of a fox, but Jesus knew him through and through. He knew also that His own life, characterized by mercy for man, was to be perfected by death and resurrection. The hatred of Herod was however a small thing. The great thing was the rejection of Christ, and of all the grace that was in Him, by Jerusalem. They were the people that God had appealed to by the prophets, and that now He would gather together by His Son. The figure used is a very beautiful one. The prophets had recalled them to their duties under the broken law, while predicting Messiah's coming. Now He was come in the fulness of grace, and the shelter of His protecting wings might have been theirs. All however was in vain.

Jerusalem boasted of the beautiful house which was in the midst of her. Jesus had spoken of it earlier as "My Father's house," now He disowns it as "your house," and He leaves it to them desolate and empty. Jerusalem had missed her opportunity, and soon would not see her Messiah until the cry of Psalm 118: 26 is heard, which proceeds, "out of the house of the Lord." That cry will not be heard on the lips of Jerusalem until the day of His second advent.

## Chapter 14

IN THE CLOSING verses of the previous chapter the Lord accepted His rejection and foretold its results for Jerusalem; yet He did not cease His activities in grace nor His teachings of grace, as the opening part of this chapter shows. The Pharisees wished to use their law of the sabbath as a cord wherewith to tie up His hands of mercy and restrain them from action. He broke their rope and showed that He would at least have as much mercy on the afflicted man as they were accustomed to show to their domestic animals. His grace abounded above all their legal prejudice.

From verse 7 Luke resumes the account of His teachings, and we do not find any further record of His works until we come to verse 11 of chapter 17. In the first place, the Lord emphasized the behaviour which should characterize those who are the recipients of grace. Fallen human nature is pushful and self-assertive, but grace can only be received as humility is manifested. The guest invited to a wedding enters the feast as a matter of bounty and not as of right or of merit, and should behave accordingly. It may be remarked that in worldly society today bold self-assertiveness would not be considered good form. We admit that, and it is a witness to the way in which Christian ideals still prevail. In pagan circles such pushfulness would be applauded, and we shall see it increasingly manifested as pagan ideals prevail.

The abasement of the self-exalted and the exaltation of the humbled is sometimes seen in this life, but it will be fully seen when the One, who in supreme measure humbled Himself, even unto the death of the cross, is highly exalted in public, and every knee bows before Him. In verse 11 we can discern the two Adams. The first attempted to exalt himself and fell: the Last humbled Himself, and sits at the right hand of the Majesty on high.

In the three verses which follow we find the Lord instructing not the guest but the host. He too is to act in the spirit which befits grace. Human nature is selfish even in its benefactions, and will issue its invitations with a view to future profit. If, under the influence of grace, we think of those who have nothing to offer us, we aim at no earthly recompense. There is recompense however even for the actions of grace, but that is found in the resurrection world which lies ahead of us.

Teachings such as these moved someone to ejaculate, "Blessed is he that shall eat bread in the kingdom of God." This was said very probably under the impression that entrance into the kingdom was a matter of great difficulty, and the one to eat bread there must be a particularly fortunate person. This remark led the Lord to give the parable of the "great supper," in which He showed that the door into the kingdom is to be opened to all, and that if any do not enter it is their own fault. In this parable there is a prophetic element; that is, the Lord looked forward and spoke of things which have their fulfilment in the day in which we live. It is pre-eminently the parable of the Gospel.

"A certain man made a great supper and bade many." The cost and labour was his; the benefit was to be conferred upon many. Those first invited were people who were already possessed of something—a piece of ground, oxen, a wife. These represent the Jews with their religious leaders in the land, who first heard the message. Taken as a whole they refused the invitation, and it was the religious privileges they already possessed that blinded them to the value of the Gospel offer.

When their refusal was reported by the servant, the master is represented as "being angry." In Hebrews 10: 28, 29, the doing of "despite unto the Spirit of grace" is said to be worthy of "sorer punishment" than the despising of Moses' law. What we have here is in keeping with that. The anger of the master did indeed mean that none of those who thus despised his invitation should taste of his supper, as verse 24 states, yet it did not shut up his bowels of kindness. The servant was the rather bidden to go out quickly and gather in the poor and needy—those most disqualified from a human standpoint.

But these were to be gathered from "the streets and lanes of the city;" so they represent, we judge, the poor and afflicted and undeserving of Israel—the publicans and sinners, as contrasted with the scribes and Pharisees. The Lord Himself was now turning to these, and amongst such the work continued into the days recorded in the earlier chapters of the Acts of the Apostles. Then the moment arrived when the invitation had been fully declared amongst them, and though many responded, the happy announcement was made by the servant, "Yet there is room."

This led to an extension of the kindly invitation. Still the word is "Go out," and now the poor derelicts of the highways and hedges, outside the bounds of the city, are to be brought in, to fill the house. This pictures the going forth of the Gospel to the Gentiles. It carries us to the end of Acts, where we have Paul saying, "The salvation of God is sent unto the Gentiles, and . . . they will hear it."

The parable definitely sets forth the matter from God's side rather than man's. He makes the supper, He sends the Servant, He has His own way, and fills His house in spite of man's perversity. The Servant He sends is the Holy Spirit, for no one less than He can wield a power which is absolutely compelling. The under-servants, even so great an one as the Apostle Paul, cannot go beyond the persuading of men (see 2 Cor. 5: 11); only the Spirit of the living God can so effectually work in the hearts of men as to "compel them to come in." But this, blessed be God, is what He does, and has done for each of us.

Hearing things such as these, great multitudes went with Him. Many there are who like to hear of something which is to be had for nothing. The Lord turned, and set before these the conditions of discipleship. The grace of God imposes no conditions, but the Gospel which announces that grace does conduct our feet into the path of discipleship, which can only be trodden rightly as we submit to very stringent conditions. Four are mentioned here. (1) The Master must be supreme in the affections of the disciple; so much so that all other loves must be as hatred compared with it. (2) There must be the bearing of the cross in our following of Him; that is, a readiness to accept a death sentence as from the world. (3) There must be a counting of the cost as regards our resources; a correct appraisal of all that is ours in the Christ whom we follow. (4) There must equally be a correct appraisal of the powers arrayed against us.

If we do not reckon rightly in either of these directions we shall very likely go beyond our measure, on the one hand, or be filled with fear, and compromise with the adversary, on the other. If, as verse 33 says, we do indeed forsake all that we have, we shall be wholly cast upon the resources of the great Master whom we follow, and then the path of discipleship becomes gloriously possible for us.

Now the true disciple is salt; and salt is good. In Matthew 5, we find Jesus saying, "Ye are the salt of the earth" (ver. 13), but He said that to "disciples" (ver. 1). If the disciple compromises he becomes like salt that has lost its savour, and he is fit for nothing. What a word for us! Grace has called us, and our feet have been placed in the path of discipleship. Are we complying with its solemn conditions, so that we become disciples indeed? May we indeed have ears to hear!

# LUKE

## Chapter 15

FROM THE TWO verses that open this chapter, it would seem that these words about grace and discipleship drew the publicans and sinners toward Him, while repelling the Pharisees and scribes. He did indeed receive sinners and eat with them: such action is according to the very nature of grace. The Pharisees flung out the remark as a taunt. The Lord accepted it as a compliment, and proceeded by parables to show that He not only received sinners but positively sought them, and also to demonstrate what kind of reception sinners get when they are received.

First the parable of the lost sheep. Here we see in the shepherd a picture of the Lord Himself. The ninety and nine, who represent the Pharisee and scribe class, were left not in the fold but in the wilderness—a place of barrenness and death. The one sheep that was lost represents the publican and sinner class; those who are lost, and know it—the "sinner that repenteth." The Shepherd finds the sheep; the labour and toil is His. Having found it, He secures it and brings it home. His shoulders become its security. He brings it home, and then His joy begins. Never does He have to say, "Sorrow with Me, for I have lost My sheep which was found."

It is impossible to find on earth the "ninety and nine just persons, which need no repentance," though sadly easy to find ninety and nine who imagine themselves to be such. Yet if they could be found there is more joy in heaven over one repentant sinner than there could be over them. All the myriads of holy angels in heaven have never caused such joy as one repentant sinner. What astounding grace this is!

The parable of the lost piece of silver pursues the same general theme, but with a few special details. The woman with her operations in the house represents the subjective work of the Spirit in the souls of men, rather than the objective work of Christ. The Spirit lights a candle within the dark heart and creates the disturbance which ends in the finding of the silver. The joy is here said to be in the presence of the angels; that is, it is not the joy of the angels but of the Godhead, before whom they stand.

Then follows the parable of the "prodigal son." The opening words are very significant. The Lord had been saying, "What man of you . . . doth not . . . go after?" "What woman . . . doth not . . . seek diligently?" He could not now say, "What man of you," if he have a prodigal son and he returns, will not "run and fall on his neck and kiss him"? We doubt if any man would go to the lengths of the father of this parable: the great majority of men certainly would not. This parable sets forth the grace of God the Father. Once more it is a picture of the sinner who repents, and we are now permitted to see in parabolic form the depths from which the sinner is raised, and the heights to which he is lifted according to the Father's heart, by the Gospel.

In the best robe we see the symbol of our acceptance in the Beloved: in the ring the symbol of an eternal relationship established: in the shoes the sign of sonship, for servants entered the houses of their masters with bare feet. The fatted calf and the merriment set forth the gladness of heaven and the Father's joy in particular. The son had been dead morally and spiritually but now he was as one risen into a new life.

If the younger son pictures the repentant sinner, the elder son accurately represents the spirit of the Pharisee. The one was hungry and went in: the other was angry and stayed out. The arrival of grace always divides men into these two classes—those who know they are worthy of nothing, and those who imagine themselves to be worthy of more than they have got. Said the elder son, "Thou never gavest me a kid, that I might make merry with my friends." So he too found his society and pleasure in a circle of friends outside his father's circle. The only difference was in the character of the friends—the younger son's were disreputable, while his presumably, were respectable. The self-righteous religionist is no more in real communion with the heart of the Father than is the prodigal; and he ends up still outside while the prodigal is brought within.

### Chapter 16

These parables were spoken to the Pharisees but the one that opens this chapter was spoken to the disciples. They were instructed by it as to the position in which men find themselves before God, and the behaviour that befits them in that position. We are stewards, and have been unfaithful in our stewardship. The steward was accused to his master that he had "wasted his goods." This phrase gives us a link with the previous parable, for the younger son had "wasted his substance with riotous living." All that we possess has reached us from the hand of God, so that if we squander upon ourselves that which we may have, we are really wasting our Master's goods.

The unfaithful steward found himself under notice to quit, whereupon he resolved he would use certain opportunities, still within his reach in the present, with a view to his advantage in the future. Verse 8 is the close of the parable. The steward was unjust—the Lord plainly calls him so—yet his lord could not but commend the subtle wisdom with which he had acted, in spite of it being to his own detriment. In matters of worldly shrewdness the children of this age excel the children of God.

Verses 9-13 are the application of the parable to us all. Earthly possessions, money and the like, are "the mammon of unrighteousness," because they are the things in which man's unrighteousness is mostly displayed, though in themselves they are not intrinsically unrighteous. We are to use the mammon in such a way as to lay up "a good foundation against

# LUKE

the time to come" (see 1 Tim. 6: 17-19), or as our verse says, "when it fails ye may be received into the eternal tabernacles" (New Trans.).

Verse 9 therefore shows that we are to act upon the principle so wisely adopted by the steward; verse 10 shows that we are to wholly differ from him in this, that what he did in unfaithfulness we are to do in all good fidelity. The "unrighteous mammon," which men struggle to obtain so earnestly, and often so dishonestly, is after all "that which is least." It is not properly ours at all but "another man's," inasmuch as "the earth is the Lord's and the fulness thereof." But there is "the true" mammon, which the Lord speaks of as, "that which is your own." If we truly realize that our own things are those which we have in Christ, we shall use all that we have in this life—money, time, opportunities, mental powers—with a view to our Master's interests. At all events, we cannot serve two masters. Either God or mammon will dominate us. Let us see to it that God dominates us.

Though all this was said to the disciples, there were Pharisees listening and they openly mocked Him. To their covetous minds such teaching was ridiculous. They were great sticklers for the law, and the law had never stipulated things like these. The Lord's answer to them was twofold. First, they were all for that which was outward before the eyes of men, merely concerning themselves with that which men esteemed. They ignored the God who is concerned with the state of men's hearts, and whose thoughts are wholly opposed to men's. Ultimately God's thoughts will be established and men's thoughts overthrown.

But second, the law in which they boasted was being superseded by the kingdom of God. The law had stipulated the things necessary for man's life on earth, and the prophets had predicted God's coming kingdom on earth. The time of the visible, world-wide kingdom was not yet, but nevertheless it was being introduced in another form by preaching, and already in this spiritual form men were beginning to press into it. The Pharisees were blind to all this, and were staying outside. But, though the law was being superseded in this way, not one tittle of it was going to fail. In its own domain it stands in all its majesty. It is "holy, just and good," and its moral enactments still remain. The particular enactment which the Lord emphasized in verse 18, was no doubt a tremendous thrust at the Pharisees, who were very slack in such matters, while busily occupied with their tithes of mint and anise and cummin.

This home-thrust was followed by the tremendous parable of verses 19-31, if indeed it is a parable. The Lord uses a few figurative expressions such as "Abraham's bosom," but He relates it all as fact. Verses 19-22 relate very ordinary facts of this life ending in death and burial, and there for us the curtain drops. As we begin verse 23 the Lord lifts the curtain and brings into our view the things which lie beyond.

# LUKE

The rich man acted on precisely the opposite principle to the steward at the beginning of the chapter. All that he had he used for selfish, present enjoyment and he left the future to care for itself. The Lord is not inveighing against riches, but against man's selfish use of riches without God. The rich man was all for the present, all for this world; God's kingdom was nothing to him.

The word Jesus used for "hell" here is *hades;* not the lake of fire, but the unseen world of the departed. He therefore shows us that even *that* is for the unsaved a place of torment. Four times over does He state that *hades* is a place of torment.

He also shows that once the soul enters *hades* no change is possible. The "great gulf" is "fixed." No transference from torment to blessedness is possible. No "larger hope" is here.

The rich man became quite evangelistic in hell. He desired his brethren to have a supernatural visitation to stop them reaching that awful place. The Lord shows us that no such supernatural event, were it possible, would stop people, if they are not stopped by the Word of God.

Today God is appealing to men by the New Testament as well as by Moses and the prophets, and in the New Testament is the record of the One who rose from the dead. If men reject the Bible, which is the full Word of God for today, nothing will persuade them, and they will reach the place of torment.

Oh, that a God-given conviction of this may possess us! Then, the "love of God our Saviour toward man" also possessing our hearts, we should be full of zeal for the souls of men. We should be more like Joseph Alleine, one of the devoted men ejected from their livings under the Act of Uniformity, who was said to be, "insatiably greedy of the conversion of precious souls!" And we should have the zeal for the souls of men while still it is the accepted time and the day of salvation.

## Chapter 17

THE LATTER PART of the previous chapter, verse 14 to the end, was spoken to the Pharisees: at the beginning of this chapter the Lord again addresses His disciples. The rich man had stumbled over his possessions into hell, and now the Lord tells His disciples that, the world being what it is, "offences," or occasions of stumbling are inevitable. The great thing is to avoid being an "offence" to anyone else, to even the least important. The consequences are so serious that anything is better than that.

Yet this does not mean that we should never speak to our brother for fear of stumbling him. The very opposite: if he should go astray into sin, we are to rebuke him, and immediately he repents forgive him; and this, even if it should repeatedly happen. We might imagine that we should run the risk of stumbling him by rebuking him, but we should really do so by

# LUKE

*not* rebuking him. It is of course assumed that the rebuke is administered not in human anger but in the power of Divine love.

Teaching such as this made the disciples feel that they needed to have their faith increased. The Lord's reply seems to infer that it is not a question of the *quantity* of faith but of its *vitality*. A mustard seed is very small but it is alive! Live faith accomplishes results of a supernatural order. Many a time have heavy paving stones been forced up by tender sprouts, proceeding from live seeds embedded beneath them. Even vegetable life has powers which appear miraculous, and much more so faith which is living. Nevertheless no faith that we have and no service that we render gives us any kind of claim upon God. We can never accomplish more than it was our duty to do. This seems to be the truth inculcated in verses 7-10.

The Lord was now on His way to Jerusalem, and we come to the touching incident concerning the ten lepers. All of them had some measure of faith in Him, for they appealed to Him as Master and they obeyed His direction to go to the priests, in spite of the fact that there was at the moment no change in their condition. Yet when the cleansing reached them nine of them continued their journey to the priests, so as to complete their ceremonial cleansing at the earliest moment. Only one deferred the ceremonial part in order to give the first place to his Benefactor. The Jewish mind was more bound by what was ceremonial: the poor Samaritan was free to render praise and thanksgiving to the Saviour in the first place and receive his ceremonial cleansing afterwards. Sovereign mercy had been dispensed, and he got lifted above the customs of the law by a glimpse of the Person who dispensed the mercy. In result he got the assurance of being made whole from the Lord's own lips, with the acknowledgement that his faith had been the instrument of it. This was worth far more than any assurance he could get from the priests. Intelligent faith always puts Christ first.

In verses 20 and 21, Luke sets the obtuse unbelief of the Pharisees in contrast with the faith of the Samaritan. They only thought of the kingdom of God arriving with outward show, so as to be observed of all. The Lord told them that it was not at that time coming in that way, but that already it was amongst them, inasmuch as He—the King—was in their midst. The kingdom was amongst them for He was amongst them. The Pharisees were quite blind to this, but the Samaritan had evidently got a sight of it, hence his hurried return to give thanks at His feet.

In verse 22, Jesus again turns to His disciples, speaking of "the days of the Son of Man," and of course it is the Son of Man who is to take the kingdom, when the hour does arrive for its public establishment, as had long before been made known in Daniel 7: 13, 14. Now they, like the Samaritan, had faith and already saw the power and authority of God vested in the Lord Jesus. They would also in due season see the Son of Man revealed in His glory, and of this verse 30 speaks as well as verse 24. But meanwhile His rejection was going to supervene, and the sayings reported to the end of the chapter were evidently addressed to them as representing saints who should be here until the time in which He is revealed in glory. Many there have been who have desired to see one of His days, and have not seen it.

As the time of His advent approaches two things will become prominent. First, there will be much activity on the part of the powers of evil. Imposters will present themselves in this place and in that, as verse 23 indicates. Second, there will be on the part of men generally absorption with the things of earth. In the days of Noah and of Lot men were absorbed in their pleasures, their business and their schemes; consequently judgment caught them unawares and they all perished. Thus it will be in the day of the revelation of the Son of Man.

The great thought embodied in verse 33 occurs no less than six times in the Gospels, and the Lord seems to have uttered it on four different occasions. The context here makes it very striking. Men immerse themselves in the things of earth seeking to save their lives. In result they only lose them. The believer is to let go these things in favour of the far greater things that are revealed to him. He preserves his life, as will be very manifest when the Lord comes. Lot's wife illustrated this principle. The angels pulled her body out of Sodom, but her heart was still there. She lost everything, and her own life as well. We do well to remember her.

Those who are on earth when the Lord comes will do well to remember her also. If they do they will not think of attempting to retrieve their stuff from the house, or to return from their field. That day will come with the swiftness of an eagle's swoop. Just as the eagles congregate wherever their prey is found, so the judgment of God will reach all who are subject to it. The kingdom, when established, will be marked by discriminating judgment against evil. The sinner will be taken in judgment, and the righteous left to enjoy the blessing, no matter how closely they have been associated together. Had the Pharisees realized that the public establishment of the kingdom would involve this, they might not have wished to raise the question as to when it would come.

It is worthy of note that the three cases mentioned by the Lord in verses 34-36, suppose night-time, early morning and full day-time respectively. When He comes men will be instantaneously arrested in all parts of the earth, just as they are.

## Chapter 18

IN SPEAKING THE parable, with which this chapter opens, the Lord was continuing the same line of thought, as is shown by His application of the parable in verses 7 and 8. When the kingdom arrives it will mean judgment for the evil-doers, but the days just before its arrival will mean tribulation for saints. Their resource will be prayer. Even an unjust judge will be moved to right the wrongs of a widow, if she is sufficiently importunate; so the saint may continue waiting upon God with the assurance of being heard in due season.

There is not the smallest doubt about the coming of the Son of Man to answer the cries of His elect. The only doubt is as to faith being found in lively exercise amongst them. The Lord asked the question, "Shall He find faith on the earth?" but He did not answer it. The inference seems to be that faith will be at a low ebb, which agrees with His own plain statement elsewhere that, "the love of many shall wax cold." If we are right in believing that the end of the age draws very near, we shall do well to take this very much to heart, and stir ourselves up to faith and prayer. Only if we *always* pray shall we *not* faint.

The man who prays trusts in God. The trouble with so many is that they trust in themselves and in their own righteousness. To these the next parable is addressed. The Pharisee and the publican are typical men. The Lord takes for granted that God's grace, which brings justification for men, was available, but shows that all depends on the attitude of the one who needs it. The Pharisee exactly represents the elder son of chapter 15, the rich man of chapter 16, the unrepentant thief of chapter 23. The publican represents the younger son, Lazarus, and the repentant thief.

With the Pharisee it was himself, his character, his deeds. With the publican, the confession of sin, and of his need of propitiation — the word translated, "be merciful," is literally, "be propitious." How full of significance is verse 13! His *position:* "afar off," indicating he knew he had no right to draw hear. His *attitude:* not lifting "his eyes unto heaven,"— heaven was no place for such a man as he. His *action:* "smote upon his breast," thus confessing that he was the man who deserved to be smitten. *His words:* "me, *the* sinner," for it is *the* rather than *a* here. The Pharisee had said, "I am not as other men," smiting other men rather than himself. The publican hit the right man, and humbling himself was blessed.

How strikingly all this fits in with the special theme of this Gospel. Grace was there in abundance in the perfect Son of Man, but except there be on our side the humble and repentant spirit, we miss all that it offers.

The next incident, which Luke relates briefly in verses 15-17, enforces just the same thing. Mere babes do not count in the world's scheme of things, but of such the kingdom is composed. It is not, as we should have thought, that the babe must reach up to full-grown estate to enter, but that the full-grown man must reach down to the babe's estate to enter. The former might have suited the law of Moses, but grace is in question here.

Again the next incident, concerning the rich young ruler, lays its emphasis on the same point. The Lord had just spoken of *receiving* the kingdom as a little child, when the ruler asks, "What shall *I do* to inherit eternal life?" His mind swung back to the works of the law, not knowing what Paul tells us in Romans 4: 4, "To him that worketh is the reward not reckoned of grace, but of debt." Approaching on this basis, the Lord referred him to the Law, as regards his duty to his neighbour, and on his claiming to have complied from his youth up, He tested him further as to his relation to Himself. "Come, follow Me." Who is this *Me*? That was the supreme question, on which everything hinged, whether for the ruler or for ourselves.

The ruler had addressed Him as "Good Master," and this complimentary epithet the Lord had refused apart from the acknowledgment that He was God. In truth He *was* God, and He *was* good, and He presented Himself to the young man, bidding him relinquish what he possessed and follow Him—just as Levi had done some time before. Even the law demanded that God should be loved with all the heart. Did the ruler love God thus? Did he recognize God in the lowly Jesus? Alas, he did not. He might claim to have kept commandments relating to his neighbour; he utterly broke down when the first of all the commandments was in question. In his eyes his riches had in them greater value than Jesus.

With great difficulty does a rich man enter into the kingdom of God, since it is so difficult to have riches without the heart becoming absorbed by them to the exclusion of God. To those who thought of riches as tokens of God's favour all this seemed very disturbing, but the truth is that salvation is impossible to man, yet possible to God. This brings us back to the point which is in question. The kingdom cannot be earned, much less eternal life. All must be received as gifts from God. And if, in receiving the gift, other things are surrendered, there is an abundant recompense both now and in the world to come.

This saying of our Lord, recorded in verses 29 and 30, is a very sweeping one. In the *present* time there is *manifold more* for *everyone* who has given up good things of earth for the sake of the kingdom. Any difficulty we may have in understanding this is based upon our failure to appraise rightly the spiritual favours which make up the "manifold more." Paul illustrates that saying for us. Read Philippians 3, and see how he reckoned up the spiritual wealth poured into his bosom after he had "suffered the loss of all things." Like a camel stripped of every rag it had carried, he had passed through the needle gate, only to find himself loaded with favours on the other side.

All this would sound very strange to the Jewish mind, but the fact, which explained it all, was that the Son of Man was not at this time going to take the kingdom, but rather to go up to Jerusalem to die. So again at this point Jesus spoke of the death which was just before Him. The prophets had indicated that this was the way in which He would enter into His glory, though the disciples failed to understand it. And even though He thus again instructed them, they failed to take it in. Such is the power that preconceived notions can attain over the mind.

# LUKE

The Lord was now on His final journey to Jerusalem, and He approached Jericho for the last time. The blind man intercepted Him in faith. The crowd told him that Jesus of Nazareth was passing by, yet he at once addressed Him as the Son of David, and asked for mercy. The rich ruler had asked what he should *do*, when the Lord had just spoken of the kingdom being *received*. The blind beggar said that he would *receive* when the Lord enquired what *He should do to him*. No transaction came to pass in the case of the ruler: a transaction was completed on the spot in the case of the beggar. The contrast between the two cases is very decisive.

The beggar received his sight, and, said the Lord, "Thy faith hath saved thee." This shows that the transaction went deeper than the opening of the eyes of his head. He became a follower of the Jesus, who was going up to Jerusalem and to the cross; and there was glory to God, both on his part and on the part of all the beholders. An equally distinct case of spiritual blessing met the Lord when He entered and passed through Jericho.

If, at this point, Luke's Gospel be compared with Matthew 20: 29-34, and Mark 10: 46-52, a serious discrepancy becomes evident. Luke most definitely places the cure of the blind man as Jesus *approached* Jericho, and the other two Evangelists as definitely place it as He *left* Jericho. With our limited knowledge it seemed impossible on this point to reconcile the different accounts. But during the last few years the archaeologists have been digging in the Jericho area, and have laid bare the foundations of two Jerichos; one, the old original city, the other, the Roman Jericho, a short distance off. The blind man understood the begging business and planted himself between the two! Luke writing for Gentiles, naturally has the Roman Jericho in his mind. The other Evangelists very naturally are thinking of the original city. We mention this to show how very simply what looks like an insuperable objection vanishes, when we know all the facts.

## Chapter 19

ONLY LUKE TELLS us about the conversion of Zacchaeus, which fits in so strikingly with the theme of his Gospel. The publican, though so despised by the leaders of his people, was a fit subject for the grace of the Lord, and he was marked by the faith which is ready to receive it. Zacchaeus had no physical or material needs; his was a case of spiritual need only. The people flung the epithet, "sinner," at him. It was a true epithet, and Zacchaeus knew it, yet it provoked him into an attempt to accredit himself by recounting his benevolences and scrupulous honesty. Jesus however put his blessing on its proper basis by proclaiming him to be a son of Abraham—that is, a true child of faith—and Himself to be the One come to seek and save that which was lost. Zacchaeus was in himself a lost man, yet he was a believer, and so salvation reached him that day. On exactly the same basis has it reached every one of us since that day.

## LUKE

The Lord had shown the Pharisees that the kingdom was already in their midst in His own Person; He had also again told His disciples about His impending death and resurrection. Yet they still cherished expectations as to the immediate appearing of the kingdom in glory. So the Lord added the parable, of verses 11-27, as a further corrective to these thoughts of theirs. The time of the kingdom would come, when all His enemies would be destroyed; but first comes a period of His absence, when the faithfulness and diligence of His servants would be tested. To each servant the same sum is entrusted, so that the difference in the result sprang from their diligence and skill, or otherwise. According to their diligence they were rewarded in the day of the kingdom. The servant, who did nothing, only showed that he did not really know his Master. In result, he not only had no reward but he suffered loss.

This is another reminder that grace calls us into a place of responsibility and service, and that our place in the kingdom will depend upon the diligence with which we have used that with which we have been entrusted.

Having spoken the parable of the pounds, the Lord led His disciples on the ascent towards Jerusalem, and reaching Bethphage and Bethany He sent for the ass colt, on which He made His entry to the city, according to the prophecy of Zechariah. The colt was unbroken for no man had sat upon it, and consequently it was tied up under restraint. It was loosed from restraint, but only in order that He might sit upon it. Under His powerful hand it was perfectly restrained. A parable this, of how grace sets us free from the bondage of the law.

Though the kingdom was not at this time to be established in glory, He did in this way most definitely present Himself to Jerusalem as its rightful and God-sent King. His disciples assisted in this, and as they approached the city they began to praise God and rejoice. We are told quite plainly in John 12: 16 that at that time they did not really understand what they were doing, yet it is evident that the Spirit of God took possession of their lips and guided them in their words. They acclaimed Him as the King, and they spoke of "peace in heaven, and glory in the highest."

At the incarnation the angels had celebrated "on earth peace," for the Man of God's good pleasure had appeared, and they celebrated the whole result of His work. But now it was clear that death lay before Him and that His rejection would entail a period of anything but peace on earth. Nevertheless the first effect of His work on the cross would be to establish peace in the highest Court of all—in heaven—and to display glory in the highest, Himself going up there in triumph. This note of praise had to be struck at this juncture. God could have made the stones cry out, but instead He used the lips of the disciples, though they uttered the words without full intelligence of their meaning.

Now comes a striking contrast. As they approached the city the disciples rejoiced and shouted blessings on the King. The King Himself wept over the city! In John 11: 35, the word used indicates silent tears; here the word used indicates breaking forth in lamentation, visible and audible. The lament of Jehovah over Israel, as recorded in Psalm 81: 13, reappears here, only greatly accentuated as they approached the greatest of all their terrible sins. Jerusalem did not know the things that belonged to her peace, hence peace on earth was impossible at that time, and the Lord foresaw and predicted her violent destruction at the hands of the Romans, which came to pass forty years later. The Dayspring from on high had visited them, and they did not know the time of their visitation.

As a consequence, everything in Jerusalem was in disorder. Entering the city, the Lord went straight to its very centre, and in the temple found evil enthroned. The house of Jehovah, intended to be an house of prayer for all nations, was just a den of thieves, so that any stranger, coming up there as a seeker after God, was swindled in the obtaining of the necessary sacrifices. Thereby he would be repelled from the true God instead of being attracted to Him. Thus in the hands of men the house of God had been wholly perverted from its proper use. Moreover the men who held authority in the house were potentially murderers, as verse 47 shows: so it had become a stronghold of murderers as well as a den of thieves. Could anything be much worse than this? No wonder God swept it away by the Romans forty years later!

## Chapter 20

YET IN THE precincts of the temple the Lord taught daily during this last week of His life, so it is not surprising that He came into conflict with them. The whole of this chapter is occupied with details of the conflict. The chief priest and scribes began the conflict, and at the end they were left silenced and unmasked.

They started by challenging His authority. They were the people in authority there, and to them He was but an upstart "Prophet" from Nazareth. Their question assumed that they had the ability to judge of the Lord's credentials, if He produced them; so He called upon them to settle the preliminary question as to the credentials of His forerunner, John. This at once put them in a quandary, for the answer they wished to give would have been resented by the people. They were time-servers, courting popularity, so they pleaded ignorance. To such men as these the Lord did not produce His authority. Instead He proceeded to speak with all the authority which omniscience gives, and they were very soon made to feel its power. There could be no doubt about His authority by the time the verbal conflict ceased.

In the parable, which occupies verses 9-16, He set forth with great clearness the exact position of things at that moment. It reads like a continuation of the historical statements made in 2 Chronicles 36: 15, 16. There it was

# LUKE

God appealing by His "messengers, rising up betimes and sending;" but all were mocked and misused until "there was no remedy," and "He brought upon them the king of the Chaldees." Here the story is carried a step further and the "Beloved Son" is sent, only to be cast out and killed. Hence a worse chastisement than the Chaldeans was to come upon them. The Psalmist had prophesied that the rejected "Stone" should become the Head of the corner, and Jesus added that all, who fall upon that Stone, or upon whom it shall fall, would be destroyed. They were at that moment stumbling on the Stone, as Romans 9: 32 declares. The falling of the Stone upon them, and upon the Gentile powers, will take place at the Second Advent, as Daniel 2: 34 shows.

The chief priests and scribes felt the point and authority of His words, as we see in verse 19, but they were only thereby stirred up to more determined opposition; and they sent forth men of craft and deceit to entrap Him in His words, if possible. They came with the question as to paying tribute to Cæsar; and in this both Pharisees and Herodians united, sinking their animosities in common hatred of the Lord.

The Lord's question, "Why tempt ye Me?" showed that He was thoroughly aware of their craft. His request for the penny reveals His own poverty. The superscription on the penny was a witness to their subjection to Cæsar. His reply thus was that they must render to Cæsar his rights, and yield to God the rights that were His. It was because they had not rendered to God the things that were His that Cæsar had acquired the rights of conquest over them. All this was so indubitable, when pointed out, that these crafty questioners were silenced.

The question with which the Sadducees thought to entrap the Lord was founded upon ignorance. No doubt they had often perplexed the Pharisees with it, but then they had no more light than the Sadducees on the essential point which the Lord made so plain. He contrasted "this world" and "that world," using really the word which means "age." Now it will be the portion of some to "obtain that age" as living men on earth, without passing through death and resurrection; but those who "obtain that age *and the resurrection*" will enter upon altogether new conditions of life. They will be deathless as the angels, and marriage will have no application to them. The Lord was here beginning to bring "to light life and incorruptibility" (2 Tim. 1: 10. N.Tr.); and in result the Sadducees' question, which to their ignorance seemed so unanswerable, became merely ridiculous.

The Lord proceeded to prove the resurrection from Exodus 3: 6. If the patriarchs were alive to God, centuries after they were dead to this world, their ultimate resurrection was a certainty. Thus He answered not only the foolish question of the Sadducees, but the unbelief that lay behind their question. And He answered it with such authority that even a scribe was moved to admiration and approval, and they all feared to ask Him any more questions.

# LUKE

The Lord then asked them His great question, based upon Psalm 110. Matthew records that no man was able to answer Him a word. No answer was possible save to the faith that perceived the Divine glory of the Christ, and they had no faith. They were silent in stubborn unbelief. Answer His question they *could* not: ask Him any further question they *dared* not.

It only remained for the Lord to unmask these evil men, and this He did in few words, as recorded in the two verses which close the chapter. They were hypocrites of the most desperate type, using religion as a cloak to cover their self-seeking and rapacity. He unmasked them, and pronounced their doom. He did not speak of a *longer* damnation, as though judgment were bounded by time and not eternal. But He did speak of *greater* damnation, showing that judgment will differ as to its severity. They suffer "more abundant judgment" (N.Tr.).

## Chapter 21

THEN HE LOOKED up, and here were some of these rich men ostentatiously casting their money into the temple treasury, and amongst them came a poor widow casting in her two mites. We must not allow the break of the chapters to divorce in our minds these opening verses from the closing two of chapter 20. The widow was presumably one of those whose "house" had been devoured, yet instead of repining, she cast her last two mites into the temple treasury. Under these circumstances her gift was truly a great one, and the Lord pronounced it to be so. She went to the utmost limit; casting in her *all*.

Nor must we divorce this touching incident from the verses that follow, particularly verse 6. The widow expressed her devotion to God by casting her two mites into the collection for the upkeep of the temple fabric; yet the Lord proceeds to foretell its total destruction. Already it was displacde by the presence of the Lord. God was in Christ, not in Herod's temple. In her understanding the widow was, as we should say, behind the times; yet this did not mar the Lord's approval of her gift. Whole-hearted devotion He *does* appreciate, even if the expression of it is not marked by complete intelligence. This should be a great comfort to us.

Luke now gives us the Lord's prophetic discourse, putting on record that part of it which specially answered the disciples' question, as recorded in verse 7. As Matthew's account shows, both their question and the Lord's answer contained in them a good deal more than Luke puts on record. Here the question is as to the time of the overthrow of the temple, and the sign of it. The answer divides itself into two parts: verses 8-24, events that led up to the destruction and treading down of Jerusalem by the Romans, verses 25-33, the appearing of the Son of Man at the end of the age.

It is very noticeable how the Lord presents the whole matter not as a mass of details, appealing to our curiosity, but as predictions which sound

# LUKE

a note of warning, and convey instructions of the utmost importance to His disciples. Everything is stated in a way to appeal to our consciences and not our curiosity.

The first part of the discourse, verses 8-19, is occupied with very personal instructions to the disciples. The Lord does indeed make predictions. He foretells (1) the rising up of false Christs, (2) wars and commotions, together with abnormal happenings in the physical world around, (3) the coming of bitter opposition and persecution, even unto death. But in each case His disciples are to be forearmed by His warnings. They are not for one moment to be deceived by false Christs, or follow them. They are not to be afraid of the violent movements of men, nor imagine that these convulsions mean that the end is coming *immediately*—for that is what "by and by" means here. They are to accept the persecution as an occasion for testimony, and in testifying are not to rely on a prepared defence but on supernatural wisdom to be granted to them when the moment arrives.

Verse 18 is evidently intended to convey the personal and intimate way in which God would care for them. The closing words of verse 16 show it does not mean that all of them would escape; but even if death claimed them, all would be made good in resurrection. By patient endurance they would win through, whether in life or in death. This seems to be the meaning of verse 19. We can see in the Acts how these things were fulfilled in the Apostles.

Then, verses 20-24, He predicts the desolation of Jerusalem. No word appears here as to the setting up of "the abomination of desolation," for that is only to happen at the end of the times of the Gentiles: all the things the Lord specifies were fulfilled when Jerusalem was destroyed by the Romans. *Then* the city was compassed with armies. *Then* those who believed the words of Jesus did flee to the mountains, and so escaped the horrors of the siege. *Then* there commenced "days of vengeance" for the Jew, which will not cease for them until all that is predicted is fulfilled. *Then* started the long captivity which has persisted, and will persist, with Jerusalem under the feet of the nations, until the times of the Gentiles are ended. Those times began when God raised up Nebuchadnezzar, who dispossessed the last king of David's line, and they will be ended by the crushing of Gentile dominion at the appearing of Christ.

Consequently verse 25 carries us right on to the time of the end, and speaks of things which will just precede His advent. There will be signs in the heavenly regions, and on earth distress and perplexity; "sea and waves" being expressions figurative of the masses of mankind in a state of violent unrest and agitation. In result men will be "ready to die through fear and expectation of what is coming" (N.Tr.). In view of the state of things that prevails on earth as we write, it is not difficult for us to conceive the condition of things which the Lord thus predicts.

# LUKE

This is the moment when God is going to shake the heavens as well as the earth, as Haggai predicted; and when only things which cannot be shaken will remain. All will lead up to the public appearing of the Son of Man in power and great glory. The day of His poverty will be over, as well as the day of His patience; and the day of His power, of which Psalm 110 speaks, will have fully arrived. Previous to His coming, the hearts of unconverted men will be filled with fear: when He has come, their worst fears will be realized, and "all kindreds of the earth shall wail because of Him" (Rev. 1: 7).

But to His saints His coming will wear another aspect, as verse 28 makes happily manifest. For them it means a final redemption, when all creation will be delivered from the bondage of corruption. That being so, the first signs of His advent are to fill us with glad anticipation. We are to "look up," for the next movement that really counts is to come from the right hand of God, where He sits. We are to "lift up our heads," the opposite of hanging them down in depression or fear. The very things that frighten the world are to fill the believer with the optimism of holy expectation.

Next comes the short parable of the fig tree. It is said to be "a parable," you notice, not a mere illustration. The fig tree stands for the Jew nationally. For centuries he has been dead nationally, and when at last there are signs of national reviving with them, and signs of reviving too with other "trees," of ancient nationalities, we may know that the millennial "summer" is near. Until that time comes there shall be no passing away of "this generation"—by this term the Lord indicated, we believe, that "froward generation . . . in whom is no faith," of which Moses spoke in Deuteronomy 32: 5, 20. When the kingdom is established, that generation will be gone.

Luke's short account of the Lord's prophecy ends with the solemn words in which He asserted the truth and reliability of His words. Every word of His lips has something in it, something to be fulfilled, and is more stable than the heavens and the earth. Thus verse 33 furnishes the striking thought that the words of His lips are more enduring than the works of His fingers.

He closed with another appeal to the consciences of His disciples, and our consciences as well. No doubt those three verses, 34, 35, 36, have special application to saints who will be on earth just before His appearing, but they have a great voice for the believer today. A multiplicity of pleasures surrounds us, and we may easily become over-charged with a surfeit of them. On the other hand, there were never more and greater dangers on the horizon, and our hearts may be laden with forebodings, so that we lose sight of the day that is coming. It is very possible to be occupied so much with the doings of dictators and the progress of world movements that the coming of the Lord is obscured in our minds. The word for us is, "Watch ye therefore, and pray always." Then shall we be thoroughly awake, and ready to greet the Lord when He comes.

# LUKE

In the closing verses of the chapter, Luke reminds us that He, who thus foretold His coming again, was still the rejected One. By day, during that last week, He diligently uttered the word of God: at night, having no home, He abode on the Mount of Olives.

## CHAPTER 22

AS WE COMMENCE to read this chapter, we reach the closing scenes of our Lord's life. The Passover was not only a standing witness to Israel's deliverance from Egypt but also a type of the great Sacrifice which was yet to come. Now at last the climax approached, and "Christ our Passover" was to be sacrificed for us precisely at the Passover season. The religious leaders were scheming how they might kill Him in spite of the fact that many of the people viewed Him with favour. Satan inspired their hatred, and Satan it was who presented them with a tool wherewith to carry out their wishes.

John, in his Gospel, unmasks Judas for us before the end is reached. In his twelfth chapter he tells us that, consumed with covetousness, he had become a thief. He also tells us in his thirteenth chapter the exact moment at which Satan entered into him. Luke relates that dreadful fact in a more general way; and it shows that the prince of the powers of darkness considered that to encompass the death of Christ was a task of such importance that it should be delegated to no lesser power: he would take charge of the business himself. Yet he undertook the work to his own overthrow. The compact between Judas and the religious leaders was easily settled. They were consumed with *envy*, and Judas with *the love of money*.

For many centuries the Passover had been observed with more or less faithfulness, it was now, *in its full significance*, to be observed for the last time. Within twenty-four hours its light grew pale in the shining of its Antitype, when the true Lamb of God died on the cross. It is a remarkable fact that the last time it was celebrated in its full significance, there was present to partake of it the One who instituted it—the perfect, holy Man, who was Jehovah's Fellow. He ordered the Passover to be prepared, and He decided the very place where they should eat it. The time, the manner, the place, were all His appointment. The choice lay not with the disciples but with Him, as verse 9 shows.

The Lord's foreknowledge is strikingly displayed in verse 10. Carrying the water was the task of the women; a man bearing a pitcher of water was a very uncommon sight. Yet He knew that there would be a man performing this unusual act, and that Peter and John would meet him as they entered the city. He knew also that the "goodman of the house" would respond to the message delivered by the disciples in the name of "the Master." Doubtless he recognized *the* Master as being *his* Master; in other words, he was one of the godly in Jerusalem who acknowledged His claims, and the Lord knew how to lay His hand upon him. This man had

# LUKE

the privilege of furnishing a guest-chamber for the use of the One who had no chamber of His own, and when the hour was come He sat down with His disciples.

In the account which Luke gives, the distinction between the Passover Supper and the Supper which He instituted is very clear: verses 15-18 give the one, and verses 19, 20 the other. The Lord's words as to the Passover indicate the closing up of that old order of things. His sufferings would mean its fulfilment, and when a spared remnant of Israel enters at last into the blessedness of the millennium, it will be as sheltered by the blood of Christ. As to the cup (verse 17), this does not appear to have been any part of the Passover as instituted through Moses, and the Lord apparently did not drink of it. Instead, He indicated that His day of joy, which the fruit of the vine symbolized, would only be reached in the coming kingdom.

Then He instituted His own Supper in remembrance of His death; the bread symbolizing His body, the cup, His shed blood. The account is very brief, and, for the full significance of it all, we have to go to 1 Corinthians 10 and 11. *Remembrance,* was what the Lord emphasized at the moment, and in view of His long absence we can see the importance of this. Through the centuries the memorial of His death has been with us, and the abiding witness of His love.

The verses which follow (21-27) witness to the folly and the feebleness which was found amongst the disciples. The hand of the betrayer was on the table, and He knew it, though the rest of the disciples were quite unaware of it. There was also strife amongst them, each wishing for the foremost place, and this just as their great Master was about to take the lowest place. Such, alas! is the heart of man, even of saints. It served however to bring out very clearly the fundamental difference between the disciple and the world. *Worldly* greatness is expressed and maintained by taking a *lordly place: Christian* greatness is found in taking a *servant's place.* In that greatness Jesus Himself was pre-eminent. Few words are more touching than this—"I am among you as he that serveth." Such had been His life of perfect grace; and such, in supreme measure, His death was about to be.

It is also most touching to observe how He spoke to the disciples in verses 28-30. They were indeed foolish, and their spirit far astray from His, yet with what graciousness He brought into the light the good feature that had characterized them. They were firmly attached to Him. In spite of His temptations, culminating in His rejection, they had continued with Him. This He would never forget, and there would be an abundant recompense in the kingdom. In the coming day He will take up the kingdom *for* His His Father, and take it up *by* His saints, and these disciples of His will have a very special place of prominence. In the light of this gracious pronouncement they must surely have felt how mean and sordid had been their previous strife for a great place. And, *may we feel the same.*

# LUKE

Next, verses 31-34, comes the Lord's special warning to Peter. At this moment he was thinking and acting in the flesh, so Jesus used his name according to the flesh, and His repetition of it conveyed the urgency of His warning. Self-confidence marked him as well as desire for pre-eminence, and this laid him open to Satan: yet the Lord's intercession would prevail, and there was wheat there and not chaff only. This wheat would remain when the winnowing was passed.

The four verses which follow, 35-38, were addressed to all the disciples. They had to bear witness that they had possessed an absolute sufficiency as the fruit of His power, though sent without any human resources; and He intimated that with His death and departure another order of things would supervene. Men would reckon Him among the transgressors in this world, but the things concerning Him had an end in another world. He would be exalted to glory, and His disciples left as His witnesses, having to resume the ordinary circumstances of this world. Their response to these words showed that they were likely to miss the spirit of what He said, by seizing upon one literal detail; so for the moment He left it.

Thus far it has been the dealings of His *love* with His own; now we see the *perfection* of His Manhood displayed in Gethsemane. He faced, as before the Father, the full bitterness of that cup of judgment which He had to drink; and His full perfection is seen in that, while shrinking from it, He devoted Himself to the accomplishing of the Father's will, whatever it might cost Him. Luke, alone of the Evangelists, tells us of the appearance of the angel to strengthen Him. This emphasizes the reality of His Manhood, in keeping with the special character of this Gospel. So also His sweat being as great drops of blood is only mentioned in this Gospel. The horror of that which was before Him was entered into in communion with the Father.

With verse 47 the last scenes begin, and now all is *calmness* and *grace* with the Lord: all is *confusion* and *agitation* with His friends, His adversaries, and even with His judges. The *communion* in the garden led to the *calmness* in the great hour of trial. Judas reached the heights of hypocrisy in betraying his Master with a kiss. Peter used one of those two swords they had just alluded to, in ill-conceived and ill-directed violence. What he did in his violence the Lord promptly undid in His grace. The violence was to be left to the multitude with the swords and staves. It was their hour, and the hour in which the power of darkness was to be displayed. Against that dark background the Lord displayed His grace.

The account of Peter's fall follows. The way for it had been prepared by his previous desire for the first place, his self-confidence, and his violent action. Now he followed afar off, and soon got amongst the enemies of his Master. Satan set the trap with consummate skill. First the maid and then the other two servants pressed home their identification of him, leading

# LUKE

him to denials increasing in emphasis; though Luke does not tell us how he broke into curses and swearing. That after all was incidental; the essential thing was that he denied his Lord.

Precisely at that moment, just as Jesus had predicted, the cock crew; and then the Lord turned and looked upon him. Just what that look conveyed we may not know, but it spoke such volumes to the fallen disciple that he went out from the enemies of his Master with bitter tears. Judas was filled with remorse, but we do not read that he wept. Peter's bitter weeping was a witness that after all he did love his Lord, and that his faith was not going to fail. The prayer and the look were beginning to prove their efficacy.

This Gospel makes it clear that the trial of Jesus was divided into four parts. First, there was the examination before the chief priests and scribes, as they sought for some plausible pretext for condemning Him to death. The account of this fills the closing verses of the chapter, and it is given with brevity. It is made very plain however that they condemned Him on His own plain confession of who He was. They challenged Him as to being the Christ, and the Lord's answer showed that He knew they were fixed in their unbelief and in their determination to condemn Him. Still, He claimed to be the Son of Man, who should presently wield the very power of God, and this they interpreted as meaning that He must also claim to be the Son of God. This indeed He was, and His reply, "Ye say that I am," was an emphatic, "Yes." As claiming to be *the Christ, the Son of Man, the Son of God*, they condemned Him to death,

## CHAPTER 23

THEN SECOND, THEY led Him to Pilate to get the Roman sanction for the execution of this sentence. Here they changed their ground completely, and charged Him as being an insurrectionary and a rival to Caesar. Jesus confessed Himself to be *the King of the Jews*, yet Pilate declared Him to be faultless. This might seem a surprising declaration, but Mark gives us a peep behind the scenes when he tells us that Pilate knew that the fierce hatred of the religious leaders was inspired by envy. Hence he began by refusing to be the tool of their grudge, and availed himself of the Lord's connection with Galilee to send Him to Herod. The accusation, "He stirreth up the people," was indeed true; but He stirred them up towards God, and not against Caesar.

So, third, there was the brief appearance of the Lord before Herod, who was eager to see Him, hoping to witness something sensational. Here again the chief priests and scribes vehemently accused Him, but in the presence of that wicked man, whom He had previously characterized as, "that fox," Jesus answered nothing. His dignified silence only moved Herod and his soldiers to abandon all pretence of administering justice, and descend to mockery and ridicule. In His humiliation His judgment was taken away.

# LUKE

Hence Herod returned Him to Pilate, and here the fourth and last stage of His trial began. But before we are told of Pilate's further efforts to placate the accusers and release Jesus, Luke puts on record how both he and Herod buried their enmity that day in condemning Him. The same tragedy has been often repeated since. Men of wholly different character and view have found a point of unity in their rejection of Christ. Herod was given up to his pleasures and utterly indifferent: Pilate, though possessed of some sense of what was right, was a time-server and hence ready to do wrong for popularity's sake; but they came to an agreement here.

The story of the final scenes of the trial are given with brevity in verses 13-26. Not one word spoken by our Lord is put on record: all is presented as a matter lying between Pilate and the people instigated by the chief priests; yet certain things stand out very clearly. In the first place, abundant witness is given that *Jesus was faultless*. Pilate had stated this during the earlier examination (verse 4), and now he repeats it twice (verses 14, 22), and states it for a fourth time as being Herod's verdict (verse 15). God took care that there should be abundant and official witness to this.

Then the *blind unreasoning fury* of His accusers is made abundantly manifest. They merely shouted for his death. Again, the choice they made as an alternative to His release stands out with crystal clearness. Twice in these verses Barabbas is identified with *sedition and murder;* that is, he was the living embodiment of the two forms in which evil is so frequently presented in Scripture—corruption, and violence; or, to put it in another way, we see the power of Satan working, both as a serpent, and as a roaring lion. Lastly we see that the condemnation of Jesus was the result of the *weakness* of the judge, who "delivered Jesus to their will." He represented the autocratic power of Rome, but he abdicated it in favour of the will of the people.

The crucifixion scenes occupy verses 27-49. We are struck by the fact that right through nothing happened in an ordinary way. Everything was unusual — supernatural, or bordering upon the supernatural. It was quite usual for professional wailing women to appear on these occasions, but wholly unusual for them to be told to weep for themselves, or to hear a prophecy of coming doom. Jesus Himself was the "green tree," according to Psalm 1, and perhaps He was alluding to the parable of Ezekiel 20: 45-49. In that scripture God predicts a flame upon every green tree and every dry tree. Judgment fell upon the "green tree" when Christ suffered for our sakes. When the fire breaks out in the dry tree of apostate Jews, it will not be quenched.

Then the prayer of Jesus as they crucified Him was wholly unexpected and unusual. He desired the Father, in effect, that the sin of the people might be counted not as murder, for which there was no forgiveness, but as manslaughter, so that there might yet be available a city of refuge, even for His murderers. An answer to that prayer was seen some fifty days later,

# LUKE

when Peter in Jerusalem preached salvation through the risen Christ, and 3,000 souls fled for refuge. The prayer was unusual because it was the fruit of such Divine compassions as had never come to light before.

The actions of the various people involved in His crucifixion were unusual. Men do not ordinarily taunt and revile even the worst criminals undergoing capital punishment. Here all classes did so, even rulers, soldiers, and one of the malefactors who suffered at His side. The power of the devil and of darkness had seized their minds.

Pilate's superscription was unexpected. Having condemned Him as a false claimant of kingship amongst the Jews, he wrote a title proclaiming Him to be the King of the Jews, and, as another Gospel shows, he refused to alter it. This was the overruling of God.

The sudden conversion of the second thief was wholly supernatural. He condemned himself, and justified Jesus. Having justified Him, he owned Him as Lord and proclaimed—virtually, though not in so many words—his belief that God would raise him from the dead, so as to establish him in His kingdom. He fulfilled the two conditions of Romans 10:9, only he believed that God *would raise* Him from the dead, instead of believing, as we do, that God *has* raised Him from the dead. The faith of the dying thief was a gem of the first order, beside which our faith today loses its sparkle. It is much more remarkable to believe that a thing shall be done, when as yet it is not done, than to believe that a thing is done, when it is done. And further, it was most unusual that a malefactor should wish to be *remembered* by the King, when His kingdom was established. Malefactors usually slink into the dark and wish to be forgotten by the authorities. His wish to be remembered shows his faith in *the grace of the suffering Lord* equalled his faith in *His coming glory*.

The response of Jesus to the thief's prayer was wonderful and unexpected indeed! Not merely in the coming kingdom but that very day he was to experience grace reaching beyond death, and landing his ransomed spirit into companionship with Christ in Paradise. Now Paradise and the third Heaven are identified in 2 Corinthians 12: 2-4. These words of the Lord were the first definite revelation of the fact that immediately death supervenes the spirits of the saints are to be in conscious blessedness *with Christ*.

If everything was unusual, on the human side, when Jesus died, there were also supernatural manifestations from the hand of God; and of these verses 44 and 45 speak. The three brightest hours of the day were darkened, by the sun being veiled. There was something very fitting in this, for the true "Sun of Righteousness" was bearing our sin at that time. Also the veil of the temple was rent by a Divine hand, signifying that the day of the visible temple system was now over, and the way into the holiest about to be made manifest—see, Hebrews 9: 8. Our true "Sun" *was veiled* for a moment, enduring our judgment, that there might be *no veil* between us and God.

## LUKE

Luke does not record the Saviour's cry as to the Divine forsaking, uttered about the time that the darkness passed away, nor the triumphant shout, "It is finished," though he does put on record that He "cried with a loud voice," and that then His closing words were, "Father, into Thy hands I commend My spirit." In these closing words on the cross we see the One, who all along had been marked by prayerful submission to the will of God, closing His path as the perfect, dependent Man. Having said this, He yielded up His spirit; yet we see He is more than Man, for at one moment there was the loud voice, His vigour unimpaired, and the next moment He was dead. In every sense His was a supernatural death.

Testimony to this was borne by the centurion who witnessed the scene by reason of his official duty. Even the crowds drawn together by morbid curiosity were moved to uneasy fear and foreboding, and those who were His friends retreated into the distance. The centurion became a fourth witness to the perfection of Jesus, joining Pilate, Herod and the dying thief.

The prophetic writings had said, "Lover and friend hast Thou put far from Me" (Psalm 88: 18); but they had also said, "He made His grave . . . with the rich in His death" (Isaiah 53: 9). If verse 49 gives us the fulfilment of the one, verses 50-53 give us the fulfilment of the other. In every emergency God has in reserve an instrument to effect His purpose and fulfil His word. Joseph is mentioned in all four Gospels, and John informs us that up to this point he had been a secret disciple for fear of the Jews. Now he acts with boldness when all others were cowed, and the new, untainted tomb is available for the sacred body of the Lord. Not even by the faintest contact did He "see corruption." Men had intended otherwise, but God serenely fulfilled His word.

### CHAPTER 24

THE CLOSING VERSES of chapter 23, and the opening part of this chapter makes it very plain that none of His disciples in any way anticipated His resurrection. This makes the testimony to it all the more pronounced and satisfying. They were not enthusiastic and visionary, inclined to believe anything, but rather of materialistic mind and despondent, inclined to doubt everything.

The women are brought before us in the first place. They had no thoughts but those suitable to an ordinary funeral. Their minds were occupied with the sepulchre, His body and the spices and ointments that were customary. The Jewish sabbath intervened however, and put a stop to their activities — this was of God, for their activities were wholly unnecessary, and by the time they could have resumed them, the sacred body was not to be found. Instead of the dead body they found two men in shining garments, and heard from their lips that the Lord was now "the living One" and not among the dead. So the first testimony to His resurrection came from the lips of angels. A second testimony was found in the words He Himself had spoken during His life. He had predicted His death, *and His resurrection.* When reminded of His words, they remembered them.

The women returned and told all these things to the eleven; that is, they presented to them the evidence of the angels, and of the Lord's own words, and of their own eyes, as to the body not being in the sepulchre; yet they did not believe. The modern sceptic might call these things "idle tales;" well, that was just how they appeared to the disciples. Peter however, with his usual impulsiveness, went a step further. He ran to the sepulchre to see for himself, and what he saw so far verified their words. Yet in his mind wonder rather than faith was excited.

Next we are carried on to the afternoon of the resurrection day, and Luke gives us in full what happened with the two going into the country, to which Mark just alludes in verses 12 and 13 of his last chapter. The incident gives us a very striking insight into the state of mind that characterized them—and doubtless they were typical of the rest.

Cleopas and his companions were evidently just drifting away from Jerusalem to the old home, utterly disappointed and dejected. They had entertained very fervent expectations which centred in the Messiah, and in Jesus they believed that they had found Him. To them Jesus of Nazareth was "a prophet mighty in deed and word before God and all the people;" and at that point evidently their faith stopped. They did not as yet perceive in Him the Son of God who could not be holden of death, and so to them His death was the mournful end of His story. They did think that "it had been He which should have redeemed Israel," but then that to them meant redeeming them by power from all their national foes, rather than redeeming them to God by His blood. His death had shattered their hopes of this redemption by power and by glory. This disappointment was the fruit of their having cherished expectations which were not warranted by the Word of God. They expected the glory without the sufferings.

Not a few believers may be found today who have drifted off into the world in rather similar fashion. They too have drifted because disappointed, and they are disappointed because of entertaining unwarranted expectations. The expectations may have been centred in Christian work, and the conquests of the Gospel, or in some particular group or body of believers with whom they were linked, or perhaps in themselves and their own personal sanctity and power. However, things have not happened as they expected, and they are in the depths of dejection.

This case of Cleopas will help in the diagnosis of their trouble. In the first place, like him they have some little "Israel," which engrosses their thoughts. Had Israel been redeemed, just as Cleopas had expected, he would have been in the seventh heaven of delight: as it was not so, he had lost his enthusiasm and interest. He had to learn that though Israel was right in the centre of the bright little picture that his fancy had painted, it was not in the centre of God's picture. *God's picture is the real one, and its centre is Christ risen from the dead.* When Jesus had joined Himself to them, drawn out their thoughts and gained their confidence, He opened up to them, not things concerning Israel, but "things concerning HIM-SELF." A certain cure for disappointment is to have Christ filling every picture that our minds entertain:—not work, even Christian work, not brethren, nor even the church, not self in any of its many forms, *but Christ.*

But there was a second thing. True, these unwarranted hopes of Cleopas, which led to his disappointment, had sprung from this thinking too much of Israel and too little of Christ; yet this wrong emphasis was the result of his *partial reading* of the Old Testament Scriptures. Verse 25 shows that their foolishness and the slowness of their hearts had led them to overlook some parts of the Scriptures. They believed *some* things that the prophets had spoken—those nice, plain, easy-to-be-understood things as to the glory of the Messiah—whilst they set on one side and passed over the predictions of His sufferings, which doubtless seemed to them to be mysterious, peculiar, and difficult to understand. The very things they had skipped were just what would have saved them from the painful experience through which they were passing.

In speaking to them, three times did the Lord emphasize the importance of *all* Scripture — see verses 25 and 27. He so dealt with them as to make them see that His death and resurrection were the appointed basis of all the glory which is yet to come. "Ought not Christ to have suffered these things . . . ?" Yes, *indeed He ought!* And as He ought, *so had He done!*

What a walk that must have been! At the close of it they could not bear the thought of a separation from this unexpected "Stranger," and they besought Him to abide. Going in to tarry with them, He of necessity took the place which is ever intrinsically His. He must be Host and Leader and also the Blesser; and then their eyes were opened and they knew Him. What joy for their hearts when suddenly they discerned their risen Lord!

But why did He withdraw from their sight just as they had recognized Him? For the same reason doubtless as He had told Mary not to touch Him earlier in that same day (see, John 20: 17). He wished to show them from the outset that He had entered into new conditions by resurrection, and that consequently *their relations with Him must be upon a new basis.* The brief glimpse they had of Him however, coupled with His unfolding of all the prophetic Scriptures, had done its work. They were completely revolutionized. A new light had dawned upon them: new hopes had arisen in their hearts: their disconsolate drifting was over. Though night had fallen, they retraced their steps to Jerusalem, to seek the company of their fellow-disciples. Sick at heart they had sought solitude: faith and hope being revived, the company of saints was their delight. It is ever thus with all of us.

# LUKE

Back they came to tell their great news to the eleven, but they arrived to find themselves forestalled. The eleven knew the Lord was risen, for He had also appeared to Peter. The proofs of His resurrection were rapidly accumulating. They now had not only the testimony of the angels, and the remembrance of His own words, and the account given by the women, but also the witness of Simon, almost instantly corroborated by the witness of the two returned from Emmaus. And, best of all, even as the two were telling their story, in their very midst, with words of peace on His lips, stood *Jesus Himself*.

Yet, even so, they were not at the outset wholly convinced. There was about Him in His new risen condition something unusual and past their comprehension. They were fearful, thinking they saw a spirit. The truth was they saw their Saviour in a spiritual body, such as 1 Corintians 15: 44 speaks of. This fact He proceeded to demonstrate to them in very convincing fashion. His was a body of "flesh and bones," yet though conditions were new, it was to be identified with the body of "flesh and blood," in which He had suffered, for the marks of the suffering were there in both hands and feet. And while the truth was slowly dawning in their minds, He made it yet more manifest by eating before them, that they might see that He was not merely "a spirit." Thus the reality of His resurrection was fully certified, and the true character of His risen body made manifest.

Then He began to instruct them, and first of all He emphasized to them what He had already stressed with threefold emphasis to the two at Emmaus, that ALL things written concerning Him in the Scriptures had to be fulfilled, as indeed He had told them before His death. They were to understand that all that had happened had transpired according to the Scriptures, and was in no way a contradiction of what had been written. Then, in the second place, He opened their understandings so that they might really take in all that had been opened up in the Scriptures. This, we think, is to be identified with that in-breathing of His risen life, which is recorded in John 20: 22. This new life in the power of the Spirit carried with it a new understanding.

Then, thirdly, He indicated that, having this new understanding, and being "witnesses of these things," a new commission was to be entrusted to them. They were no longer to speak of law but of "repentance and remission of sins ... in His Name." Grace was to be their theme—forgiveness of sins through the Name and virtue of Another—and the only necessity on the side of men is repentance—that honesty of heart which leads a man to take his true place as a sinner before God. This preaching of grace is to be "among all nations," and not confined to the Jews only, as was the giving of the law. Yet it was to begin at Jerusalem, for in that city man's iniquity had risen to its climax in the crucifixion of the Saviour; and where sin had abounded, there the over-abounding of grace was to be manifested.

# LUKE

The basis, on which rests this commission of grace, is seen in verse 46—the death and resurrection of Christ. All that had just happened, which had seemed so strange and a stumbling-block to the disciples, had been the laying of the necessary foundation, on which the superstructure of grace was to be reared. And all was according to the Scriptures, as He again emphasized by saying, "Thus it is written." The Word of God imparted a Divine authority to all that had transpired and to the message of grace which they were to proclaim.

So, in verses 46 and 47, we have the Lord inaugurating the present Gospel of grace, and giving us its *authority*, its *basis*, its *terms*, the *scope* it embraces, and the *depths* of sin and need to which it descends.

Verse 49 gives us a fourth thing, and by no means the least — the coming gift of the Holy Spirit, as the *power* of all that is contemplated. The Scriptures had been opened up, their understandings had been opened too, the new commission of grace had been clearly given; but all must wait until they possessed the power in which alone they could act, or rightly use what now they knew. Luke draws his Gospel to an end, leaving everything, if we may so put it, like a well-laid fire waiting for the match to be struck which will produce a cheerful blaze. He opens his sequel—the Acts—by showing us how the coming of the Spirit struck the match, and lit the fire with wonderful results.

We have just seen how this Gospel ends with the launching of the Gospel of *grace*, which is in striking contrast with the way in which, in its opening verses, it brings before us the temple service in working order, according to the *law* of Moses. The four verses which close this Gospel also present us with a striking contrast, for the first chapter gives us a picture of godly people with *earthly* hopes, waiting for the Messiah who would visit and redeem His people. It shows us a God-fearing priest, engaged in his temple duties, but possessed of only a little faith, so that he was struck *dumb*. Not believing, he could not speak: he knew nothing worth speaking about, at all events for the moment. Verses 50-53 show us the risen Saviour ascending to engage in His service as High Priest in the *heavens*, and leaving behind Him a company of people whose hearts have been carried from earth to heaven, and whose mouths are *opened* in praise.

Bethany was the spot from which He ascended, the place where, more than any other, He had been appreciated. He went up in the very act of blessing His disciples. When we remember what they had proved themselves to be, this is indeed touching. Six weeks before all had forsaken Him and fled. One had denied Him with oaths and curses, and to all of them He might have said what He did say to two—"O fools, and slow of heart to believe." Yet upon these foolish, faithless, cowardly disciples He lifted up His hands in blessing. And upon us too, though very like to these men in spite of our living in the day when the Spirit is given, His blessing still descends.

# LUKE

He blessed them, and they worshipped Him. They returned to the spot that He appointed for them until the Spirit came, and in the temple they were continually occupied in the praise of God. Zacharias had been dumb: no blessing could escape his lips, either Godward or manward. Jesus went up on high to assume His priestly office in the fulness of blessing for His people; and He left behind those who proved to be the nucleus of the new priestly race, and already they were blessing God and worshipping Him.

This Gospel has indeed carried us *from law to grace* and *from earth to heaven.*

# JOHN

## Chapter 1

THE GOSPEL OF JOHN was evidently written some time after the other three Gospels. Matthew, Mark and Luke had each told, in their divinely appointed way, the story of the birth, early years and entrance into ministry of Jesus Christ, and John takes their record for granted, since without it his opening paragraphs would be hardly intelligible. As the first century drew to its close, sufficient time had elapsed for the launching of attacks on the Person of Christ, as being the very citadel of the faith, and there were philosophic, semi-pagan notions floating about and attaching themselves to the doctrine, which would have been disastrous if they had not been met in the energy of the Spirit of God. Hence that energy was put forth in the writings of the Apostle John, about a quarter of a century, it would seem, after both Paul and Peter had finished their course.

The early Christians were much troubled by the so-called "Gnostics;" that is, the "Knowing-ones." We have been made familiar with agnostics, that is, people who deny that any certain knowledge of God and His things is possible. The Gnostics were at the opposite pole: they claimed to be initiated and have the superior knowledge, but their theories denied both the essential Godhead and the true humanity of Jesus. Then there were those who separated Jesus from the Christ. The Christ was to them an ideal, a state into which man might graduate; whereas Jesus was the historic Man who appeared at Nazareth. The Gospel that John wrote meets these errors, and was designed to do so.

Before considering the opening words it may be well to read the two verses that conclude chapter 20, for in them the design before the mind of the Spirit in inditing this Gospel is stated. The miracles recorded are all "signs" that prove Jesus to be the Christ—so that there is no separation between the two. They prove Him also to be the Son of God; thus establishing His Deity. In the faith of these things life is found; while to refuse them is to abide in death. This is the objective of the Spirit of God in this Gospel and we shall need to keep it continually before us as we travel through it. We shall find it a very important key to the unlocking of its treasures.

The opening words of the first verse carry us back to the most remote moment that our minds are capable of conceiving: the moment when there began the first thing that ever had a beginning: the moment on the further side of which there was only—GOD. In that moment of "beginning" the Word "was," that is, existed. He did not begin then; He existed then. His *eternal Being* is proclaimed, and we are carried back before the opening words of Genesis 1. Further He was "with God." Our minds are still back at that remote moment, and we discover that then He was possessed of *distinct Personality*. The Word is not a title of the Godhead in a general way, apart from any special distinction, for in being "with God" a special, distinctive place is definitely stated.

# JOHN

This being so, the reasoning mind would be inclined to argue: then we cannot speak of the Word as being God in any full or proper sense; even if He is not exactly a creature, seeing He existed before creation. Such reasoning is flatly contradicted by the closing words of verse 1, "the Word was God." *Essential Deity* was His. Attempts have been made to weaken the force of this great statement, and translate it, "the Word was Divine," or, "the Word was *a* god," based upon the omission of the definite article; i.e., it does not say, "the Word was *the* God." But we are told by those who know the Greek that there is in that language no indefinite article, and the word translated "God" is a strong one, denoting proper and absolute Deity; and had it stated that the Word was *the* God, it would have confined Deity to the Word and excluded therefrom the other Persons of the Godhead. The words are chosen with Divine exactitude: the Word was properly and absolutely God.

Then the second verse carries us back to the first and second statements of verse 1. This distinct Personality which characterizes the Word is not something assumed at some subsequent point of time. *Eternal Personality* was His. In the beginning He was thus "with God," for this distinction of Personality lies in the very essence of the Godhead. Thus we have had four things stated of the Word. His eternal Being; His distinct Personality; His essential Deity; His eternal Personality. Whatever else we may have to learn about the Word, here are four things that should bow us in lowly adoration.

A fifth thing confronts us in the third verse: He is the *creatorial Originator*, and that in the fullest sense. Now we come to things that were made; that is, came into being. In verses 1 and 2 a different word is used. The Word did not come into being: He *was*, for His being was eternal. But He originated all that came into being, for He created "all things." To leave not the smallest loophole for an error, this is emphasized in the second part of the verse. The language is remarkable in view of the modern "science falsely so called," so widely popularized, which endeavours to account for everything "without Him." Unbelieving minds cling to the theory of evolution, in spite of a pathetic paucity of facts to support it, and the supports, that are alleged, being of the most fragile description, because while glorifying man it eliminates HIM. But in truth He cannot be eliminated. Of all the untold things that originally received being, not one received it apart from Him.

Ponder this fact; for here we have the explanation of the heavens declaring the glory of God, and of the fact that God has been made known to some extent in creation, as is indicated in Romans 1: 19, 20. The Word created all things and hence in creation there is a true expression, as far as it goes, of God Himself and of His mind. We give expression to our thoughts in words; and the import of this great name, WORD, is that He who bears it is the *expression of all that God is;* and, as verses 1 and 2 show, *He Himself essentially IS all that He expresses.* Creation, as it sprang into being

# JOHN

through the Word, was not a meaningless jumble but a declaration of the power and wisdom of God.

We reach a sixth great fact in the fourth verse. The Word has *essential vitality*. In Him life is not derivative but original and essential. Coupling this with all that has gone before, we perceive how fully the proper Deity of the Word is stated and guarded. The words used are of the utmost brevity and simplicity—every word in the first four verses except three is a monosyllable—yet they are charged with a Divine fulness of meaning, and like the sword of the cherubim in Genesis 3: 24, they turn every way to keep inviolate in our minds the truth concerning the One who is the Tree of Life for man. This Gospel will presently show us how truly the life of the believer is derived from Him, but the point in verse 4 is not that but rather, "the life was the *light* of men." This is the point which is taken up more fully in the opening verses of John's first Epistle. The life has been manifested, and consequently the God who is light, has come forth into the light, and in that light the believer walks.

The light in which men are to walk is not merely that of creation—wonderful as that is—but in that which has been displayed in the actions and words of the Word. When the Word was manifested, the light shone, but the scene, wherein the manifestation was made, was one of darkness. In Genesis 1 we read how by the Divine word the light of creation burst upon the darkness; and, lo! the darkness vanished. Here, we have light of a far higher order and it appears amidst moral and spiritual darkness, which could only be dispelled by a true apprehension of the light. Alas! that apprehension was lacking. Yet though the darkness remained there was no other light for men than "the life." There is no contradiction in these statements for, as so often, John is speaking here of things according to their abstract nature, and has not yet arrived at the historical relation of events.

But how came it to pass that the life in the Word did actually shine in the darkness and become light to men? The answer to this question is in verse 14. Before we reach that verse we have the important paragraph, verses 6-13, where we do begin to view things from an historical standpoint, and John the Baptist is introduced in order to throw into relief the supreme importance of "the true Light." This John was just a man who came into being as sent from God; his mission being to bear witness to the Light. It is true that he is spoken of as "a shining light" in verse 35 of chapter 5, but the word used there is "lamp" rather than "light." John shone as a lamp and bore witness, but the true Light is He who, "coming into the world, lightens every man" (New Trans.). It is not that every man is enlightened, or verse 5 would be contradicted, but that He was not a partial light, but rather like the sun which sheds its beams universally. No one nation could have a monopoly of the true Light; so at once this Gospel carries our thoughts beyond the narrow boundaries of Israel.

# JOHN

In the remainder of this paragraph (vv. 10-13) we have further statements of an historical nature which amplify and clarify what we have been told in verses 4 and 5. We have already learned that the Word is a Person in the Godhead, that His life shone as light for men, though in the midst of darkness; now we find that the world was the seat of that darkness, that He entered it, and that, though He had made the world, it had become so alienated that it did not know Him. In this verse again it is not Israel or the Jew, but the world. Such light as was shed through the prophets might be confined to Israel, but not the shining of the true Light.

The Apostle John often mentions the world in his writings, and he always uses a word which we have adopted in English when we speak of the "cosmos," meaning, the universe as an ordered whole, or sometimes, in a more restricted sense, just our world as an ordered whole. That is the sense of the world in this verse. As Creator He had made the universe as an ordered whole, and a wonderful moment arrived when He was found in that cosmos in a special way. He was there by entering this smaller restricted cosmos, which sad to say had become perverted and alienated by sin—so perverted that it did not even know Him.

Then, further narrowing down the point, He came actually to a rather obscure corner of that cosmos, where were found His own things such as had been indicated by prophecy, but His own people—Israel—with whom those things were connected, did not receive Him. He was rejected, for the darkness could not apprehend Him. But, though that was so, there were exceptions, as this Gospel will proceed to show us. Some did receive Him, believing on His Name. They were not of the darkness. Their eyes were open and they apprehended Him, as seeing and believing the glory of His Name. As a consequence these received from Him authority to become children of God, and not better and more enlightened Jews. The word here is definitely "children," another word that John uses habitually, rather than the word for "sons," which is used more by Paul. There is a shade of difference between the two. The same blessed relationship with God is in view, but as sons our maturity and position in that relationship is more in view: as children the emphasis is laid on the fact that we have been truly and vitally born of God.

That is the emphasis here, as verse 13 shows. The Jew boasted of having Abraham's blood in his veins, just as today a man may boast of being born of aristocratic or even royal blood. Those humble souls, who as exceptions to the rule received Christ when He came, were born of God. The will of the flesh never *would* have produced it, for the flesh is altogether opposed to God. The will of man, not even of the best of men, *could* have produced it: it is wholly beyond man's powers. Their birth was of God, as a Divine act; and the One whom they received in faith gave them the right formally to take the place that was thus vitally theirs.

# JOHN

How came it that the pious souls, of whom we get a glimpse in Luke 1 and 2, received the Christ the instant He appeared? Not because they had Abraham's blood: not because the flesh in them was of so superior a type that it urged them to do so: not because they were influenced by the powerful will of some good man. Simply because they were born of God. It was a Divine act. When we reach chapter 10 we shall find the same basic fact stated in another way. When the Shepherd came to the fold He found there some who were "His own sheep," who heard His voice and were led out by Him. Many there were who were His sheep nationally, who were not *His own sheep* in the sense in which Mary Magdalene and the disciples and the Bethany family and Simeon and Anna were. These people born of God were the ones that received Him.

Now, in verse 14, we pick up the theme from verse 5, and find a seventh great fact as to the Word. He became flesh and tabernacled among us. Verses 1 and 2 tell us what He *was* essentially and eternally. Verse 14 tells us what He *became*. He became flesh; that is, He assumed *perfect Humanity;* and thereby all the other six great facts are revealed to us and become available for us. Only when in this manner He put Himself into relation with the creature could this absolute and self-existent One be properly known by men.

The fact that the Word became flesh guarantees not only that He possessed a real human body (which was denied by some of the earliest heretics), but also that having passed by angels and "taken hold of the seed of Abraham," He had become in every proper sense a Man. It is significant that it is in this Gospel, which starts with such a full assertion of His Deity, that He speaks of Himself as "a Man" (8:40). At last all that God is was revealed to men in a Man. He dwelt among us "full of grace and truth." The basis of all truth lies in the knowledge of God. Had that knowledge reached us apart from grace it would have overthrown us; but here was One full of both grace and truth, and dwelling among us.

In verse 14 there is a parenthesis, placed in brackets in our Bibles, but verse 15 is also a parenthesis, though not placed in brackets. The first tells us that the Apostles, and as many others "as received Him" (v. 12), beheld His glory, and it was "as of an only begotten with a father" (New Trans.), and not like the glory of Sinai. That was the glory attached to Majesty and righteous demand; this the glory connected with a dear and intimate relationship.

The second parenthesis briefly brings in John's witness, which is referred to more fully a few verses later, to show that he discerned the pre-existence and therefore the Divine glory of the One to whom he bore witness. Historically He came after him, both in His birth and in His entrance upon ministry, but He existed before him, and so took the first and supreme place.

# JOHN

Eliminating in our minds the two parentheses, we get, "the Word was made flesh, and dwelt among us, full of grace and truth; and of His fulness have all we received." Again here is stated the result for the believing "we." Only "as many as received Him" can truly say, "we received" of His fulness; but such *can* say it, and *all* of them can, thanks be to God! Fulness of grace and fulness of truth are the portion of each, even of the feeblest, though they will never have explored all the fulness thereof. Grace is specially emphasized. We needed it, piled mountains high—"grace upon grace." Through Moses the law was given, formulating God's demands but establishing nothing. Grace and truth came into being down here and were actually established by the advent of Jesus Christ.

At last John has definitely identified the Person, known amongst men, who is the Word. The Word was made flesh, dwelling among us, full of grace and truth: and, lo! this fulness is in Jesus Christ. This magnificent preface to the Gospel has led us straight to JESUS.

Having arrived there, we are given a further glimpse of His glory. He is the revealer of the God whom no man had ever seen. As the only begotten Son who is in the bosom of the Father, He could fully declare Him as the Father. In the word, "bosom," we have *a human figure*, but we must not use it in *a human way*. The figure is used elsewhere in Scripture as indicating *closest union* and *completest intimacy*. The Son is so wholly one with the Father and in the intimacy of His mind, that He can declare Him to perfection. Our verse does not say that He *was*, as though it were a place that He might have left, but that HE IS. It is an eternal *is*;—He ever was, He is, He ever shall be in the Father's bosom. So the Word becoming flesh meant the coming of grace and truth, and the full declaration of God as Father.

Verses 19-28 give us John's testimony, rendered while he was baptizing in Jordan; a wholly different side of it from that recorded in other Gospels. There was first the negative side, since the religious leaders were curious about him and wished to know if he were the Christ, or Elijah, or the prophet of whom Moses had spoken. His testimony was steadfast; he was none of these but only the voice crying in the wilderness, of whom Isaiah had spoken. Then, when they questioned his baptism, came his positive testimony. There was One already among them whom they did not know, so much greater than himself that he was not worthy to unloose His sandal. By the use of this graphic figure John expressed his sense of the *supreme glory* of the One about to be manifested.

This was the beginning of John's witness. It increased in definiteness and intensity as the succeeding verses show.

Some of the mighty implications of the incarnation come before us in the latter part of the chapter. We find in John's first chapter not only many of His Names and Titles, but also an unfolding of the varied offices and capacities that He fills.

## JOHN

The great ones of the earth fill various capacities. The Queen, for instance, appears on one occasion as a Commander-in-Chief, on another as a Patron, and so on. As Head of the State she fills these capacities, and more besides. It is not surprising therefore that the Word, becoming flesh, should assume offices and fill capacities of immense range and eternal significance. As we read verse 29 and note John's further witness, we meet with the first of the series. He is "the Lamb of God, which taketh away the sin of the world."

John said in effect, "Here is the one effectual, never-to-be-repeated SACRIFICE of eternal value." In the Old Testament the lamb had been specially marked as the animal devoted to sacrificial use: hence the title here. Jesus is the Lamb of God's providing, and if He takes away by sacrifice the sin of the world—not merely your sin or mine, or Israel's sin, but the sin of the whole "cosmos"—then there has been effected a work of such magnitude that the settlement abides to eternity. The thing is to be DONE, and here is the Doer of it. We usually think of sin in its manifestations and myriad details, but here it is regarded as one gigantic and terrible problem, meeting its complete solution and removal. God will have a cosmos—the universe as an ordered whole—totally and eternally purged from sin; and here is the One who by His sacrifice accomplishes this. He is the Sacrifice of the Ages, and in this we see the basis of all that follows. Were He not this, there would be nothing to follow in the way of blessing and glory.

John proceeded to identify Jesus as the One of whom he had previously spoken, and to declare that the object of his baptism was not merely the manifestation of the godly remnant *in* Israel, but the manifestation of the Lamb of God *to* Israel. Upon Him he had seen the Spirit as a dove descending and abiding—not descending and returning, like the dove that Noah sent forth. When commissioned John had been told that this was to be, as it were, the hall-mark on the One to whom he was to act as forerunner; the One who would baptize not merely with water, but with the Holy Ghost.

In saying this, John evidently presented Jesus as the great BLESSER. As the Sacrifice He takes away the sin of the world: as the Blesser He fills it with the light and energy of the Spirit of God. It is plain therefore that here we have two parts of one whole, and both statements are on broad, comprehensive lines. Each believer today has his sins taken away and he receives the Holy Ghost: a tiny item within the compass of the whole. But the point here is the whole, considered abstractly. We do not yet see sin wholly removed historically and the Spirit poured upon all flesh; but here was the One who brings both to pass.

John's conclusion, stated in verse 34, is of much importance. It verified to John the witness he bore in verses 15 and 27. Here was the Son of God, and to His Sonship he could bear witness. The Holy Ghost is a Person in the Godhead, and here is a Man who has this Divine Person at His disposal, so as to shed Him forth as a baptism. Who can this Man be? No one less than the Son of God, another Person in the Godhead. Thus we are at once conducted to the point which is the main objective of this Gospel (see 20: 31). The Son was here in Manhood; hence such a thing could be. The Son of God and the Word are One.

The following day John bore similar testimony, only concentrating upon the Person Himself rather than His work. Still, it was the Person in His character as the sacrificial Lamb, and it is when He wears this character that He becomes specially attractive, as Revelation 5 shows. This attractiveness was felt here, for two of John's disciples heard him thus speak and they at once turned from John to attach themselves to Jesus. No truer service can be rendered to God than that which diverts the hearers from the human servant and attaches them to Christ. A very true servant was John the Baptist.

Jesus did not check the two disciples in their desire to be with Him; rather He encouraged them to *abide* with Him. He is not only the Sacrifice and the Blesser, but also the CENTRE to whom all must gather. The two disciples had discovered this by a kind of instinct, and their action suffices to set Him before us in this capacity. Presently we have the Lord saying, "I, if I be lifted up from the earth, will draw all men unto Me" (12: 32); and in days to come this will be visibly accomplished. But amongst all the myriads Andrew and the other disciple will have the distinction of being the first to discover the Divinely appointed Centre in Jesus.

Verse 41 shows us that what had transpired had revealed to the soul of Andrew that Jesus was the Christ. Again we must think of that verse in chapter 20—He was Baptizer with the Holy Spirit, therefore the Son of God; He was the Centre, appointed by God, therefore the Christ. Andrew's first action was to seek his own brother Simon and testify to him of his discovery, and thus "he brought him to Jesus." It has often been the case since, that the more forcible and distinguished man has been led to the Saviour by someone of very ordinary type. As far as we have any record, this is the most striking thing that Andrew did.

Simon was a ready talker, and amongst the disciples usually the first to speak, but when brought to Jesus he did not have the first word. Jesus at once showed that He knew his name and ancestry, and then gave him a new name. As we see with Daniel and his three friends, great kings asserted their ownership over servants and slaves by changing their names; in like manner when Simon came to Jesus He asserted His claim over him. But by giving him a name which meant "A stone," He did more than this: He annexed him for the building that He had in view, and of which at that moment Simon knew nothing. Simon indeed, as far as the record goes, had nothing to say. What the Lord had in view and what He said was of all moment.

We have only to turn to 1 Peter 2, to find that presently Simon did know, and had something to say to us about it. Coming to Christ, the Living

# JOHN

Stone, he became a living stone in view of God's building, which is proceeding during the present epoch; and, as he shows us in that chapter, that which was true for him is true also for us, as we come to the Living Stone each in our turn. Clearly then, Jesus revealed Himself as the BUILDER of God's house by the way He met Simon, though Simon himself and the rest did not know it at the time. This is another capacity that Jesus fills.

Jesus Himself took the initiative in finding Philip, as verse 43 shows, introducing Himself with the two words, "Follow Me." The two words evidently were sufficient. They presented Him to Philip as the LEADER, who rightly commands loyal obedience from each and all. Philip followed and became a seeker of others, though as yet he did not know much. To Nathanael he could only speak of "Jesus of Nazareth, the son of Joseph;" neither a very lofty nor a very correct designation of the One whom he had just begun to follow. It had the effect at the outset of slightly prejudicing Nathanael: still it sufficed to lead him to an interview with the Lord.

Again Jesus took the initiative and by His opening exclamation as to Nathanael revealed Himself as the Discerner of the hearts of men. Here was an Israelite, not without sin, but without guile; that is, without deceit or dishonesty. Here was a man who was straight and honest in his spirit before God; and Jesus knew this, as He showed by His answer to Nathanael's startled question, "Whence knowest Thou me?" The Lord was showing Himself to be the JUDGE of all, before whom all men are naked and open, who can put every man in his proper place. Nathanael came to see Jesus of Nazareth, and he discovered One who knew all about him and read him through and through like an open book. Who could this Jesus be?

Nathanael's answer is given in verse 49, and we are carried on again to that verse in chapter 20. He is "the Son of God," and He is also "the King of Israel." As an earnest and godly Israelite he was waiting for the King, and would have been inclined to lay all possible emphasis there. But evidently in the presence of this Judge of men and Searcher of hearts all the emphasis lay on the fact that He must be the Son of God; and if that, then the King of Israel. Then note how in verse 50 Jesus accepted Nathanael's homage as not misplaced but as the fruit of faith. Hearing the words of Jesus he had believed, and his homage was the fruit of this.

In verse 50 there seems to be a contrast between *hearing* and *seeing*. Hearing induces faith, but a day is coming when we shall see greater things than we have heard. When the day arrives for sight we shall view the Son of Man as the great ADMINISTRATOR of God's universe of light and blessing. Angels will have their place of service, but their every movement will be regulated and performed in reference to Him. This capacity He will fill as Son of Man in keeping with what is predicted in Psalm 8. That Psalm indeed speaks of Him as made "a little lower than the angels," but this was for the suffering of death, as Hebrews 2 informs us. It also speaks of His having dominion over Jehovah's works in earth and sea. Our verse in

# JOHN

John 1 shows that the angels will be subject to Him, but Hebrews 2 carries it even further, saying that "all things" being in subjection means that there is "nothing that is not put under Him." The Son of Man will dominate the heavens as well as the earth.

Before passing from the first chapter let us note that not only do we have these glimpses of the various capacities that are filled by the Word become flesh, but also we get all His main Titles brought to light:—Jesus, the Messiah; the Christ; the only begotten Son; the Lamb of God; the Son of God; Jesus of Nazareth; the King of Israel; the Son of Man. The whole chapter is like a mine richly shot through with these veins of gold.

## Chapter 2

THIS CHAPTER BEGINS, "And the third day." If we work back we find the second day was that on which Philip was found, and the first that on which Andrew and his companion found their Centre in Jesus. Viewing these things in a typical or allegorical sense, we may say that the first day is that in which the church is gathered to Christ; the second that in which He is recognised as Son of God and King of Israel by the godly remnant in Israel; the third that of millennial blessedness and joy as the fruit of the Son of Man being set over all things.

On the occasion of the marriage at Cana no external glory marked the presence of Jesus. His disciples were there and His mother also, but He soon showed, by the answer He gave His mother, that the initiative was His and not hers; and also that His hour was not yet come—neither the hour of His suffering, nor the hour of His glory, when "all things" will be at His disposal. However, He quickly manifested His glory by showing that water was at His disposal, and that He could make of it that which He pleased. He turned the water of purification into the wine of rejoicing. This was the beginning of His miracles or signs, and as a sign it looked on to the ultimate result of His work. There can be no gladness of an abiding sort save on the basis of a purification which He brings to pass, and the gladness which will spring forth when at last the marriage day comes for a cleansed Israel, will be the best of all. The "good wine" is kept until that day. This sign, demonstrating His glory, confirmed the faith of His disciples, and may well confirm ours.

After a short period still in Galilee, He went up for the Passover to Jerusalem. All these things transpired before John was cast into prison, and therefore before His more public entrance upon ministry, as recorded by the other Evangelists. The scene in the Temple, recorded here, took place therefore right at the beginning of His ministry. He was at the heart of things when He arrived at the Temple, and here at the very heart the need for a work of purification was most strongly manifest. The house of God, His Father, had been turned into a house of merchandise—a place of trading and worldly profit.

# JOHN

This illustrates how the kindly provisions of the law could be and were corrupted to serve man's covetous ends. There was instruction on this point in Deuteronomy 14: 22-26, and they might plead that they were only doing what the law allowed. The law told them to bring their money and purchase what they needed, but did not countenance the covetous practices they had introduced, turning the house of God into a money-making centre. The same thing in principle can be seen in our day; such as Romish shrines with shops attached where the devotees buy candles and other paraphernalia at high prices!

The Lord did not yet disown the Temple. He treated it as God's house, and He was filled with zeal for it. No one could resist Him and His scourge of small cords, and the evil-doers had for the moment to go. The Jews, however, challenged what He did and demanded a sign, as though the irresistible authority of His action was not sign enough. In reply He gave them the great sign of His own death and resurrection, only couched in symbolic language. The fact was that the Temple, as God's dwelling-place, was about to be superseded by Himself. His body was a far more wonderful "Temple" than that which had stood on Mount Moriah. The Word dwelt among us in flesh, and hence "God was in Christ" in a far deeper and more intimate way. The fulness of the Godhead was dwelling in Him. The Temple had served a certain capacity in Israel, but He was now filling that capacity in an altogether new way.

From the outset of this Gospel He is viewed as rejected. So here Jesus takes their deadly animosity for granted. His words were a prediction that they would set their hands to His death; destroying, as far as in them lay, the temple of His body. They would destroy, and in three days He would raise it up. Mark how He says that He would do it. It is equally true, of course, that God raised Him from the dead, but in chapter 10 He again speaks of His resurrection as His own act. This is in keeping with the Gospel which presents Him as the Word who was God and became flesh. Of all the signs He showed, His own resurrection was the greatest.

At the moment no one, not even His disciples, understood Him. This is another characteristic feature of John's Gospel. He is continuously misunderstood, by friends as well as by foes. It was only after His resurrection and the consequent gift of the Spirit that the real meaning of these things dawned upon the disciples. But this again is not surprising. If the Word becomes flesh, He will speak to us in human accents it is true: but He will also speak of the lofty things which He knows as in the bosom of the Father. Hence His utterances are bound to have in them a depth utterly beyond any plumb-line which man possesses—depths which only the Holy Ghost can reveal.

When the Lord spoke figuratively of His resurrection His words were not understood by any, yet the works of power that He did had their effect on many minds. The verses which close the second chapter show that miracles may produce a "belief" of a certain kind. Many in Jerusalem at that time would have subscribed to the dictum that "Seeing is believing;" yet the belief that springs from the sight of facts, which cannot be denied, is not the God-given faith which saves. It is merely intellectual conviction which, when tested, easily collapses, as we see in the sixty-sixth verse of chapter 6.

For the moment things in Jerusalem must have appeared quite promising, but Jesus saw beneath the surface and the Evangelist seizes the opportunity to tell us so. He makes the twofold statement that Jesus "knew all men," and that He "knew what was in man." He makes again a very similar statement in verse 64 of chapter 6; but this in our chapter is the first of a series of similar remarks which disclose to us the omniscience of our Lord, and are very much in keeping with the character of this Gospel. Knowing these men Jesus did not commit Himself to them. The word translated *commit* is the same as that translated *believed* in the previous verse, which helps us to see that true faith is not a mere mental conviction, but the committal of oneself in simple trust to the One in whom one believes.

## Chapter 3

THIS CHAPTER REALLY begins with a word, which may be translated, *But*, though it is omitted in the Authorised Version. Nicodemus was amongst those impressed with the miracles, *but* in his case something further existed. The signs he had witnessed had led him in his thoughts to God, and after God he sought. The orthodox way of seeking God was to go to the Temple, and that Nicodemus would have done by day. He chose the unorthodox way of seeking an interview with this "Teacher come from God," who was not popularly accepted; hence he did it by night. He himself was a leader and teacher in Israel, and he assumed that all he needed for himself was further instruction. It was no small thing for this proud Pharisee to take the place of a humble scholar!

The Lord met him at once with that great and emphatic pronouncement concerning the absolute necessity of the new birth. Without it no one even sees the kingdom of God. He may see the miracles and signs, but he does not see the kingdom. Nicodemus needed the new birth and not teaching, for at once he showed himself quite incapable of understanding the Lord's words, and thereby he illustrated their truth. He could not see anything in them but a mystifying reference to natural birth. This called forth a second emphatic pronouncement in which the matter is carried a step further. The kingdom is not only to be seen but entered, and the birth for this must be of water and of Spirit.

What is imperative is not merely new behaviour or new principles of action, but a new birth, and this signifies an entirely *new origin*. The origin

# JOHN

and pedigree of Nicodemus was of the best, since he came of true Abrahamic stock. Moreover he had acquired all possible culture in the Jew's religion. If he, a cultured son of Abraham needed a new birth then it shows that all flesh, even Abrahamic flesh, is condemned before God. The fact that new birth is universally needed puts the sentence of condemnation upon us all. By our first birth we found our origin in Adam, partaking of his life and nature. Only by experiencing new birth, which brings us into another life and nature, can we see or enter the kingdom.

The Lord's words in verse 5 are clearly a reference to the prophecy of Ezekiel 36: 24-32, which foretells the deep and fundamental cleansing which will reach Israel in the beginning of the millennial age, when God will "sprinkle clean water" upon them, giving them "a new heart," and putting within them "a new spirit," and then putting His Spirit within them. As a result of this they will be so cleansed in their very being that they will loathe themselves as in their former corruptions, and then they will be blessed of God. This passage does not give us the full truth of the matter, but it gives so much that Nicodemus ought to have felt no surprise at the things he had just heard. As a master in Israel he should have known what Ezekiel had said.

A good deal of sprinkling was enjoined under the law, generally of blood, but sometimes of water, as in Numbers 8 and 19. By sprinkling the blood or water was *applied*. Water is the great cleansing *agent*. Ezekiel used these familiar figures to teach that God would apply His cleansing agent to Israel for their spiritual renewal. His spiritual cleansing agent is *His word*, as is indicated in Psalm 119: 9.

So here we find the Lord in His earliest utterances linking His teaching with what had been made known through Ezekiel, and at the same time clarifying and expanding the truth. Yet more is revealed to us about it in the epistles, and we must remember that what we read as to it, in verses 12 and 13 of chapter 1, were written by the apostle John years after full light had been granted on the subject. To Nicodemus Jesus stated that new birth is an imperative necessity for every soul that would see or enter the kingdom; that it is of the Spirit as the active Agent, and of the water of the Word as the passive agent. Such is the state of all men that nothing less fundamental and drastic than a new birth will suffice.

He also stated that flesh always remains flesh, and that which is born of the Spirit partakes of His nature and remains spirit. Verse 6 makes it very plain that the two natures are altogether distinct and never merge into one another. The phrase, oft repeated in Genesis 1, applies—"after his kind." There is no more trace of evolution here than there is in Genesis 1: by no amount of cultivation or natural selection can flesh be transmuted into spirit.

A good deal of reasoning and controversy has taken place as to the new birth which might have been avoided if verse 8 had been duly noted. The

Greek word for "wind" and "Spirit" is the same. Like wind the Spirit is invisible, and only to be apprehended by *hearing* Him in the word He gives, or *feeling* the effects of His operations. Like the wind, too, He is not subject to our control, and His actions beyond all our thoughts. The same thing applies to all those who are spirit as born of Him. There must therefore be about the new birth, and about those born again, elements that are incomprehensible to us; consequently our reasonings may easily be futile or even erroneous.

In verse 11 we get the note of special emphasis—"Verily, verily," for the third time in this chapter. Nicodemus was specially to note that the Lord was not speaking as a mere prophet. He had inward conscious knowledge of the things of which He spoke: He had actually seen that concerning which He testified. He was ever "in the bosom of the Father," as before intimated. Nevertheless His witness was not received by man, apart from the operation of the Spirit of God. And of what did He bear witness? He had spoken of things intimated by Ezekiel as necessary for earthly blessing in the millennial age, giving an expansion to Ezekiel's prophecy, and here was Nicodemus full of hesitancy and doubt. He had yet to speak of things related to God's purposes for heaven; were these things then likely to be received in faith?

Heavenly things in their very nature must be wholly inaccessible to men. Their feet tread the earth and they have a familiarity with it, but to heaven they have never come. But here was One wholly competent to reveal heavenly things. An astonishing paradox greets us. He came down *from* heaven, yet He was *in* heaven. If however we remember how the Gospel started, the paradox disappears. Here is the Word who was God and became flesh. In becoming flesh He certainly came down from heaven: yet He never ceased to be God who is in heaven. But He said, "the *Son of Man* which is in heaven." Yes, and evidently we are intended to learn thereby that we are not at liberty to dissect in our minds His person, as some are inclined to do. We must not say, In *that* position He is wholly as God; or, *That* He did altogether as Man. We may distinguish of course, but we must not divide. Even when in Manhood His personality is one and indivisible. Hence the Son of Man is the completely competent Spokesman of heavenly things. How different from all who had gone before!

Having mentioned heavenly things, the Lord at once proceeded to foretell the great event that must take place before they could be available for men, and the full revelation of them be made. The event had been typified by the brazen serpent in the wilderness—even the lifting up of the Son of Man on the cross. This is the work wrought *for* us, outside of ourselves. New birth is a work wrought *in* us. As to both Jesus used the word, MUST; for both are imperative if we are to have to do with God in blessing. The sacrificial death of the Son of Man is the only possible way of eternal life for man; a way that becomes effective for "whosoever believeth in Him;" that is, by faith.

# JOHN

Verses 16 and 17 both begin with "For," and thus are connected closely with verses 14 and 15. We discover that this Son of Man, who came down from heaven, yet is in heaven, who was lifted up on the cross, is the only begotten Son whom God gave. How strikingly all this fits in with Romans 8: 3, where also is set forth the truth typified by the brazen serpent. Just as Moses made the brazen serpent in the likeness of the fiery serpents that were the source of the mischief, so God had sent His own Son in the likeness of sinful flesh, that sin in the flesh might be condemned in His sacrifice for sin. Sin was resident in our flesh, dominating and corrupting our old life. Believing in Jesus, the Son of God, eternal life is ours; but it rests for its basis on God's condemnation of sin at the cross. There the governing power, active in our old life, was condemned, the pledge that ultimately it will be removed for ever. On that basis eternal life is given.

In the gift of the only begotten Son the love of God is revealed; a love which embraced not Israel merely, but the world. The way in which the grace made known in this Gospel overleaps the narrow boundaries of Israel is very striking. In the opening verses we saw that "the life was the light of *men*," not of Israel merely; as also that the true Light "lighteth *every man*." So here, "God . . . loved *the world*," and the gift of the Son is the measure of the love. Further the term, "only begotten," expresses the supreme and exclusive place He holds in God's love. The type of Abraham and Isaac helps us here. Hebrews 11 tells us that Abraham offered "his only begotten son," though as a matter of fact he had Ishmael at that time, and subsequently many more sons. Isaac however stood solitary and alone in God's purpose and in Abraham's affection. After this striking fashion the term is used of the Son of God, and it is intended to enhance in our minds the greatness of God's gift. God gave the One supreme and unique in His affections.

Verse 17 furnishes a further thought. Perishing is at the end of the course the world pursues, as verse 16 indicates. Now we find that judgment and condemnation lies ahead of it. To perish is to lie eternally in utter alienation and separation from God; that is, in a state of eternal death. Life is consequently an urgent necessity for men and the gift of the only begotten Son has made it possible for the believer in Him to have not merely life of some sort, but "eternal life," life of that Divine and surpassingly wonderful quality. So too, the coming of the Son into the world was not for the purpose of condemnation; the law of Moses had already brought that in very effectively. He came to save. The godly in Israel expected the raising up of "an horn of salvation" in the house of David, that would save them from their enemies (see Luke 1: 68-71), but this is something much greater. The salvation is from sin and its effects, and the scope of it is the world.

Still though the Son of God had not come to earth with the object of condemning, His presence here did incidentally bring in condemnation, inasmuch as He was the Light, and light makes everything manifest, and so brings all men to the test. Light acts in illumination and manifestation, and in its presence man reacts in one of two ways. If he is a doer of evil he loves darkness and hates light because it reproves him. If a doer of truth he welcomes the light and comes to it. These verses (18-20) assume that "he that believeth on Him" is the doer of truth; whilst "he that believeth not" is the doer of evil. The one comes to the light and there is no condemnation for him; the other remains in the darkness, and this is sufficient to condemn him. The light has appeared in the coming of the Son of God and he has not believed. That is enough, and there is no need to wait until the arrival of the actual day of judgment. He is condemned *already*.

Verses 22-24 make it quite clear that the foregoing things transpired before John was cast into prison, which is the point from which the Lord's public ministry started according to Matthew 4: 12; Mark 1: 14; Luke 3:20. For a short time baptism was being administered by both the Lord— through His disciples (see 4: 2)—and John. Certain Jews took occasion to apprise John of this activity of the Lord, as though they would stir him to jealousy. If this was their object, they wholly failed to achieve it.

With real humility and fidelity John kept his place as a servant of God who had nothing but that which he had received from heaven. They had to bear witness that he had never claimed to be the Christ. He had claimed to be the *forerunner* of the Messiah; he was also the *friend* of the Bridegroom. In this second claim he evidently spoke figuratively by way of illustration. Truth, such as we have in Revelation 19: 7, was not yet revealed, but doubtless he was inspired to express himself in terms which exactly suit that truth, when revealed. He had no link with the bride, but as the friend of the Bridegroom he had in Him the deepest interest and affection. To hear the Bridegroom's voice filled up his cup of joy to the brim.

Then John uttered words which should be graven upon the heart of everyone who loves the Lord Jesus — "He must increase, but I must decrease." For the third time in this chapter we get "MUST." In verse 7 it is connected with man's great need; in verse 14 with God's great love; here with the devotion of the true-hearted servant. Like the sun, Christ was to rise to his zenith with increasing glory; thus, like the moon, John was to fade out and disappear. He knew it and rejoiced, for at that moment in his thoughts Christ was all. He knew Him as One coming from heaven and not of earth at all. Being such, He spoke in a way impossible to all others. He was in touch with the full range of heavenly things in a way impossible to the greatest of the prophets, such as John.

John's words came true, and soon he had to decrease and drop out of sight in prison. In this he was no exception to the rule. It is the rule for all the servants of God: in one way or another they decrease and depart. It was so with Moses in the Old Testament, and with Paul in the New. Great servants as they were, we must not think too much of them. Paul had his day as an ardent evangelist and founder of churches. But then came prison

# JOHN

for him, and failure in the churches, and so he drops out of our sight. Paul decreases, but only to increase the supreme excellence of Christ. So it must be for all of us, and we should rejoice in it, as John did.

The opening words of verse 33 appear to contradict the closing words of verse 32, but the paradox is a purely verbal one, and based upon one of those abstract statements which appear so repeatedly in John's writings. Man in his natural condition is wholly dead and unresponsive to the Divine testimony. The fact is stated *abstractly* at the close of verse 32. But then on the other hand God works by His Spirit in the hearts of some; and so from a practical standpoint we do find those who receive the testimony, and by so doing set to their seal that God is true. At the beginning the devil impugned the testimony God gave to Adam, and thus sin was introduced. Faith vindicates the truth of the testimony, and thus life and salvation are brought in.

Testimony from God had existed from the time that God spoke to Adam about the trees of the Garden, but now it was reaching its climax in this One whom God had sent, who knew by observation the heavenly things of which He spoke, who uttered them in "the words of God," possessing the Spirit without any measure or limit. At last therefore there was a testimony of infinite range and incomparable fulness. Of course it wholly transcended the powers of the natural man, yet the simple believer can accept it, attaching his seal to it as the truth of God.

Verses 35 and 36 appear to be a separate paragraph in which the words of the Baptist are supplemented by the Evangelist, who could speak in the full light of all that had been revealed in the Word become flesh. The Son having been manifested, the Father had been made known, together with the relations between these Divine Persons. Three great facts concerning the Son meet us here. He is the Object of the Father's love. By the Father's gift all things are in His hand, to be disposed of as He sees fit. He is the Object of faith, and therefore the test of every man. To believe on Him is to become possessed of life eternal. To refuse the subjection of faith to Him is to be excluded from life and lie under the wrath of God.

Thus quite early in this Gospel do we discover that the Son is not only the *Creator* of all things and the *Revealer* of all things as the Word, but He is also the *Operator* in all things, the *Disposer* of all things, and finally as the Object of the Father's love He is manifested amongst men, becoming the *Criterion* for all. We notice that, in verse 36, life is to be possessed and also to be seen, which shows how comprehensive a term "eternal life" is: and further, that the antithesis to seeing life is abiding under the wrath of God. Here again things are stated abstractly, but the language is such as to negative both the theories by which men endeavour to escape the solemn fact of eternal punishment. The words, "shall not see life," negative universal reconciliation, which declares that in some way or other all shall ultimately see it. The theory of conditional immortality, which means the

# JOHN

annihilation of impenitent unbelievers, is negatived by the fact that the wrath of God "abideth" on such—therefore they exist abidingly. At this point let us again recall chapter 20: 31. This Gospel is written that we may be amongst those who believe and have life. The terrible alternative to this is put before us very plainly here.

## Chapter 4

THE CLOSING PARAGRAPHS of the third chapter spring out of the intermeddling of the Jews in the matter of John's baptism, and his reaction to it: this chapter opens with the Lord's reaction to their interference. John gladly took the place of decreasing that his Master might increase. The Master withdrew Himself to Galilee lest rivalry should be instituted, which would be so hurtful to His servant. Such was His thoughtful care for John. Moreover the Lord himself would have been belittled if treated thus. It would have put Him beside John as a kind of party leader, akin in principle to the error of the Corinthian saints who coupled the name of Christ with Paul, Apollos and Cephas. This must never be.

The direct route to Galilee lay through the district of Samaria so "He must needs go" that way as a geographical necessity. But there was also a necessity connected with the grace of God which imposed upon Him a road which brought Him to a particular city of Samaria, called Sychar. Jesus, the Word made flesh, was wearied with His journey; a testimony this to the reality of His Manhood: and not weary only, but hungry and thirsty too. He sat on the well-side about midday, as the time of greatest heat approached. Nicodemus sought Him by night. He sought a Samaritan sinner at midday. John's Gospel specializes in the record of His conversations and dealings with individuals. It also records His conversations—usually of a controversial nature—with groups of persons, but not once does it put on record His more formal preachings, such as the Sermon on the Mount or the parables of Matthew 13. Many of us would own that it takes more spiritual skill to deal rightly with an individual than to address a crowd, and makes a bigger demand upon our courage. A perfect example of personal dealing is presented to us here.

Jesus began by requesting a drink of cold water. The Word made flesh takes the place of a humble suppliant before a very sinful specimen of His creatures! A marvellous sight indeed! Regarding Him merely as a Jew, the woman felt He was belittling Himself; but in the light of the true situation we can see how truly He had made Himself of no reputation and emptied Himself. But this very lowly and humble approach to the woman gave a most advantageous start to the conversation. If we, who aim at serving the souls of men today, could always approach them with humility, we should be wise indeed.

The woman, awakened to astonishment and curiosity, could not resist asking how such a request came to be made. The answer of Jesus in verse 10 set before her three things. First, the fact that God is a Giver. She had known a little of the law, but this set Him before her in a new light altogether. Second, He indicated the mysterious greatness of His own Person, since He was the Dispenser of God's gift. She saw in Him but a Jew who asked for a drink of water. When she knew Him she would discover that He was really the Giver of a Gift of surpassing value. Third, He indicated the Gift to be "living water," thus turning her thoughts from the natural to the spiritual. Both Nicodemus and this unnamed woman were alike in having at the outset no conception of the meaning of the Lord's words, let alone the things of which He spoke. Yet here again, there had been some indication of these things in the Old Testament. Twice in the Book of Jeremiah, for instance, Jehovah had presented Himself as "the Fountain of living waters" (2: 13; 17.13).

The misunderstanding of the woman led to further unfoldings contained in verse 14, which again seem to range themselves under three heads. First, the one who drinks of the living water as the gift of Christ will have it "in him," abiding in his very being. Then, it will be in him as a "well," or "fountain," of water, "springing up into everlasting life." A fountain of life within, which springs up to the level of its Source! Lastly, the drinking of such water and the possession of such a fountain will produce abiding satisfaction. The Lord used a very strong expression—"shall never thirst for ever."

By "living water" the Lord indicated the Spirit of God as is quite evident when we reach chapter 7: 39. In the previous chapter the only begotten Son is God's gift to the world but in this chapter, the Spirit of God is God's gift to the believer, but a gift which is administered by the Son of God; who was the Speaker, seated on Sychar's well. By the Spirit we have the life within—He is spoken of elsewhere as "the Spirit of life in Christ Jesus" (Rom. 8: 2)—and by Him the life within springs up to the Source of the life above. In this way did the Lord indicate the life of communion and worship and satisfaction which He was about to make available for the believer. As a result, the believer today may anticipate the millennial joy, set forth figuratively in the beginning of miracles at Cana of Galilee: and not only anticipate, but also know it in truer measure and a more spiritual way.

Before proceeding with our chapter let us note the remarkable sequence of the teaching since the record of that first miracle. We have had *the work wrought in us*—new birth by the Spirit and the word. Then *the testimony rendered to us*, receiving which, we set to our seal that God is true. Thirdly, *the gift of the Spirit bestowed upon us*, to be in us as an ever-flowing fountain, springing up to the eternal Source. Here we have presented to us in a germinal way great realities which find expansion in the Epistles.

Pursuing our chapter we notice that though the woman was still in the dark as to the significance of "living water," the Lord's further words had

# JOHN

at least sufficiently stirred her desires to lead her to ask for it. Before He gave it, her conscience had to be reached and conviction of sin produced. In bidding her call her husband the Lord put His finger upon a specially sore spot in her life, and followed this by letting her see that her sad story lay like an open book before His eye. On her side she at once saw and confessed that He was a prophet; thus by implication pleading guilty to His indictment; yet as is so often the way when a wounded conscience exists, she endeavoured to sidetrack the conversation into a religious discussion, thus eliminating the personal element.

The place where worship was to be offered to Jehovah had long been a burning question. Had Gerizim displaced Moriah, as the Samaritans claimed? The Lord seized the opportunity to show the woman not only her personal sin but also the futility of the "worship" in which she and her people had engaged. In saying, "Ye worship ye know not what," He disowned it; and in saying, "Salvation is of the Jews," He convicted her of her unsaved condition. She stood amongst the Gentiles—"strangers from the covenants of promise, having no hope, and without God in the world" (Eph. 2: 12). So even in discussing the question of worship she was not beyond the reach of rapier-like thrusts at her conscience.

The Lord, however, lifted the whole matter of worship on to a far higher plane. He spoke of worshipping Jehovah in the light of the revelation that He was bringing—even as "the Father." This at once lifted it out of that ceremonial order of things which connected it with a holy place on earth. The law had tied people down very strictly to a holy place where Jehovah's name was set; hence the prolonged dispute between Jew and Samaritan: He lifted her thoughts to God who is a Spirit, revealing Him as Father.

This new revelation was ushering in a new "hour," which had indeed already begun. The worship which is to characterize that hour must be in keeping with the revelation that has formed it. God who is Spirit is seeking that worship as Father, so now worship to be acceptable must be "in spirit and in truth." Notice this further "MUST." Worship is not something optional, or to be varied as suits our tastes. God *must* be worshipped in the way He Himself prescribes. All else that may claim to be "worship" is no worship at all.

True worship is "in spirit"; that is, not in flesh, not in bodily posture. This word of our Lord negatives the *ritualistic* and ceremonial line of things which has been a snare to so many. Our capacity to offer worship in spirit lies in the possession of the Spirit of God—the Fountain of living water springing up into everlasting life—as is also indicated in Philippians 3: 3. The Spirit of God may engage our spirits in true worship at any time and in any place; not merely in some sacred shrine as in Judaism.

Then again worship must be "in truth"; that is, in the light of all that God has revealed Himself to be in Christ. This negatives the *rationalistic*

# JOHN

line of things, which is also so common. Men speak, for instance, of worshipping "the great First Cause" in the light of the beauties of nature, while ignoring or refusing the truth concerning Him, as made known in Christ. Only in Him do we know the Father who is to be worshipped. If we do know the Father thus, our hearts are bound to be filled with worship of that spiritual nature which is acceptable to Him.

The Father seeks worshippers of this sort. He has made Himself known in order to produce this response. The downward flow of His love, in the revelation made to us, produces the upward flow of responsive love in worship. This is acceptable to Him and He seeks it.

The Samaritan woman knew of the promise of the Messiah, and these wonderful words of the Lord, coupled with the inward conviction of sin that had reached her, turned her thoughts to His advent. Her response seems to indicate that she felt a Messiah-like character about the Lord's utterances. The Lord at once and with the utmost plainness revealed Himself to her as the Christ. That revelation she evidently accepted at once; and going back to the city, in her words to the men, she divulged what lay behind her ready faith. He must be the Christ, for had He not told her all things that ever she did? Not in detail, of course; but rather He had shown to her as in a flash that all she had ever done was to be summed up in the one word—*sin*. It is just the same today. Faith in Christ goes hand in hand with true conviction of sin.

The beautiful paragraph, verses 31-38, comes as a parenthesis in the story. The Lord's words to the disciples, in verse 32, have been rendered, "I have found food to eat which ye do not know." He was labouring for "fruit unto life eternal," as He indicates in verse 36, and to see this end being reached in the bestowal of blessing on the Samaritan sinner was delectable food for Him. It was "the will of Him that sent Me," said He, to do this. The light He brought was to shine for every man, as we learned at the beginning of this Gospel, so here we see it shining upon a sinner outside the bounds of Judaism. The will of God, the work of God, and life eternal for man go together here; and how blessed for us it is that they do. Further, the Lord indicated to His disciples that in their turn they were to have a share in this most blessed work, whether by sowing or reaping. In this case the Lord Himself was doing the sowing. When the reaping time came, recorded in Acts 8, the harvest was very great.

The paragraph, verses 39-42, concludes the story. The men came to Christ as the result of the woman's testimony, and reached for themselves the same conviction. Many believed because of what she said, and many more as the result of listening to Him. They believed and they greatly desired His company.

In their confession they went even further than the woman. He was not only the Christ but also "the Saviour of the world." Mere religious pride might have made them boast that here was the Saviour of the Samaritan equally with the Jew; but only faith could have led them thus to seize God's large thought for "the world," according to John 3: 16. They had *heard*, and they *knew;* and beneath both hearing and knowledge lay faith.

In relating all this the Evangelist has led us to the fact that Jesus is *the Christ*. The next chapter, as we shall see, conducts us to the fact that He is *the Son*. Putting both together, we are again brought to the point indicated in the last verse of chapter 20 of his gospel.

In the last paragraph of this chapter, we find the Lord back again in Galilee, and it brings us to the second of the miraculous signs that John mentions. In Galilee He met with a reception that had not been accorded to Him in Jerusalem, and this second sign also had a connection with the town of Cana of Galilee.

The first sign prefigured the time predicted in Isaiah 62: 4, 5, when Israel's marriage day shall have come, and from the purifying water the wine of gladness will be produced. The second sign presented the Lord as the One who can bring life and healing when death seems imminent. This Jewish nobleman did not exhibit the strong faith that marked the Gentile centurion of Matthew 8. His tendency as a Jew was to demand signs and wonders before believing; and belief of that sort is not genuine faith, as we saw at the end of chapter 2. Still, though feeble, faith was there in this man's heart.

It manifested itself in two ways. First, it persisted in its appeal, when at first the Lord's answer seemed unfavourable, fully exposing the desperate need of the son. Second, when the answer he received was a simple command to return because his son lived, he took Jesus at His word without any sign before his eyes. Here indeed are the marks of true faith; it persists, and it takes God at His word without signs or wonders or feelings.

The Lord verified His own word, and the next day the man saw that his confidence had not been misplaced. Jesus had said, "Thy son liveth;" the next day his servants met him saying "Thy son liveth," though they had not heard Jesus speak. Life granted even at the point of death is evidently the leading thought. And this is just what man in general needs, and Israel in particular: not just healing but *life*. This was the second sign, and we shall find much instruction about life—about Jesus as its Fountain Head and Giver—in the chapters that follow.

## Chapter 5

But first we are brought back again to Jerusalem that we may consider a third sign that He gave in the healing of the impotent man at Bethseda. The Jew reading this Gospel might say, "Well we are as a nation sick to the point of death, and need life; but we have the law. Ought we not to find healing there." The third sign furnishes us with a reply to this.

# JOHN

A way of blessing was brought within man's reach by the law of Moses. Only one thing was necessary on man's part, but that one thing was wholly lacking. It demanded that he should have power to avail himself of the benefit provided. The case of the impotent man by the pool aptly sets forth the state in which every man lies, if tested by the law. Sin has destroyed our power to do the necessary thing which the law demands. This was so obvious in the case of the man that he made no reference to his own powers, which had vanished, but only acknowledged that no one was available to do for him what he could not do himself. "I have no man," said he.

Yet by his confession he acknowledged his desire to be made whole, and complete soundness was granted to him at once by the word of the Lord. What the law could not do for him, inasmuch as it was weak through the impotence of his flesh, was accomplished in an instant as the work of the Son of God, now present on earth. The man was able not only to walk but also to carry the bed which formerly had witnessed to his helplessness. The Lord bade him do this though it was the Sabbath.

The law of the Sabbath was very strict. All kinds of work were prohibited, even to picking up sticks and lighting a fire. The Jews therefore were up in arms at once when they saw the man carrying his bed. He had however a ready and sufficient answer. The Man who had healed him had told him to do it; and a little later he was able to name that Man—Jesus. Their zeal for the Sabbath was such that from that moment He became the Object of their hatred and persecution.

The Lord uttered no word of apology or even explanation; He simply asserted that which cut at the root of this legal institution. Under the law of Moses the Sabbath was instituted as a sign between Jehovah and Israel, as is made clear in Exodus 31: 12-17, though it was based upon His rest when creation was finished. As far as it concerned Himself Jesus brushed it aside. Since the creation had been invaded by sin His Father was working not resting, and He was working in communion with His Father, and not keeping Sabbaths as linked up with them.

This pointed declaration stirred up the Jews to murderous hatred for the two reasons stated in verse 18. He had broken the sign of the covenant in which they boasted, and He had coupled with His action the assertion that God was His Father; thus claiming equality with God. Verse 18, be it noted, is John's explanation of why the Jews sought to kill Him, and not his record of the explanation furnished by the Jews—though of course it may have been the explanation which they gave. It is therefore the comment of the Holy Spirit through John, and proves that in the Sonship of our Lord there is no thought of any kind of inferiority to the Father. On the contrary it is the assertion of equality.

The answer Jesus gave to their murderous hatred, in verse 19, is very striking. The Son, who was here in Manhood, had taken the place of carrying out in perfection all the Father's will and work. Hence He could do nothing "of Himself," as originating it independently of the Father: but rather He acted in all things as directed and ordered of the Father. But this is intended to conduct us, we believe, to the still deeper truth that this necessity was rooted in His perfect oneness with the Father. Though Man He was so wholly and perfectly and altogether in the unity of the Godhead that it was impossible for Him to act apart from the Father. In that sense, "The Son can do nothing of Himself;" and therefore this saying far from being any confession of impotence or even inferiority is an assertion of His unqualified Deity.

"The Father loveth the Son." These five words occur as the statement of the Evangelist at the end of chapter 3. They now occur in verse 20 as the voice of Jesus Himself. The Son, now on earth in Manhood, was in full cognizance of all the Father's actings, and was to engage in works greater than any yet manifested. He would act as the Giver of life and as the Executor of judgment. To quicken is to give life; and in this the Son acts according to His sovereign will, though of course His will is ever in complete harmony with the Father's will.

Raising the dead and quickening are distinguished in verse 21. The wicked dead are to be raised, but it is not said that they will be quickened. Again, quickening takes place when resurrection is not in question, as verse 25 shows. The Son will raise the dead, as He states in verses 28 and 29, but the point in verse 21 is that He gives life just as the Father does. In the opening verses of the Gospel we viewed Him as having life inherently, and as displaying that life so that it should be the light of men. Here we go a step further: He is the Giver of life to others. In this He acts *with* the Father.

But in the matter of judgment He acts *for* the Father, as verse 22 states. There are things which the Son disclaims, such as the fixing and revealing of "times and seasons," as we see in Acts 1: 7, Mark 13: 32; here we find that the Father disclaims all judgment, committing it into the hands of the Son. These facts, however, must not be used in any way to detract from the honour and glory of either Father or Son. This is specially pointed out as regards the Son in verse 23, inasmuch as the fact of His assuming Manhood lays Him open to unwarranted depreciation in the minds of those who neither understand nor love Him. He will be honoured by all in the hour of judgment; and not to honour Him today is to dishonour the Father who sent Him. The Father evidently will accept no honour save that in which the Son is honoured conjointly.

In this wonderful discourse the Lord made three statements on which He laid special emphasis, expressed by the words "Verily, verily." In verse 19 He emphasized His essential oneness with the Father in all His works, as we have seen. In verse 24 the emphasis again lies on His connection with the Father. As the Word became flesh He was the sent One of the Father, and in His word the Father was made known. So He did not just say, "He that heareth My word and believeth *it*," but, "believeth *on Him that sent Me*." We believe on the Father through the word of the Son; so that presently Peter writes to saints, "who by Him do believe in God" (1 Pet. 1: 21). Now here He announced that such simple hearing of faith produced three amazing results: the possession of life eternal; preservation from judgment; passage out of death into life.

How many ten thousand times has this great verse been used to bring light and assurance to the souls of anxious and enquiring sinners! May it yet be used many thousand times more! The authoritative assurance it breathes lies on the very face of it. We are well rewarded, however, when we look a little more closely into its depths. The Son gives life to whom He will and He executes all judgment. He speaks the life-giving word, which conducts the soul in faith to God, and at once the life is ours and into the judgment we shall never come. We have become the subjects of the first of those greater works of which He has spoken, and into the second we never enter. He laid emphasis on the positive side by speaking of life in a twofold way. It is not only that which the believer *possesses*, but that also into which he *passes* out of the realm of death.

If we speak of life as connected with this lower creation, we deal with something which defies our analysis and definitions, yet obviously the word on our lips has more senses than one. We contemplate, for instance, not only the vital spark in man or beast but also the conditions needed for that spark to exist. There is no fish life without water; no human life without air. Even so there is no spiritual and eternal life without the knowledge of God; and no knowledge of God without the revelation which reaches us in the word of the Sent One and the faith which receives it. Because of this, we believe, Jesus spoke not only of the believer having eternal life but of his passing out of that spiritual death which is marked by utter ignorance of God into the realm of life which is filled with the light of the knowledge of the Father. No wonder He laid such emphasis on this wonderful statement.

And in the next verse He emphasized the further statement that a period of time was then dawning in which this great life-giving work of His would specially be carried on. In this verse we view the work more from the side of His own sovereign action, and faith is not specially mentioned, though of course no one does "hear the voice of the Son of God" apart from faith. This "hour" has lasted till the present moment, and through the centuries multitudes have heard the voices of the preachers of the word without hearing His voice in the word. Only those who have heard His voice have lived. They have lived because, as the next verse tells us, the Son now come forth in Manhood, has life in Himself, as given of the Father. Life was in Him essentially, for the statement, "In Him was life" (1: 4), is connected with His eternal existence, and His incarnation is not mentioned till verse

14; but here we see that in Manhood the Son is given of the Father as the Fountain Head of eternal life for men. We possess it derivatively, whereas only that which is possessed inherently and essentially can be communicated to others. This great life-giving work is His alone and now is the time of His so acting. In the deep-seated silence of innumerable hearts His voice has sounded: they have heard and lived. We must not invert the order of the words, as some have been inclined to do. It is not, "they that live shall hear," but, "they that hear shall live."

But further, the Son of God is also the Son of Man, and so He is not only the Fountain of life but also the authoritative Judge of all. As Son of Man He was to be "lifted up" as under man's judgment. Presently we shall hear the people saying, "How sayest Thou, The Son of Man must be lifted up? Who is this Son of Man?" (12: 34). Well, in the coming day they will know who He is to their irretrievable ruin! Though at first sight it seems most marvellous that all judgment should be vested in A MAN, yet we are not to marvel. Another hour will strike when the voice of the Son of Man will be heard, and this not only by some but by all—whether good or evil.

Only those who heard the voice of the Son of God and lived had the power to do good. The life expressed itself in the good, as its product and proof. The rest simply did evil. The voice of the Son of Man will lift out of the grave all without exception, for there is a resurrection of judgment as well as a resurrection of life. They are distinguished here, though we have to go to other scriptures to discover that a wide interval of time separates them. Both however are in the future, for the words, "and now is," do not occur in this connection. The words in verses 22, 24, 27, 29, translated variously, judgment, condemnation, damnation, are fundamentally the same. It is well to bear this in mind.

But though all judgment is in His hands, He does not even in this act independently or apart from the Father. Having taken up Manhood, He does not leave the place He has taken but carries it out in perfection. Had He said, "My judgment is just; because I am the Word who became flesh," He would have stated what is absolutely true; but He based the assertion on this—"because I seek not mine own will, but the will of the Father which hath sent Me." All judgment may safely be committed into the hands of a Man of this order, and in this sense He said, "I can of mine own self do nothing."

In Matthew 20: 23, Jesus uttered the actual words, "Not mine to give." In Mark 13: 32, He said in effect, "Not mine to know." Here He says in effect, "Not mine to do." All three statements are made in view of the lowly place of dependence which He took for the glory of the Godhead and our salvation, and they do not in the least militate against His supreme place in the unity of the Godhead. They show us something of what is meant by His making Himself "of no reputation," or, "emptying Himself," according to Philippians 2, and thus we get a glimpse of the true

# JOHN

"kenosis" of which the Scripture speaks, and we find it far removed from the evil "kenosis theory" formulated by unbelieving theologians, which attributes fallibility and error to our Lord.

The truth was that, though Himself so great, He was here wholly for the will of the Father, and all His judgments were according to the Father's thoughts. Even as regards witness to Himself all was left in the Father's hands. It is customary among men to advertise themselves, but thus it was not with Him.

The first witness, John, was just a man. Jesus needed no such testimony, yet He mentioned it, if thereby some might listen and be saved. In verses 33-35, Jesus is really bearing witness to John, who had borne witness to the truth as a burning and a shining lamp. John's witness was marked by both warmth and light, yet he was only a lamp—for that is the word the Lord used—whilst Jesus was the true light, like the sun shining in its strength. Now the sun needs no witness from a mere lamp, even though it burns and shines.

The works, which the Father had given Jesus to finish, were like beams of light thrown off by the sun; they were a greater witness to Him than anything that John could say. They were so obviously Divine that they proved Him to be the Sent One of the Father. And then, in the third place, the Father Himself had borne witness to Him—notably at the time of John's baptism—but they, being utterly carnal, had no appreciation of it. They wanted something which would appeal to their natural powers of sight or hearing, and knew nothing of that word of the Father, which brings spiritual illumination.

Lastly, there were the Holy Writings. These did indeed testify of Him, and they searched them. They thought they had eternal life in the Scriptures, but Christ is the Giver of it, and to Him they would not come. If by searching the Scriptures men are conducted to Christ, then indeed they have eternal life through the Scriptures, otherwise they merely gain knowledge of a technical, theological sort and remain in spiritual death. These words are most illuminating as to what the true function of Scripture is.

The Lord proceeded to show that He thoroughly knew His opponents. He was here in His Father's name, and hence the honour and glory that man can offer was nothing to Him. They had nothing of the love of God in them, and hence were greedy for honour, one of another, instead of seeking that which comes from God. In their minds they glorified men, and this was as ever an effectual barrier to faith, and they *could not* believe. Jesus came in His Father's name; which means He was seeking His Father's glory. All that was foreign to them, and they refused Him. Another would come in his own name, and therefore seeking his own glory; that would exactly suit them and they would receive him. In these words the Lord predicted the coming of antichrist, in whom the false glory of man will reach its climax.

## JOHN

In these words also were exposed the evil motives lying deep in the hearts of His opponents, yet He was not their accuser. Moses was that through the law that had been given by him. They boasted in Moses, because they felt that great man conferred some honour upon themselves, but they did not really believe him. Had they done so they would have received Christ. Verse 39 applies to all Old Testament scriptures: they "testify of Me." Verse 46 alludes specifically to the early books written by Moses; and he "wrote of Me." This, then, is the key which unlocks all the Old Testament—the main theme is the Christ, who was to come.

The way in which the Lord linked His words with Moses' writings is very striking. If men refuse the earlier testimony through the servant, they will not receive the Son, when He speaks. And so indeed it is. The men today, who disbelieve the books of Moses and even deny his authorship, do not believe the words of Jesus. This is perfectly clear, inasmuch as He endorses here the very thing they deny. We must make our choice between the rationalistic modernists and Christ. They have stepped into the shoes of His Jewish opponents: that is all. The two questions, "How can ye believe?" and, "How shall ye believe?" are very striking. As the love of God is in us, as the glory of man fades in our eyes, we shall accept and believe the Holy Writings, and they will lead us in faith to Christ.

### Chapter 6

THIS CHAPTER BRINGS us back again to Galilee, and we read of another of the great "signs" which Jesus did. The miracle of feeding the five thousand has evidently a special importance, since it is related in each of the four Gospels. Our chapter gives us the teaching, based upon it and relating to it, which makes apparent its significance. The miracle itself is described in such a way as to emphasize the Lord's resource and foreknowledge.

Jesus first addressed Himself to Philip. Now this was the disciple who did believe Moses' writings, as we saw in chapter 1: 45; yet when tested here he did not look beyond the purchasing power of money. Jesus Himself "knew what He would do." In such an emergency the best that could be said of other servants of God would be that not knowing what to do, they looked to God for direction, and got it. But here was One, who knew what to do, and knew He had the power to do it. Before Andrew spoke of the lad with his small loaves and fishes, He knew about them. To have such knowledge, and wield such power as to know with absolute certainty what one will do, is the prerogative of Deity. Statements such as this are common in this Gospel: see 2: 24, 25; 13: 3; 18: 4.

Though His knowledge and power were such, He did not disdain the small supplies which the lad offered, nor did He ignore the disciples with their small understanding and feeble faith. He made them the distributors of His bounty. The original food supply was the lad's; the hands that distributed it were the disciples'; the power and grace were His, and His alone. So manifest was this to the men that partook of the bounty, that they connected it with heaven, and declared that He must be the Prophet that should come into the world, as Moses had said. People were led to that conclusion on a number of occasions—see, 4:19; 7:40; 9: 17—yet to be lasting it had to be a stepping-stone to deeper conclusions. In chapter 4, it led to the conviction that He was *the Christ:* in chapter 9, to the conclusion that He was the *Son of God.*

With these men the loaves and fishes had acquired too much importance, and desiring a continuance of supplies so easily procured, they took counsel to force kingship upon this Prophet. Now we have just heard Him say, "I receive not testimony from man," and again, "I receive not honour from men," so we are not surprised to find that He will not receive a kingdom from the hands of men. The glory of the greatest earthly kingdom, that man can erect, is but tinsel before Him. So He departed into the solitude of a mountain, while His disciples set out to cross the lake. Matthew 14: 22, tells us that He constrained His disciples to enter the ship, while He dismissed the crowds by Himself. John's account explains His actions. They would easily and enthusiastically have fallen in with the proposals of the people, but He thoughtfully removed them from the scene of temptation.

But though He would accept no earthly kingship by democratic vote, He showed Himself to be complete Master in other spheres, though the display of this was for the eyes of His disciples only. Both wind and sea can display a force in the grip of which man is but a toy and a plaything, but over which He is supreme Lord. The disciples in their day, and we in our day, need to apprehend Him in this light. An earthly kingdom with plenty of food easily appeals to a carnal mind. The spiritual mind is formed by knowing Him as the Master of both wind and wave, and the powers they represent. Revealing Himself thus to the disciples, their fears were dispelled, and they found themselves conducted at once to their destination, when they willingly received Him into the ship. Ponder this incident with care, for we very specially need to know Him in this way. He is today not dealing with an earthly kingdom, but proving Himself supreme *above* adverse forces, while conducting His saints *through* them.

The crowd knew nothing of His miraculous crossing of the sea, yet they sensed that something unusual had happened, and they sought Him on the further side, wishing to satisfy their curiosity as to the mode of His transit. The Lord did not satisfy it, but rather at once showed them that He knew the unspoken thoughts of their hearts. The seeing of miracles is not enough, as we learned in chapter 2: 23-25, but even that was in their minds supplanted by the food that perishes: He, the Son of Man, sealed by the Father, was the Giver of food that endures to life eternal. They should seek that.

His answer to these men bears a strong resemblance to His approach to the Samaritan woman, in chapter 4. There water was in question, here bread; but in both cases the well-known material substance was turned into a symbol of great spiritual reality, and the hearer brought face to face with that, though there is no evidence of these men receiving blessing as the woman did. The "living water" was the Spirit, that He would give. The "living bread" was Christ Himself, come down from heaven, the food of eternal life for men. That food can only be received as a gift in which the whole Godhead is concerned, since it comes from the Son of Man, sealed by the Father—and that seal, we know, was by the Spirit.

The woman no more understands at first the import of the Lord's words than did these men, but her response was, "Sir, *give* me . . ." whereas theirs was, "What shall we do that we might *work* . . . ?" A tell-tale difference this! The men's question at once drew forth the assertion that faith in the Sent One of God is the very beginning of all work that is according to God. If men do not believe on Him whom God sent, in no proper sense do they believe in God; and they remain in spiritual death, since life is presented to them in Him. Alas! they did not believe, as verse 30 shows, but instead they demanded a sign, suggesting that if it were spectacular enough it would create faith in their hearts. And then, anticipating that He might refer them to the sign of the multiplication of the loaves and fishes, which they had just witnessed, they attempted to discount that by referring to the miracle of the manna, ministered to their fathers in the wilderness through Moses for the space of forty years.

This called forth the emphatic statement of verse 32. It was not Moses but God who gave that bread from heaven, which was only a figure of the true. The true bread out of heaven is the gift of God, and He was now being revealed as Father by the One who was that gift. He had Himself come down out of heaven as the Giver of life to the world. In natural things bread only sustains life and in no sense gives it; but the spiritual always transcends the natural. The material figure serves to direct our thoughts to the Divine fact, but can never contain its fulness. Jesus was here as both the Giver and the Sustainer of life; and this in relation to the world and not merely to the small Jewish nation, amongst whom He moved. We have noticed this feature before: the Word having become flesh, He cannot be confined in His light and life-giving powers to any circle less than the world.

Their response to this, in verse 34, looks more encouraging, yet in it there was no faith, as verse 36 shows. It led, however, to the Lord very definitely and plainly presenting Himself as the bread of life, and stating that in coming to Him in genuine faith every desire would find its satisfaction. The gift from Him of the Spirit leads to heart satisfaction in chapter 4. Here, the reception of Himself in faith leads to the same blessed consummation. In the knowledge of Himself all the fulness of the Godhead is revealed to us, and may be appropriated by us. This it is that satisfies. These men showed no sign of coming to Him, but the Father was active in His purposes and grace, and hence a response there was going to be.

# JOHN

In this setting stands that great and assuring gospel statement, "Him that cometh to Me I will in no wise cast out." In chapter 3, we saw that though "no man receiveth His testimony," yet some did receive His testimony. Now, for the first time we discover what lies behind the paradox. There is the sovereign grace of the Father, which has given certain to the Son, and these without any exception come to Him. These happy individuals are impelled towards Him, as far as their own consciousness is concerned, by a variety of things, differing in almost every case; yet beneath all, as the ultimate explanation, lies this gift of the Father to Christ—a love gift, we may call it.

All that the Father has given come, and *none* that come are cast out by the Son; and that not only because of His own grace and personal love for such, but because they are the Father's gift, and because the very object of His coming down from heaven was to carry out the Father's will, and thus reveal the Father's heart. The Father gave them in order that, coming to the Son, He might be to them the Giver and the Food of life and thus, the Father made known to them, they might be satisfied indeed. There is no possibility of any slip between the Father's gift and the Son's reception. As we observe thus the context and bearing of the passage, we see how rightly and happily the evangelist directs the anxious soul, who is turning towards Christ and about to come to Him, to the golden words, "Him that cometh to Me I will in no wise cast out."

Then again, the Father's will is not only that the Son should receive in life-giving power the one who comes to Him now, but that all should be consummated in resurrection at "the last day." The Jews had the light of the Old Testament, and looked forward to the time of Messiah's presence and glory as the last day. The Lord's words here amply confirm the thought and show that though we may have the life now in a world that is marked by death, we are to know the fulness of it in the age that is to come. How delightful is the connection between verses 37 and 39—*no one* will be cast out now, and *nothing* will be lost as we move on to the day of glory; and both in keeping with the Father's will.

Verse 40, while expressing the same truth as verse 39, amplifies it somewhat. The same persons are in view, but described first as, "all which He hath given Me," and then as, "every one which seeth the Son, and believeth on Him." The first describes from the viewpoint of Divine purpose; the second shows the corresponding action of faith in our responsible lives here. This "seeing" the Son is, we believe, as much faith as believing on Him. Many there were who saw Jesus as He walked on earth without "seeing the Son" in any true sense. But where eyes were spiritually opened, and they saw the Son and believed on Him, eternal life was received in the present (see also 20: 31), and the world of resurrection life will be entered at the last day.

# JOHN

The Jews promptly displayed themselves as being wholly without faith. They only did see the Man Jesus, thinking they knew His parents; that He was the Son, come of David's seed according to the flesh (see Rom. 1: 3), was utterly unperceived by them. Thereby they made it plain that they had no part nor lot in this matter. They were strangers to that drawing of the Father, apart from which no man actually does come to Christ.

Verses 39, 40, and 44, each end with resurrection. They set before us the Father's gift to the Son according to His purpose, His drawing to make the gift effective, and the resultant faith on our side, which leads to the present possession of eternal life, and the certainty of its fulness in resurrection. The Lord found in Isaiah 54: 13, a forecast of this inward work of the Father; and He knew that what He is going to do in Israel's children, who shall be redeemed and restored when the age to come dawns, He was doing then, and He is still doing today. No man has seen the Father in a natural way. Only those who are "of God" see Him, and that by faith.

Verses 40 and 46 are linked together by the two expressions, "seeth the Son," and "seeth the Father." Faith is needed for both, and the Father is only seen if the Son be seen. Let us beware, therefore, of theories which tamper with the Sonship of Jesus. The Divine and eternal Fatherhood cannot be retained if the Divine and eternal Sonship be discarded.

The murmuring of the Jews called forth another of those weighty statements of especial emphasis, which are frequent in this Gospel. Jesus is the bread of life, and those who appropriate Him by faith have life eternal. This great fact stands, without any reservation or qualification whatever. The manna in the wilderness had been recalled by the Jews; the Lord now uses it as in sharp contrast with Himself. Their fathers were dead, though they partook of the manna. He was the bread come down from heaven, and to partake of Him meant deliverance from death. Their fathers were dead spiritually as well as physically, for they had not faith (see Heb. 3: 19) though they ate the manna. The man who eats the bread come down from heaven never dies spiritually, whatever happens to him physically.

In verses 50-58, the Lord speaks of eating Himself or His flesh as the living bread no less than seven times, and of drinking His blood three times. His language is figurative, yet really very simple. That which we eat and drink we appropriate in the fullest and most intense way. It is wholly and irrevocably ours, and ultimately becomes part of ourselves. It is consequently a very appropriate figure of faith, for that is just what faith effects in a spiritual way. By incarnation the Son of the Father was amongst men, truly come down from heaven, and thereby all that was revealed in Him was made available for men, but only to be actually appropriated by faith. Hence men must eat of that bread, and eating they live for ever.

The latter part of verse 51 brings in a further thought. This "bread" is His flesh, to be given not for the Jewish nation only but for "the life of the world." Here the Lord indicates that His incarnation was in view of His death. Wholly blinded, the Jews plunged into arguments among themselves, and this brought forth another statement of extreme emphasis. Apart from the death of the Son of Man, appropriated by faith, no one has any spiritual life in him. The Son having come in flesh as Son of Man and died, life depends upon faith in Him. Before He came there were many who believed in God, according to the testimony He had given, and they lived before Him. But now that the Son of God is come, He is the testimony and everything hinges upon Him.

The tense of the verb, "eat," in verses 51 and 53, is worthy of note. Darby's "New Translation" renders, "if any one shall have eaten . . ." and "unless ye shall have eaten . . ." respectively. It signifies an act of appropriation, once for all accomplished. This act there must be if a man is to live toward God—no life without the faith-appropriation of the death of Christ. This, however, does not militate against eating as an habitual thing, which is set forth in the four occurrences of the word in verses 54, 56, 57, 58. The life that is received has to be nourished and sustained; hence the one who has eaten still eats; in other words, he who has received the life by the original appropriation of faith now lives on the same principle— "The just shall *live* by faith." He has believed, and he goes on believing.

The habitual eater has eternal life and, in verse 54, for the fourth time resurrection is brought before us. What underlies this fourfold mention undoubtedly is that eternal life is to reach its fullest expression and fruition in resurrection at the last day. It is only mentioned twice in the Old Testament: "life for evermore" (Psa. 133: 3), "everlasting life" (Dan. 12:2), and in both cases Messiah's day, which is "the last time," is anticipated. Daniel 12 speaks of a national resurrection for Israel, how they shall rise up from amidst the dust of the nations; but in our chapter we have individuals in view, and the resurrection is not figurative but vital and real. When Paul mentions eternal life he usually has in view its future fulness in resurrection; for instance, "the end everlasting life" (Rom. 6: 22). In John it is habitually presented as a present reality though, as the Lord's words here show, its fulness in the age to come is not excluded from our thoughts.

He who thus eats and drinks not only has the life but he "dwells" or "abides" in Christ, and Christ in him. Moreover, as verse 57 shows, he is put into the same relation with Christ as He was in with the Father. As the Sent One of the Father, commissioned to reveal the Father, the whole life of Jesus was lived on the Father's account, as drawing everything from Him. Just so, in regard to Christ, shall live the one who appropriates Him habitually by faith; and so living he abides in Christ and Christ in him. One can only exclaim, What a marvellous character of life is thus opened to the simple believer, and how little we have entered into it experimentally! This is indeed, in contrast to the manna, the true bread that came down from heaven; and the life, into which by eating we are introduced, abides for ever.

## JOHN

These remarkable teachings of our Lord had a very testing and sifting effect upon His disciples, and many were offended. His saying was "hard" to them; but wherein did its hardness consist? In that it cut at the roots of their national religious pride. To be told, "Ye have no life in you" except there be this eating and drinking, was intolerable to them. Why, they took it for granted that life was theirs as the nation owned of God, and they had not abandoned that idea though they thought they had found the promised Messiah in Jesus. Now He knew "in Himself" that these disciples were thus objecting under their breath, since He knew all things, and as a consequence He proposed to them an even greater test.

That of which He had spoken had involved His incarnation, by which the fulness of the Godhead had been brought down to us, and His death, by which life has been made available for us: now He speaks of His exaltation and glory. If they stumbled at the thought of the Son of God coming down, what would they say to the Son of Man going up? In our chapter then we have the first and last items in that "mystery of godliness" of which 1 Timothy 3: 16 speaks—"God was manifest in the flesh... received up into glory." Note that He ascends as Son of MAN. It was a wonder that God should descend to earth: it was no less a wonder that Man should ascend to heaven. Jesus of Nazareth is in heaven (see Acts 22: 8). And He is "where He was before." A striking witness this to the fact that His Person is one and indivisible, however much and rightly we may emphasize the force and meaning of His various names and titles, as well as distinguish between what He ever was and what He became, as we did when considering the opening verses of this Gospel.

The teaching of this chapter is completed by verse 63, where the Holy Spirit is brought in. Nothing proceeds from the flesh that profits in this matter: it is the Spirit who gives life. The Father is the Giver of the true bread of life: the Son is that bread, and as Son of Man gives His flesh for the life of the world: the Spirit quickens. All is of God, and nothing proceeds from man. How dead man is this chapter shows, for the Lord's words, which are spirit and life, were only an occasion of stumbling to them. The Evangelist interrupts his record in verses 64 and 65, to tell us that Jesus spoke in the full knowledge of this, and that not only did He know in Himself what they thought and said, but also who believed and who did not, from the very beginning, and who should betray Him.

It was at this point apparently that many of those spoken of in chapter 2: 23-25, revealed themselves in their true character. Vital faith was not theirs, and they disappeared. Jesus then tested the twelve, and Peter, their spokesman, uttered a fine confession of genuine faith. He recognised the Sent One of God, who had the words of eternal life. Mere men may have the words of science or the words of philosophy, and occasionally words of wisdom, but only the Son of God has words of eternal life. So there was no alternative, no possible rival upon the horizon of Peter's faith. Christ was unique and alone. Surely, by the grace of God, He is that for us too. Yet

# JOHN

He was not that even for each of the twelve, and the Lord took the occasion to show that the heart of Judas Iscariot was completely open to His eye. He had not placed him amongst the twelve under any misapprehension of his true character. At this time Galilee was still the scene of the Lord's ministry, and in a remarkable way the hearts of all men were being manifested. We have seen spurious disciples going back, a genuine disciple making the confession of faith, the traitor disciple being unmasked.

## Chapter 7

HERE WE FIND the Jews of Jerusalem adopting an attitude of murderous hostility, and then His brethren according to the flesh are seen in a sceptical frame of mind. They really did not as yet believe in Him, they did not understand His methods and His avoidance of ostentatious publicity. They wished Him to display His powers in the capital city in a way that would capture the world for Himself. Their advice the Lord refused. The world could not hate them, for they were not as yet in any way separated from it. It hated Him because from the outset He was essentially separated from it and testified against its evil works.

Moreover, He only acted according to the Father's will, and hence His time was not yet come. They acted according to their own thoughts, and hence any time was their time, according to the spirit of the world. If we read 1 John 3: 12, 13, we see that the situation in which the Lord was found had been typified by that of Abel. His righteous works in His Father's name testified against the evil works of the Jews and they were aiming at His death, and would encompass it when His hour was come. At the appropriate moment He did go up to the feast of Tabernacles, while many were seeking Him and discussing Him in private. This shows us that the mass of the people, though not identified with the leaders who wanted to kill Him, were all too indifferent. They were full of curiosity and questions, and they argued their varying opinions, yet they were not sufficiently moved to reach decision. How like the situation today! Some murderously opposed, some sceptical, false disciples prepared to sell out, the masses indifferent, but some, like Peter and the ten, discovering the Lord of life, who is without a rival.

In the midst of the feast Jesus appeared and taught. At once the power of His words was felt and enquiry raised. He had not been through the schools of men yet He spake thus! How was it? He answered their question by saying that His teaching proceeded from the One who sent Him. He had come forth to utter His words and was doing so to perfection. Any difficulty that His questioners felt sprang from their own attitude. If only they had a real desire to do the will of God they would have recognised that His teaching was of God. If we desire to do God's will we are of necessity marked by *sincerity* and *subjection*, and our convictions become clear and correct. The mists of doubt shroud the minds of those who are merely triflers or curious.

Jesus was indeed speaking not from Himself but from God, and thus His truth and righteousness were manifest. He had come to seek the glory of God instead of seeking His own by speaking as from Himself. If it had been unrighteousness for Him to have sought His own glory, though all glory was rightly His, how much more unrighteous is it for any of us who serve Him to seek our own glory, seeing that rightly we have no glory at all. A very searching and convincing thought for all of us! The standard that the Lord set is the test for us.

For the people, however, Moses was the test, and judged by that all were guilty. Jesus knew they sought to kill Him, and here was a most flagrant violation of Moses' law. The crowd repudiated what He said, and it is possible they were ignorant of the devices of their leaders; but they showed their animosity by the terrible charge that He had a demon. Jesus replied by referring to the miracle of chapter 5, performed on His previous visit to Jerusalem, and by showing them how unrighteous and superficial their judgments were by their practices in regard to circumcision. Others intervened at this point, and by their remarks corroborated the Lord's assertion of their murderous intent and overthrew the people's repudiation of it. Yet they did not believe in Him; they were stumbled by imagining they knew His human origin. Still the reality of things was made clear by these men thus cancelling each other out.

Knowing their words, Jesus took them up in His teaching in the temple, to show that while they knew Him and knew He had come from the carpenter's shop in Nazareth, they did not know the One that sent Him. They had some knowledge of the human side, but to the Divine side they were wholly blind. Yet there were those impressed by His miracles and inclined to believe that He might be the Messiah. The Pharisees and chief priests remained in implacable hostility and sent to apprehend Him, but His hour was not yet come. They had no real power against Him, and verses 33 and 34 show this. When His hour was come very shortly, He would go to Him that sent Him, and pass into a region that they would never enter—a region in which He ever dwelt. He spoke thus of His death and resurrection from a very exalted standpoint. Verses 35 and 36 reveal to us once more their utter incapacity. They had not the smallest inkling of the meaning of His words.

The eighth day of the feast of Tabernacles was to be "an holy convocation," according to Leviticus 23. On that day, when the gladness of the people was supposed to reach its climax, Jesus made His second great pronouncement about the "living water." He knew that none of these Jewish festivals slaked men's thirst, and that there were some who were conscious of this. So He invited them to come to Him and drink, since through faith in Himself the Spirit was soon to be ministered. He had

## JOHN

spoken to the woman of Samaria of the Spirit indwelling as a Fountain; now He speaks of that same Spirit causing the flowing forth of rivers. Out of the inward parts of the believer these rivers are to flow. The significance of the figure seems to be that the Spirit is to be not only received but spiritually assimilated if the outflow is to take place. Out of the "belly" and not out of the head the rivers will flow.

This is to take place "as the Scripture hath *said;*" that is, it is not the quotation of a written statement, but rather something indicated in a more general way. For instance, Ezekiel 47: 1-9, had predicted that waters should flow from the Millennial Temple, and that its waters should be living since, "everything shall live whither the river cometh." Further, "the name of the city from that day shall be, The LORD is there" (Ezek. 48: 35). The living waters will signalize the fact that the living Lord is in their midst. But the Spirit was to be given when Jesus was glorified on high, long before the Millennial Day is reached, and He signalizes His presence and His indwelling of believers by the outflow of the living waters in a spiritual and not a material way. The Scripture thus had spoken of these things. Again and again we see verified the fact that what Israel will enjoy in a more material way in that age is to be known by the believer in a spiritual way in this age.

Verse 39 is important as clearly defining the relation between the glorification of Jesus and the shedding forth of the Spirit. By that act the church was to be formed, and as the body united to its Head. Jesus was here incarnate but, before as Lord and Christ He takes up that intimate headship, four further steps were necessary—death, resurrection, ascension, glorification. Then the Holy Ghost was shed forth, and the living waters began to flow in Jerusalem and elsewhere. Looking forward, the Lord Jesus promised this, and attached no qualifications to "he that believeth on Me." It was not for the apostolic age only but for us also. Why are the rivers so little seen? Is it because our inward parts have been clogged with other things, and but little open to the operations of God?

Verses 40-44 show us the people still hesitant and mystified. Some expressed one opinion and some another. Some would have apprehended Him yet no one did so. It appeared to end in futile discussion; but it revealed the presence of a deep rift of division. There are many ways of being against Christ and only one way of being for Him—the way we saw Peter take at the end of chapter 6. The rift, like some great canyon of Colorado, exists today, and all other cleavages among men are but shallow ditches compared with it. There is still a division among the people *because of Him.*

At the end of the sixth chapter, we had Peter's tribute to the supernatural power of the Lord's words; they were "words of eternal life." We now find that the same power was felt by men who were on the opposite side of the deep cleavage that ran through the nation. The religious leaders had sent men to arrest Him but they returned without Him. The only explanation they gave of their failure to touch Him was, "Never man spake like this Man." They did not understand what He said, but they felt that no mere man ever spake as He did; that His words placed Him in a different category altogether. They might be ignorant, but their sensibilities were not wholly deadened.

Their leaders, who had sent them, lacked not only sensibilities but scruples also. They did not lack an immense conceit of themselves; so much so that they were sure that their own rejection of Jesus was incontestable, and so final that everybody ought to accept it. If the crowd, or any of them, did not, it only showed them to be ignorant and accursed. So these false shepherds just cursed the sheep, and left it at that. Yet their own ignorance began to peep out, for the effect of their triumphant question as to whether any of the rulers or Pharisees had believed in Him, was spoiled by Nicodemus who was both a Pharisee and a ruler. Though not yet prepared to come out as a definite believer, he revealed by his question that he did not conform to their unbelief. Further, their sneer as to Galilee only revealed their ignorance as to whence Christ had come.

The scene presented to us, in these closing verses shows what an astonishing likeness exists between the present-day, modernistic religionist and these men. True, the written Word of God is more in question now, rather than the Living Word as then, but there is just the same triumphant assertion of the supreme place of human cleverness and knowledge. The modern phrase is, "All scholars are agreed . . ." agreed in denying or even ridiculing the Word of God. But now as then all scholars are NOT agreed, and the dissentients are not just a unit like Nicodemus in the Sanhedrim, as also their faith in Christ and His Word is far clearer and more definite than his. Moreover, like the ancient religionists, our modern specimens are just as wrong in their basic facts. Christ was not "of Galilee" as they ought to have known; but they did not trouble to look beneath surface appearances. Modern unbelief is wealthy in speculations, guesses, fancies, and sadly bankrupt in solid facts.

## Chapter 8

However, they felt that they had decisively settled the point, and they retired to the comfort of their own homes, whilst Jesus, the Word made flesh, without a home, spent the night on the Mount of Olives. Returning early in the morning to the temple, He was confronted by some of these very opponents with a case which, they hoped, would impale Him on the horns of a dilemma. The crowd might be ignorant of the law and cursed; they knew the law right well and thought themselves blessed by it; they also knew the kindness and grace of Jesus. So they set the sinning woman in the midst and quoted the law of Moses against her. The result was not what they expected. The Lord turned the law like a searchlight upon them,

# JOHN

and its convincing power reached even their hardened consciences. These double-dyed, religious hypocrites, who talked glibly enough of the curse coming on the crowd, now saw the curse of the law looming up against themselves, and they disappeared.

The action of Jesus in stooping down and writing on the ground is very significant. Here was, if we may say so, the finger that once wrote the law on two tables of stone—the law that wrote a sentence of doom against Israel. The same finger had written a sentence of doom against a proud Gentile monarchy in the days of Daniel, upon the plaster of the wall. The writing substances are striking. The inflexible law written on inflexible stone; hence the despiser of Moses' law "died without mercy," since the law cannot be twisted as rubber is twisted. Plaster is friable and easily broken, like the strongest and proudest human kingdoms. Jesus wrote on the ground. What He wrote there we are not told, but we do know that He was going "into the dust of death" (Ps. 22: 15), where He wrote a full declaration of the love of God.

In Revelation 5, the book of judgment is produced, and a strong angel with a loud voice issues the challenge, "Who is worthy to open the book, and to loose the seals thereof?" Jesus issued just that challenge, though in different words. The result of the challenge then will be that "no man in heaven, nor in earth, neither under the earth" was able to open or even look upon that book; just as here every accuser slunk away. Then the "Lion" who became the "Lamb" is left to execute the judgments alone. Here "Jesus was left alone, and the woman standing in the midst;" yet it was not the hour of judgment but of grace, and so the One who had the right to condemn did not exercise it. He was "full of grace and truth." He turned the searchlight of truth on the hypocrites, and extended grace to the sinner, with a view to her deliverance from the sin.

Out of this incident sprang a solemn controversy between the Lord and the Jews, and the account of it fills the rest of the chapter. His opening words, in verse 12, refer to the incident and are the key to what follows. In the beginning of the Gospel we saw that the Word was the Originator of life, and was the Light which shone in the darkness. Chapters 3-7 have presented Him to us as the Source of life eternal. Now He comes before us as the Light, and at the end of chapter 12 the result of that presentation is summed up for us. Jesus is the light not of Israel only but of the world, and the one who follows Him will have the light of the life manifested in Him, no matter whence he may have come. The one who did not follow Him remained in darkness, even though he were the most orthodox Jew imaginable.

In chapter 5 the Lord had pointed out how ample was the witness borne to Him, so that He was not in the position of coming to them with self-produced credentials. The Pharisees now seized upon the words He then used and attempted to convict Him on the ground of verbal inconsistency.

# JOHN

He neither withdrew His words nor explained them. He simply appealed to things of a far higher nature which convicted them of ignorance and error. In mere men their self-knowledge is small. What is behind them and what is before, both are shrouded in a veil of impenetrable mystery. There was no such limitation with Him. His self-knowledge was Divine and eternal. These Pharisees were as ignorant of themselves as they were of Him. They were also in error, since all their judgments were formed by the flesh, in which no good dwells. In their fleshly judgment of His words they were wrong, though clever in pouncing upon what looked like a contradiction.

In the case of the woman the Lord had refused the place of Judge. It will be His in a coming day, but not today; and He disclaims it again to the Pharisees in verse 15. Yet in His disclaimer He again commits Himself to a verbal paradox, since He asserts the truth of His judgments, seeing He is so wholly one with the Father who had sent Him. In the age to come all judgment will be His, yet He will execute it in fullest concert with the Father. So also in the matter of witness to Himself, the full weight of the Father's authority lay behind it. This reference to the Father on His part only served to bring to light complete ignorance on their part. The Father can only be known in the Son, whom they would not receive. If only they had known the Son they would have known the Father.

Verse 20 bears witness to the power of these words of our Lord as also to the power of His Person. His words made them wish to apprehend Him, but there was that about Him which hindered them, until the hour came when He gave Himself up to their will. The Lord however continued His witness to them.

He had been going their way and seeking them in grace. A moment was now coming when He would go His own way and they would seek Him fruitlessly and die in their sins. Then they would be cut off from Him and from God for ever. This complete turning of the tables would be not only just, but appropriate. Again in verse 22 we see complete ignorance with the Jews, and that their minds were sordid to the last degree. They were indeed "from beneath" in every sense of the words. This led the Lord to draw the sharp contrast between them and Himself. First as to *origin:* they from beneath; He from above. Second, as to *character:* they of this world; He not of this world. Third, as to *end:* they were about to die in their sins and be excluded from God; He was going to the Father, as He had already inferred. Only faith in Him could avert their doom—the faith that would discover in Him, "I AM." There is no word representing the "he" in the original, hence it is printed in italics. In Exodus 3: 14, God had revealed Himself as the great, "I AM," hence this statement of Jesus was virtually a claim to Deity.

The Jews had not discerned this for the moment but they evidently saw His claim was a great one, for they at once asked, "Who art Thou?" They received an astonishing answer, "Altogether that which I also say to you"

# JOHN

(New Trans.). He was the truth, and His speech was a true and exact presentation of Himself. This could not be said of the best and wisest of men. If we would, we cannot accurately manifest ourselves in words. If we could, we should shrink from doing it, being what we are. His words were the true revelation of Himself; as we might expect when we know that He is the Word who became flesh. Let us ponder this word of Jesus very deeply, for it carries with it the assurance that in the Gospels we have a real and true revelation of Christ. They give us what He did as well as what He said; but *by His words alone* we may truly know Him, though we never saw Him in the days of His flesh. What He said, *that He is altogether.*

Verse 26 shows us that all that He had to say concerning men was equally the truth, because all was spoken of and from the Father. They were wholly ignorant of the Father, and wholly unbelieving as to the Son present amongst them. When they had lifted up the Son of man there should be a demonstration of the fact that He really was "I AM," and that in every sense the Father was with Him. His lifting up was His death, and, that accomplished, resurrection would supervene, which would declare Him to be, "the Son of God with power, according to the spirit of holiness" (Rom. 1:4). Then they would know, in the sense of having perfectly ample demonstration before their eyes. Some few did know, in the sense of being enlightened by the demonstration, but the mass deliberately closed their eyes against the light. Still the demonstration that He was wholly and ever pleasing to the Father was there for every eye to see.

The power of His words was felt and many took the place of believing on Him. The Lord tested them by telling them that one who was not a mere nominal follower but a disciple indeed is characterized by continuing in His word; that is, in the whole truth that He brought. Continuance is ever the test of reality, and where that exists the truth is known in its emancipating power. The devil enslaved by the power of his lie: Christ liberates by the power of God's truth. He did not flatter them by telling them that as God's nation they were free. He set before them that true spiritual freedom which is the result of the knowledge of the truth. *That* they needed, and so do we.

Many failed under the test, for their national and religious pride was wounded. They might be Abraham's seed after the flesh, but to claim they were never in bondage to any, while in complete subjection to the Romans, only proved their blindness. By His emphatic statement of verse 34, Jesus directed their thoughts to the slavery of sin. Men cannot practise sin without being enslaved thereby—a tremendous thought for every one of us. Now the place of the slave is outside, but in contrast to him is the Son, whose place is inside and that for ever. And the Son not only has that abiding place Himself but He can set free the slave, introducing him into that which is liberty indeed. Thus he who is one of the "disciples *indeed*" becomes "free *indeed*."

# JOHN

In these words of our Lord, recorded in verses 32 and 36, we may surely see the germ of that which is more fully expounded in the epistles. Romans 6 unfolds our death with Christ, leading to our being "made free from sin," which in its turn leads to "newness of life." This answers to verse 32 of our chapter; while verse 36 finds its counterpart in Galatians 4: 1-7, connected with 5: 1. The redemption from under the law, wrought by the Son, coupled with the sending forth of the Spirit of the Son into our hearts, has brought us into the liberty in which we are to stand fast. The Son has set us free indeed.

In verses 37-44, the Lord very solemnly exposes the hollowness of their claim to be Abraham's children. There would have been some value in their claim if they had shown themselves to be his children in a spiritual sense by displaying his faith and doing his works. Actually they were marked by hatred and the spirit of murder. Cain had shown that spirit, and he was "of that wicked one, and slew his brother" (1 John 3: 12); so, too, they were doing the deeds of their father, and thus manifesting themselves to be of their father the devil, who was a murderer from the beginning and had no truth in him. Hatred and lying are both fathered by the devil, and those characterized by these two things thereby betray their spiritual origin.

Jesus speaks of Himself, in verse 40, as "a Man that hath told you the truth." Others spoke of Him as a Man, and saw no more in Him than that; but it is striking that in this Gospel, which presents Him as the Word made flesh, He should speak of Himself as a Man. Thus the truth is balanced for us, and both His essential Godhead and His perfect Manhood made abundantly clear. He set forth the truth, and those who had God for their Father would both love the truth and love Him. His opponents had an evil origin, and could not hear His *word*—the revelation that He brought. Consequently they were wholly unable to understand His *speech*—the words in which He clothed the revelation. This is what verse 43 tells us.

Notice how the Lord's words totally destroy the false idea held by so many concerning the "universal Fatherhood of God," though these Jewish religionists only went so far as to claim a universal fatherhood of Abraham, and therefore of God, for their nation. Jesus said, "If God were your Father . . ." It was a denial. The devil was their father. The Fatherhood of God is limited to those that believe, as Galatians 3: 26 states.

Before these Jews stood One whom not even His bitterest foes could convince of sin, and He told them the truth. That truth honoured the Father and delivered men from death, yet they refused the truth, dishonoured Him, called Him a Samaritan, and said He had a demon. They gloried in Abraham though they admit he was long since dead. The Lord met them as One who knew He had come forth from the Father, was honoured of the Father, and was going to enter upon His own day, to which Abraham had looked forward, and which by faith he saw.

# JOHN

The Jews, as ever, utterly misunderstood His words. He spoke of Abraham seeing His day, and they thought it meant a claim on His part to have seen Abraham. Their mistake served to bring out the great and emphatic pronouncement, "Before Abraham was, I AM." At a certain moment Abraham "was." The verb used here is the same as in chapter 1:14, where we read that the Word "was made" or "became" flesh. The verb for "am" is the one signifying abiding existence, as used in 1:18; the Son "is" in the bosom of the Father; and it is used in the past tense, as to the Word in the bygone eternity, in 1:1 and 2. Jesus therefore said, Before Abraham came into existence, I eternally AM.

This tremendous claim moved the Jews to attempt His death by stoning, and had it been false they would have been quite right. It surely moves our hearts to adore Him, and to adore the grace that brought Him into Manhood and so low for our salvation.

## CHAPTER 9

THE MURDEROUS INTENTIONS of the Jews did not fail because they lacked fixity of purpose but because He was beyond their reach until His hour was come. Hiding Himself from them, Jesus left the temple, and as He passed on He encountered a blind man who was to bear striking witness to the leaders of Israel, and in his own person become another "sign" that here amongst them was indeed the Christ, the Son of God.

The question which the disciples raised may seem curious to us, but it expressed thoughts which were common among the Jews, finding their basis in Exodus 20:5, which speaks of the iniquity of the fathers being visited upon the children. The Lord's reply shows that affliction may come without there being any element of retribution in it, but simply in order that God's work may be manifested. It was manifested here in working a complete deliverance from the affliction. It may just as strikingly be manifested by complete deliverance from the depression and weight of the affliction, while the affliction itself still persists; and so it is often seen today. It was then the "day," marked by the presence on earth of "the Light of the world." Jesus knew that the "night" of His rejection and death was approaching, but until that time He was here to do the Father's works, and this blind man was a fit subject for the work of God, though he had made no appeal for it, as far as the record goes.

The action taken by the Lord was symbolic, as is shown by the name of the pool being interpreted for us. Jesus was the "Sent One," who had become flesh, and of His flesh the clay mixed with His spittle was the symbol. Now seeing eyes would be blinded if plastered with clay, and blind eyes rendered doubly blind. Just so it was for the spiritually blind; the flesh of the Word was a stumbling-block and they saw only the carpenter's Son. For us who believe in Him as the Sent One the reverse is true. It is by

# JOHN

His revelation in flesh that we have come to know Him, as 1 John 1: 1, 2 shows. His flesh is darkness to the world: it is light to us. We can adopt the language in a spiritual sense and say we "washed, and came seeing." The rest of the chapter shows that the blind man got the eyes of his heart opened as well as the eyes of his head.

Once his spiritual eyes were opened his measure of light increased. The very opposition he encountered served to produce the increase. The questioning of the neighbours sprang from curiosity rather than opposition, and it served to bring out the simple facts with which he started. He knew how his eyes were opened and that he owed it to a Man called Jesus, though His whereabouts he knew not.

His case was so remarkable that they brought him to the Pharisees, and here at once the antagonistic spirit prevailed. There was no difficulty in finding ground for their opposition for the miracle had been wrought on the sabbath. Again Jesus had broken the sabbath, and this at once condemned Him in their eyes. To fail in this matter of ceremonial observance was fatal: He could not be of God—a conclusion quite typical of the Pharisaic mind. Others, however, were more impressed by the miracle, and so a division was again manifested, which led them to ask the man what he had to say of Him. His reply showed that the Man called Jesus was to him at least a Prophet. This was more than they would admit, so they questioned the truth of his miraculous cure.

The parents were now called into the discussion, only to testify that he was indeed born blind, so his cure was beyond question, though fear led them to refer all further enquiry to the man himself; and the fact comes out that the verdict of the Pharisees on the case was a foregone conclusion. Anyone confessing Jesus to be the Christ was to be excluded from all the religious privileges of Judaism. Thus their base motives stood revealed, and they pursued their examination of the man not to elicit the truth but to discover some possible ground for condemning either Jesus or the man, or both.

Would he ascribe the praise to God, while agreeing that the Man by whom God's power was exercised was a sinner? The man avoided this subtle trap by simply affirming again the one point as to which he was immovably certain. Like a skilful general who declines battle on ground chosen by the enemy and will only meet the foe in his own impregnable position, so he declined mere theological discussion, in which he was no match for them, and took his stand on what he knew had been wrought in himself. The man's words in verse 25 are full of instruction for us. The unlettered ploughboy of today can humbly yet boldly confront the numerous counterparts of both Pharisees and Sadducees, if content just to testify of that which the grace of God has done for him and in him.

Next they attempted to extract from the man more exact details of the method Jesus employed, if perchance they might find a point of attack. By now, however, he had perceived their antagonism, and his question, "Will ye also be His disciples?" had in it a touch of sarcasm. This stung them to the point of losing their tempers, so much so that while declaring their adherence to Moses they committed themselves to a declaration of ignorance as to the origin and credentials of Jesus. They took the "agnostic" attitude, just as so many do today. This, however, was a fatal admission. The loss of their tempers was followed by the loss of their case from an argumentative point of view. The simple believer, if he sticks to the foundation facts as to which he can bear witness, will suffer no defeat when he encounters the agnostic.

These Pharisees, who posed as the supreme religious authorities of the day, not only professed ignorance as to this most vital question, but also demanded a verdict on the question wholly contrary to the evidence. Beneficent power had undeniably operated, working deliverance from evil: they professed ignorance of its source, yet demanded that He who wielded it should be denounced as a sinner. The man, however, had felt the action of the power; he knew it was of God, and the wicked opposition he encountered only helped him to the further conclusion that Jesus Himself was "of God" indeed.

Having lost their case and failed to corrupt the thoughts of the man, they resorted to violence and cast him out. As regards Judaism he was excommunicated: was there anything for the poor man except heathenism with its blank darkness? *Yes, there was.* Jesus Himself was morally outside it already; from the outset of this Gospel He has been so viewed, as we have remarked before; though He was not outside it in the fullest sense till He was led outside the gate of Jerusalem to die the malefactor's death. In verse 35 we see the rejected Saviour finding the rejected man and propounding to him the greatest of questions—"Dost thou believe on the Son of God?" The question reached him in an abstract form. The man hesitated, for he wished the Son of God to be before him in concrete shape. Where should he find Him that he might believe? Thus challenged, Jesus plainly presented Himself *as the Son of God.* The man at once, and as plainly, accepted Him as such in faith, and worshipped Him.

So once more we are conducted to the main point of this Gospel as expressed in verse 31 of chapter 20. The man had been led step by step to the faith of the Son of God and to life in His name, and the opening of his physical eyes had been a sign of the greater work of opening the eyes of his mind and heart. In verse 39 we have the comment of the Lord on the whole scene. He had come into the world for judgment—not in the sense of condemning men, but as producing a discrimination that cut down beneath surface appearances and reached men as they really were. Some, like this man, had their eyes opened to see the truth. Others who professed to be the seeing ones, like the Pharisees, might be blinded and manifested as being blind. Some Pharisees who were present suspected that He referred to

# JOHN

them, and their question gave an opportunity for their perilous position to be shown. Their sin lay in their hypocrisy. They had *intellectual* sight yet were *spiritually* blind and their sin remained; whereas those really blind, and confessedly so, are rather objects of compassion.

## Chapter 10

THERE IS NO real break where this chapter commences in our Bibles. The Lord's answer which commenced in the last verse of the ninth chapter, continues to the end of verse 5 of this chapter. He propounded to them the parable of the Shepherd and the fold, and it illustrated the point, inasmuch as there were not only "the sheep" but also "His own sheep." These last knew the Shepherd's voice and so recognized Him. The man of the previous chapter was one of "His own sheep."

The religious system instituted through Moses was like a fold. Thereby the Jews were penned up apart from the Gentiles awaiting the coming of the true Messiah. The door of entrance had been prescribed by the voices of the prophets: He must be born of a virgin, at Bethlehem, etc. Imposters had appeared, but lacking these credentials they had sought an entrance in some other way and thereby betrayed themselves. Now the true Shepherd had appeared, and entering by the door, it had been kept open for Him by the providence of God. It had been said, "Behold, He that keepeth Israel shall neither slumber nor sleep" (Psa. 121: 4), and that watchful eye and hand had prevented Herod from closing the door of entrance against Him. God saw to it that He had full access to the sheep.

But now comes what no one had anticipated: He enters the fold not to reform or improve it but to call an election from the mass—"His own sheep"—and lead them *out* into something new. Israel had been the elect nation but now it is entirely individual, for He calls His own sheep "by name," establishing personal contact with each of these. Further, He leads them out by first going out Himself: they follow Him because this contact exists and they recognize His voice and trust Him. In the beginning of this Gospel these elect souls were referred to as, "born ... of God," being, "as many as received Him" (1: 12, 13).

Christ's sheep do not follow strangers, not because they have a wide acquaintance with them and know their voices right well, but because "they know not the voice of strangers." They know the Shepherd's voice well and that suffices. As to all others they simply say, That is not the Shepherd's voice. We have here in parabolic form the same basic fact as John stated, when he wrote to the babes in the family of God, saying, "I have not written unto you because ye know not the truth, but because ye know it, and that no lie is of the truth" (1 John 2: 21). As Paul also says, we are to be "wise unto that which is good, and simple concerning evil" (Rom. 16: 19). Let us cultivate this acquaintance with our Lord, for it develops a spiritual instinct which preserves against straying feet.

# JOHN

Blind as ever, the Pharisees understood none of these things; but that did not hinder the Lord pursuing His parable somewhat further. He was the door Himself; for all exit from the fold, and all entrance into the new place of blessing to be established, must be by Him. That new blessing we generally speak of as Christianity, in contrast with Judaism. Verse 9 begins to enumerate the blessings. Parabolic language is still used, as evidenced by the word "pasture," yet in saying, "if any *man* enter in," Jesus showed that He was speaking in accord with that great Old Testament chapter which ends, "Ye My flock, the flock of My pasture, are men" (Ezek. 34: 31).

The initial blessing of Christianity is salvation. It meets us as we enter by Christ the door. Most of the references to salvation in the Old Testament have to do with deliverance from enemies and troubles. The spiritual emancipation which comes to us by the gospel could not be known then, since the work on which it rests was not accomplished. Let Hebrews 9: 6-14 and 10: 1-14 be read and inwardly digested, and this fact will be very plain. Only by the death and resurrection of Christ is the door opened into salvation in its fulness.

The words, "shall go in and out," indicate liberty. In Judaism there was no liberty of access to God since "the way into the holiest of all was not yet made manifest;" nor had they permission to go out to the nations and spread any knowledge of God they had. They were enclosed within the fold of the law of Moses and its ordinances, and there they had to stay. As Christians we have "boldness to enter into the holiest by the blood of Jesus," and we may go out as did those early believers who "went everywhere preaching the word" (Acts 8: 4). In both directions we are carried far beyond the privileges of the Jewish fold.

Then, thirdly, we may "find pasture." This may carry our thoughts back to Ezekiel 34, where we find a tremendous indictment of the former shepherds of Israel. These religious leaders fed themselves and not the sheep, and set so bad an example, that the stronger among the sheep oppressed the weaker and had "eaten up the good pasture," and with their feet had trodden down "the residue of your pastures" (verse 18). Consequently for the poor of the flock there was no pasture at all. Jesus, the true Shepherd of Israel, leads His own sheep into an abundance of spiritual food.

In verses 10 and 11 we get the contrast between the thief and the Good Shepherd. These thieves and robbers were men such as those mentioned by Gamaliel, in Acts 5: 36, 37; self-seeking imposters who brought in destruction and death. The true Shepherd brought in life; laying down His own life in order to do so. If He had not come and died, there would have been no life at all for sinful men; having done so, life is made available, and it is bestowed in abundant measure upon His sheep. We live in the light of the abundant revelation of God which has reached us in the Word made flesh, hence we have life abundantly. The life given to saints in all ages may be intrinsically the same, yet its fulness can only be known as God is fully revealed. This is indicated in 1 John 1: 1-4.

Next we have, in verses 12-15, the contrast between the hireling and the Good Shepherd. The hireling is not necessarily evil like the thief; but being a man who works for wages, his interest is primarily a monetary one. The sheep are of interest to him in so far as they are the means of his livelihood. He does not really care for them to the extent of risking his skin on their behalf. It is far otherwise with the Shepherd, who lays down His life for them and establishes a link of wonderful intimacy. His sheep are men, and hence capable of knowing Him in an intimate way; so much so that His knowledge of them and their knowledge of Him can be compared to the Father's knowledge of Himself and His knowledge of the Father. And we must remember that it is by the knowledge of Him that we come to know the Father. Nothing at all approaching this had been possible in the Jewish fold before the Shepherd came.

The Lord's words in verse 16 add another unexpected development. He was about to find sheep who had been outside that fold. There was to be the calling of an election from among the Gentiles. We see the beginning of this early in the Acts—the Ethiopian in chapter 8; Cornelius and his friends in chapter 10. We have often dwelt upon the "must" which occurs several times in chapter 3: have we ever praised God for the "must" here? —"them also I MUST bring." Sinners of the Gentiles become the subjects of the Divine work. They hear the Shepherd's voice and are attached to Him. Then, as a result of this two-fold calling—from Jewish fold and from the straying Gentiles—there is to be established one flock, held together under the authority of the one Shepherd. The word in this verse is definitely "flock" and not "fold." Sheep held together by outward restrictions: that was Judaism. Sheep constituted a flock by the personal power and attraction of the Shepherd: that is Christianity.

But for this not only death but resurrection also was needful. The Shepherd truly had to be smitten as the prophet had said, but it is in His risen life that He gathers His flock out of both Jew and Gentile. Jesus proceeded to show that His death was in order to His resurrection. Both are viewed here as His own act. His death was His laying down of His life: His resurrection His taking of it again, though under new conditions. In both He was acting according to the Father's commandment; and furnishing the Father with a fresh motive for His love to the Son.

The Lord's words, recorded in verse 18, are thoroughly in keeping with the character of this Gospel. As recorded in other Gospels, He spoke again and again to His disciples of how He should be delivered by the chief priests and rulers to the Gentiles, that they should put Him to death; yet here He asserts that no man should take His life from Him, since both death and resurrection would be His own acts. Men did to Him that, which

# JOHN

for any mere man, made death inevitable; yet in His case nothing would have had any effect, if He had not been pleased to lay down His life. His Deity is emphasized, but also the true Humanity which He assumed in subjection to the will of God, for all was in keeping with the Father's commandment. Life was in Him, and it was "the *light* of men" (1: 4), even while He was here; but now He is to take up His life in resurrection, and thus He was to become the very *life* of His own in the power of the Spirit, as indicated in chapter 20, verse 22.

By these parables the Lord had furnished the Jews with a condensed summary of the great changes that were impending as the result of His coming as the true Shepherd into the midst of Israel. The Divine programme was opened out to them, but God's purposes so cut across the grain of their self-sufficient thoughts that His words sounded to many like the words of a madman or worse. Others, impressed by the miracle on the blind man, could not accept this extreme opinion. As the succeeding verses show, they took the place of "honest doubters," yet wished to insinuate that His ambiguity lay at the root of their vacillation. The trouble lay, however, not in *His words* but in *their minds*. It was thus with their forefathers when the law was given and they "could not steadfastly look to the end of that which is abolished" (2 Cor. 3: 13); that is, they never saw God's purpose in it all. Now religious pride was lying as a veil on the minds of these Jews and they could not perceive "the end" of the Lord's words. In just the same way does "the god of this age" impose a veil on the minds of the unbelieving today; no matter how able and acute they may be in the ordinary matters of the world.

Their demand was, "If Thou be the Christ, tell us plainly." Jesus at once asserted that He had told them plainly, and that His works equally with His words had borne plain witness to Him. Then He told them plainly that their unbelief had put the veil over their eyes. The evidence was there plainly enough, but they could not see it; and what lay behind that fact was that though of Israel nationally they were not the true Israel (see Rom. 9: 6): they were not "My sheep," though sheep within the Jewish fold. They were spiritually dead and hence unresponsive. Thus Jesus told them *plainly* not only the truth *about Himself* but *about themselves*.

Having put a sentence of condemnation upon them, He added words of the greatest comfort and assurance for the benefit of His own sheep. On their side they hear His voice and follow Him. On His side He knows them and gives them eternal life. This ensures that they shall never perish as under God's judgment, nor can any created power seize them out of the Shepherd's hand. This assurance is reinforced by the perfect oneness subsisting between the Son and the Father. The Son had taken the subject place on earth and the Father remained "greater than all" in heaven, but this did not militate against Their oneness. Being in the hand of the Son involved being in the hand of the Father, and the purpose of the Godhead in securing the sheep is guaranteed by both the Son and the Father. The same glorious fact confronts us in that great passage, Romans 8: 29-39.

These words moved the Jews to murderous intentions. They did not understand their drift, but they did see that in saying, "I and the Father are one," He was claiming equality with God. It might have been slightly less offensive had He put the Father first by saying, "The Father and I;" but no, it was "I and the Father." This was intolerable to them, for there was no mistaking the drift of such words as these. To them it was atrocious blasphemy—a man making himself God. We accept His words in the spirit of worship, for we know He was truly God, yet had made Himself Man. We reverse the terms of their accusation and find in it soul-saving truth.

In His reply Jesus referred to His own words, "I am the Son of God," in such a way as to identify them with their accusation of making Himself God. He did not defend His claim by one of His own emphatic assertions but by an argument based on their Scripture. Those acknowledged as "gods" in Psalm 82: 6, were authorities "unto whom the word of God *came*." He who had been set apart and sent into the world by the Father *was* the Word Himself—"the Word . . . made flesh." How vast the difference! It was not blasphemy but sober truth when He said, "I am the Son of God." Moreover His works bore witness to His claim, as being unmistakably the works of God. They plainly set forth the fact that the Father was in Him, livingly declared and revealed; and He was in the Father, as to essential life and nature. Once let that be known and believed, and there is no difficulty in receiving Him as the Son of God; for both statements set forth the same foundation fact, though in different words.

But the moment was not yet come for their murderous hatred to take effect, and in His retirement to the place of John's baptism beyond Jordan the faith of a number was made manifest. John's witness was recalled and the truth of his words acknowledged. John was the last prophet of the old dispensation, and amidst its ruins miracles were not in season. They were in season, and in full measure, directly the Christ the Son of God appeared. Still John bore a true and faithful and unswerving witness to Christ, which was better than miracles. We too are at the end time of a dispensation, so let us not crave for miracles but emulate John in faithfulness of testimony. If it could be said of any of us before the judgment seat, that all things we have spoken of Christ are TRUE—that were commendation indeed!

CHAPTER 11

THE TWO VERSES with which this chapter opens indicate that this Gospel was written when the other Gospels were well known. In naming Bethany as the town of Martha and Mary, it is assumed that the readers will be more familiar with the women than the village. Again, in verse 2, Mary is identified by her action in anointing the Lord, though John does not tell us about this till the next chapter is reached: he evidently knew he could safely identify her thus, since the story was so widely known.

The brief message sent by the sisters indicates very strikingly the intimacy into which the Lord introduced His friends in the days of His flesh. It was a *reverential* intimacy, in which He ever held the supreme place, for they did not address Him, with undue familiarity as Jesus, but as "Lord." Yet they could with all confidence speak of their brother as "he whom Thou lovest." He had made the Bethany household quite conscious of *His love*, so that they could count upon it with confidence. That their confidence was not misplaced is confirmed by the comment of the Evangelist in verse 5. Jesus did indeed love them. He loved each individually; and Martha, whom, we might consider, He had least cause to love, is placed first on the list. Lazarus, whom most evidently He loved, as shown by this chapter, is placed last. Mary, whom we might have placed first, is not even mentioned by name; she is just "her sister." Let us learn that the love of Christ is placed upon a foundation lying far deeper than the varying characteristics of saints. Proceeding from what He is in Himself, it is a wonderfully impartial thing.

In spite of it, however, the sisters' appeal did not meet with an immediate response. There was a deliberate delay, which gave time for the sickness to terminate in death; and death have time to produce corruption. Why was this? Here we have answered for all time this question which so constantly arises in the hearts of saints. Death was not the real end of this incident, but the manifestation of the glory of God and the glorifying of the Son of God. It was for the good of the disciples, as verse 15 shows: it was also to be turned into a great blessing to the sorrowing sisters, as indicated by the Lord's words recorded in verse 40. Hence what seemed so strange and inexplicable worked out for glory to God and good for men. There was a response of the highest kind in the apparent lack of response on the part of the Lord.

When the Lord did turn His steps again towards Judæa His disciples feared, for they were like men walking in the dark, and they had no light in themselves. But He, on the other hand, was like one walking in the day, for He was in the light—not indeed of this world, but of that other world where the Father's will and way is everything. Hence He never stumbled, and now He went up to Bethany to do the will of God. The disciples followed Him thinking of death, as Thomas indicated; but He went up into scenes of death in the power of resurrection.

The action of the two sisters, when Jesus drew near, was characteristic. Martha, the woman of action, went out to meet Him. Mary, the woman of meditation and sympathy, still sat in the house awaiting His call. Both, however, greeted Him with the same words when they saw Him. Martha had genuine faith. She believed in His power as Intercessor with God, and in the power of God to be exerted in resurrection at the last day. Doubtless she was impetuous, but her impetuosity called forth one of the greatest pronouncements on record. Of old Jehovah had called Himself "I AM." Now the Word has been made flesh, and He too is "I AM," but He fills it out in detail. Here we have, "I AM the resurrection and the life." Since the point here is what He is in relation to men, resurrection comes first. Death lies upon Adam and his race, hence life for men can only be in the power of resurrection.

The fact itself is twofold, and there follows a two-fold application to the believer. If he have died he shall yet certainly live, for his faith reposes in One who is the resurrection, and who consequently quickens with life beyond death. But then Jesus is also the life, and His quickening power reaches men so that they "live by the faith of the Son of God"—or, as the Lord puts it, "liveth and believeth in Me"—then such shall never die; that is, shall never taste death in its full and proper form. The earthly house of this tabernacle may be dissolved, but death is not for us; it is rather a falling asleep. The whole utterance was somewhat enigmatical in form, and wholly beyond any light that had hitherto been granted to men. He was not as yet revealing truth as to His coming again, to which He does allude when the opening of chapter 14 is reached, and which is expanded for us in 1 Thessalonians 4: 13-18. But though not the primary interpretation of His words, we can see, when once the truth of His coming is revealed, a striking secondary application of them. At His coming for His saints there will be in fact the great public demonstration of the truth of His words, "I am the resurrection and the life."

When the Lord challenged Martha as to her belief she at once showed that it was all an enigma to her. Probably she viewed resurrection at the last day as being a restoration to life in this world, in common with the mass of the Jews. So in replying she fell back, very wisely, upon what she did believe with certitude—that He was the Christ the Son of God who had been announced as coming into the world. She had already arrived at the faith to which this Gospel conducts us, and so possessed "life in His name." But mentally out of her depth as to other matters, she proceeded to call her sister secretly to go to the Master.

With Mary a special bond of sympathy existed. We do not read of Martha falling at the feet of Jesus, nor of her tears. The sorrow of death lay on Mary's spirit very heavily, as indeed it lay upon His. Though He was on His way to lift the weight of it for a season in this particular case, He felt its weight in a measure infinitely deep, moving Him to groaning in spirit and even to the shedding of tears. He wept, not for Lazarus, for He knew that in a few minutes He would recall him to life, but in sympathy with the sisters and as feeling in His spirit the desolation of death brought in by sin.

The word used here is the one for the shedding of silent tears, not the word for vocal lamentations, which is used in Luke 19: 41. But those silent tears of Jesus have moved the hearts of sorrowing saints for nearly two thousand years.

Death had drawn forth a groan in the spirit of Jesus, and again (verse 38) we find the grave doing the same. But now He was about to bring the power of His word into action and display. Verse 39 begins, "Jesus said." There are five striking couplets in this chapter which would serve to summarize the whole story. They occur in verses 4, 5, 17, 35, 39—"Jesus heard," "Jesus loved," "Jesus came," "Jesus wept," "Jesus said." The sorrowing saint of today has to wait for the fifth to be verified in that "shout" which will raise the dead and change the living, and catch up all to be with Him. The other four are valid and efficacious for us at all times.

At the word of the Lord men could roll the stone from the mouth of the cave. This they did in spite of Martha's rather officious remonstrance, but their power stopped at that point. The display of the glory of God, which Martha was to see if she believed, was His work alone. Quickening and resurrection are wholly His work, though men may be used to remove obstructions. Yet the power that brought Lazarus back to life was only exercised in dependence on the Father. Full testimony was rendered in the presence of the crowd to the fact that here was the Son of God in power, and also to the fact that He was here on the Father's behalf and in full dependence upon Him.

He uttered but three words and the mighty sign came to pass. Death and corruption disappeared and Lazarus, still bound in grave-clothes, came forth. Now again human instrumentality came into play and Lazarus was freed from his bonds; just as today the servants of God may so preach the word as to remove spiritual obstructions and release souls from bondage, while the life-giving work remains altogether in the hands of the Son of God. In this great sign, the sixth that John puts on record, the glory of God had been manifested, since the giving of life is His glorious prerogative. Brutish man can kill all too easily: only God can "kill *and make alive*" (see 1 Sam. 2: 6; 2 Kings 5: 7). In it, too, the Son of God had been glorified, for His oneness with the Father in the wielding of this power had been displayed.

Taking place so near to Jerusalem this sign had a deep effect. It moved many to faith, and it stirred the chief priests and Pharisees to a fiercer resolve to slay Him. They had to admit that He had done many signs, yet they only considered the effect these things might have on their own place in the presence of the Romans. God was not at all in their thoughts. The council they held gave occasion for the prophecy of Caiaphas.

God can lay hold on a false prophet like Balaam and force him to utter words of truth. But here was a man who, save for being high priest that

# JOHN

year, had no pretensions to anything of the kind; a man who prophesied without knowing that he was prophesying. As far as he was concerned his words were sarcastic, filled with the spirit of cynical, heartless, cold-blooded murder; yet they were used by the Holy Spirit to convey the fact that Jesus was about to die for Israel, in a sense of which they knew nothing. Verse 52 gives us a further commentary on his words through the Evangelist. Israel was indeed to be redeemed through His death, but there was a further purpose shortly to come to light. Children of God existed, but as yet without any special bond of union. That bond was to be created as the fruit of His death. More light as to this will reach us in the next chapter.

## Chapter 12

For the third time in this Gospel a Passover feast is mentioned. In Leviticus 23, it is spoken of as one of the "feasts of the Lord," but in John's Gospel it is always a feast of the Jews, in keeping with the fact that Jesus is regarded as refused by His people from the outset, and consequently they and their feasts are disowned by God. The religious leaders were now about to crown their infamy by using the Passover as an occasion for encompassing the death of the Son of God. Their guilt was not lessened by the fact that God overruled their action to the fulfilling of the type, and that thereby "Christ our Passover is sacrificed for us."

Six days before the Passover Jesus came to Bethany, so that all recorded between verse 1 of this chapter and verse 25 of chapter 20 falls into a brief period of seven or eight days—surely the most wonderful week in the world's history. In the home at Bethany dwelt the three who were *objects of His love* and who loved Him in return. A suitable opportunity had now arrived for them to testify of this. Behind them lay the death of Lazarus and His calling to life by the voice of the Son of God. Just ahead lay the death and resurrection of the Son of God Himself.

At the close of Luke 10 we see this household marked by some measure of disorder and complaint; but *here*, after the display of the Lord's resurrection power, all is found in order and harmonious. The simple proceedings of that evening centred in Christ. He was the honoured Object of each and all, for, "they made HIM a supper." We may indeed see a parable in this. When Christ is the supreme Object and His resurrection power is known, everything falls into its right place.

Martha was hostess and served Him. Lazarus had his part with Him at the supper table. Mary expressed her heart's devotion to Him by expending upon Him her costly ointment. Thus we see how the knowledge of Him and of His resurrection power led to service, to communion, and to worship. All was happily in order, and, just because it was, the voice of hostile criticism was heard, centred upon Mary's action. It originated with Judas Iscariot, though the other disciples echoed his words, as Matthew's Gospel shows.

The world is incapable of appreciating true worship, and in spite of his fair exterior Judas was wholly of the world. Ruled by covetousness Judas had become a thief; and not only a thief but a hypocrite, masking his self-seeking by the profession of care for the poor. He posed as an eminently practical man, fully alive to the value of solid, material benefits for the poor, whilst Mary was in his view squandering valuable substance, moved by silly sentiment. The world is exactly of that opinion today. The religion which suits its taste is one which lays all the emphasis upon material and earthly benefits for mankind. And today, as much as then, carnally minded believers are very prone to be in agreement with the world and echo its opinions.

In saying, "Let her alone," Jesus silenced the hostile criticism. The three words may well be written upon our memories. True worship lies between the soul of the believer and the Lord, and no other may interfere. In Romans 14 the believer is viewed as a servant and the spirit of that chapter again is, "Let him alone." Further, the Lord knew how to interpret her action. He gave, no doubt, a fuller explanation of it than Mary herself could have offered; though she knew the hatred of the leaders and intuitively perceived His death approaching. It is significant too that Mary of Bethany did not join the other women in visiting His grave with the spices they had prepared.

Of Mary we may say that what she did, was done "for Jesus' sake only." With Judas it was "the poor," and even with the other disciples, it was "Jesus and the poor." With many of the Jews who flocked to Bethany at this time it was "Jesus and Lazarus," for they were curious to see a man who had been raised from the dead. The Bethany household had concentrated upon Jesus their true affection. In contrast therewith the chief priests concentrated upon Him the deadliest hatred, which so blinded them that they contemplated slaying Lazarus, the witness to His power. They were most religious but most unscrupulous. They forgot the warning of Psalm 82: 1-5.

The next day Jesus presented Himself to Jerusalem as Israel's King, just as Zechariah the prophet had said. No mere Sovereign of earth could afford to formally present himself to his capital city in such humble fashion; but to Him who was the Word made flesh all such glory, as was possible then, would have been loss, not gain. This occasion is recorded in each of the four Gospels, but John records two special details. First, there is the contrast between the disciples and their Master, who ever knew exactly what He would do (see 6: 6). They took part without any understanding of what they were doing. The significance of it all only dawned upon them when they had received the Holy Spirit, consequent upon the glorification of Jesus. Second, there is the fact that the measure of popular

# JOHN

enthusiasm manifested had been stirred by the raising of Lazarus, wherein His glory as the Son of God had been displayed.

We are next permitted to see the effect of all this in three directions. The Pharisees were bitterly mortified, attributing to the demonstration of the people a depth of conviction which was non-existent. But among certain Greeks who had come up to the feast there was a spirit of enquiry and their desire to see Jesus was the pledge of a day when "the Gentiles shall come to Thy light, and king's to the brightness of Thy rising" (Isa. 60: 3). And indeed now was the moment when He should have been received and acclaimed by His own people. The hour had struck when as the Son of Man He should have been glorified. As regards the Lord Himself, He knew well that as the rejected One nothing but death lay before Him—the death which would be the foundation of all the glory in days to come. Of that death therefore He proceeded to speak.

In verse 24 we find another of His great statements introduced with special emphasis. The life that abides and blossoms forth into much fruit is only reached through death. If fruit for God is to be ingathered—fruit which will be of the same order as Himself—He must die. Emmanuel was here, the Word made flesh, and His intrinsic worth and beauty is beyond all words; but only through death will He "be fruitful and multiply," so that a multitude of others "after His kind" may be found to the glory of God. This was what filled His thoughts while others were still thinking of earthly glory.

Fruit for God, then, is the first result of His death which He mentioned. The second was the new order of life on earth, which thereby would be entailed upon His disciples. He was about to lay down His life in this world, all perfect as it was. Life in this world is for us wholly marred by sin, and under judgment. If we love it we shall only lose it. Seeing it in its true light we learn to hate it, and thereby we keep life—the only life worth having—unto life eternal. This is for us an hard saying, but of extreme importance, as we may glean from the fact that Jesus uttered words of similar import on three other occasions, and these four sayings are recorded six times in the four Gospels. No other saying of our Lord is repeated for us like this. It is not too much to say that our spiritual stature and prosperity are determined by the measure in which this saying leaves its impress on our hearts and lives.

Verse 26 springs naturally out of verse 25. We can only really serve the Lord as we follow Him, and we only really follow Him as our attitude to life is the same as His. He did not love His life in this world when as the grain of wheat He fell into the ground and died. The Apostle Paul entered into the spirit of this, as we can see by such scriptures as 2 Corinthians 4: 10-18 and Galatians 2: 20; 6: 14. And as a servant of Christ he greatly surpasses us all. The servant's reward is to be with his Master, and to be honoured of the Father.

# JOHN

On another occasion Jesus had said that every servant when perfected is to be "AS his Master" (Luke 6: 40). Here we find he is to be WITH his Master. And there is yet something more. "If any man serve Me" — who is this ME? The humbled and rejected Son of God! Who serves Him in the hour of His unpopularity and rejection? Such are honoured of the Father, and the honours will be publicly theirs when the day of the great review arrives. The highest honours of the world are but tinsel compared with this.

John's Gospel makes no mention of the sorrows of Gethsemane, but we are permitted to see here how the weight of His approaching death lay upon His soul. His Deity did not mitigate His trouble; it rather gave Him an infinite capacity to feel it. He could not desire the hour that drew near: His perfect knowledge and infinite holiness caused Him of necessity to shrink from it, yet to be saved from it was not His prayer, but rather that the Father's name should be glorified in it. This desire was so perfect, so wholly delightful to the Father, that a voice was heard from heaven. The other Gospels have told us how the Father's voice was heard at His baptism and His transfiguration. These were more private occasions, and there seems to have been no difficulty in understanding what was said. Here in view of His death the voice was more public and intended for the ears of the people; yet they did not receive it, and explained the sound they heard either as the voice of an angel or a peal of thunder. God spoke to men audibly and directly, yet they made nothing of it! In man's fallen condition it would ever be thus.

The Father's response was that His name had already been glorified in the whole pathway of Jesus down here, and more particularly in the raising of Lazarus; and He would glorify it again in the death and resurrection of His Son. This then is another great result of the dying of the single "corn of wheat." There is the production of much fruit; which involves the entrance upon a new kind of life and service by the disciple: there is the glorifying of the Father's name. And there is yet more, for verse 31 brings both the world and its prince into view.

At the cross was the judgment of this world. Our language has appropriated both the Greek words used here. There came to pass the *crisis* of this *cosmos* at the cross. Cosmos signifies an ordered scene in contrast with chaos, but alas! this cosmos has fallen under the leadership of the devil. Now the death of Christ exposed the world in its true character, thus bringing it under righteous condemnation. It also broke the power and legally dispossessed the usurper, who had become its prince. It appeared to be his greatest triumph: it was really his utter defeat.

This wonderful unfolding of the results of His death came from the lips of the Lord, and characteristically He placed last its result as regards Himself. In mentioning this He signified crucifixion as the manner of his death. Now this was the Roman way of executing the death sentence; but seeing that all the animosity against Him was in the breast of the Jew, it signified

# JOHN

that He would die a death of utmost shame, repudiated by both Jew and Gentile. He was lifted up from the earth in order that He might be contemptuously dismissed—the extinguisher dropped, so to speak, upon His cause and His Name. And the result to be attained is precisely the opposite. He who once was crucified is to be the universal and everlasting Object of attraction! All who are drawn into God's mighty circle of blessing will be drawn by Him and to Him. Here we have in germinal form what is more fully expounded in Ephesians 1: 9-14. Far from extinguishing His glory the cross becomes the foundation upon which it rests, the basis for its most perfect display, as is so movingly witnessed by Revelation 5: 5-14.

The opening words of Jesus spoke of the Son of Man being glorified, and the closing words of His being lifted up. The Jews knew that the Messiah was to abide when He came, and the title "Son of Man" was not unknown to them for it is found in the Old Testament. The Son of Man who was to receive the kingdom according to Daniel 7, they knew, but who was this Son of Man who was to suffer? They had overlooked the Son of Man made a little lower than the angels, according to Psalm 8. This humbled Son of Man was the light of men. Except they believed in the light and became children of light, utter darkness would come upon them and they would be lost. With this warning Jesus withdrew Himself from them.

A summary of the situation up to this point is furnished by the Evangelist in verses 37-43. Jesus had done many signs before them, yet they did not believe on Him. The fact was this: their eyes were blinded. The blinding of the eyes of men is the work of the god of this age, as we learn from 2 Corinthians 4: 4. Yet there are times when God specially permits it to take place in governmental retribution, and so it can be attributed to Him. Such was the case here; such it had been in the days of Isaiah; and such it was again some 35 years later, when the testimony to the glorified Christ was refused (see Acts 28: 25-27). The unbelieving generation persists, and will still be found when the final judgment falls at the end of the age.

In Isaiah 6 the prophet records how he saw the King, *Jehovah* of Hosts. John tells us, however, that Isaiah "saw His glory and spake of Him;" evidently referring to *Jesus*. Again, verse 40 of our chapter is recorded in Isaiah 6 as "the voice of the Lord." In Acts 28 Paul quotes it as that which was said by the *Holy Ghost*. This casts a helpful light on the unity of the Divine Persons. We may not divide, though we may distinguish.

The effect of this blinding was that "they could not believe." Their minds were so befogged that faith had become a moral impossibility. No matter how brightly the light shone before them, they had no eyes to perceive it. There were, however, some—and these among the chief rulers—who were not completely blinded in this way. Their minds were open to evidence and the signs displayed wrought intellectual conviction in them. Now intellectual conviction, though an essential ingredient of living faith, is non-living, if by itself alone. It does not fructify in works but it is "as the body without spirit" (Jas. 2: 26). Living faith conducts the soul to God through Christ. This was unknown by these rulers for had they experienced it they would not have loved the praise of men more than the praise of God. The same test applies today. He who really believes in his heart that God has raised Christ from the dead, will not fail to confess Him with the mouth as Lord. If men do not confess, they do not really believe.

In verses 44-50 we get the Lord's own summing up of the situation as He brought to a close His testimony to the world. In chapters 3-7 the prominent thought is life, and Jesus is seen as the Life-giver. From chapter 8 to this point light has been a great theme, and Jesus is seen as the Light-bearer. Chapter 8: 12 gives the Lord's opening pronouncement as to this, and verse 46 of our chapter the closing word. We only emerge from the darkness as we come into the light of Christ. But the light that shone in Him was the full revelation of God so that he who comes into His light believes on, and sees, Him that sent Him. Being the Word made flesh He was not less than the Father whom He revealed, yet He had come into the place of subjection in order to make Him known and carry out His every commandment.

At that moment the Father's commandment was not judgment but life everlasting, hence He had hidden Himself from His adversaries instead of breaking them by His power. Still judgment will come in due season; the Judge is appointed, and on the basis of the revelation He had brought will they be judged. The Lord now addressed Himself to the work immediately before Him, to "save the world," and to bring in "life everlasting." So He still continued to *speak* after the Father's commandment and also, as He declares in chapter 14: 31, to *do* His commandment, which involved the cross as the necessary basis of both salvation and life. The immediate thing before Him was the gathering together of His disciples for the last time, that He might fully communicate to them the present purposes of the Father's love.

## Chapter 13

THIS CHAPTER THEREFORE begins with a description of the spirit in which Jesus gathered His disciples together for the last Passover Supper. The other Gospels have told us all we need to know as to the surrounding circumstances; here we are made aware of the atmosphere of Divine love which graced the occasion. He was in the full knowledge of His approaching death, which is viewed as a departure out of the judged "cosmos" to the Father whilst He leaves behind in the "cosmos" a few who are recognized as "His own." He had spoken of these in chapter 10 as "His own sheep," indicating that He would lay down His life for them; now we discover how His love had been set upon them. He loved "unto the end," which as regards this world was death; but since death itself is but the door into life eternal for them, the love abides to eternity.

# JOHN

The first three verses uncover to our eyes things which otherwise were only known to God. Who could adequately read the love that filled the heart of Christ? Who could discern the hatred and craft of the devil which led him at that moment to inject the fatal thought of treachery into the heart of Judas? And who else was privy to that which filled the mind of Jesus in that sacred hour? We are permitted to know, however. As He faced the death by which He would depart to the Father, nothing was hidden from His eyes. He knew that He had come from God in order that He might carry to perfection both the revelation of God and the redemption of men. He knew that He was going to God in risen life as the firstfruits of a great harvest of blessing, the Head of a new creation. And He knew that though He was going forth to submit Himself to the hands of evil men, the Father had in reality given all things into His hands of perfect administration. Everything lies at His disposal, and the prediction of Isaiah, "The pleasure of the Lord shall prosper in His hand," shall surely be fulfilled.

In the full consciousness of all this He took the humble place of service in the midst of His gathered disciples. The pleasure of Jehovah is to prosper in the hand of "the Servant of Jehovah." In the coming day of glory He will cause that pleasure to prosper throughout a wide universe of blessing, but on the eve of His suffering He caused it to prosper by using His hands to wash the disciples' feet. In this He was the servant of the Lord as much as He will be in the coming day; and both forms of service are alike wonderful. He was serving God in serving them.

Peter's impetuous remonstrance was overruled to make plain the significance of all this. The marvellous humility of it was very obvious to him, and it prompted his remonstrance. He was plainly told, however, that he did not know the real meaning of the Lord's action, but that when the Spirit was come he should know it. We should understand it too. What then was its significance? The words of Jesus, recorded in verse 8, provide us with the key. He spoke of "part with Me," and if we are to have the happiness of sharing with Him, He must render to us the service symbolized by feet-washing. By our feet we come into contact with the earth, and the dust and defilement which this involves must be removed from us.

The Lord's words in verse 10 throw further light on the matter. He used two words for *wash*, the first of which means to wash all over, or bathe. He said, therefore, that he who is bathed needs only to wash his feet, thus alluding very evidently to the twofold washing of the priests—the bathing when they were consecrated (Lev. 8: 6), which was once for all, and the subsequent frequent washings of hands and feet whenever the sanctuary was entered (Exod. 30: 19). This once-for-all bathing is ours when we are born again. We are then born of water and the Spirit; and so, after reminding the Corinthians of the evils in which once they had been sunk, Paul could write to them, "But ye are washed," even though they were still mainly of a carnal mind. So here, the Lord said to the disciples, "Ye are clean," adding, "but not all"—with Judas in mind. In spite of all his profession no new birth had ever reached Judas.

This symbolic action of the Lord, together with His explanatory words, was the suited prelude to the marvellous chapters that follow. His communications to the disciples in chapters 14-16, so to speak, introduced them into the sanctuary while in chapter 17 we see Him going alone into the Holiest of all. When His death was accomplished and, having gone up on high, the Holy Ghost was given, we find that boldness to enter the Holiest is the common privilege of believers. But whether it was the disciples then, or ourselves today, this cleansing from the defilement of earth is needed, in addition to the new birth, if there is to be the enjoyment of part with Him in the sanctuary of God's presence.

This gracious service is still rendered to us by the Lord Himself just as we need it. It is part of His work as our High Priest and Advocate on high. Yet He is our Lord and Master, and therefore an Example to us that we should follow His steps in this. The Word is the great cleansing agent, as Psalm 119: 9 has told us. It requires, we believe, more divinely given skill to use it as cleansing water than as a shining light or a cutting sword. If we acquire this skill and exercise it in our intercourse with saints we shall be happy indeed. It is easier to gain knowledge about this thing than to DO it, as verse 17 indicates. Doing it, we should be restored and refreshed.

In keeping with this is the exhortation of Galatians 6: 1, yet spiritual "feet-washing" would deal with defilements which, though touching the heart and mind, have not as yet led to being "overtaken in a fault." If we knew better how to DO this thing we should often be instrumental in preserving one another from being overtaken and suffering a fall.

The moment had now come for Judas to be exposed in his true character. At the close of chapter 6 we find words of the Lord recorded which show that He thoroughly knew him from the outset. In His choice of the disciples He acted with Divine foreknowledge, and Judas was the man to fulfil the prediction of Psalm 41: 9. Nevertheless he had been commissioned and sent by the Lord as much as the others and those who received him and them had received his Master, and God Himself, from whom the Lord had come. The personal unworthiness of the servant did not vitiate this great principle.

Yet the terrible fall of Judas was a real grief to the heart of the Lord, which was not lessened by His Divine foreknowledge, which enabled Him to see the end from the beginning. The Lord's emphatic pronouncement that one of the chosen twelve was about to reveal himself as a traitor also carried trouble into the minds of the disciples, and verse 22 bears witness to the fact that no suspicion of Judas was lurking in their minds. He appeared perfectly sincere to their eyes, so much so that the common purse had been entrusted to him. The craft of Satanic camouflage is well-nigh perfect. Has there ever been a more striking illustration of what is stated in 2 Corinthians 11: 13-15?

"Who is it?;" that was the delicate question, and only one disciple was at that moment qualified to ask it. The bodily position of "the disciple whom Jesus loved" was an index of the state of his mind. Peter felt this and prompted the enquiry. The answer was given in a symbolic fashion. It was a mark of distinction for a guest to receive a dipped morsel from the host. But the honoured disciple was to prove the traitor.

We can discern three steps in his fall. First there was the unjudged covetousness which led him to become even a thief (12: 6). Then came the action of Satan, putting it into his mind to recoup himself in part (13: 2), since the three hundred pence which the ointment represented had not come into his hands; and he finally settled for ten per cent of this sum. Lastly Satan entered into him. The master spirit of evil took personal control, that there might be no slip in the arrangements that should encompass the Lord's death.

The Lord accepted the situation and bade him act quickly. It seems that even Satan could not freely move in the matter without Divine permission; but that granted, under the imperative control of Satan, Judas rose and left. He went out into the night, in more senses than one.

Within the upper chamber a sense of ease prevailed when Judas had gone out into the night. Relieved of his presence, the Lord at once began His farewell discourse, which shed Divine light on all that was impending. At last He could speak with all freedom, though His disciples as yet had but little apprehension of His meaning. The first two sentences that He uttered present us with a marvellous summary. Each sentence furnishes two great facts.

The hour had just struck when the Son of Man should have been glorified in public fashion, as the prophets had said. Instead of that He was on the point of going into death. But—wondrous fact—in that very death He was going to be glorified, inasmuch as every Divine and human excellence, which was intrinsically His, would there be brought into brightest display. Connected with this is the second fact, that God was perfectly glorified in Him. In the first man and in his race God had been utterly misrepresented and dishonoured: in His death the perfect revelation of God was carried to its climax; His character and nature vindicated and displayed.

Then further, in answer to this glorifying of God, there is to be the glorifying of the Son of Man in God Himself. Christ is now hidden in God, as Colossians 3: 3 infers, but He is hidden there as the glorified One. That the Son of Man should be glorified in this way had not been previously revealed. So this fact gives an unexpected turn to events; as does also the second fact of this verse that this hidden glorification should take place straightway. No waiting until the visible kingdom for this! But on the fact of this present and hidden glory hangs the shedding forth of the Spirit to indwell believers, and consequently all the privilege and blessing which is properly Christian.

The glorifying of Christ in this heavenly and immediate way involved, however, the severing of existing links upon an earthly basis with His disciples, for at that moment they could not follow Him into His new place. Here for the first time does the Lord address His disciples as "children," viewing them as those who had been introduced into the family of God, according to verse twelve of chapter 1. It is remarkable how much of John's first Epistle is based upon the Lord's words recorded in verse 34. We enter the Divine family by being born of God, and the very life of the family is love, for God is love. The Lord makes it plain that while He is in the hidden glory of heaven, the children, left in the world of darkness and hatred, are to prove their discipleship by manifesting love. Glory there, and love here, was the Divine thought. The former is perfect, but, alas! how imperfect the latter!

This approaching separation was a puzzle as well as a grief to the disciples, and Peter voiced their difficulty. His question drew forth the assurance that neither he nor any other could follow Him then, as He passed through death into His risen glory, yet ultimately they should be there. There was a special meaning in the remark in Peter's case, as we can see by turning to chapter 21: 18, 19; yet it surely has an application to all of us. He has made a way through death into resurrection that we all have to tread. Peter, not being content with the Lord's assurance only revealed his own foolish self-confidence. In that solemn hour the self-confident boaster was exposed, just as the traitor had been.

## Chapter 14

THE WORD OF warning was at once followed by a word of exceeding grace. Jesus knew well that these disciples in spite of all their failures did really love Him, and the thought of His departure was a sore grief to them. Hence the words that open our chapter. It was beginning to dawn upon them that they were to lose His visible presence with them; that was the trouble that burdened their hearts. But then the invisible God had ever been to them real, as an Object of faith. Might not Christ from henceforward be the same? He would indeed be so. As an Object of faith He would be a living, bright reality to countless millions, whereas He could only be an Object of sight to a few in one locality at a time, did He remain as He was. The first item of comfort troubled hearts then is this: Christ, as the risen Victor over death, the Object of simple faith.

# JOHN

And the second item is this: a place prepared and secured in the many abodes in the Father's house on high. Now the disciples were men who had staked all on their belief that they found the Messiah present on earth in flesh and blood. They had given up such place as they had possessed on earth and, if He was going to leave them, for what? As they learn here, for a place of nearer relationship, of far greater elevation, abiding eternally beyond the reach of death. What a marvellous exchange! The earthly Temple had been "My Father's house" (see 2: 16); this is now disowned, and the true "Father's house" is found on high, into which He was about to enter. In it there are many abodes, as had been indicated by the many chambers in the earthly type. Their particular place and ours was to be prepared by His entering in. He holds it for us as our Forerunner, as is shown by Hebrews 6: 20.

Of necessity therefore a time must come when the saints enter into their prepared place; so in verse 3 we find a third item of comfort—His personal coming to receive us unto Himself, that we may be with Him in the Father's house. The disciples must have known from the Old Testament that there was to be a personal coming of Jehovah: for instance, "His feet shall stand in that day upon the Mount of Olives ... and the Lord my God shall come, and all the saints with Thee" (Zech. 14: 4, 5). But they had not realized that "Jehovah" was "Jesus," and they knew nothing of this coming *in order to receive saints unto Himself*, for it had not been announced. It was as much a new revelation as that saints should have a place *in heaven* or that the Messiah should be *there* as an Object of faith, instead of being visibly present on the earth.

We may say then that verse 1 gives us in germ that life "by the faith of the Son of God," of which Paul speaks in Galatians 2: 20. Verse 2 gives us in germinal form the truth of the heavenly calling, more fully expounded in Ephesians 1: 3-6 and in Hebrews 2: 9; 3: 1. Verse 3 gives us the first intimation of the coming of the Lord for His saints. Their rapture into His presence above is more fully expounded in 1 Thessalonians 4: 14-18. There also, as here, this truth was made known to bring comfort to troubled hearts.

Jesus credited His disciples with knowing both where He was going and the way. Thomas was the disciple of materialistic and therefore of doubtful mind. His objection served to bring forth one of the Lord's greatest pronouncements. He is the way to the Father, the truth about the Father, the life, in the energy of which the Father can be really known. There exists no other avenue of approach than the Son. Moreover, being in the fallen life of Adam, we have no capacity to enter into the knowledge of the Father: such knowledge is only possible for those who are in the life of Christ. The more we meditate on these words the more we shall perceive the all-sufficiency of Christ; as also that they yield their tribute to the fact that the fulness of the Godhead dwelt in Him (see Col. 1: 19; 2: 9).

# JOHN

Philip's plaintive request in verse 8 shows that he too desired to have the Father displayed before his eyes in a material way. He was not wrong in this, but only in failing to discern the display that had been made in Christ, who was the Word made flesh. As John says in the opening words of his first Epistle, the Word thereby became *audible, visible* and *tangible.* The Father therefore had been perfectly shown forth. The words of Jesus were the Father's words, and His works were done by the Father who dwelt in Him. In verse 17 of our chapter we have an allusion to the fact that the Spirit was with them dwelling in Christ; and here it is the Father who dwells in Him: thus our thoughts are again conducted to Colossians 1: 19.

His words and works corroborated the great claim which the Lord twice makes here. As to essential being and life and nature, He was "in the Father," as also the Father was in Him, in manifestation and display. The disciples should believe this just because His own lips stated it; but if not, they should receive the evidence of His works, which so plainly declared it. And more than this, the day was coming, as stated in verse 12, when similar and even greater works should be done through the disciples, and that because He was going to the Father, which as we have learned in chapter 7, meant the coming of the Spirit. At that day the disciples would discover themselves to be in Christ and Christ would be in them (see verse 20), and this doubtless explains the "greater works." Before His death and resurrection the Lord was "straitened" (Luke 12: 50); but once that was accomplished and the Spirit given, He could freely operate by the Spirit through His disciples. There was no day in the Lord's ministry when 3,000 souls were converted as on the Day of Pentecost; nor did His labours cover the mighty circuit of "from Jerusalem, and round about unto Illyricum," as did those of Paul.

In verses 13 and 14 the Lord comforted His disciples with the power of His name. He indicated thereby that He was going to leave them to serve as His representatives. Their requests, if really in His name, would be certain of fulfilment. He would Himself act on their behalf though absent from them. His object in so doing would be not only the maintenance of His own interests, but that the Father should be glorified. Thus the Father would be glorified in His activities in resurrection and glory, just as He was also in the dark hour of His death.

No doubt this acting and asking in His name had special reference to His apostles, yet it surely applies to us all. We have to remember that we can only rightly use our Master's name in connection with His cause and interests. If we attempt to use it merely for the furtherance of our own personal desires, we are guilty of what our Law Courts call a misfeasance, to which serious penalty is attached. The promise here only applies, of course, where the prayer is genuinely in His name.

Thus far we have had five items of great comfort before us, calculated to assure the sorrowful hearts of His disciples that there was going to be great gain for them, in spite of the fact that they were to lose His presence amongst them. Let us recapitulate them: the fact that He would still be accessible to them as an Object of faith; that there was a place assured to them in the Father's house; that He would come again that they might be with Him in that place; that meanwhile the Father had been fully made known to them in Him; that they were to remain in the world as His representatives, with the authority of His name to give potency to their prayers. We now pass to a sixth item of equal comfort.

The coming of the Holy Spirit is definitely promised. The Lord only presumed one thing—that they really loved Him, for genuine love always expresses itself in obedience; and love is itself the Divine nature. Just that is taken for granted. And taken for granted, He would pray the Father when He ascended on high, and in response to His request the other Comforter would come. Now "Comforter" means, "One who stands alongside to help." Jesus Himself had been this amongst them on earth, and would yet be it, though absent from them *in heaven;* for "Advocate" (1 John 2: 1) is the same word. The Spirit would be this with us here *on earth*, and once come, He abides with us for ever.

The Comforter is also the Spirit of truth. Truth, together with grace, "came by Jesus Christ" (1: 17), and He is the truth, as we have just seen, presented to us in an objective way. The Spirit of truth is now to come, indwelling the saints, and thus bringing truth into them subjectively. Hence when we come to 2 John 2, we read the truth "dwelleth in us" by the Spirit, as well as being "with us for ever" in Christ. The world does not share in this. It has not the Divine nature, nor does it walk in obedience; hence it cannot receive the Spirit. It neither sees nor knows Him, occupied as it is with material things.

All this was an assurance to the disciples that they were not to be left "comfortless," or "orphans," but that by the Comforter He would come to them, and thus His presence be a reality to their hearts.

The Comforter is given as the seal of love and obedience, and in keeping with this the full blessing of His indwelling is only enjoyed as obedience is perfected in us. Verse 15 had indicated that, being the fruit of love, obedience is the proof that the love exists: now we find that the fruit of obedience is a special place in the love of both the Father and the Son, together with a special manifestation of the Son, which must carry with it a special manifestation of the Father, inasmuch as we only know the Father as revealed in the Son. The objective manifestation is perfect, complete and abiding, but the subjective manifestation to each of us individually, in the power of the Comforter, depends on the measure in which we are characterized by obedience and love.

The question of Judas (verse 22) evidently was prompted by the fact that the thoughts of the disciples were wholly concentrated on the public manifestation of the Messiah, as announced in the Old Testament, and they did not as yet grasp the character of the dispensation about to dawn, in which the knowledge of Himself would be by faith in the power of the Spirit. The Lord answered by amplifying His previous words, speaking now of the keeping of His word—not "words," but singular, "word," the truth that He brought viewed as a whole—as the fruit of love. Such loving obedience incites the appreciation and love of the Father, so that both Father and Son make their abode; through the indwelling Spirit doubtless, for these great pronouncements come in the section of the discourse devoted to the Comforter. Thus His sayings, in which His word is conveyed to us, become the test of our love. They conduct us to the word of the Father who sent Him. If we disregard them our protestations of love toward Him are proved to be vain and insincere.

This leads us to another function of the Comforter: being "the Spirit of truth," He is the Teacher of the disciples. We must not miss the contrast in verses 25 and 26 between *"these* things" and *"all* things." When, as the fruit of His work, Jesus should be glorified and the Spirit given, there should be a larger revelation of Divine truth. All things that come within the scope of revelation should be made known and effectually taught to the disciples by the Comforter. *Much* had been made known to them by Christ, present amongst them in flesh and blood: *all* should be made known to them in the coming day of the Spirit. Here we find promised as to *revelation* and *teaching* the same expansion by the coming of the Spirit as we found stated in verse 12 as to *works*. In addition, the Spirit would bring to their remembrance all the things they had heard through Christ.

We are now in the happy position of seeing how literally and perfectly these things were fulfilled. The four Gospels were written as the fruit of things He said being brought to their remembrance; whilst as the fruit of the further and newer teachings of the Spirit we have the Epistles, ministering the full light of the Christian faith and of the counsels of God.

We had previously noted that the coming of the Comforter furnished the sixth item in the comfort which Jesus was ministering to His disciples. We now find the seventh and last in this chapter; namely, *peace*. In departing He left peace with them, bequeathed as the result of His atoning work. Further, He gave them that peace which He called peculiarly His own— the peace of perfect confidence in the Father, as the result of knowing Him, and of submission to His will. And all that He gives is out of His own fulness and linking them with Himself, and not according to the poor standards of this world.

Having thus unfolded to the disciples all these great items of encouragement the Lord ended on the same note as He began—"Let not your heart be troubled, neither let it be afraid." Exactly the same word comes to us as we face the great difficulties of our day.

But the disciples were to know not only peace, but joy. This indeed they did when the Spirit was given, and even before, as Luke 24: 52 testifies.

# JOHN

They were grasping the fact that He was going away and they were to realize that nevertheless He was coming to them by the advent of the Comforter. Yet there was a further thing: He was going to the Father, and into all that would be involved thereby—infinite approbation and glory, in the Father's love. That would be exceeding joy for Him, and loving Him it would be for their joy as well. Have we not known that joy also? Is not the thought of *His* joy among the deepest of *our* joys?

The last words of this verse, "My Father is greater than I," have been made into an occasion of stumbling to some. But here we have speaking the Word made flesh, and He speaks in His estate as the lowly Man upon earth. Hence in *position* or *station* the Father was greater than He, whilst as to *being* and *nature* He and the Father were one.

The Lord's words in verse 29 shed great light upon all that is contained in this chapter. The things of which He had been speaking had not yet come to pass, for the first there must be accomplished His redemption work. That accomplished, they would come to pass, and He was telling them now so that in the coming days they might *believe*. In saying this the Lord again indicated that our day is one in which faith is all-important. Israel's day had been characterized by things visible and tangible, but all the things of which He had just spoken to them are to be apprehended by faith and not sight. Both the peace and the joy reach our hearts by faith. So presently we find Paul speaking of "all joy and peace in *believing* . . . through the power of the Holy Ghost" (Rom. 15: 13), and Peter saying, "though now ye see Him not, yet *believing*, ye rejoice with joy unspeakable and full of glory" (1 Pet. 1: 8).

The Lord now indicated that His talks with the disciples were coming to an end. What lay before Him was the full accomplishment of the work that the Father had commanded. But before that end was fully reached Satan, the prince of this world, was again coming, wielding the power of darkness; but he would find no point of attack in Him. Satan had *nothing* in Christ because the Father had *everything*—all His love and obedience. He was meeting not man in a state of innocence, as was Adam in Eden, but Man in absolute holiness and righteousness, and withal the Word who was God. The great Antitype of the Hebrew servant, depicted in Exodus 21: 2-6, was found here saying, "I love the Father," the equivalent of "I love My Master . . . I will not go out free;" just as in John 13: 1 we had the declaration of His love to those typified by the wife and children in Exodus.

It would seem that the words, "Arise, let us go hence," mark their departure from the upper chamber, and that what we have in the following two chapters was spoken on the way to Gethsemane. The change in position was matched by a change in the themes and in chapter 15 Jesus contemplates His disciples as in the world with corresponding privilege and responsibility rather than as in their new place and state as before the Father,

# JOHN

which was the theme in chapter 14. Just as there He gave them His place before the Father so now they are identified with Him in His place before the world. He is the true Vine and they the branches.

## CHAPTER 15

IN SPEAKING OF Himself as the Vine the Lord adopted a figure which in the Old Testament had been applied to Israel, notably in such passages as Psalm 80: 8-18; Isaiah 5: 1-7. In the Psalm the desolation of the vine is declared, but mention is made of "the Branch" and "the Son of Man," that "Thou madest strong for Thyself." In Isaiah the reason for the desolation is made plain. Israel as the vine brought forth nothing but wild and worthless grapes. There was no fruit for God. Jesus Himself was the Branch made strong for Jehovah, and He now presents Himself as the real Source of all fruit for God on the earth.

He was the Stem, His disciples were the branches, His Father the Husbandman. Each branch that was vitally in Him brought forth fruit. Branches in Him there might be whose connection was not vital, and these bore no fruit. The action of the Husbandman bore in each direction. Where the branch bears fruit He cleanses it that it may bring forth more fruit. Where no fruit is borne He takes the branch away and the ultimate end is destruction, as verse 6 indicates. Of this latter class Judas Iscariot had just been a sad example.

The word in verse 2 is "purgeth," not "pruneth." The Father cleanses the fruitful saint, though such are already clean through the Word. The Lord had indicated a double cleansing by His words recorded in 13: 10-14, and we meet with the same thought here. As the branch is cleansed by the action of the Father, obstructions are removed and the life of the Stem flows more freely, the production of more fruit being the result. The surest proof that we are in Christ is that we abide in Christ; and the surest proof that we abide in Christ is that we produce fruit in life and service, the very character and ways of Christ coming out in us. Without Him we can do nothing. Abiding in Him there is much fruit; we are brought into communion with His mind so that we ask with liberty and have our desires granted, the Father is glorified, and our discipleship is proved genuine beyond all question.

It is a great privilege, as well as a great responsibility, to be left on earth to bear fruit; it is even a greater privilege to know ourselves to be the objects of Divine Love. The love of Jesus rested upon these disciples—and upon us also—just as the Father's love rested upon Himself. In the knowledge, the consciousness, the enjoyment of His love we are to abide. This abiding is maintained by obedience to His commandments. Do we not know only too well that the moment we disobey His plainly expressed word our consciences smite us, and we are out of communion with His mind and out of the enjoyment of His love. Walking in obedience, we abide in His love, we enter into His joy and our own joy is full.

Verse 12 is evidently connected with verse 10 in a very intimate way. Jesus spoke of keeping His commandments in a general way, but there was one commandment that He had already signalized in a special way (13: 34), and He returns to it again. Love is to flow between His disciples after the character of His perfect love towards them. Love that springs from the possession of the Divine nature is to circulate amongst the Divine family. The flesh is in each and the diversities amongst us are innumerable; hence the opportunities for clashes and prejudices are endless. It is His commandment that the love of the Divine nature triumph over the antagonisms of our fleshly nature. How have we obeyed this commandment? Our failure here accounts for the small measure in which we abide in His love and have His joy abiding in us. It also means poor discipleship and lack of glory to the Father.

Human love has its limit, as verse 13 states; but the Lord teaches His disciples to regard each other as friends because they are each and all *His* friends, as being marked by obedience to His commands. He was indeed going forth to lay down His life for them, but in Him was found a love which far exceeded all that was known among men. His love and not mere human love was to stamp its character on their love, one for the other.

From the first moment of their attachment to Himself the disciples had been His servants, but the Lord now indicates that henceforward He was going to treat them as standing on a higher basis of friendship. This friendship was a real thing, inasmuch as He had made known to them all that He had heard of the Father, as the Revealer of the Father's love and purposes. In saying this we believe the Lord had also in view the coming of the Comforter, who would endow them with the capacity to discern these things, as He had already told them. This privileged place is open to all believers today on the same simple ground—love and obedience. Hence we have the Apostle John using the term in the last verse of his third Epistle. As the first century drew to its close Paul's prediction, as to men speaking perverted things "to draw away disciples after them" (Acts 20: 30), was being fulfilled, and Diotrephes was an example of such men. Yet there were found saints marked by love and obedience—shining contrasts to Diotrephes, and acknowledged as "friends." Some were with John, joining in the salutation: some with Gaius, to be greeted by name.

Though Jesus thus gave His disciples so exalted a place, He did not cease to be absolutely pre-eminent among them. Friends they were, but wholly of *His* choice and not theirs, and therefore His sovereign rights remained unimpaired. They were chosen as friends and appointed to bear fruit of a sort that should remain, in contrast with the transient world in which they were found. Then as friends and fruit-bearers a further happy result follows. They should have access to the Father in the name of the

Son with the assurance of a favourable answer. It may be thought that "Whatsoever ye shall ask . . . in My Name" covers a very wide range. So it does, but we must remember that "friends" are in view, who have had revealed to them all the Father's things. Those things have to do with the Name and glory of the Son, and it is taken for granted therefore that, identified in heart with Him, every request will be in line with the Father's purposes, and hence be sure of an answer.

As a reminder of how intimately connected with these things is love among the disciples, the Lord, in verse 17, repeats His command that they love one another. The Lord foreknew how great would be the need of this word in the history of His people, so He utters this command no less than three times in these closing words before He suffered.

The command of our Lord, that love be manifested as the bond between His disciples, gains force from the fact of the world's hatred. Love circulating within and hatred pressing from without: this is the situation contemplated as the result of His rejection and death. Let us take this to heart for all through the centuries the tendency has been to reverse the situation; and as the hearts of believers stray into loving the world without and courting its favours, so do coldness, disintegration and even hatred find a place within.

Both the love and the hatred spring out of the intimate relation that exists between the disciples and their Lord. We have already seen this as to the love and now we see it as to the hatred. The world hated Christ before ever it hated them, and it hated them because they had been chosen out of the world and hence were not of it. At the moment when the Lord spoke the hatred had only been manifested by the Jews to whom He had presented Himself, but as we have before noticed He is viewed as rejected from the outset of this Gospel, and the Jew is viewed as having consequently lost his distinctive place nationally. A Nicodemus with all his advantages needs to be born again as much as the degraded Gentile; and so here, in keeping with this, the Jews are just the world—the former distinctions swept away in the presence of the rejected Christ.

Moreover, hatred generates persecution, and so that is predicted in verse 20. The servants must expect just the treatment meted out to their Master, and all has ultimately to be traced up to the world's ignorance of God, and the fact that they hated Him when they saw Him revealed perfectly in Christ. This revelation brought all things to a clear issue. The Lord speaks of His words in verse 22 and of His works in verse 24; both combined to bring their sin to light in a way that was beyond all question and excuse. In seeing the Son they saw the Father: in hating the Son they hated the Father, and all was without any cause as the Scripture had said.

There remained, however, one further testimony, that of the Comforter. Sent by the glorified Jesus, yet proceeding from the Father, He would complete the witness as the Spirit of Truth. The Son incarnate upon earth, had revealed the Father and His testimony had been refused. Yet the testimony would still be maintained by the Comforter, for proceeding from the Father He would now testify of the Son gone up on high and thus maintain the revelation that He had made. They could cast out the Son: they did so by way of the cross. But there was to come One that they could not eject in this fashion, and so an abiding witness would be secured. The Spirit's testimony is the last to be rendered. Hence the exceeding gravity of sin against the Holy Ghost or doing despite to the Spirit of grace.

Verse 27 speaks of the witness to be borne by the apostles and differentiates it from the testimony of the Comforter. They bore witness to all that they had seen and heard "from the beginning," as we see at the opening of John's first Epistle; in which the weight and value of this witness is revealed to us. They were also the appointed witnesses of His resurrection. Their witness to the great facts and realities on which all is based is of the last importance, yet something more was needed, and it was supplied by the fresh testimony of the Spirit of Truth, which we have recorded in the Acts. That was specially given through Stephen in the first place, and then through the converted arch-persecutor, Saul of Tarsus, who became the Apostle Paul. We may express the difference by saying that the main witness of the twelve was to the great facts connected with the life, death, resurrection and ascension of Christ: the witness of the Comforter was to be concerning the significance and bearing of those facts; of the whole purpose of God established in them.

## Chapter 16

FURTHER WORDS OF warning follow in the opening verses of this chapter, lest the disciples should be stumbled by being unprepared for persecution. Acts 8: 3; 9: 1, 2; 1 Timothy 1: 13, furnish us with a commentary on verses 2 and 3 of our chapter. Saul of Tarsus persecuted this way unto the death, and he did it ignorantly in his unbelief. At that time he certainly knew neither the Father nor the Son.

Jesus was going to Him that sent Him, and the disciples had sufficient sense of the loss they would suffer to be filled with sorrow, but if only they had enquired more as to where He was going, and what would be involved in His presence with the Father, they would have seen things in a different light. His departure was going to be profitable for them. Loss there was going to be, but also gain which would outweigh the loss. This was a startling statement, but the Lord proceeds to support it by giving further unfoldings of the benefits which would flow from the coming of the Comforter, which coming was contingent on His departure. He speaks first of what His coming would mean as regards themselves.

Being come, He will, by His very presence and activity, be a standing witness against the world. The word "reprove" does not mean that He will

# JOHN

bring such conviction to the world as would result in its conversion, but that His coming will bring such a demonstration of these three great realities as shall leave the world without excuse. He comes as the direct consequence of the going on high of Jesus, the One cast out by the unbelieving world. Perfect goodness embodied in the Son of God had been before their eyes and had been totally rejected. Here was sin, an outrageous missing of the mark—and demonstrated by the presence of the Comforter, who came because He was gone.

But Jesus was going through death and resurrection and by ascension into the glory of the Father. Thus Divine righteousness would be vindicated and displayed. The point here is not remission of sins and justification for us, as it is in Romans 3, but of righteousness to be publicly established in every sphere that has been touched and marred by sin. Christ's death was the supreme act of the world's unrighteousness: His glorification was the supreme act of God's righteousness, and the guarantee that ultimately righteousness shall everywhere prevail, in keeping with Paul's words in Acts 17: 31. Now the Spirit is come from the glorified Christ as the standing Witness to this. To have merely demonstrated sin would not have been enough: righteousness its antithesis, and that which will ultimately abolish it, must be demonstrated too.

The third thing, judgment, follows as the appropriate sequence. If human sin be dealt with in Divine righteousness, judgment cannot be avoided. Paul reasoned before Felix of "judgment to come" and the Roman governor trembled, but the point in our passage is that the prince of this world has been judged by his attitude to Christ, and in the power of His cross. In chapter 12, Jesus had spoken of the judgment of the world and the casting out of its prince. These solemn facts are demonstrated by the presence of the Spirit, for if the prince and leader of the world is judged, the world that he controls is judged too. Satan is also called "the god of this world" (2 Cor. 4: 4), as men ignorantly worship him in turning aside to all the things that they idolize: he is "the prince" as being the originator and leader in the world's great schemes.

Now it is indeed expedient and profitable for us that the Comforter should have come with plain demonstration of these things. To see the devil in a true light, to see the world as it really is, to have things brought to an issue as between sin and righteousness, are matters of the deepest moment. The witness truly is against the world but it stands for our benefit and instruction. Had it been more fully heeded by ourselves, and by the church all through its history, we should have kept ourselves far more unspotted from the world than we have done. The strong words that we read in James 4: 4 are more easily understood in the light of the Lord's words here.

How profitable too is that ministry of the Spirit indicated in verses 13-15. It seems to fall under three heads—"He will guide you . . . He will shew you . . . He shall glorify Me."

He is to guide the disciples into all truth. In the previous verse the Lord indicated that there were many things yet to be revealed, but that they were not yet in the condition to receive them. When by the reception of the Spirit they should have that anointing, spoken of in 1 John 2: 20 and 27, they would have the capacity to understand. So, when the Spirit of Truth was come, the Lord said through Him the many things He had yet to say, and all truth was revealed, and into that the Spirit guided them. The Apostles doubtless are primarily in view here, but as the fruit of this guiding into all truth, the Epistles were written, and thus the saints of all ages down to our own have had all truth brought within the circle of their knowledge. With what diligence have we given ourselves to these things so as to be guided into them?

Then He was to show the disciples "things to come." As the fruit of this particular ministry to the Apostles, we have the book of Revelation as well as certain passages in the Epistles, and thus this ministry has been made available to us. By these prophetic writings the drift of things both in the church and in the world is made known to us, and hence we are not in darkness, though the rejection and absence of Christ has introduced an epoch in the world's history characterized as "the night."

Then, thirdly, the mission of the Comforter is to glorify the Christ who has been dishonoured by the world. This He does by announcing to us the things that are Christ's, so that we make the discovery that all the Father's things are also His. Let us not miss the tremendous scope of this great declaration. We have already heard twice that the Father has given all things into His hand (3: 35; 13: 3), but that might carry us no further than the fact that, like Joseph in Egypt with Pharaoh's things, all administration is committed to Him. This does carry us further. All the Father's things ARE HIS! And this was said by the Son whilst on earth in His pathway of humiliation. That "ARE" is timeless: it breathes the air of eternity. The Father's things ever were His, they are, and ever will be. He who speaks thus lays claim to Deity, One in the unity of the Godhead. The acknowledgment of this by the ministry of the Comforter does indeed glorify Him.

The transition of thought from verse 15 to 16 may not be apparent at first sight, but we believe the Lord is still pursuing the thought of how profitable for them would be His departure because it involved the advent of the Comforter. Soon they would no longer see Him, and then again a little while and they would see Him. But this second seeing was to be "because I go to the Father"; that is, because then the Spirit would be given. In this remarkable statement the Lord used two different words: the first meaning to behold or view as a spectator, the second to perceive or discern. A little while and they would no longer see Him, beholding His ways and works as spectators; then another little while and the Spirit being given, they would see Him in this new fashion, perceiving Him by faith with the inward eye of their Spirit-filled hearts, in a measure unknown before. Blessed be God that it is possible for us too to say, "But we *see* Jesus... crowned with glory and honour" (Heb. 2:9).

This saying of His was dark at the moment to the disciples and therefore further explanation was given. The world was going to have its way with Him and His death was impending. It would rejoice in getting rid of Him, but for them the outlook was one of weeping and lamentation. Yet beyond death lay resurrection and His ascension to the Father. This would reverse everything. The travail of childbirth is used as an illustration, for not only does it set forth the idea of joy supervening on sorrow, but also that of new life springing up. Now their sorrow was just a reflex of His sorrow, and His was so deep and of such a nature as to be called "the travail of His soul" in Isaiah 53:11, whilst the previous verse predicts, "He shall see His seed," evidently in resurrection and in glory. They could not share His atoning sufferings yet they were dimly sharing His sorrow, though largely, without a doubt, in a selfish way. They should soon very really share His joy.

The context of verse 22 would indicate that the Lord was referring, not only to the gladness that would fill the disciples when they met Him in resurrection, but also to their joy when, by the Spirit given, they should have the knowledge of His glory. This is yet more plain when we consider verse 23, for "In that day" does not indicate merely the forty days during which they saw Him before Pentecost, but rather the whole period characterized by His absence and the Spirit's personal presence in the church. That day has not yet run its course, and it is still our privilege to pray in the Holy Ghost, and thus to ask of the Father in the name of the Son.

The word "ask" occurs twice in this verse, but actually the Lord used two different words, which might be distinguished by using "demand" or "enquire" for the first and "ask" or "petition" for the second. The Lord had been meeting all their demands, and they had run to Him with all their enquiries, but now that day was closing. But He had revealed the Father *before* them, and directly the Spirit should be given that revelation would become effective *in* them. They would be empowered to take their place as representatives of the Son, and so ask in His Name. Asking thus under the direction of the Spirit, their prayers would be sure of an affirmative answer, as being according to the Father's mind. Striking instances of prayers of this kind are given us in the latter part of Acts 4, and again in Acts 12. Indeed the prayer of the dying Stephen, in the last verse of Acts 7, illustrates it; for the conversion of the man who presided, like an evil genius, over his martyrdom was an answer to the spirit of the request, "Lord, lay not this sin to their charge."

The change that would be introduced by the coming of the Comforter is still the dominant thought in verse 25. It would affect the very way in which the truth as to the Father was to be presented. He had been making known the Father by doing the Father's works. All the miracles, or "signs" recorded in this gospel, had been a setting forth of the grace and power and glory of the Father, in a parabolic or allegorical way. When we turn to the Epistles we read plain declarations of the Father, His purposes and glory and love, given by inspiration of the Holy Ghost. All this came to pass in the day of which the Lord was speaking, when they should be able to ask with all freedom in His Name as knowing the Father's love.

The words in the latter part of verse 26 are no contradiction of the fact that Jesus is our Intercessor on high. They only emphasize the fact of the Father's love for the saints and the place of intimacy that they have in His presence. The attitude of the disciples to Jesus was, as verse 27 shows, one of *love* and *faith*. Is that our attitude? Then we too come under the benediction of the Father's love. Hence, though we deeply need Christ's gracious intercession for us, in view of our weakness and constant failure, as those *in this place* of love and favour, yet we have no need for intercession *that we may be in this place*. Souls brought up in the darkness of Romanism may imagine they need just the kind of intercession that is precluded here, only so often they sink still lower by thinking that the Virgin Mary or some lesser "saint" must undertake it. Blessed be God, we need no intercessor of that kind at all!

The disciples believed that He had come forth from God, but as yet they had hardly risen to the thought of His coming forth from the Father, though, as their words show, they did not as yet realize their limitations. Until the Spirit was given they were limited in understanding, as verse 31 shows, and also in power and courage, as verse 32 shows. The very men who were groping in their minds here, and in a few hours' time were scattered and running away, were gathered with minds of clear understanding, and with hearts as bold as lions, when the Day of Pentecost was fully come. Understanding and courage: these two things should characterize us today. But do they?

Though the Lord had no support from His disciples in the dark hour before Him, He could go forth in perfect dependence on the Father and in the assurance of His abiding presence. Hence He confronted the world's hatred and opposition in perfect peace and wholly overcame it. Now all these communications the Lord had made that His disciples in their turn might have peace in Him, just as He had possessed peace in the Father. His overcoming the world, moreover, was the pledge that overcoming power was also at their disposal. He had just been speaking of the world's hatred and persecution. To us perhaps its seductions and smiles are more dangerous. But, whichever it be, our safety lies in Christ. Only as begotten of God and as believing that Jesus is the Son of God do we overcome the world, as 1 John 5: 4, 5, tells us.

## Chapter 17

WE NEED TO have in our minds the five words that close the previous chapter as we read the opening words of this chapter. He who had over-

# JOHN

come the world "lifted up His eyes to heaven, and said, Father." In the knowledge of the Father and in the light of heaven, what is the world worth? And what are its threats or persecutions? Here was the Son of God Himself in the absolute fulness of both, and hence the world was, so to speak, beneath His feet. He is now going to present Himself before the Father, and to present His disciples also; so that they, begotten of God, and knowing Himself as the Son of God, and the Father revealed in Him, might be kept from the world through which they were to pass. When Bunyan in his allegory pictured a man with a crown of glory "before his eyes," he very rightly placed the world "behind his back."

In the fourth verse of the next chapter we have the Evangelist's testimony that Jesus knew "all things that should come upon Him." Here He addresses the Father in the consciousness that the hour, for which He specially came into the world, was come. In this matchless chapter we are permitted to hear the Son communing with the Father, and lifted thus into this Divine region, we view His great work as a completed whole and pass in spirit beyond the Cross. Here are words that defy all human powers of analysis and submerge all human powers of thought. Yet we may consider them. Let us do so, as we pass through the verses, by noting the things for which He made request of the Father, and also His emphatic statements as to what He had already accomplished.

His first request is, "Glorify Thy Son." The Son had been here as the Servant of the Father's pleasure and glory, to which fact this Gospel has borne special and abundant witness. So, in keeping with this, His first request is, that no longer in humiliation on earth but amid the splendours of heaven He may still serve and glorify the Father by exerting the power over all flesh conferred upon Him in a way of peculiar wonder and blessedness. By-and-by He will exert that power over all flesh in the execution of judgment: at present He exerts it in the bestowal of eternal life to all that have been given to Him of the Father. Of that life He is the Source and Fountain for men. We have life and we have the Spirit from the glorified One, and the Father is glorified in this in a way that surpasses the solemn glory that will be His in the hour of judgment.

Now all life takes character from the conditions that surround it—from its environment. Eternal life can only be lived in the knowledge of the only true God as Father, and of Jesus Christ the Sent One of the Father. This it is doubtless that accounts for the fact that life of an eternal sort is only mentioned twice in the Old Testament, and then simply as hinting prophetically at that which will be enjoyed in the millennial age to come. It was promise rather than known and enjoyed blessing. The law offered life on earth. The age of life eternal began when the Son of God appeared, and having finished His work on earth He was glorified in heaven.

Ten times over in this chapter does Jesus utter the words, "I have," in declaring the fulness of all that He had accomplished. The first two occurrences are in verse 4, where He urges the completeness of His work in support of His request for glory. He had glorified the Father, be it noted, *on the earth*—that particular corner of the wide universe where He had been most signally dishonoured by the sin and breakdown of the first man and his race. That great work had been entrusted to Him, together with the parallel work of making propitiation for sin, so that there might be redemption for sinners. Passing in spirit beyond the Cross, He declared the completeness and perfection of His own work. No mere man could utter words like this. The work of the most eminent servants of God has been but fragmentary and incomplete. And had it been otherwise not one of them would have dared to approach God, the Searcher of hearts and ways, and pronounce on their own work, declaring its finished perfection, for it would have betokened impertinent presumption of the worst kind. But here the Son is speaking, and it was no presumption for Him.

Yet He was truly Man; and that is what strikes us as we read verse 5, where He repeats His request for glory—that particular glory which He had along with the Father before the world came into being. He is to be re-invested with that glory, only now as the Son in Manhood—*risen Manhood*. Here is a fact of greatest wonder and weightiest moment: a Risen Man, Christ Jesus, is invested with the uncreated glory of Deity. In that glory is the church's Head, the Leader of the chosen race to which we belong. Who can measure the consequences that are going to flow from this great fact?

The chosen race come into view in the next verse. They are designated, "the men which Thou gavest Me out of the world." So at the outset they are sharply differentiated from the world, as taken out of it by the Father and given to the Son. They were the Father's according to His counsel before time was, but they were given to the Son that He might bring them to the knowledge of the Father by manifesting His Name to them. At the end of His prayer Jesus speaks of *declaring* the Father's Name, which lays the stress upon His words. Here however it is *manifesting*, and that was accomplished more in His life and works; as He had said previously, "He that hath seen Me hath seen the Father." Of these men He says, "They have kept Thy word."

This was very touching, for think what these men had been, how slow, how obtuse, how unresponsive! And think what they were on the point of showing themselves to be. What cowardice, what denials, in a few hours time! But the Son viewed them in the light of the Divine purpose, and He knew that the Father had power ultimately to effect in them all that He had purposed. So He credited them with the possession in fulness of that which they as yet only realized in a very feeble measure. And does He not treat His saints today, and intercede for them, in just the same way? He credits them also, in the next verse, with tracing up to the Father all that they had seen displayed in Him. All through this Gospel we find Him attributing

# JOHN

everything to the Father. His words and His works were the Father's. He neither spoke nor acted as from Himself, though He was the Word and the Son. So real was the Humanity that He took: so real the place of subjection He assumed that He might manifest the Father's Name and glory.

In verse 8 He speaks not of "the word" but of "the words" that had been given to Him and handed on to the disciples. The one is the revelation, considered as one whole; the other the many and varied sayings in which He had communicated the word to them. These sayings they had received, and thereby had been directed to the Father Himself. They had indeed received them, but had they really grasped the tiniest fraction of their meaning? How much have we grasped—we who have the Spirit? Yet it is no small thing if we implicitly receive and believe what He says because He says it. All that He has said will put us into touch with the Father who has sent Him.

Thus far we have heard the Son making His first and greatest request; that He should be glorified in His risen Manhood, in order that He might glorify the Father in a new way. We have also heard Him state four things which He had perfectly accomplished. He had glorified the Father on the earth. He had finished the work given Him to do. He had manifested the Father's name to the disciples; and given them the words which the Father had given to Him. In verse 9 we meet with His second request, not for Himself but for His disciples. He begins by dissociating them from the world in the most decisive fashion.

The old line of cleavage had been between Jew and Gentile, but that, though it had been sharp enough up to this point, was now disappearing, and was being replaced by the cleavage between the disciples who received Him and the world that rejected Him. If a Jew rejected Him, his place of privilege disappeared, and he was just one of the units of which the world was composed. Note how the Lord characterizes His disciples here. They were the Father's by His purpose and choice, and then given by Him to the Son. As thus given they were held as belonging jointly to the Father and the Son. But they were peculiarly the vessel or vehicle in which the Son is to be glorified.

"All Mine are Thine, and Thine are Mine." Ponder these words. A mere man may say, "All mine are Thine," but no mere man could say, "All Thine are mine," or he would be guilty of unpardonable and blasphemous presumption. But the Son could so speak with seemliness and truth; for He is One with the Father.

Having placed the disciples before the Father as the objects of His second request, Jesus mentioned as the occasion of it that He was leaving the world and coming to the Father, while they were to be left in it. They had very little conception of what the world was, with its dangers and snares; He knew it perfectly. Nothing but the keeping power of the Father, according to His own holiness, would be sufficient to preserve them. They were not merely to be preserved but kept in a unity after the pattern of the Father and the Son. The Son had revealed that holy name of Father, and in it there was binding power and grace, as also there was in the life eternal which the Son gives, coupled with the gift of the Spirit, soon to be. These men moreover were left to be witnesses to their Lord who was going, and it was essential that their witness should be marked by unity, in order to be effectual. The Acts and the Epistles show us how fully this unity of witness was preserved.

Hitherto they had been kept by the Son in the Father's name, and the only one missing was no true disciple at all but the son of perdition, and even this sad happening was in fulfilment of Scripture. As to all those really given to Him of the Father, Jesus could say, "I have kept;" the fifth occurrence of "I have" in the chapter. Now as going out of the world He puts the disciples in His own place, as verse 13 shows. He had been here in His Father's name, finding His joy in serving His interests. They were henceforward to be here in His Name and have that same joy fulfilled in themselves as they served the Father in representing the Son.

But for this they would need to be in the knowledge of the Father's mind and purpose; hence the Son had given to them the Father's word. For the sixth time we have the words, "I have," and this time concerning not "the words" but "the word;" that is, the whole revelation which He had brought. They had as yet but little entered into its fulness, but thereby they had been separated from the world as to their knowledge, just as they were separated also in their origin, for they were not OF the world even as He was not. Yet as to place they were IN the world, and the Lord did not desire that they should be taken out of it, but rather kept from the evil.

Here we have very explicitly a thing for which the Lord did NOT make a request. Yet the thing, with strange perversity, has been sought by earnest souls—and many true believers among them—through the centuries, as embodied in the monastic idea. That idea may be pursued by the aid of walls of thick masonry, or it may be pursued without them. The result, however, is the same. If we turn Divinely-ordained separation into monastic isolation, we shall always end by generating within the area of our seclusion the very evils we are supposed to be avoiding. The world indeed presents us with a deadly peril. But why? Because of what we are in ourselves. A holy angel would neither court its favours nor fear its frowns: it would leave him wholly unmoved. The world does present, so to speak, the infectious germs from without; but the main trouble lies in ourselves—the susceptibility of the flesh within. No monastic isolation affects that.

What the Lord did request was, "Sanctify them through thy truth," for the truth separates by building up that spiritual immunity which preserves from spiritual disease. The root idea of sanctification is setting apart. The Son has given the Father's word, which introduces us to all His love, His thoughts, His purposes, His glory. All this is truth; that is, reality of the

Divinest sort. The world lives so largely in a region of unreality and make-believe, striving to establish its systems which have no solid basis and which eventually must pass away. If we know Divine realities we must of necessity be set apart from the world's unrealities. This will expose us to the world's hatred, but it will build up strong spiritual resistance to its snares. It will immunize us against its germs. This is the kind of separation that endures, because effected by the Father's word and truth.

The seventh "I have," is found in verse 18. As the holy and perfect One, Jesus had been sent into the world by the Father, that He might represent Him and make Him known. Now He sends His disciples into the world in similar manner. They were to represent Him and make Him known. What qualified them for this was the sanctification of which the previous verse had spoken. Had it been His plan to place them in monastic isolation, no such mission would have been possible, and it would not have been possible had they not been sanctified by the truth. But with the spiritual immunity which the truth confers *it was possible*.

But a further thing was needed as indicated in verse 19. The Lord Jesus must Himself be set apart in the glory of heaven, that He might shed upon them His Spirit, that He might become the attractive Object for their hearts, and the Pattern to whom they are to be conformed in due time. Being intrinsically and Divinely holy, the only sanctification possible for Him was such a setting apart as this; and let us notice that, according to this verse, *He does it Himself*. Another tribute to His Deity, for no mere man could set himself apart in the glory of heaven!

Verse 17, then, gives us the sanctifying power of truth, reaching us through the Father's word, which had been ministered by the Son, as verse 14 has stated. Verse 19 adds the sanctifying power of Christ's glory, to be ministered by the Spirit, who was to come to the disciples as the consequence of His glorification. To state the matter more briefly: it is the revelation of the Father by the Son, and the knowledge of the glory of the Son in risen Manhood by the Spirit, that sanctifies the believer today.

Verse 20 should touch all our hearts. The Lord Jesus had been praying for the little band of disciples that surrounded Him at that moment: He now enlarged His requests to embrace even ourselves. Though nineteen centuries have passed since the first disciples went forth with the word, we have believed on Him as the result of it. Their spoken word has long since died away, but their word in the shape of inspired New Testament writings abides, and it has been the authoritative basis of all Gospel preaching through the years, and it is still that today. It should also touch our hearts that the first of the two requests, which He made for us, was for our unification.

The oneness He desired is of a fundamental nature. We are to be one as the Father is in the Son and the Son is in the Father. Between the Father and the Son there is the unity of essential being, and consequently of life and nature and manifestation. We so truly derive life and nature from the Son and the Father that the Lord Jesus could say, "One in Us"—this very expression showing the equality which exists between Them—and without oneness of this sort nothing of a more outward kind would have been of value. Ecclesiastical union without this would have been only the binding together of a mass of heterogeneous material. This request being granted, the Divine nature would characterize *all* saints; and the formation of such an underlying unity in those who on the surface were so different (Jews and Gentiles; as had been intimated in chapter 10: 16) was a satisfying proof of the Divine mission of Christ. He does not say that the world *would* believe, but there was sufficient proof so that they *might*.

The oneness for which the Lord prayed, is to be perfected in glory, though first established in grace. Again we find the words "I have" and this time connected with glory. To His disciples, ourselves amongst them, He has donated the glory given to Him of the Father. Questions of time do not enter into the intercourse of the Divine Persons, so He does not say, "I will give," but, "I have given." When things are viewed from the standpoint of God's counsel and purpose we find similar statements of an absolute kind—Romans 8: 30 and Ephesians 2: 6, for instance. It is indeed a marvellous fact that the glory given to Him as Man by the Father is now irrevocably ours by His gift to us; and this with a view to the perfection of our oneness in Him. In verse 23, then, we have the unity displayed: the Father displayed in the Son; the Son displayed in the glorified saints. This will be a perfected unity indeed! The world of that day will *know* that the Father sent the Son, and has loved the saints even as He loved Him. The glory will declare the love.

This leads to the second request of the Lord which was framed to embrace all the saints of this present period. He had given His glory to them, and now He asks the Father to place them in association and company with Himself. Glory with Himself above is His desire, yet the crowning point of it for us will be to behold the supreme glory which shall be His. Earlier in His prayer He had asked to be glorified along with the Father with the glory that He had with Him before the world was. That uncreated glory had been His from eternity as being in the unity of the Godhead: He has now been re-invested with it, but in a new way; receiving it as a gift from the Father in His risen Manhood. As glorified with Him we are to behold His glory, which will witness to us for ever, not only the perfection of all that He wrought in Manhood, but also of the Father's love, of which He had been the Object from all eternity.

The world was sunk in ignorance of the Father. When Jesus prayed for the preservation of His disciples in the world, He addressed the Father as "Holy" (verse 11), for *their separation* from it was to be governed by *His* holiness. In verse 25 He contemplates the world itself in its sin and blindness, so He addresses the Father as "Righteous." Thus the Divine righteousness is set over against the world's sin, as before it had been—

chapter 16: 9, 10. He had come as the Sent One, bringing the knowledge of the Father, and the disciples had received it in receiving Him, for He had declared to them the Father's Name. Here are the closing occurrences of, "I have"—"I have known Thee ... I have declared unto them Thy name."

He had spoken, in verse 6, of the *manifestation* of the Father's name, and this was accomplished in the life He had lived and needed no addition. But He also had made a *declaration* of His name by lip and word, and this He would supplement in the future, when risen from the dead. We are permitted to hear of it in this Gospel: chapter 20: 17. And all this was to the end that the Father's love, which supremely centred in Him, might be "in them;" that is, their consciously realized portion. As the Father's love thus dwelt in them, they would be qualified to be an expression of Christ: He would be "in them" in display.

This wonderful prayer—the outbreathings of the Son in communion with the Father—must of necessity be beyond all our thoughts, yet it is effective beyond all else in bringing the warmth of Divine love into our hearts. It is a joy to notice that just as it begins with the Son glorified *by* the Father, it ends with the Son manifested and thus glorified *in* the saints.

CHAPTER 18

HAVING COMMUNED WITH the Father and expressed His desires, Jesus went forth to meet His foes, who were led by the traitor, and then to the death that He should die. True to the character of this Gospel, striking witness is borne to His *omniscience*. He went forth in the full knowledge of "all things that should come upon Him"—not only of outward circumstances but of the inward weight of all involved. If we refer back to chapters 6: 6, and 13: 3, we shall find statements of similar import.

But the scene in the Garden also furnishes us with a display of His *omnipotence*. They sought Jesus of Nazareth, but when He replied, "I am," reminiscent of the way Jehovah declared Himself in the Old Testament, they were felled to the ground. Thus irresistibly, yet unwillingly, they did obeisance before Him. So the signs of His Deity were present even while He submitted to their hands, since He was here as the Man subject to the Father's will. His desire was to extend protection to His disciples according to His own word, and Peter's zealous but mistaken action only gave occasion to the display of His complete oneness of mind with the Father. He accepted all as coming from His hands, even though the highest religious authorities in Jewry were His chief opponents. The servant of the high priest, Malchus, was prominent in His arrest, and to the tribunal of Annas and Caiaphas was He first led. Caiaphas had the decisive voice and was already determined upon His death.

Verses 15-18 are parenthetical, as again are verses 25-27. Taken together they give us the sad story of Peter's downfall, in which the Lord's pre-

## JOHN

diction of 13: 38 was fulfilled. That this should be one of the few episodes recorded by all four Evangelists is worthy of note. God does not take pleasure in recording the sins of His saints, so we may be sure that there is in it warning and instruction much needed by all saints in all ages, for self-confidence is one of the commonest and most deep-seated tendencies of the flesh: a tendency which, if not judged and refused, invariably leads to disaster. True spiritual circumcision involves "no confidence in the flesh," (See, Phil. 3: 3), but that is a lesson we do not learn save through a good deal of painful experience.

The "other disciple" known to the high priest was pretty evidently John himself. His acquaintance with the high priest gave him a little worldly status and privilege, which he used to introduce Peter into the place of danger. The word "also" in verse 17 seems to imply that the damsel keeping the door knew that John was a disciple of Jesus. He had not been tempted to deny the fact as Peter had. That which trips up one disciple may leave another unmoved. Moreover, Satan knows just exactly how to set his traps. That the third questioner should be a relation of the Malchus, who had suffered in the Garden at Peter's hands, was a masterstroke of his craft. That encompassed Peter's third and worst denial, and his sin and discomfiture were complete.

Verses 19-24, give details of what transpired in the palace of the high priest, and they are the connecting link between verses 14 and 28. The question raised as to His disciples and doctrine was an attempt to obtain from His lips something incriminating as a basis for the death sentence they had determined to pronounce. The other Gospels tell us that they sought for witness against Him and found none, which accounts for the fact that when He referred them to the witness of His hearers they were so irritated as to strike our Lord. Matthew tells us that they went so far as to seek for *false* witness against Him.

It is well to note the contrast between Jesus in verse 23 and Paul in Acts 23: 5. There is a gulf between the Master and the most devoted of His servants. The reply of Jesus was conclusive. There was no evil to which any could bear witness: no one could convince Him of sin.

John's account of the proceedings before the high priest is very brief. In contrast to this he gives us a fuller account of what transpired before Pilate than any of the others. Paul writes of "Christ Jesus, who before Pontius Pilate witnessed a good confession," and the details of that good confession come particularly to light here.

First however, we are given a sight of the fearful hypocrisy of the Jewish leaders. To have walked inside the judgment hall would have defiled them, so they felt. Yet they had no scruple as to committing themselves to murder, and hunting for liars in order to give some semblance of decency to their action. Alas! Alas! to such lengths will religious flesh proceed.

# JOHN

Pilate rightly desired a definite accusation, but, having none to offer, they attempted in the first place to rush Pilate into a verdict on the general plea that He was an evildoer. To denounce on general grounds, whilst avoiding any specific charge, is a common trick of the religious persecutor. This irregularity made Pilate wish to throw the case back on their hands. Their answer showed that they were determined upon His death, yet it led to the fulfilment of the Lord's own predictions as to the death He should die—see, 3: 14; 8: 28; 12: 32. However, they eventually fixed on the charge that He sought to make Himself a King. The Lord's question in verse 34 infers this; and it comes clearly to light in the next chapter, verse 12.

The "good confession" before Pilate covered at least four great points. First, the Lord boldly confessed that He *was* a King. The context shows that in saying this He referred not merely to the fact that He was the true Son of David according to the flesh, but that He held the place as Son of God, just as Psalm 2 predicted.

But secondly, He affirmed that His kingdom was neither "*of this world,*" nor "*from hence.*" It does not bear the character or stamp of this world nor does it derive its authority and power from this place. His Kingdom of course derives all its authority and power from Heaven, and it bears the heavenly character; but instead of stating this positively He put the matter in that negative light which tacitly put a sentence of condemnation and repudiation upon this world and this place. It was a bold statement to make in the presence of the man who represented the greatest existing earthly power.

Thirdly, He asserted that He was born to Kingship inasmuch as He came into the world as *the Witness to the truth.* He who brings the light of truth is the only One fitted to hold the Royal power, as David stated in 2 Samuel 23: 3. We started this Gospel with the fact that grace and truth came by Jesus Christ, but in this moment of crisis grace had been rejected and truth was the matter in question. Outside were the men who embodied lying and hypocrisy. Pilate held the judicial authority, and therefore was responsible to discern truth and judge accordingly, but his question, "What is truth?" was evidently uttered in a vein of flippant scepticism, and showed how judgment was divorced from righteousness in his mind. As a Roman judge he knew all too much of men and their deceits, and he felt that to pursue truth was to chase a mirage. But this did not excuse his folly, manifested in turning his back on Christ and going out to the lying Jews directly he had asked his question.

Fourthly, He claimed to be not merely the Witness to the truth, but *the very embodiment of truth itself.* In the farewell discourse He had said, "I am ... the truth," to His disciples; now before His adversaries the same thing is implicit in the remarkable words, "Every one that is of the truth heareth My Voice." He is the truth in such absolute fashion that He is the test of every man. Those of whom it can be said, "Of His own will begat

He us with the word of truth" (Jas. 1: 18), are "of the truth," and such hear His voice. It is remarkable how often in this Gospel our attention is called to hearing His voice or hearing His word — see, for instance, 3: 34; 4: 42; 5: 24, 25, 28; 6: 68; 7: 17; 8: 43; 10: 4, 16, 27; 12: 48-50. Everything hinges upon it for us, as these scriptures make manifest, and (to use a modern illustration) we must be on the right wave-length in order to hear. Nothing but being begotten of God with the word of truth can put us on the right wave-length.

Pilate had no real ear for His voice, as his words and action plainly showed. He walked out from the presence of the Truth that again he might establish contact with the world of unreality, yet he had sufficient judicial sense to perceive how false was the case against the Lord and to pronounce Him to be without fault. His effort, however, to side-track the accusers by the Passover custom failed, yet it was over-ruled to bring out in the plainest possible fashion their implacable hostility.

Five words sufficed to express their utter rejection of the Lord—"Not this Man, but Barabbas," and they were wholly unanimous for this was the cry of *all*. The Evangelist's comment on this cry is equally terse and also compressed into five words, "Now Barabbas was a robber." Without exaggeration we may designate this cry as the most fateful in all history. It has controlled the course of the world for nearly two thousand years and will ultimately seal its doom—more particularly we might say it has controlled the sad course of Jewish history. What have they not endured at the hands of the spoilers during the centuries! But if they cry out and even wish to complain against God, it is sufficient answer to refer them to this unanimous demand of their leaders. The One who was the embodiment of grace and truth they rejected. Barabbas, the robber, they demanded. Incidentally, he was also a revolutionary and a murderer, as other Gospels show. Robbery, revolution and murder has been their portion with a vengeance, right through the centuries.

The fact is that in the holy government of God they have just reaped what they have sown. And the same thing has been true of the Gentile world generally, though perhaps on not quite so intensive a scale. Still, again and again through the years there have arisen men of striking personality in whom the Barabbas spirit has reappeared. At the present moment the earth is groaning beneath this very thing. As we contemplate the sufferings of many peoples, we have to remind ourselves, "Now Barabbas was a robber."

CHAPTER 19

IN THE FIRST verse of this chapter the word, "therefore" is to be noted. Pilate had pronounced already the verdict of "No fault" as to Jesus, but *because* the Jews shouted for Barabbas and rejected Him, he took Him and scourged Him. All attempt at a display of ordinary human justice was thrown to the winds, all public decencies were outraged. Taking their cue from the action of the judge, the soldiers followed suit in their own rough way. Yet the hand of God was so over even Pilate that a second and yet a third time was he constrained to pronounce the verdict of "No fault" over the Lord. This was a much more sweeping pronouncement than if he had merely declared Him to be not guilty of the particular offences alleged against Him. He attempted to throw the onus of the death sentence on to the Jews. They repudiated it however, while declaring that His claim to be the Son of God demanded death according to their law.

They said He should die because He said He was *the Son of God*, while demanding that Pilate should condemn Him because He said He was *the King of Israel*. At the start of the Gospel we heard Nathanael owning Him in that twofold way, as we, thank God, own Him today. But on those two counts He was condemned.

The remark of the Evangelist in verse 8, throws a flood of light on the situation as far as Pilate was concerned. Secular history informs us that he badly antagonized the Jews in the earlier years of his governorship and therefore he feared to irritate them further. Yet he was convinced of the innocence of the Prisoner, whose serene bearing made him even more uneasy. The accusation relating to "the Son of God," raised fears which were probably superstitious, but nonetheless potent, and which prompted the question, "Whence art Thou?"

Had this question sprung from real spiritual exercise the Lord doubtless would have responded, as He did to the two disciples with their question, "Where dwellest Thou?" in the first chapter of this Gospel. As it was prompted by superstition and fear the Lord gave no answer. This led Pilate to the threatening assertion of the power of life and death which he held under Cæsar. The Lord's reply to this evidently increased his fears—for lo! the Prisoner calmly assumed the judicial position, and with an air of finality pointed him to a higher Power than Cæsar as the real Source of any transient authority that he possessed, and also adjudicated on the degree of guilt attaching to himself and to the Jewish leaders respectively. The desperate animus lay with the Jews and he was but their tool. Still, though less guilty than they, he was definitely a guilty man. It was a shattering situation for Pilate, who found himself without knowing it in the presence of the Word become flesh. What then was the answer to Pilate's unanswered question? Surely that Jesus was Himself "from above," come from the Fountainhead of Pilate's authority.

This episode greatly increased Pilate's desire to release Jesus but the crafty Jews knew how to exert decisive pressure. In view of the tension previously existing between himself and the Jews he could only regard their cry, recorded in verse 12, as a direct threat to impeach him to Cæsar if he let Jesus go. The Jewish leaders themselves "loved the praise of men more

# JOHN

than the praise of God," (12: 43); Pilate had much more regard for the praise of Cæsar than for judgment according to truth and justice.

He made, however, one more appeal. In the last chapter, verse 31, we saw him making a suggestion calculated to appeal to their national pride; again in verse 39, he asked a question, appealing to their custom. Now in our chapter, verses 13 and 14, he makes an appeal to their sentiment. All, however, was in vain as regards his wish to divest himself of the responsibility of pronouncing jusdgment against the Lord. All was ordered so that the guilt of the Jews, and more especially of the chief priests, should be proclaimed in clearest fashion by their own lips. They crown their cry, "Not this Man, but Barabbas," with the statement, "We have no king but Cæsar."

Hosea's prediction had been, "The children of Israel shall abide many days without a king, and without a prince . . . " (3: 4). The two tribes had had the kings of the God-appointed line, and the ten tribes princes of their own selection. Hosea declared that soon they should have neither. But as if that were not enough for these evil men they now deliberately accepted Gentile despotism. They appealed unto Cæsar, and under the iron heel of a succession of despots God has seen fit to leave them. For nineteen centuries the two names, Barabbas and Cæsar, might serve to sum up their history of misery. The lawless and insurrectionary spirit of mankind had been headed up in Barabbas: the order which is enforced by powerful autocracy was expressed in Cæsar. For nineteen centuries the Jews have suffered; now from the organized cruelty of the authorities, and then from the unorganized rabble—ground, as it were, between this upper and nether millstone. They have yet to suffer under the last forms of Cæsar and Barabbas, which will prove to be worse than the first.

When Pilate brought Jesus forth to make his last appeal, he seated himself in the judgment seat on the Pavement, which indicated that he was about to pronounce judgment in the case. John pauses here to give us the note as to time, which is recorded in verse 14. The fact that there is an apparent clash between it and that given so plainly in Mark 15: 25, has occasioned much discussion and controversy. We cannot but enquire, If he was crucified at the third hour, how comes it that Pilate should be said to deliver his sentence about the sixth hour? The solution would appear to be that our Evangelist, dealing with what transpired before the Roman judge, uses the Roman reckoning, which was similar to ours, whereas Mark reckons according to Jewish custom. If this is so, all is simple. It was about 6 a.m. when Pilate's examination drew to a close, and about 9 a.m. when Jesus was crucified. The "preparation of the Passover" was the 24 hours, starting at 6 the evening before. Into that 24 hours were crowded the most tremendous events in time, or indeed in eternity.

In our Gospel nothing is said as to the further mockery of the Roman soldiers, when He was handed over to them, for these were but the crude actions of pagans and lay upon the surface. What we are told in verse 16 is that Pilate delivered Him "unto them," that is, the chief priests and officers, of which verse 6 had spoken. They were His persecutors and prosecutors. The animus lay with them. They it was who hated both Him and His Father. Pilate delivered Him into their hands that they might perpetrate their greatest sin by handing Him over to the Gentile executioners.

As the other Gospels show, the Lord had used such expressions as "taking his cross," and "bearing his cross," as figurative of the fact that His disciple must be prepared to come under the death sentence of the world. The full force of that figure is seen here, for, "He bearing His cross went forth into a place called the place of a skull." The place got its name from the peculiar configuration of the rock, but it is significant for all that! A skull speaks of the humiliating end of all man's power and glory. In some living man it may once have held as brilliant and powerful a brain as ever existed; and it has come to this! The Son of God accepted the judgment of death as from man's hand, and to a place which set forth symbolically the end of all man's glory He went to bear it.

Moreover, He accepted death from the hands of men in its most shameful form. Crucifixion was peculiarly a death of repudiation and shame. As a Roman invention it expressed the haughty contempt with which they put to death the conquered barbarians, nailing them up as though they were vermin. To such a death was Jesus delivered by the leaders of the Jews. John gives us but the briefest and plainest statement of that tremendous fact. The Lord of glory was crucified. That fact needs no embellishment of any kind.

But when this was accomplished Pilate intervened, writing a title and putting it on the cross. It would appear that not one of the Evangelists quotes every word of the title, though John comes nearest to doing so. In full it seems to have been, "This is Jesus of Nazareth, the King of the Jews." As regards the Jews this act of Pilate was definitely provocative, and intended to be so. They had forced his hand in the condemnation of Jesus and he retaliated by the public statement that the hated Jesus of Nazareth was the King of the Jews. This was the last thing they wished to admit, hence their expostulation. But here Pilate was adamant. He refused to alter one jot or tittle, and his curt answer, "What I have written I have written," has become almost proverbial.

In all this we can see the hand of God. The Word had become flesh and had dwelt among us. God had so loved the world as to give His only begotten Son. He was known among men as Jesus of Nazareth—a title of disparagement. When He entered Jerusalem a week before there had been some testimony to His glory, and had there not been the stones would immediately have cried out—so Luke tells us. But here indeed there was no human testimony and so a piece of board, inscribed by the hand of Pilate, or by his order, cried out that the despised Jesus of Nazareth was

# JOHN

indeed King of the Jews. It is remarkable how our Lord Himself adopted the title of shame, and weaved it as a chaplet for His brow when risen and glorified. It is an astounding fact that, JESUS of NAZARETH IS IN HEAVEN—see, Acts 22:8.

The title was written in the three prevailing languages of that day. Hebrew, the tongue in which the Law of Moses had appeared, the language of religion. Greek, the language of Gentile culture. Latin, the language of Gentile imperialism. In this representative way the whole world was involved in His death.

In verse 23, the Roman soldiers do appear as the instruments of His death, and also as fulfilling prophecies that had stood in the Scripture for about a thousand years and of which they knew nothing. In Psalm 22, David had foretold the parting of His garments among them and the casting of lots upon His vesture. These two things the four soldiers did, and John puts on record the circumstances which led to so exact a fulfilment. His coat was without seam, woven from the top throughout. Things which to us might seem quite trivial lead to the fulfilment of the Word of God.

We cannot but think, however, that this feature is mentioned because it has a symbolic value. Everything about our Lord, both as to His Person and work, was of one piece, woven throughout without seam. With man in his fallen condition it is otherwise. The appropriate symbol for man and his work is the fig leaf apron to which Adam and his wife had recourse after their sin. They sewed fig leaves together, and anyone who knows the shape of the fig leaf will realize how many a seam there must have been. All was patchwork of an elaborate sort. *Theirs* was the *patchwork apron: His* was the *seamless coat*.

In that coat Jesus appeared before men, the symbol of His perfection and it was not to be rent. It is remarkable that John only speaks of this coat, telling us it was woven *"from the top* throughout," for unlike the other Gospels he omits any mention of the vail in the temple that was "rent in twain *from the top* to the bottom." Everything about the Lord testified to the fact that He came from above and was above all. And the stroke that at the hour of His death set aside the old order of things came from above also.

Verses 25-27 are particularly striking as occurring in this Gospel, written as it was to declare His divine glory that we might believe Him to be the Christ, the Son of God. Viewing Him thus we might have supposed that such lower things as human relationships would be disregarded. But it is just the opposite. All through the Gospel we have noticed how the reality of His Manhood is stressed. Every human perfection reached its fullest display in Him, and hence we see the affection connected with near human relationship fully displayed even in the hour of His deepest agony. The hour had struck when the words of the aged Simeon to Mary were fulfilled —"Yea, a sword shall pierce through thy own soul also." The sword of

# JOHN

Jehovah, according to Zechariah, was about to awake against the true Shepherd of Israel, but a sword of another kind would also pierce the soul of His mother, and the Shepherd thought of that.

Only seven words were spoken—four to Mary, and three to John; but their significance was plain, and they struck a chord of love which met with a ready response. Jesus entrusted His mother to the disciple whom He loved, and who in the knowledge of His love, loved in return. Love can be trusted, especially when it is not mere human affection but divine in its source, as springing from the appreciation of the love of Jesus.

In verse 28 we get another of those flashes of omniscience which characterize this Gospel. A few verses earlier we saw the soldiers fulfilling Scripture, though utterly unconscious that they were doing so. We now see Jesus Himself in that dark hour surveying the whole field of prophecy, and well aware that of all the predictions centring on His death only one remained to be fulfilled. In Psalm 69 David had written, "In my thirst they gave me vinegar to drink." A small thing in itself, but every word of God must be verified in its season, and we are informed that in that hour of suffering He was able to rise above His circumstances and not only discern the one thing lacking but also utter words that at once brought it to pass. No mere man could have done either the one or the other.

The remarkable thing is also that just before He was crucified the soldiers gave Him vinegar mixed with gall and myrrh, but He would not accept it, as recorded in Matthew and Mark. This was doubtless becuase He would have nothing of any human device to lessen the physical suffering involved, and also because at that moment there was *no thirst* on His part. Divine predictions must be fulfilled with exactitude and precision.

John makes no mention of the three hours of darkness, nor of the forsaking with the bitter cry that it called forth, which had been predicted in the first verse of Psalm 22. Those things did not particularly illustrate the Deity of Jesus, upon which the Spirit of God had led him to lay such emphasis. What did illustrate it was the triumphant cry with which His earthly life closed. Psalm 22 ends with the words, "He hath done," and of this the New Testament equivalent is, "It is finished." He had come into the world in the full knowledge of all that had been entrusted to Him of the Father: He was now leaving it in the full knowledge that all had been fulfilled; not one thing was lacking. The prophet had predicted that Jehovah should "make His soul an offering for sin," and this was accomplished. As a consequence faith can now take up the language of Isaiah 53: 5, and make it its own; just as the repentant remnant of Israel will adopt it in a coming day.

In this also our Lord was unique. There have been servants of God who like Paul have been able to speak with confidence of having finished their course, but none would have dared to affirm that they had put the finishing touch to the work in their hands; they have rather handed on the work to

# JOHN

him who should succeed them. His work was exclusively His own, He carried it to its perfect completion. He could appraise His own work, and announce it as finished. All others have to humbly submit their labour to the Divine scrutiny and verdict in the day to come.

Both Matthew and Mark tell us that after crying with a loud voice Jesus expired. It would appear that Luke and John each give us a part of that last utterance. If so, it must have been, "It is finished, Father, into Thy hands I commend My spirit." The first part helps to emphasize His Deity, so John records it: the second emphasizes His perfect Humanity, in its dependence upon God, so Luke records it. True also to the character of his Gospel, John chronicles the very act of His death in a special way—"He delivered up His spirit" (New Trans.). The wise man of the Old Testament has told us, "There is no man that hath power over the spirit to retain the spirit; neither hath he power in the day of death" (Eccles. 8:8), but here is One who had that power. He is able at one moment to lift up His voice with unimpaired strength, and the next moment to deliver up His spirit, and thus fulfil His own words recorded in chapter 10. True, there He spoke of the laying down of His "life" or "soul," saying, "No man taketh it from Me, but I lay it down of Myself. I have power to lay it down, and I have power to take it again." But the two statements are entirely in agreement for we all know that when the human spirit quits the body a man's life on earth ceases. When God calls his spirit, go he must. Here is One who has full command over His spirit; He delivered it up to His Father, and thus He laid down His life.

That, having laid it down, He took it again in resurrection, we find in the next chapter: the rest of our chapter is filled with the various activities of men, some of them His foes and some His friends, but all working together to the end that the determinate counsel of God should be fulfilled, just as He had spoken in His word.

First on the scene were the Jews, the men who were His most implacable foes. They were great sticklers for the ceremonial side of things and the Passover Sabbath being an high day it was of peculiar sanctity in their eyes. They could not enter the judgment hall lest they defile themselves, as we saw in the last chapter. Now we see that the idea of the dead bodies of men they esteemed evil-doers remaining exposed in the sight of men and Heaven over that day was abhorrent to their ritualistic souls. They were right of course, for it had been so ordered in Deuteronomy 21:23, but that was the type of enactment which they loved to observe, whilst overlooking matters of greater moment. Thus from them came the request that death might be hastened by the breaking of the legs, so indirectly they played their part in bringing to fulfilment another of the many predictions which were focussed on that great day when Jesus died.

We might have supposed that life with the Lord would have been prolonged far beyond the others, but in fact it was the opposite, just because

He deliberately laid His life down. Had He not done so, man's act in crucifying Him would have had no power against Him. It is significant also that John does not designate the two men as thieves or malefactors; they were "two other" (ver. 18). No need to mention their particularly bad character to heighten the contrast. The greatness of the Divine Son is such that it is sufficient to say that they were two other men.

Pilate's order to the soldiers, at the instance of the Jews, had two effects. First, while the two other had their legs broken to hasten their end not a bone of our Lord was broken, and thus Scripture was fulfilled. The reference must be to Psalm 34: 20, and to the instructions given as to the Passover lamb in Exodus 12, and repeated in Numbers 9. This is worthy of note as showing how fully the Spirit of God identifies the typical lamb with its Antitype, inasmuch as that which is said of the type is treated as applying to the Antitype. With this agree the words of Paul in 1 Corinthians 5, when he says, "Christ our passover is sacrificed for us."

Secondly, there was the wanton and vindictive act of the soldier with a spear. Seeing that Jesus was dead, and hence he had no authority to break His bones, he thrust the spear into His side. He did it without the least understanding of the significant effect of his act. Once more, however, that which lay in the Divine counsel was brought to pass and a Scripture found its fulfilment. The prophet Zechariah had declared that at last the spirit of grace and of supplications should be poured upon the house of David and the inhabitants of Jerusalem, "and they shall look upon Me, whom they have pierced" (12: 10). Notice here how the act of the subordinate official is treated as the act of those whose determination and will lay at the root of all that happened. The Roman soldier was but the instrument of this wickedness, and in the coming day the repentant remnant of Israel will acknowledge it as the act of their nation. Even today do we not acknowledge that spear-thrust to have been the terrible expression of man's hatred and contemptuous rejection of the Son of God?

But the Evangelist specially concentrates our attention upon the result of that wanton deed—"forthwith came there out blood and water." When, in verse 35, he solemnly affirms the truth of his record, so that faith may spring up in the reader, it is to this he refers. In the first place, this piercing of His side publicly demonstrated that death had really taken place. In the second place, by it His blood was actually shed, and we have only to recall that, "without shedding of blood is no remission," (Heb. 9: 22), to realize the importance of that fact. In the third place, we know what gracious and blessed results flow to us each individually when our faith reaches out and reposes in the Christ who died and in the blood that He shed. So we are not surprised at John's strong affirmation of the truth of his witness.

But water came thereout as well as blood and we do well to study the significance of that, for John dwells on it again in chapter 5 of his first Epistle, where we read that Jesus Christ came "by water and blood," and it is emphasized that it was "not by water only, but by water and blood." If the blood speaks of judicial expiation, the water speaks of moral purification, and both are absolutely essential and only to be found in the death of Christ. There is always a tendency to separate the two. When John wrote, the tendency was to emphasize the water and ignore or belittle the blood, and this tendency is still powerfully felt, for there are many who like to think of His death as having a moral effect on us while they dislike the thought of death paying the wages of sin and thus effecting expiation. It is quite possible of course to find the opposite extreme in those who recognize nothing but the blood shed for our sins, and thus overlook the necessity of that moral cleansing of which the death of Christ is the all-essential basis.

It is remarkable too that in the Gospel we have the record of John as to the fact, whereas in his Epistle both the water and the blood are regarded as bearing witness, together with the Spirit. They bear record "that God hath given to us eternal life, and this life is in His Son." Blood and water came forth from the dead Christ. The Spirit has been shed forth from the risen and glorified Christ. Together they bear record that, while there is no life in us, we have eternal life in the Son of God.

Joseph of Arimathæa now appears at the precise moment when he can serve the purpose of God. He is mentioned in each of the Gospels, and each supplies us with some special detail concerning him. Matthew tells us that he was rich and a disciple. Mark calls him an honourable counsellor who waited for the kingdom of God. Luke says he was a good man and a just and that he had not consented to the counsel and deed of the great majority of the Sanhedrim in putting Jesus to death. John admits that he was a disciple, but a secret one for fear of the Jews. So apparently he had been in a position akin to that of the Pharisees, who are mentioned in verses 42, 43, of chapter 12. Yet, wonderful to say, in this the darkest hour, when everything seemed hopelessly lost—as witness the attitude of the two disciples going to Emmaus (Luke 24)—Joseph found his courage and went to Pilate with his request to have possession of the body of Jesus. Mark it is, who tells us that he went in boldly to Pilate, and the decision of the Governor was overruled of God. Isaiah had declared that He should be "with the rich in His death," though His grave was appointed to Him with the wicked. The Jews would have desired nothing better than that He should be flung under a heap of stones with the bodies of the malefactors. But God fulfilled His own word, firstly through the sudden boldness of Joseph, and then through Pilate's disposition to thwart the Jews by reason of his irritation with them. God everywhere has sway and all things serve His might.

At this point Nicodemus again appears. Mentioned nowhere else, he is mentioned three times in our Gospel. We see him first as an enquirer, but needing to be humbled, and brought down from his high estate as Pharisee, teacher, and ruler in Israel. He must be born again. At the end of chapter 7 we find him raising a mild objection to the evil counsel and actions of the council, and standing up for what is right, and being snubbed for his remonstrance. Now we find him taking a further step in advance. He identified himself with Jesus in His death more definitely than he ever had during His life. He too must have been rich, judging from the amount of spices that he brought. The crisis, which had paralyzed the men who had boldly identified themselves with the Lord in His life and ministry, had nerved these timid and cautious men, who hitherto had been in the background unrecognized, into boldness and action. Truly Omnipotence has servants everywhere!

One other point remains at the end of the chapter. Close by the place of the crucifixion was a garden and a tomb in the rock. Only Matthew tells us that it was Joseph's own tomb; he also says that it was new; both Luke and John are more emphatic on this point, saying no man before had lain there. It had been foretold through the Psalmist that Jehovah would not suffer His "Holy One to see corruption." That this signified that the holy and sacred body of Jesus though undergoing death was not in the least touched by the process of disintegration and corruption, we all know. But it also meant that His body should not even come into contact with it externally. When God fulfils His word, He does so with thoroughness and completeness.

Thus, as we intimated, when the Divine Son suffered, the hand of Omnipotence overshadowed all men and all things, so that all that He had declared through holy men of old might come to pass. The counsel of the Lord, it shall stand.

## Chapter 20

In our Gospel Mary Magdalene only appears in connection with the closing scenes. She was amongst the last standing by the cross and amongst the first at the sepulchre on the resurrection day. It is not easy to piece together the records of the four Evangelists so as to make out the historic sequence of events, but it would almost appear that, having come with other women very early in the morning, she ran off by herself to inform Peter and John that the sepulchre was open and empty and then returned to its vicinity.

The other women are not mentioned here at all. Our thoughts are concentrated on her, to lead us up to the spiritual instruction conveyed through her actions and by means of her lips.

That the Lord was the supreme and absorbing Object before her is quite evident from her words to the Apostles, as recorded in verse 2. Her choice of the two to whom she went is remarkable for Peter had so grievously sinned just before. Still, he did love the Lord, as the next chapter records, and John was the disciple whom Jesus loved. On their side love may have been somewhat eclipsed for the moment, but it was there, and Mary, in whom it was burning brightly, knew it.

It was declared, moreover, by the way they responded to the announcement Mary brought. It set their hearts and feet in motion. They ran with eager haste and John outran Peter. The natural explanation doubtless was that he was the younger man; but there was also a spiritual explanation. John was more deeply impressed by the Lord's love for him, as he showed by the way he spoke of himself, whilst Peter was under the cloud of having trusted in his own love for the Lord, which, when tested, broke down in such a scandalous and public way. He who is most drawn by the love of Christ, runs the fastest. It was a case of, "Draw me, we will run after Thee" (Song of Sol. 1:4).

Still Peter, in spite of his disgraceful failure, did run and, arrived at the sepulchre, was the bolder of the two and went right inside. This led John to join him and thus there were two witnesses to the fact that the linen clothes in which the sacred body had been enfolded were not lying in disorder but rather in such fashion as to suggest that, far from the body having been removed by others, Jesus had risen from death in such a condition that the grave clothes were wholly undisturbed. Verse 19 of our chapter shows that in His resurrection body closed doors were no impediment to our Lord, so doubtless the clothes similarly were left just as they were.

In verse 8, John speaks for himself—he believed, though it was only accepting the evidence of his eyes. Peter is not mentioned, for faith, though it may be there, is not active when the soul is under the dark cloud of failure and sin, and is as yet unrestored. But though John believed his faith was of an unintelligent kind, for he, as much as the rest, was not yet illuminated by an understanding of the Scripture. Had he been he would have known the Christ *must* rise from the dead (see, Acts 17: 3), which would have explained everything. So though there was faith there was also ignorance, and this accounts for what we read in verse 10. The example set by Peter and John early in the morning of the resurrection day was followed in the afternoon by Cleopas and his companion as recorded in Luke 24.

The conduct of Mary stands out in bright contrast to all the rest. The two disciples had left for their home convinced that the body of Jesus was not there. Mary was equally convinced but she left her home to linger at the sepulchre, weeping in her sense of utter desolation. They knew the Lord as One who had called them from boats and nets. She knew Him as One who had delivered her from the grip of seven demons. It had been a mighty deliverance and she loved much. To her two angels appeared and there is no record of her having been afraid of their presence.

This is remarkable since in the other Gospels fear is mentioned in connection with each appearance. Her case evidently illustrates how an overpowering affection can drive out of the heart every other emotion. Her reply to the question of the angels showed how Jesus, whom she called "My Lord," monopolized the whole range of her thoughts. She answered as though meeting with angels were an everyday occurrence. In seeking her Lord she had lost the trail, and she seems to have taken it for granted that they were as much preoccupied with the matter as she was herself. But evidently as yet no thought of His resurrection had crossed her mind. She only thought of others removing His body. She was seeking a dead Christ.

At that moment the risen Lord intervened and she turned herself back from the angels to find Him standing there, yet she did not recognize Him. The same feature characterized His meeting with the two disciples going to Emmaus that afternoon, and the rest of the disciples in the upper room that evening. It was the same Jesus but with a difference owing to His being clothed in a risen body—risen, though not yet glorified—hence they did not identify Him at once. She mistook Him for the gardener. He, the Great Shepherd risen from the dead, knew well that here was one of His sheep thoroughly devoted to Him, seeking only Himself and weeping because she knew not where to find Him.

In the simple utterance of her name He revealed Himself to her and she instantly responded to Him as her Master. All that is recorded, however, in verses 11-15, shows that she was seeking His body as dead, and hence her first thought on finding Him alive was doubtless that of a resumption of associations on the old basis, which had prevailed in "the days of His flesh." This it is which accounts for the Lord's opening word to her, "Touch Me not." In view of the new relationship which He was about to announce to her, and through her to the other disciples, He showed her in this decisive way that relations could not be resumed just as they were before. His death and resurrection had changed everything. He was no less a Man than He was before He died, yet having laid down His life, He had taken it again in a new state and condition suited to the heavens into which He was about to ascend. Hence relations with Him must be on a new basis.

The Lord added the words, "for I am not yet ascended to My Father," to His prohibition. Thus He evidently implied that when He was ascended to His Father Mary was to be in "touch" with Him. His ascension to the Father involved the shedding forth of the Holy Ghost on the disciples, as has been made abundantly clear in this Gospel—see, 7: 39; 14: 16; 15: 26; 16: 13. When, at Pentecost, Mary, along with the others, was filled with the Holy Spirit, she found herself in her spirit brought into a far more intimate touch with her risen Lord than she had ever experienced in the days of His flesh.

Doubtless the Apostles were privileged far beyond ourselves in the way they "heard," "saw," "looked upon," "handled of the Word of life" (1 John 1: 1). Yet while they were walking with Him in Palestine the real significance of what they observed was obscure to them. As chapter 14:

17, 20, has shown us, it was only when they had the indwelling of the Spirit that they *knew* that they were in Him and He in them—His life theirs and a new relationship established. Now we too have the Spirit of God, so though the objective manifestation has reached us not directly as it did with the Apostles but only through their inspired writings, the subjective realization may be ours in full measure. We do well to ponder this matter very deeply.

A further thing lies in this great verse. Jesus calls the disciples, "My brethren." They had previously been designated, "His own," (13: 1), and He had called them, "My friends" (15: 14), but neither of these indicates *relationship* in the same way as "My brethren." We should learn from this that He has established the relationship as the Risen One, who has passed through death and triumphed over it. It exists not by virtue of His incarnation but in the power of His resurrection. He truly took part in "flesh and blood," and laid hold on "the seed of Abraham," with a view to the suffering of death. Having tasted death for every man, and been made perfect through sufferings, He became the Captain of our salvation, and thus as the Sanctifier He acknowledges those whom He sanctifies as His brethren. This is brought before us in Hebrews 2: 9-16. By incarnation He came to our side, that in His perfect and spotless Manhood He might take up our case. Having taken it up, and by His death and resurrection wrought deliverance for us, He lifts us to His side in identification with Him in risen life. Thus it is that the relationship lies not in incarnation but in resurrection. This, too, is a deeply important point to remember.

The message Mary was to convey to the other disciples announced to them their new relationship with God and not only in regard to Himself. His Father is our Father, His God is our God. He places us in His own relation to God but of course in a subsidiary way. Our relationship with God springs out of His, and out of our relations with Him. He did not say, "our" Father and God, as though He and we were on the same level. This we must carefully note, for His full pre-eminence must always be acknowledged with thankfulness. Though He speaks of us as, "My brethren," we never find Him spoken of as "our Brother," nor even as, "our Elder Brother," in the Scriptures. Such terms would tend to our thinking of Him as though He came down to our side rather than His lifting us to His side. They would also obscure His pre-eminent position.

In His wonderful earthly life the Lord Jesus had revealed the Father, for the Father had dwelt in Him, so that He could say, "He that hath seen Me hath seen the Father." This we saw when we considered chapter 14. He had also taught the disciples to look up to God as their "Heavenly Father," in connection with all their needs and circumstances in this world, as the other Gospels show, but a fuller revelation comes to light here. We do not lose the blessing and benefit of the earlier revelation, any more than we do of the revelation of Him as the Almighty or as Jehovah; but we need to

## JOHN

understand and rejoice in the knowledge of God as "the God and Father of our Lord Jesus Christ" (Eph. 1: 3 and 1 Pet. 1: 3). Our Lord's words to Mary were the first intimation of this fuller and higher relationship, and once it had come to light the epistles of the New Testament present God to us in that way. He is indeed a "Heavenly Father" to us in all the vicissitudes of this life but let us not treat this as though it were everything. Our proper relationship with God as Christians is on this higher basis.

Mary Magdalene — the woman with the loving responsive heart — was the first to hear these wonderful things, and she became the messenger of them to all of us. She could testify that she had seen the Lord and that He had made these communications to her, and through her to the rest.

Later in the day the Lord appeared to Simon Peter and to Cleopas and his companion journeying to Emmaus, though John makes no mention of these manifestations. It is clear, however, from the other Gospels that as the resurrection day advanced the disciples had two witnesses to His resurrection—Mary and Peter—and that their testimony brought them together in Jerusalem as the eventide drew on. When assembled, Cleopas and his friend came amongst them, thus furnishing them with a third and fourth witness. Then, when the doors were shut, Jesus Himself stood in their midst, identifying Himself by His pierced hands and side, and filling their hearts with gladness.

The doors had been shut for fear of the Jews. His presence as risen caused joy to intervene on their fear. Even so an element was still lacking, which could only be supplied by the filling of the Spirit of God. On the day of Pentecost fear was swallowed up entirely, and they were filled with boldness coupled with power.

The Lord Jesus Christ of necessity always takes the central place. He did so in death, as recorded in verse 18 of the previous chapter. Here He does so in resurrection, and thus there was a fulfilment of His word recorded in Matthew 18: 20. On the evening of the resurrection day the disciples were gathered together in His Name, though only half believing the witnesses to His resurrection. He came into their midst in visible form. The main difference for us today is that He takes His place in invisible form where disciples are gathered in His Name. When His presence is realized the effect is as here—peace and gladness. The word of peace came from His lips. The gladness followed as their eyes corroborated the evidence furnished by their ears.

Luke tells us, in Acts 1, that He showed Himself alive "by many infallible proofs," and prominent among these was the display to His disciples of His pierced hands and side. These sacred marks identified Him beyond all dispute. Death and resurrection had both been accomplished, and they were like twin pillars on which the peace He announced was firmly established. Twice did the Lord salute them with peace on His lips for He knew full well that until that was realized in their hearts they would have little ability to receive the further things that He had to convey to them. It is just so with us today. Until we have the enjoyment of settled peace with God we can make no spiritual progress.

Having announced peace for the second time the risen Lord commissioned His disciples in words which, though very brief, are full of profound significance. Each Gospel records a commission, though with characteristic differences. Matthew records it in terms that would specially strike a Jewish reader. They were no longer to make disciples from the very limited sphere indicated earlier in that Gospel (10: 5-11), but from *all nations*, and they were to baptise in the Name that had come to light in Christ, and not with John's baptism or one akin to that. The commission there is so worded as to have an application to those who may make disciples after the church is gone. In Mark also the universal aspect of the Apostolic preaching and service is emphasized. This is the case also in Luke, where the fulness of grace seems to be the point; grace which could begin at Jerusalem, the worst spot, and extend to all nations. The three synoptic Gospels have this in common however; the commission in each is concerned with the apostles' preaching and service.

But in John, as befits that Gospel, a deeper note is struck. The Lord Jesus had been sent forth from the Father, that in Him the Father might be made known. As the fourteenth chapter made so plain, He was in the Father as to His being, His life, His nature, and consequently the Father was in Him, and so was fully made known. Now, having died and risen again He was going to the Father, but He was leaving in the world disciples, whom now He sent that they might be for Him after the pattern of the way He had been sent forth to be for the Father. If, therefore, we are to understand their mission, we must first understand the Lord's own mission as sent of the Father.

It is remarkable how many times in this Gospel the Lord is referred to as the One who had been sent of the Father into the world. In slightly varying words this is referred to upwards of forty times, and we can see how relevant it is to the fact that He is presented to us as One who was God, and was with God. He was, therefore not indigenous to the world, as though He sprang out of it. He came from above, and all that He was He brought with Him. His words and His works were all the Father's. Now a new thing is brought to pass, and in its institution the Lord was fulfilling His own statement in His prayer to the Father—see, 17: 18. He was departing, and they now were to be sent as from Him.

What lay behind this sending was the fact that they too were not of the world as He had not been. This is also stated in chapter 17—see, verse 16. There was this difference, however; once they had been indigenous to the world, so in their case there was a link that had to be broken, and there were new links that had to be formed. This at once leads us to that which is set forth in verse 22 of our chapter.

## JOHN

The words of commission were followed by words of impartation, coupled with a peculiar action. He breathed on—or, more correctly, *into*—them, and said, "Receive ye Holy Ghost," for the definite article "the" is lacking in the original. We must observe the connection between this and what is recorded as to the creation of Adam in Genesis 2: 7. As to his body, he was formed of the dust of the ground but the spiritual part of him came into being by the Lord God breathing into his nostrils the breath of life, and thus it was he became a living soul. Now our Lord, who is the last Adam, is a quickening or life-giving spirit, as we read in 1 Corinthians 15: 45, and here we see Him breathing into His disciples His own risen life.

But this being so, why did He say, "Receive ye Holy Ghost"? Because His own life as the risen Man is in the energy of the Holy Ghost. He was, "put to death in the flesh, but quickened by the Spirit" (1 Pet. 3: 18). On the Day of Pentecost, as recorded in Acts 2, the disciples did indeed receive *the* Holy Ghost, as a Divine Person indwelling their very bodies, but here we have something preliminary to that. On the very day that Jesus entered upon His risen life as quickened in and by the Spirit of God, He imparted it to His own.

We must connect this great act with both what precedes and what follows. How could they be sent into the world, to be for Him as He had been sent of the Father, except they possessed His risen life? The natural life which they had from Adam gave them no competency for such a mission. They did not have *power* till the Holy Ghost was shed forth abundantly at Pentecost, but they now had the *life* and *nature* that rendered the mission possible. We do not read of this action in the other Gospels but we do read in Luke 24, "then opened He their understanding, that they might understand the scriptures" (verse 45). This opening of their understandings was, we judge, the result of the inbreathing of His risen life.

In our Gospel, however, there are the two things connected with it: first it gave them capacity to be witnesses in the world as sent of Him; and second, to be entrusted with administrative powers as to remitting or retaining sins, not eternally of course, but governmentally. In Matthew's Gospel we see that the Lord before His death and resurrection had indicated that such powers should be conferred upon Peter (16: 19), and upon the Apostles as a whole (18: 18), on each occasion looking forward to the future. Here the power is actually conferred. Primarily, no doubt, the power was apostolic, and we see Peter wielding the power in Acts 5: 1-11, and the Holy Ghost ratifying it in no uncertain way. But in 1 Corinthians 5: 3-5, 12, 13, we have Paul wielding it and calling upon the church to act with him in retaining the evil-doer's sin. In 2 Corinthians 2: 4-8, we find him calling upon the church to reverse the action as the evil-doer had repented. They were to remit, or forgive; and verse 10 of that chapter is very instructive in connection with it.

# JOHN

In the other Gospels the name of Thomas only appears in the list of the apostles: all that we know of him is contained in our Gospel. This is significant. He is mentioned in chapters 11 and 14 and his words on those occasions prepare us for the light in which his character appears here. He was evidently a man of plain, unimaginative, matter-of-fact mind, too inclined to be materialistic, and, therefore, hard to convince of anything lying off the plane of ordinary human experience. We are now very close to the verse which avows the goal to which this Gospel is designed to conduct us, and we are considering the last and greatest of the signs that John has brought before us. Hence the case of Thomas is of particular value in this Gospel.

He was not present on the evening of the resurrection day, and hence when he heard the testimony of the other disciples, which they condensed into five words of deepest import, "We have seen the Lord," he was not prepared to accept it. In a spirit of stubborn doubt he declared that except he had visible and tangible evidence of a most indubitable sort, evidence that most clearly identified the One who appeared with the One who died upon the cross, he would not believe. In thus challenging the disciple's testimony, he was really flinging down a challenge to his risen Lord, which, if accepted, would place His resurrection beyond all question as far as he was concerned.

The Lord in condescending grace did accept it a week later. Again He appeared in their midst though the doors were shut. Again He saluted them with the words, "Peace unto you." Then He bade Thomas do exactly as he had said, that he might have not only the visible, but also the tangible evidence he desired. And not only this, for He gave a spiritual sign also. His words to Thomas revealed that the challenge flung down when He was not visibly present was perfectly known to the risen Lord. At the end of chapter 1, we had a similar incident. Jesus showed Nathanael that He had seen him when he thought himself unobserved under the fig tree, and Nathanael was convinced and confessed Him as the Son of God and the King of Israel.

That was in the days of His flesh yet He revealed Himself as *the all-seeing One*. Here the days of His flesh are over and He is risen, but He is revealed as *the all-hearing One*. The effect on Thomas of all this was overwhelming. The stubborn doubter, when he is convinced, is convinced indeed! A few minutes ago he was dragging far behind the other disciples, now in his rapturous confession he goes at one bound definitely beyond them. Nathanael had been explicit in his confession at the outset: Thomas at the close is even more explicit. Only five words again! But what words they were—"My Lord and My God."!

Deniers of our Lord's deity have sought to avoid the force of this by treating this as a mere exclamation, addressed to no one in particular, but the record distinctly states that the words were said to the Lord, the form

## JOHN

of them in the original being very emphatic, since he used the definite article twice. The risen Jesus was *the* Lord and *the* God to him. And what is more significant still, the Lord replied, "Thomas . . . thou hast *believed.*" Beyond all question then He treated Thomas' joyful exclamation as *faith* laying hold of FACT. In other words, He accepted the confession as being true. There is no greater sin than for a mere man to accept Divine honours or adulation, as witness the drastic smiting of Herod, recorded in Acts 12. When John fell down before a holy angel as about to worship him, the instant reply was, "See thou do it not" (Rev. 22: 9). Instead of rebuking Thomas, Jesus approved of his confession and called it faith.

The full Deity of Jesus thus being acknowledged, we have reached the end to which this Gospel is designed to conduct us. Very appropriately, therefore, do verses 30 and 31 close this chapter. We are reminded that all the miraculous signs put on record are but a tiny fraction of the whole. Those that are recorded are quite sufficient however, and in this Gospel they are specially selected to afford ample ground for faith in Jesus as the Christ, the Son of God, for it is the faith of this which brings life through His Name.

Note that the last and conclusive proof of Jesus being the Son of God is that He accepted the ascription of Deity to Himself. We may say that if He is God, He is the Son of God; and conversely, that if He is the Son of God, He is God. Note also that His Sonship is the great point in the Gospel which traces Him back into the unfathomable depths of past eternity, and gives no details of the Virgin Birth. If we really embrace this Gospel in faith we shall have no doubt that His Sonship is eternal, and not something assumed in time.

Before leaving this chapter we have only to remark the significance of the Lord's words in verse 29. There is something better than accepting ocular and tangible evidence, and that is *believing the word* without any such demonstration. Thomas doubtless illustrates the way in which a godly remnant of Israel will discover the truth in a coming day. The word of the prophet shall be fulfilled, "They shall look upon Me whom they have pierced" (Zech. 12: 10), and then it is that they will cry, "My God, we know Thee" (Hosea 8: 2). The greater blessedness, of those who believe without seeing, is the portion of all who receive in faith the Gospel today, whether Jew or Gentile.

We can render to God no tribute that is more grateful to Him than that of taking Him fully and simply at His word without asking any corroboration by sight or by feeling. As light may be resolved into the colours of the rainbow so the Divine Name comprises many features of equal value and importance, yet He specially emphasizes the verity and reliability of His word — "Thou hast magnified Thy Word above all Thy Name" (Psa. 138: 2). Seeing that at the outset sin came in through disbelief

# JOHN

of the Divine Word, how fitting this is! The present Gospel epoch is peculiarly the time when men believe without seeing—"Whom having not seen, ye love; in whom, though now ye see Him not, yet believing ye rejoice with joy unspeakable and full of glory: receiving the end of your faith, even the salvation of your souls" (1 Pet. 1: 8, 9).

This scripture gives us a glimpse of the special blessedness of which the Lord spoke to Thomas. It may be ours, and the keener and more simple our faith the deeper the measure in which it will be ours. May the full blessedness of it be known by each reader of these lines.

## CHAPTER 21

THE CLOSING VERSES of the previous chapter indicate that the evidence furnished, showing that Jesus is the Christ, the Son of God, is now complete. This is therefore taken for granted in the closing chapter, which puts on record dealings with certain of His disciples wholly unrecorded in the other Gospels. It may be considered in two ways: first, as having a figurative or typical meaning; second, as showing His gracious dealings with them in view of their future.

Verse 14 gives us a key to its special significance from the typical viewpoint. We may remember that at the opening of this Gospel the Evangelist calls our attention to certain days, and at the beginning of chapter 2 there was a manifestation of the glory of Jesus on the *third* day, typical of the millennial age. Now here we have before us what is noted as the *third* manifestation of Jesus as risen from the dead, and again we discover it has a millennial significance.

The first manifestation, as we saw in the last chapter, was on the actual resurrection day, and all recorded in connection with it spoke of the portion of *the Church* in association with the risen Lord. The second, in the same chapter, gave us the awakening of faith in *the remnant of Israel*, when at last they look upon Him whom they have pierced. That was set forth in Thomas. Now we come to the third, when *the millennial morning* will break and the Lord be revealed as the Master of every circumstance and the Supplier of every need. The three days pointed out in chapters 1 and 2, had in each case the same significance.

The main drift of this Gospel has been the revelation of the Father in the Person of the Son, and the certifying to us that Jesus is indeed the Son of God, so that we may have no doubt as to the revelation but the light of it shine with undimmed radiance into our souls. It is very remarkable, therefore, that it should both open and close with these figurative reminders of dispensational distinctions, though the burden of the Gospel is that which abides eternally above all dispensational distinctions. Differences of dispensation may impose different measures upon the apprehensions of saints, but that which is to be apprehended is eternally the same.

# JOHN

John has given us an account of Peter's downfall, but has said no word as to his bitter tears immediately after as the result of the Lord's look, nor of the personal interview with his risen Lord in the latter part of the resurrection day. We open this chapter to find him reverting to his fishing and taking six of the other disciples with him. It was not for this kind of fishing that the Lord had originally called him, and it looks as if, though knowing that the Lord had forgiven him, he was assuming that his commission to service would have to lapse. The risen Shepherd, however, was about to restore his soul fully and lead the feet of all of them into the paths of righteousness.

Their expedition on the lake was a failure. Verse 3 sums it up as "night" and "nothing." When the morning was come everything was reversed for Jesus was there—net full, great fishes—and no broken net or sinking ship, as in Luke 5. Nor was there Peter falling down to confess himself a sinful man, though his sad fall had been so recent. Instead he flung himself into the sea to get to Jesus with all possible speed. Again we see how he is prominent when the *action* of love is in question, just as John displays more prominently the *discernment* of love.

Arrived on the shore, the disciples found themselves forestalled though their catch had been so great. The Lord had fire and fish and bread ready for them; the provision was all His own. Viewed typically, we may see a figure of disciples going forth and bringing in under the Lord's direction, a great harvest from the sea of nations, which will mark the opening of the millennial age. It was surely intended, too, as a lesson to Peter and the rest, showing them that their reversion to their ordinary occupation was unnecessary, even if specially blessed by Him. Their food was already prepared by His hand. The disciples knew it was their risen Lord, not by the sight of their eyes, but by His actions, which were unique.

Then began the Lord's special dealings with Simon Peter. His fall had taken place when he was warming himself at the world's fire in the company of the servants of the high priest, who was utterly hostile to his Master. He now finds himself by the fire that had been kindled by his Lord, not only warmed but also fed by Him, and in the company of fellow-servants as devoted to his Master as himself. Thrice had Peter been tested and each time with increasing emphasis he had denied his Lord. Thrice on this occasion does the Lord probe Peter's conscience and heart, each time increasing the severity of the test.

We can more fully appreciate verses 15-17 if we observe that two different words are used for "love." The first is one which, we are told, is not used for "love" outside the New Testament and Septuagint: the Spirit of God laid hold of it, and consecrated it to express the love of God. The second is one based upon the word for friends, and signifying rather the love of the feelings or of warm affection; or, as it has been put, "it indicates less of insight and more of emotion." We will quote from Darby's New Translation where the distinction is carefully observed.

The Lord addressed Peter not by that new name, which He had given him, but by his old name in nature, "Simon son of Jonas," and asked him, "Lovest thou Me more than these?" This is just what he had claimed for himself in saying, "Although all shall be offended, yet will not I," as Mark tells us. This must have been a very painful question, for judging by his performance it appeared that he loved Him far less. What could he say? Only this, "Yea, Lord: Thou knowest that I am attached to Thee." He used the lower word, showing that he had already come down in his own esteem.

A second time Jesus asked the question, using the same word as before but not instituting any comparison between Peter and the other disciples. It was simply, "Lovest thou Me?" it was as though He had said, "Do you really love Me at all?" This probed the wound in still deeper fashion. Peter was again unable to accept the challenge and adhered to his own word, "Thou knowest that I am attached to Thee."

The third question was a still deeper thrust, for this time Jesus adopted Peter's own word and asked, "Art thou attached to Me?" Thus He challenged Peter's right to go so far as saying he was even attached to Him. This cut him to the quick and probed him to the depth. He realized that he could not claim to love, and that his conduct had belied even a friendly attachment. He therefore cast himself wholly upon his omniscient Lord, saying, "Lord, Thou knowest all things; Thou knowest that I am attached to Thee." This virtually acknowledged that his attachment was of such faint and microscopical proportions that only Divine omniscience would perceive it. Still it was there! Peter knew it, and he knew his Lord would know it.

In all this Peter was being most graciously yet very pointedly conducted to self-judgment—the judgment of the state that had led to the sin and disaster. It is one thing to confess the sin committed, and another to confess the wrong state that led to it. This is the point which is so instructive and salutary for us. Self-esteem with its twin evil, self-confidence, was the bottom of the mischief, and full restoration before the Lord was not perfected till Peter reached this point. Moreover his sin had taken place with considerable publicity, and the other disciples must have had their confidence in him sadly shaken. How gracious then of the Lord to deal with Peter to his restoration in the presence of a number of the disciples.

And this was not all. Each affirmation by Peter that he really was attached to the Lord in spite of his cowardly denial, was followed by a

# JOHN

response which indicated that a very important service was to be entrusted to him. The Lord used three different expressions, which are not entirely clear in our excellent Authorised Version. They were, "Feed My lambs," "Shepherd My sheep," "Feed My sheep." The shepherding of sheep would involve seeing that they were fed, but it would go beyond that and cover many activities in the way of oversight, leading, protecting.

It is very evident that Peter was entrusted with a pastoral ministry, and the way in which he urges upon others a similar pastoral care, in the opening verses of chapter 5 of his first Epistle, is very striking. Therein he warns against the very abuses of such a ministry as have come in like a flood in the history of the church. These abuses reach their greatest development in the imposing religious body that claims their Roman Pontiff as the successor of Peter; and they are just the outgrowth of fallen human nature, for exactly similar things happened in Israel, and are denounced by the Lord through Ezekiel in chapter 34 of his prophecy. Today "Peter's-pence" means money *extracted from* the flock for the support of the supposed successor of Peter, instead of anything *ministered to* the flock. A grim perversion and parody indeed!

The under shepherds who served after Peter's departure soon forgot that the lambs and sheep belonged to the Lord. The word to Peter was not "Feed *your* sheep," but "*My* sheep," and that makes all the difference. It is noticeable further that the Lord spoke *once* of shepherding and *twice* of feeding. That is where the emphasis lies. Shepherding means a certain amount of authoritative handling and directing, and there are not a few who love wielding authority, even in the church of God. To be a dispenser of spiritual food is another matter and a far deeper one. He who can give spiritual food will not have much difficulty in exercising some measure of spiritual control.

One other thing we might note. When Peter was thus commissioned he was a broken and humbled man. To such an one, when fully restored, the Lord entrusted His lambs and sheep. We may remember the Apostolic injunction, "If a man be overtaken in a fault, ye which are spiritual restore such an one in the spirit of meekness; considering thyself, lest thou also be tempted" (Gal. 6: 1). It is assumed that a spiritual man will be meek and have a wholesome sense of his own liability to fall. Here Peter had fallen and, humbled now and restored, he had reached that tender and meek spirit which marks the spiritual man. To men of that type the Lord entrusts His lambs and sheep.

Having recommissioned Peter and indicated the special character of the service he was to render, the Lord now showed him that what he had boasted he would do in the energy of youth, he should actually do when his natural energy had abated. "I will lay down my life for Thy sake," had been his words, yet he miserably failed. His desire had been right, though his self-confidence was wrong and had to be rebuked. So his desire should be fulfilled, but in power other than his own. The Lord's words in verse 18 not only indicated that he should glorify God by a martyr's death, but also the character of that death. The allusion was to crucifixion. He was to follow the Lord in caring for His sheep and, up to a certain point, in the manner of his death. What amazing grace was this to the disciple who had failed! And what instruction for us! The case of John Mark also furnishes us with an example of how what is begun in the flesh may yet be made perfect by the Spirit: the exact opposite of Galatians 3: 3.

For the moment Peter turned his eye from his Master and fixed it upon a fellow-disciple, none other than the writer of this Gospel. John was evidently a younger man but had already been closely linked with Peter on several occasions. It was probably genuine interest and not merely curiosity that made him enquire as to his future. The reply appears to have a twofold bearing.

First, it emphasized the fact that for each disciple—whether Peter or ourselves—our great business is not with our brethren but with our Lord. What the Lord ordained for John was not Peter's concern, but to follow the Lord for himself. There are not very many today who point to their brother and say, "What shall this man do?" but plenty there are who say, "Look what this man has done!" To be exercised about somebody else's doings, especially if they are not quite right, is a cheap and easy thing, whereas to be exercised about oneself is a costly business. To each of us, as to Peter, does the Lord say, "Follow *thou* Me."

In the second place there was something cryptic or hidden in this saying about John, just as there had been in the saying of verse 18 about Peter. It did not indicate that he should not die and so remain till the second advent, but rather that his ministry should have a special character. The word here, translated, "tarry" is one that occurs in John's writings as often as in all the rest of the New Testament put together. It is variously translated as "abide," "continue," "dwell," "remain." Now John's ministry, as exemplified in his Gospel and Epistles, did specially deal with the abiding things of the revelation of God which nothing can touch or tarnish. In the Revelation we find he was the last of the Apostles to see the Lord in His glorious majesty, and to receive from Him through His angel the fullest unfolding of things to come, which things lead us up to the second advent, and even to the eternal state.

Verse 23 is a warning to us of the danger of drawing inferences from the Word of God, and then elevating those inferences into dogmatic assertions. If a saying had gone forth among the brethren that John might not die, in view of what the Lord had said, it perhaps would not have been worthy of remark. But they said he *should* not, rather than he *might* not. Inspired words stand in a class by themselves, and we must be careful how we draw inferences from them.

# JOHN

The last verse of our Gospel is very characteristic. It reminds us that what is recorded of the doings of the Lord on earth is but a tiny fraction of the whole, and this is true if we put all four Gospels together. It is also as true of His words as of His works. This is a fact that helps to explain things that are sometimes quoted as apparent discrepancies. For instance, the Lord must have done and said similar things scores of times during the years of His incessant service in various parts of Judea and Galilee. And lastly, there is no picturesque exaggeration in what is said about the world and the books. John has traced for us the matchless words and works of the Word become flesh—at least, a selection of them, which though small is ample to convince us that in Him we have the Christ, the Son of God. Though He assumed a finite form the Word who assumed it is *infinite*. He put therefore the stamp of *infinity* on all He did and said, and the world and books cannot contain that.

We shall never get to the end of all the things which Jesus did. On this most appropriate note our Gospel ends.

# ACTS

## Chapter 1

BY ITS OPENING words the Acts of the Apostles is linked in the clearest way with the Gospel of Luke. The same Theophilus is addressed, and in the first chapter the story is resumed just at the point where the Gospel left off, save that a few extra details are given of the Lord's words after His resurrection, and the account of His ascension is repeated in a somewhat different setting. The Gospel *leads up to* His resurrection and ascension. The Acts *starts from* those glorious facts and develops their consequences.

In the first verse Luke describes his Gospel as a "treatise . . . of all that Jesus *began* both to *do* and *teach*." The word "began" is worthy of note. It infers that Jesus has not ceased to do and teach by reason of His going on high beyond the sight of men. The Acts tells us what Jesus proceeded to *do*, by shedding forth the Holy Spirit from the Father, so that by Him He might act through the Apostles and others. In the same way we discover by reading the epistles what He proceeded to *teach* through the Apostles in due season. Before He was taken up He gave necessary instructions to the Apostles, and that, "through the Holy Ghost," though as yet the Spirit was not given to them. In his Gospel Luke had presented the Lord to us as the perfect Man, ever acting in the power of the Spirit, and in that same light we see Him here.

For the space of forty days He manifested Himself as the One living beyond the power of death, and thus abundant proof was furnished of His resurrection. During these contacts with His disciples He spoke to them of things concerning the kingdom of God, and directed them to await in Jerusalem the coming of the Spirit. John, who baptized with water, had pointed to Him as the Baptizer with the Holy Ghost, and that baptism was to reach them in a few days.

The Lord had been speaking of the kingdom of God; their minds however still ran on the restoration of the kingdom to Israel. In this they were like the two going to Emmaus, though now they knew that He was risen. Their question gave to the Lord the opportunity of indicating what was to be the programme for the opening dispensation, and we see again just what we saw in Luke 24; the Centre of the programme is not Israel but Christ. The coming of the Spirit would mean power, not that the apostles should be restorers of Israel, but "witnesses unto Me" — witnesses to Christ unto the utmost bounds of the earth. The four circles of witness, mentioned at the end of verse 8, supply us with one way of dividing up the book. We begin with the witness in Jerusalem, and until the end of chapter 7 we are occupied with that city and Judæa. Then in chapter 8 comes Samaria. In chapter 9 the man to carry the Gospel to the Gentiles is called; and in chapter 13 the mission to the uttermost parts begins.

There appears to be a contradiction between verse 7, and what Paul writes in 1 Thessalonians 5: 1 and 2. But there the point is that they knew well *what* was going to transpire as regards God's dealing with the earth: here that we may not know *when*, since that is a matter reserved by the Father for Himself alone. Our business is to render true and diligent witness to Christ. What that witness will effect is not plainly stated until we reach verse 14 of chapter 15.

Having said these things Jesus was taken up and a cloud—doubtless the cloud of Luke 9: 34—hid Him from their eyes. Two heavenly messengers however stood by their side to supplement His declaration of a few moments before. Their *mission* was to be witnesses to the ascended Christ; but their *hope* was to be His return just as He went. His going was not something figurative, shadowy, mystical, but actual and literal. His coming will be actual and literal in like manner.

Ten days had to pass before the coming of the Spirit, and the rest of the chapter tells us how those days of waiting were occupied. The number of avowed disciples in Jerusalem was about one hundred and twenty, and prayer and supplication filled their time. There could be no witness until the Spirit was given, but they could take and maintain the safe place of utter dependence upon God.

And further, they could refer to the Scriptures and apply them to the existing situation, inasmuch as the Lord had opened their minds to understand, as recorded in Luke 24. It is remarkable that Peter should have been the one to take the initiative in this matter, seeing he himself had so sadly sinned only about six weeks before. Still it shows that the Lord had thoroughly effected his restoration, and he was able to piece together Psalm 69: 25, and 109: 8, in this striking way. "Bishoprick" of course should be "office" or "charge," as reference to the Psalm will show. It was the office of apostleship that was in question, as also verse 25 of our chapter shows. Verses 18 and 19 are evidently not the words of Peter, but a parenthesis in which Luke gives us further details of the fearful end of Judas.

An essential feature of apostleship was first-hand knowledge of the risen Saviour. The apostle must be able to testify of Him as having personally seen Him in His risen estate: hence Paul's third question in 1 Corinthians 9: 1. Paul saw Him, not during the forty days but later in the full blaze of His glory. However, from the outset there must be the twelve apostolic witnesses, and Matthias was chosen. They had recourse to the Old Testament practice of casting lots: guidance, such as we read of in chapter 13: 2, could not be known until the Holy Ghost had been given.

### Chapter 2

IF WE READ Leviticus 23, we can see that just as the Passover was prophetic of the death of Christ, so Pentecost was prophetic of the coming of the Spirit, in whose power there is presented to God the "new meat offering"

# ACTS

consisting of the two loaves of firstfruits—an election from both Jew and Gentile, sanctified by the Holy Ghost. Just as that to which the Passover pointed was fulfilled on the Passover day, so that to which Pentecost pointed was fulfilled on the day of Pentecost. On Jesus the Spirit came as a dove: on the disciples as the sound of a mighty blowing or breathing, and as cloven tongues of fire. The wind appealed to the ear, and was reminiscent of the Lord's own inbreathing, of which John 20: 22 speaks. The tongues of fire appealed to the eye, and were quite unique. The wind filled *all:* the tongues sat upon *each.* We may connect inward power with the one; and with the other the expression of the power in the many tongues as the Spirit gave utterance. When Jesus came, He was audible, visible and tangible—see, 1 John 1: 1. When the Spirit came He was audible and visible only, and that in this mysterious way.

It is important that we should, from the outset, distinguish between the great *fact* of the Spirit's presence, and the *signs* and *manifestations* of His presence, which vary so greatly. This is the definite gift of the Spirit, referred to in John 7: 39; 14: 16, though, since here only Jews were in question, the pouring out of the Spirit upon believing Gentiles (see chapter 10: 45) was an act supplementary to this. Having come thus the Spirit abides with the saints right through the dispensation. As the result of the outpouring here, they were all filled with the Spirit, so that He was in complete control of each. We must also distinguish between the *gift* of the Spirit and the *filling* with the Spirit, since the former may be had without the latter, as we shall see later. Here both were present together.

Those upon whom the Spirit came were a *praying* people, in this resembling their Lord. They were also people of *one* accord, and consequently in *one* place. The one place is not named: it may have been the upper room of chapter 1, but more probably, in view of the crowds that heard the Spirit-given utterances, some court of the temple, such as Solomon's porch. At any rate the thing was real and powerful and could not be hid. It was, within a limited sphere, a reversal of Babel. There man's proud building was *stopped* by the confusion of tongues: here God signalized the *start* of His spiritual building by giving mastery over the tongues and reducing them to order.

We may see another contrast in the fact that when the tabernacle had been made in the wilderness and the Lord took possession of it by the cloud of His presence, He at once began to speak to Moses concerning sacrifice. This is shown by connecting Exodus 40: 35, with Leviticus 1: 1 and 2. In our chapter we have God taking possession of His new, spiritual house by His Spirit, and again He at once speaks by His inspired Apostles. Many people from different countries hear "the wonderful works of God."

The enquiry of the crowds gave the opportunity for witness. Peter was the spokesman, though the eleven stood with him as supporting his words, and he at once directed them to the scripture which explained what it all meant. Joel had predicted the pouring out of the Spirit upon all flesh in days that are yet to come, and what had just transpired was *a* fulfilment of it, though not *the* fulfilment. Peter's words, "this is that which was spoken," imply that it was *of the nature of* that which Joel had foretold, but not necessarily the full and conclusive thing which the prophecy had in view. John the Baptist had said of Jesus, "The same is He which baptizeth with the Holy Ghost" (John 1: 33). Joel had said that, after Israel's repentance and the destruction of their foes, there should be this pouring out of the Spirit on all flesh. Now on the day of Pentecost there had been a kind of firstfruits of this in the pouring out of the Spirit upon those who formed the nucleus of the church. That was the true explanation of what had happened. They were not drunk with wine, but filled with the Spirit.

But Peter did not stop there; he proceeded to show *why* this baptism of the Spirit had taken place. It was the direct action of Jesus, now exalted to the right hand of God. This we find when we reach verse 33; but from verse 22 he had been leading the minds of people through the scenes of the crucifixion to His resurrection and exaltation. Jesus of Nazareth had been most manifestly approved of God during the days of His ministry, yet they had slain Him with their wicked hands. He had been delivered up to this by God according to His "determinate counsel and fore-knowledge," for God knows how to make the wrath of man to praise Him and accomplish His designs of blessing; though this does not diminish man's responsibility in the matter. Verse 23 is a clear instance of how the sovereignty of God and the responsibility of man do not clash, when it is a question of practical results; though we may have difficulty in reconciling the two as a matter of theory.

What they had so wickedly *done* God had triumphantly *undone*. The collision between their programme and God's was complete. It presaged their own complete undoing and overthrow in due season; particularly as the resurrection had been foreseen by God, and foretold through David in Psalm 16. Now David could not possibly have been speaking of himself, for he had been buried and his grave was well known amongst them at that day. When he spoke of One, whose soul was not left in hades and whose flesh did not see corruption, he spoke of Christ. What he said had been fulfilled: Jesus was not only raised but exalted to heaven.

As the exalted Man, Jesus had received of the Father the promised Holy Ghost, and had shed Him forth upon His disciples. At His baptism He received the Holy Ghost *for Himself* as the dependent Man; now He receives the same Holy Ghost *on behalf of others* as their Representative. By shedding forth the Spirit these others were baptized into one body and became His members. This we learn from later scriptures.

In verses 34-36, Peter carries his argument a step further to its climax. David had prophesied of his Lord, who should be exalted to God's right hand. David himself was not ascended to the heavens any more than he was risen from the dead. The One of whom David spoke was to sit in the seat of administration and power until His foes were made His footstool; therefore the conclusion of the whole matter was this:—the shedding forth of the Spirit, which they had seen and heard, proved beyond the shadow of a doubt that God had made the crucified Jesus both Lord and Christ.

As Lord He is the great *Administrator* on God's behalf, whether in blessing or in judgment. His shedding forth the Spirit had been an act of administration, which had revealed His Lordship.

As Christ He is the anointed *Head* of all things, and particularly of the little handful of His own left upon earth. His reception from the Father of the Spirit on their behalf, preliminary to shedding Him forth, had revealed His Christhood.

Being "made" Lord and Christ is quite consistent with His having been both during His sojourn on earth. These things were ever His, but now He was officially installed as such, as the risen and glorified Man. Wonderful news for us; but terrible news for those who had been guilty of His crucifixion. It simply guaranteed their dreadful damnation, if they persisted on their course.

The Spirit, who had just fallen upon the disciples, now began to work in the consciences of many of the hearers. As they began to realize the desperate situation in which they were placed by the resurrection of the Lord, they were pricked in the heart and cried out for direction. Peter indicated repentance and baptism in the name of Jesus Christ as the way to remission of sins and the gift of the Holy Spirit; for, as he points out in verse 39, the promise in Joel is to repentant Israel, and to the children of such, and even to distant Gentiles. Thus in the first Christian sermon the extension of Gospel blessing to Gentiles is contemplated. Remission of sins and the gift of the Spirit carry with them all Christian blessings.

It may strike us as remarkable that Peter does not mention faith. But it is inferred, for no one would submit to baptism in the name of Jesus Christ except they believed in Him. Baptism signifies death, and consequently dissociation from the old life and connections. They would not be prepared to cut their links with the old life unless they really believed in Him who was Lord of the new life. With many words Peter testified, and exhorted them to cut their links, and thus save themselves from that "untoward generation."

Faith was present, for no less than three thousand received Peter's word. An hour before they knew the anguish of being pricked to the heart. Now they received the Gospel and cut their links by baptism. Having thus dissociated themselves from the mass of their nation, who had crucified their Lord, they took their stand by the side of the original 120, who were multiplied twenty-six times in one day. Further, not only did they *begin*, but they were marked by *stedfast continuance*.

# ACTS

The four things that marked them, according to verse 42, are worthy of note. First comes the apostles' doctrine or teaching. This lies at the foundation of things. The apostles were the men to whom the Lord had said, "When He, the Spirit of truth, is come, He will guide you into *all truth*" (John 16: 13). Their doctrine was consequently the fruit of the Spirit's guiding. The church was now in being, and the first thing that marked it was *subjection to the Spirit's teaching through the apostles*. The church does not teach; it is taught, and is subject to the Word as given by the Spirit.

Continuing in apostolic doctrine, they continued also in apostolic fellowship. *They found their practical life and society in apostolic company.* Formerly they had everything in common with the world; now their communion with the world had disappeared and communion with apostolic circles had been established — and the apostolic communion was "with the Father, and with His Son Jesus Christ" (1 John 1: 3).

They continued also in the breaking of bread, which was the sign of their Lord's death, and also incidentally—as we learn from 1 Corinthians 10: 17—*an expression of fellowship.* Thus they were in constant remembrance of their Lord who died, and preserved from reverting to the old associations.

Finally, they continued in prayers. They had no power in themselves; all was vested in their Lord on high and in the Spirit given to them. Hence *constant dependence on God* was necessary for the maintenance of their spiritual life and testimony.

These things marked the primitive church, and should no less mark the church today. The things mentioned in the closing verses of the chapter were of a less permanent character. The apostles, with signs and wonders are gone. The Christian communism, which prevailed at the outset, also passed away; as did the continuing with one accord in the temple, and the being in favour with all the people. Yet all was over-ruled of God. The selling of their possessions led to much poverty amongst the saints when years later the famine came, and thus was the occasion for that ministry of relief from Gentile assemblies (see, Acts 11: 27-30) which did so much to bind together the Jewish and Gentile elements in the church of God.

For the moment there was simplicity, gladness and singleness of heart with much praise to God. And the work of God, adding the believing remnant to the church, still went on.

## CHAPTER 3

THE ACTS IS an historical book, but it is not mere history. An immense amount of apostolic service is left unrecorded, and mention is made of just a few incidents which serve to show the way the Spirit of God operated in bearing witness to the risen and exalted Jesus, and in conducting the

# ACTS

disciples into the fulness of Christian blessing. The book covers a period of transition from the beginning of the church at Jerusalem to the full ingathering from among the Gentiles.

This chapter opens with the healing of the man who, lame from his birth, lay at the Beautiful gate of the temple. As the next chapter tells us he was above forty years old—the complete period of probation had been fulfilled in him. The man had not been healed by the Lord Jesus in the days of His flesh, though He so frequently taught in the temple; but he was healed by the power of His Name, now that He was glorified in heaven. Peter had neither silver nor gold, but the power of the Name of Jesus Christ of Nazareth he could wield, and the man was instantly healed in most triumphant fashion. Today many earnest Christian folk are mostly concerned about collecting the silver and gold for the support of the work of the Lord, and the power of the Name lies largely unused. This is to our reproach.

By reason of his deformity the lame man had lain under certain disabilities according to the law; now grace had removed his deformity and with it the disability, so that he could enter the temple with freedom; and holding on to the Apostles there was no hiding those who had been the instruments of his deliverance. This gave Peter the opportunity of testimony. He at once put himself and John out of the picture, in order that the glorified Jesus might fill it.

Peter's boldness is remarkable. He charged the people with their denial of "the Holy One and the Just," though he himself not many weeks before had denied his Lord. They had had before them "the Prince [Author] of life" and "a murderer;" that is a taker of life. They killed the One, and chose the other; yet He, whom they killed, God had raised from the dead, and thus they were caught in red-handed rebellion against God. Moreover this "perfect soundness" has been granted to the lame man in the power of His Name, through faith. They could not see the glory of Jesus in heaven, but they could see the miracle wrought in His Name upon earth. The soundness on earth was linked with the glory in heaven.

Verse 17 shows that God was prepared to treat their dreadful crime as a sin of ignorance—as manslaughter, for which a city of refuge is provided, and not as murder. This was a direct answer to the prayer on the cross, "Father, forgive them; for they know not what they do." By their sinful act God had accomplished His purpose as to the suffering of Christ, and hence there was still an offer of mercy for them as a nation. That offer Peter made, as recorded in verses 19-26 of our chapter. Everything hinged upon their repentance and conversion.

Whether Isaiah 35: 6, 7, was in Peter's mind as he spoke about "the times of refreshing," we cannot say, but it does seem as if it must have been in the mind of the Spirit who was speaking through him. When "the lame man" shall "leap as an hart," then, "in the wilderness shall waters break out, and streams in the desert." But all this refreshing predicted by Isaiah is for "the ransomed of the Lord." and for no others. Hence only repentance and a complete turning round would bring such times; if that took place God would send Jesus Christ to bring them to pass.

The term, "restitution of all things," has been misused in the service of the idea that God is going ultimately to save and restore everybody—even the devil himself. But the passage reads, "the restitution of all things, which God hath spoken . . ." It is things, not persons, and things which from the outset He had spoken by His prophets. God is going to make good every word, and to establish in Christ everything which has broken down in the hands of men. That time will not come till Jesus Himself comes, and since He is the Prophet of whom Moses spoke, all things will be brought to an issue when He does come, and everyone who disregards Him will be destroyed from among the people. There will be a time of blessing established, the like of which has not been since the world began.

In these words, then, Peter made the definite offer on God's behalf that if at this point there was repentance and turning to God on a national scale, Jesus would return and establish the predicted times of blessing. In the last verse of the chapter he also added that, whatever their response was, God had raised up Jesus to bless them in turning them from their sins. These two things we all need: first, the judicial blotting out of our sins; second, to be turned away from our sins, so that they lose their power over us.

## Chapter 4

As WE READ the opening verses we find the answer to this offer, which was given by the official heads of the nation. The offer being based on the resurrection of the Lord Jesus, it was particularly obnoxious to the Sadducees and to the priests, who were of that party. They gave it an unqualified rejection by arresting the apostles. The work of God, in converting power, went on however, as verse 4 records; and the next day, when examined before the council, Peter found fresh opportunity for testimony, in answering their question as to the power and Name in which he had acted.

The Name and power was that of Jesus Christ of Nazareth, whom they had crucified and whom God had exalted. Psalm 118:22 had been fulfilled in Him, and Peter proceeded to widen out the testimony from that which was particular to that which is universal. The power of the Name was right before their eyes in the particular case of the lame man healed: it was no less potent for the salvation of men universally. The physical healing of the man was just a sign of the spiritual healing which the Name of Jesus brings. The despised Jesus of Nazareth is the only door into salvation.

# ACTS

Verses 13-22, show most strikingly how Peter's testimony was vindicated. The apostles were unlearned and ignorant according to worldly standards, yet they had been with Jesus and were bold, and this impressed the council, who would fain have condemned them. Three things hindered however:-
  (1) "They could say nothing against it" (verse 14);
  (2) They had to confess, "we cannot deny it" (verse 16);
  (3) They found "nothing how they might punish them" (verse 21).

When men wish to discredit anything, they usually in the first place deny it, if that be at all possible. If that be not possible, they find some way of speaking against it, misrepresenting it, if need be. Lastly, if that be not possible, they attack the persons involved in the thing, blackening their characters and punishing them. These three well-known devices were in the minds of the council, but all failed them since they were fighting against God. They could merely threaten them and demand that they ceased to proclaim the name of Jesus. Peter repudiated their demand, since God had commanded them to preach in the name of Jesus, and as He was infinitely the higher Authority, they must obey Him rather than them.

There follows, verses 23-37, a beautiful picture of the early church in Jerusalem. Released by the council, the apostles went to "their own company." This shows us that at the outset the church was *a "company" distinct and apart from the world*, even from the religious world of Judaism. This point needs much emphasis in days when the world and the church have so largely been mixed together.

The early church found its resource in *prayer*. In the emergency they turned to God and not to men. They might have wished for a council less Sadducean in character with more liberality and breadth of outlook, but they did not agitate to get it; they simply sought the face of God, the sovereign Ruler of men.

In their prayer they were led to the Word of God. Psalm 2 shed its light on the situation that confronted them. The interpretation of it would refer it to the last days, but they saw the application of it which referred to their days. The early church was marked by *subjection to the Word*, finding in it all the light and guidance they needed. This also is a very important and instructive feature.

They were marked too by far more concern for the honour of the Name of Jesus than for their own ease and comfort. They did not request a cessation of persecution and opposition, but that they might have boldness in speaking the word, and that miraculous support which would exalt His Name. The church is the place where *that Name is held dear*.

As a result of this there was an exceptional manifestation of *the power of the Spirit*. All of them were filled with Him; the very building where they met was shaken, and their prayer for especial boldness was instantly answered. And not only this, that which they had not requested was granted to them, they all were "*of one heart and of one soul.*" This of course flowed out of the fact that the "one Spirit" was filling every one of them. If all believers today were filled with the Spirit oneness of mind and heart would mark them. It is the only way in which such oneness can be brought to pass.

Out of this flowed the next feature which verse 33 mentions. There was *great power in the Apostles' testimony to the world.* The church did not preach, but filled with grace and power it supported those who did. The preaching then, as always, lay in the hands of those called of God to do it, but the power with which they did it was largely influenced by the state that characterized the whole church.

The closing verses show that just as there was powerful testimony flowing without so there was the circulation of *love and care within.* The Christian communism, mentioned at the end of chapter 2, still continued. The distribution was made to each, "according as he had need." Not people's wants, but their needs were met, and so nobody lacked. At a later date Paul could say, "I am instructed both to be full and to be hungry, both to abound and to suffer need" (Phil. 4: 12), but at this time such experiences were unknown by the saints in Jerusalem. Whether, by escaping such experiences, they profited more than Paul did, by having them, may be an open question, though we incline to think they did not. At any rate, the action of Barnabas was very beautiful, and the love and care found in the church then should be known today, though there may be some variation in the exact mode of expressing it.

## Chapter 5

This chapter opens with a solemn incident which throws up in striking relief one last feature which characterized the early church: there was *the exercise of a holy discipline* by the power of God. The case of Ananias and Sapphira was exceptional without a doubt. When God institutes anything new, it seems to be His way to signalize His holiness by making an example of any who challenge it. He did so with the man who broke the sabbath in the wilderness (see, Num. 15: 32-36), and also with Achan when Israel began to enter Canaan (see, Josh. 7: 18-26), and so with Ananias and his wife here. Later in Israel's history many broke the sabbath and took forbidden Babylonish things without incurring similar penalties, just as during the church's history many have acted lies or told them without falling dead.

What lay behind the lie in this case were the twin evils of covetousness and vainglory. Ananias wanted to keep part of the money for himself, and yet gain the reputation of having devoted all to the Lord, as Barnabas had done. Such is the mind of the flesh, even in a saint. How many of us have never had the workings of similar evils in our own hearts? But in this case Satan had been at work, and by the unhappy couple he issued a direct challenge to the Holy Ghost present in the church. The Holy Ghost accepted the challenge, and demonstrated His presence in this drastic and unmistakable fashion. Peter recognized that this was the position, when to Sapphira he spoke of their doings as an agreement "to tempt the Spirit of the Lord."

In result Satan's challenge was made to serve the interests of the Lord and His gospel, as the following verses show. In the first place, this episode put great fear upon all who heard of it, and even upon the church itself. Here is indicated something which is very lacking in the church today—to say nothing of men generally. The fear of God is a very wholesome thing in the hearts of saints, and it is quite compatible with a deep sense of the love of God. Paul had that fear in the light of the judgment seat (see, 2 Cor. 5: 10, 11), though for the unbeliever it will go beyond fear to positive terror. A godly fear, springing from a deep sense of the holiness of God, is much to be desired.

Then, as the early part of verse 12, and verses 15 and 16 show, there was no slackening in the miraculous power of God, ministered through the Apostles. Indeed the power increased, so that the mere shadow of Peter wrought wonders. Within the parenthesis printed in brackets (verses 12-14) we get the statement that after such an happening men were afraid to join themselves to the Christian company; yet this was no real loss, for it stopped anything in the nature of a mass movement, that would have swept a good deal of unreality into the church. The real work of God was not hindered, as verse 14 states. People may be added to the church who are mere professors, but no one is "added to the Lord" save those in whom there is a vital work of God. Thus the sad business of Ananias and Sapphira was overruled for good, though to a superficial observer it might have seemed a heavy blow to the church's prospects.

God having wrought in this striking way for blessing, we see, in verse 17, the next counter-stroke of Satan. The priests and Sadducees, filled with indignation, again arrest them. This is met by God sending an angel to open the prison doors and liberate them. The next day, their escape being discovered, they are arrested, but in much more gentle fashion. The words of the priests confess the power with which God had been at work, for they admit that Jerusalem had been filled with the teaching; yet they manifest the awful hardness of their hearts in saying, "ye . . . intend to bring this Man's blood upon us." Why, they had themselves said, "His blood be on us, and on our children." The truth was that God was going to take them at their word, and do it.

Peter's answer was short and simple. They were going to obey God rather than men. Then he again summarized their testimony and repeated it. The Holy Ghost and they were witnesses to the resurrection of the Jesus, whom they slew. But God had exalted Him, not to be at that time a Judge,

## ACTS

meting out damnation upon their guilty heads, but a Prince and a Saviour, giving repentance to Israel and forgiveness of sins. Repentance as well as forgiveness is viewed as a gift.

Though mercy and forgiveness was still the burden of Peter's message, the proclamation of it only stirred them to fury. Mercy presupposes sin and guilt, and that they were not disposed to admit; hence they took counsel to slay them. Satan is a murderer from the beginning, and under his influence murder filled their hearts. Yet God has many ways of checkmating the evil designs of men, and in this case He used the worldly wisdom of the renowned Gamaliel, who had Saul of Tarsus as his pupil.

Gamaliel cited two recent cases of men who had risen up pretending to be somebody; the type of man to whom the Lord alluded in John 10, when He spoke of those who climbed up some other way, and who were but thieves and robbers. They came to nought indeed, and Gamaliel thought that Jesus might have been one of these spurious shepherds, instead of the true Shepherd of Israel. Had He been such, His cause also would have come to nought. Gamaliel's warning took effect and the Apostles were released, though with a beating and the demand that they ceased their testimony.

Truly the council was fighting against God, for the Apostles rejoiced in their suffering for His Name, and diligently pursued their witness both publicly in the temple and more privately in every house.

### Chapter 6

BEHIND ALL THE attacks and difficulties which confronted the early church in Jerusalem lay the great adversary, Satan himself. He it was that stirred the Sadducees to violence and attempts to intimidate. He filled the heart of Ananias to lie, and thus bring in corruption, tempting the Spirit of the Lord. Now, these earlier attacks having been defeated, he moves in a more subtle way, exploiting small differences that existed within the church itself. The "Grecians" of whom the first verse of this chapter speaks, were not Gentiles but Greek-speaking Jews, coming from the lands of their dispersion, whereas the "Hebrews" were the home-born Jews of Jerusalem and Palestine.

The first and greater trouble within the church—that of Ananias—was about money. If the second was not about money, it was over a matter very akin to it; being as to the distribution of daily necessities, entailed by having all things common. The first was about getting the money *in:* the second about doling *out* the money, or its equivalent. Those from a distance thought that partiality was being shown in favour of the local people. The greater trouble created only a small difficulty, for it was met instantaneously in the Spirit's power: the smaller trouble created the greater difficulty, as we see in our chapter. This, we believe, has nearly always been the way in the church's history: the most difficult cases to settle are those in which at the bottom there is very little to be settled.

It was only a "murmuring" that arose, but the apostles did not wait for it to become a formidable outcry. They discerned that Satan's object in it was to divert them from the preaching of the Word to social service, so they took steps to end any possible objections. They instructed the church to select seven men to undertake the business, who should be, "of honest report, full of the Holy Ghost and wisdom." Their administration was to be marked by wisdom and honesty that should be above all reproach.

In this business the church was to select its own officers; but then the business was the distribution of the funds and food that the church had itself provided. We never read of the church being called upon to select or appoint its elders or bishops or ministers of the Word; inasmuch as the spiritual grace and gifts which they distribute are not provided by the church but by God. The selection and ordination of these consequently lies in the hands of God. To the elders at Ephesus Paul said, "The Holy Ghost hath made you overseers." *God appoints* those who are to administer *His bounty*.

So the apostles continued to give themselves to prayer and the ministry of the Word. For those who are taught the Word comes first (see 1 Tim. 4: 5), for we only pray rightly as we are instructed in the Word. For those who minister prayer comes first, for apart from prayer they will not speak the Word aright.

Just as wisdom prevailed with the apostles, so grace prevailed in the church, for all the seven men chosen bore names which would suggest a Grecian rather than a Hebrew origin, and one of them is said to have been a proselyte, which infers that he came even of Gentile extraction. In this way the multitude took care that all murmurings and questionings, whether well-founded or not, should be hushed to silence. The apostles identified themselves with the church's choice, by laying their hands on the chosen men, with prayer. The adversary behind the scenes was again foiled.

He was more than foiled really; for instead of the apostles being diverted from the Word of God, it increased greatly, and many fresh conversions took place, even many priests being reached. Moreover one of the seven, Stephen, became a special vessel of the grace and power of the Spirit of God; so much so, that for the rest of our chapter, and the whole of chapter 7, we follow that which God wrought through him, until the time of his martyrdom.

The power operating in Stephen was so marked that it stirred up opposition in fresh quarters. The men of the various synagogues, mentioned in verse 9, were apparently all of the Grecian class, to which Stephen

## ACTS

himself belonged. All their argumentative skill was as nothing when pitted against the power of the Spirit in Stephen, so they had recourse to the usual device of lying witnesses and violence. In verse 11 they put Moses in front of God; but then they knew what would most appeal to the passions of the crowd, to whom Moses, being a man, was more real than the invisible God. So also, in verse 13, "this holy place" which was before their eyes, takes precedence of the law; and finally, "the customs which Moses delivered us," were perhaps dearer to them than all. Dragging Stephen before the council, they charged him with blasphemy, and with proclaiming Jesus of Nazareth as a destroyer of their holy place and customs. There was this much truth in this charge, that the advent of Jesus had indeed inaugurated a new departure in the ways of God.

In this public way the controversy between the nation and God was carried a step further. They threw down the gauntlet, and God accepted their challenge by so filling Stephen with the Spirit that even the fashion of his face was altered, and everybody saw it. Through his lips the Holy Ghost proceeded to give a closing word of testimony against the nation. The council found themselves arraigned at the bar of God by the Holy Ghost, speaking through the very man that was being arraigned at their bar.

### Chapter 7

THEIR HISTORY BEGAN with God calling Abraham out of his old place and associations, that he might go to the land of God's choice and there be made a great nation. This is shown in Genesis 12: 1-3, and it was an epoch-making event, as is evident when we note that a rather longer period of time is compressed into Genesis 1-11, than the period expanded to fill all the rest of the Old Testament. The call of Abraham marked a new departure in God's ways with the earth, and with that new departure Stephen began his address.

Genesis tells us that Jehovah appeared to Abraham, but Stephen knew Him and spoke of Him in a new light. The Jehovah who appeared to Abraham was the God of glory, the God of far more glorious scenes than can be afforded by this world, even at its fairest and best. This it is, doubtless, which accounts for Abraham's faith embracing such heavenly things as are spoken of in Hebrews 11: 10-16. Called by the God of glory, he at least had glimpses of the city and country where glory dwells. On this high note Stephen began, and he ended, as we know, with Jesus in the glory of God.

The main drift of his remarkable address was evidently to bring to the people the conviction of the way in which their fathers and they had been guilty of resisting the operations of God by His Spirit all through their history. He dwells particularly upon what happened when God had raised up servants to institute something new in their history. There had been a series of new departures, of greater or less significance. The original one had been with Abraham, but then followed Joseph, Moses, Joshua, David, Solomon; all of whom he refers to, though giving far more attention to the first three than to the second three. To none of these had they really responded, and Joseph and Moses they had definitely refused to start with. He ends with the seventh intervention, which threw all the others into the shade — the coming of the Just One—and Him they had just slain.

Stephen made it very plain that the Jewish rulers of his day were but repeating in a worse form the sin of their forefathers. The patriarchs sold Joseph into Egypt because they were "moved with envy;" and Matthew records the efforts of Pilate to deliver Jesus, "for he knew that for envy they had delivered Him." So too with Moses; the saying at which he fled, "Who made thee a ruler and a judge over us?" was uttered by one of his brethren, and not by an Egyptian. The rejection came from amongst his own people, and not from outside. Thus too it had been with Jesus.

Exodus 2 does not give us such an insight into the fame and prowess of Moses at the end of his first forty years as is given in verse 22 of our chapter. He was a man of learning, oratory and action, when it came into his heart to identify himself with his own people, who were the people of God. Having made the plunge, it must have come to him as a terrible shock to be refused by them. At that saying he fled. He did not fear the wrath of the king, as Hebrews 11: 27 tells us, but he could not stand this refusal. He had acted in the consciousness of his own exceptional powers, and now needed forty years of Divine tuition at the back side of the desert to learn that his powers were nothing and the power of God everything. In all this he stands in contrast to our Lord, though he typified Him in the rejection he had to endure.

This Moses was again rejected by their fathers, when he had brought them out of captivity and into the wilderness. In rejecting him, they really rejected Jehovah, and they turned aside into idolatry of a very gross kind. Even in the wilderness, and not only when in the land, they were slack about Jehovah's sacrifices, and tampered with idols, thus paving the way to the Babylonish captivity. Still God had raised up David, and then Solomon built the house. Now in the house they boasted (see Jer. 7: 4) as though the mere possession of these buildings guaranteed everything, when really God dwelt in the Heaven of heavens, far above the most gorgeous buildings on earth.

Stephen's closing words—verses 51-53—are marked by great power. They are like an appendix to the Lord's own words, recorded in Matthew 23: 31-36, carrying the indictment on to its dreadful conclusion in the betrayal and murder of the Just One. Their standing before God was on the basis of the law, and though they had received it by the disposition of angels, they had not kept it. The law broken by flagrant idolatry, and the Messiah murdered; there were the two great counts in the indictment against the Jew, and both are prominent in Stephen's closing words.

The Holy Ghost, by the lips of Stephen, had completely turned the tables upon his persecutors, and they found themselves arraigned, as though they were in the dock instead of sitting upon the judicial bench. The very suddenness with which Stephen dropped his historic recital, and launched God's accusation against them, must have added tremendous power to his words. They were cut to the heart and stirred to fury.

The only calm person evidently was Stephen. Filled with the Spirit, he had a supernatural sight of the glory of God, and of Jesus in that glory, and he testified at once of that which he saw. Ezekiel had seen, "the likeness of a throne" and "the likeness as the appearance of a man above upon it" (1:26), but Stephen saw not a mere "likeness" or "appearance," but rather the MAN Himself, standing on the right hand of God. Jesus, once crucified, is now the Man of God's right hand: He is the mighty Executive, by whom God will administrate the universe!

In his address Stephen had pointed out that though Joseph had been refused by his brethren, he became their saviour and ultimately they all had to bow down to him. He also reminded them that though Moses was at first rejected, he ultimately became both ruler and deliverer of Israel. Now he testifies a similar, but vastly greater thing in connection with Jesus. The Just One whom they had murdered, is to become their Judge, and ultimately, for those who receive Him, their great and final Deliverer. In token thereof He was in glory, and Stephen saw Him.

Utterly unable to refute or resist his words, the Jewish leaders rushed into the murder of Stephen, thus fulfilling the Lord's words, recorded in Luke 19: 14, as to the citizens hating the departed nobleman and sending a message after him saying, "We will not have this Man to reign over us." Jesus was still "standing" in glory, ready to fulfil what Peter had said in chapter 3: 20, if only they had repented. They did not repent, but gave a violent refusal by stoning Stephen and sending him after his Master. Prominent in connection with this wicked act was a young man named Saul, who consented to his death, and acted as a kind of superintendent at his execution. Thus where the history of Stephen ends, the story of Saul begins.

Stephen, the first Christian martyr, ended his short but striking career in the likeness of his Lord. Filled with the Spirit, his vision was filled with Jesus in glory. He had nothing more to say to men; his last words were addressed to his Lord. To the Lord he committed his spirit, and assuming the attitude of prayer, he desired mercy for his murderers. Who could have anticipated so astounding an answer as was given by his exalted Lord in the conversion of Saul, the arch-murderer? The prayer of the Lord Jesus from the cross for His murderers was answered by the sending forth of the Gospel, to begin at Jerusalem: the prayer of Stephen was answered in the conversion of Saul. That Saul himself never forgot it, is shown by chapter 22: 20.

## Chapter 8

NOT CONTENT WITH slaying Stephen, the religious leaders in Jerusalem at this point launched the first great persecution against the church, and in this Saul was especially prominent. He ravaged the church like a wolf, invading the privacy of homes to secure his victims. In result, the disciples were scattered abroad through the provinces of Judaea and Samaria. Now, according to the Lord's words to His disciples in chapter 1: 8, these provinces were to come after Jerusalem, and before their mission widened out to the uttermost parts of the earth; so again it was a case of God making man's wrath to serve His purpose. Yet, remarkably enough, the Apostles, to whom the commission was given, were the exceptions to the rule. They still remained in Jerusalem.

This being so, the narrative leaves them unnoticed and continues with those who went everywhere evangelizing, and particularly with Philip, another of the seven. He went to the city of Samaria and preached; the power of God was with him, and wonderful blessing followed, as is always the way when a servant of God moves in the direct line of God's purpose. The sowing among the Samaritans had been done by the Lord Himself, as recorded in John 4. Then many had said not only, "Is not this the Christ?" but also, "This is indeed the Christ." Now Philip, coming to them, "preached Christ," as the One who had died, was risen again, and now in glory; as a consequence, a great time of reaping took place. There was great joy in that city.

Philip's message being received, he began to preach among them, "the things concerning the kingdom of God," and this led to multitudes being baptized. Amongst them was Simon the sorcerer, who also "believed" and was baptized. He found himself, as verse 7 shows, in the presence of a Power far mightier than the unclean spirits, with whom he formerly had traffic.

The remarkable thing about the work in Samaria was that although so many had believed the Gospel, and been baptized, none had received the gift of the Holy Ghost. The order that Peter had propounded in chapter 2: 38, was not observed in the case of the Samaritans. God so ordered, we believe, for a special reason. There had been religious rivalry between Jerusalem and Samaria, as John 4 witnesses, and therefore there must have been a strong tendency to carry over into the new conditions this ancient prejudice. This would have meant a Samaritan church independent of, if not in rivalry to, a Jerusalem church; and thus any practical expression of the "one body" would have been imperilled even before the truth of it had been revealed. As things were, they only received the Spirit when Peter and John had come down and laid hands on them; thus formally identifying the Apostles and the church in Jerusalem with these new believers in Samaria. The oneness of the church was preserved.

When the Holy Ghost was given, there was the drawing of the line between reality and unreality. Not all baptized prove to be real, but the Spirit is only given to those that are real. Hence at Samaria the baptized Simon was left without the Holy Spirit. Verses 12 and 16 show us that the baptized person professes an entrance into the kingdom of God, and to take upon himself the name of the Lord Jesus, as his new Master, just as Israel of old were baptized to Moses—see 1 Corinthians 10: 2. Simon submitted to all this, nevertheless, when the test came, reality was not found in him. He would never have said, "Give me also this power," had he already possessed it. Nor did he understand it, as proved by his offer of money.

It must have been a great blow to Simon, who formerly had dominated the people of Samaria by his supernatural doings, to find a multitude now possessing a power, in the presence of which his own dark acts were as nothing. They possessed the gift of the Holy Spirit, and he had been left out. This led him to expose himself very thoroughly by offering money to the Apostles. He wished to purchase not only the Spirit for himself but also the power to convey Him to others by the imposition of his hands. He felt doubtless that if such a power as that could be his, any money laid out in its purchase would prove a very profitable investment.

This is the third recorded uprising of evil within the circle of those who had been baptized: first, Ananias; second, the murmuring as to the neglected widows; third, Simon the sorcerer. In each case, you notice, *money* was involved. In this third case we see the beginning of the Satanic endeavour to turn the pure faith of Christ into a money-making religion. In Samaria it was but a trickling stream, flowing through one man. It soon increased into a flood, sweeping immense riches to Rome. In the religious system which has its centre there, everything which is supposed to be a gift of God may be purchased with money.

Peter did not spare Simon the sorcerer. He told him plainly that this atrocious thought of his meant that his heart was not right with God, that he was entirely outside the true faith of Christ, and that both he and his money would perish. Peter's words surely were prophetic of the doom that ultimately will overtake the great ecclesiastical system, which through the centuries has turned Christianity into "the religion of money."

There was a ray of hope for Simon, which Peter held out for him, in verse 22. He might repent, and therefore forgiveness for him was still a

## ACTS

possibility. Notice how the very thought of his heart is characterized as wickedness, without referring to his words; an illustration this, of the statement, that, "the thought of foolishness is sin." Being still in bondage to money, he was still in the bond of iniquity and bitterness. The love of money being "the root of *all evil;*" that is, of *every kind of evil*, a large part of the bitterness which fills the earth, springs from it. Peter told Simon to pray to God; but from his answer, recorded in verse 24, it looks as if he lacked the repentance which would lead him to pray for himself, and wished to make sure of Peter's intercession on his behalf without paying for it. Multitudes since that day have paid handsome sums hoping to obtain the intercession of Peter!

The Apostles had been slow to go forth from Jerusalem, as verse 1 of our chapter told us. Philip had been the pioneer at Samaria, but now that Peter and John had come down they further ministered the Word to the converts, and also evangelized in many Samaritan villages on their return journey. However there was more pioneer work to be done, and as to this the angel of the Lord spoke not to the Apostles but to Philip.

Philip's ready and simple obedience to the Lord's instructions is very striking. He was told to leave the place of his successful labours and depart to the desert region south west of Jerusalem. The record is that told to, "Arise and go," he "arose and went," though his brethren may have thought him misguided and eccentric in doing so. If he did not know, when starting, the object of his journey, he soon discovered it, for his steps were guided so that he should intercept an important Ethiopian official who was a seeker after God. This man had taken a toilsome journey to Jerusalem according to the little light he had. He arrived there too late to get any benefit from the temple, for as the house of God it had been disowned. He was too late to find the Lord, for He had been rejected and had gone to heaven. He did however get an important book of Old Testament scripture, and he was on his return journey needing but one thing more.

That one thing more Philip was sent to supply, for God was not going to allow an Ethiopian to stretch out his hands to Him without getting an answer. He needed New Testament light, so, as the New Testament was not yet written, Philip was sent with the New Testament message. The Spirit of God was in control, hence everything moved to time with smooth perfection. The Ethiopian had just reached the middle of Isaiah 53 when Philip addressed him, and his keen mind was filled with the question which that chapter inevitably raises in the thoughts of every intelligent reader— Is the prophet speaking of himself, or of "some other man?" The Ethiopian raised his question: Philip found there his text, and preached unto him "JESUS."

All that Philip told the Ethiopian is summed up for us by Luke in that sacred Name, and this is easily understood when we remember how Matthew 1:21 introduces us to it and to its significance. All that the man needed—the light and the salvation—was found in JESUS; and while Philip was speaking he found it! Now Isaiah 53 presents Jesus as the One who died an atoning and substitutionary death, the One whose life was taken from the earth, and the Ethiopian, who evidently knew something of baptism and its significance, desired to be identified with Him in His death. In baptism we are "identified with Him in the likeness of His death" (Rom. 6: 5), and he felt that nothing hindered him being identified in this way with the One on whom he now believed. Verse 37 is to be omitted as lacking any real manuscript authority: nevertheless nothing did hinder, though he was not a Jew, and Philip baptized him.

In this way the first Gentile was reached and baptized and sent on his way back to his own people with the knowledge of the Saviour. Philip disappeared from his sight more rapidly than he had appeared but, since he had believed not on Philip but on Jesus, this did not unduly disturb him, and he went on his way *rejoicing*. His faith was not entwined around Philip but around the One whom he had preached. For him it was not Jerusalem but Jesus, and also it was not Philip but Jesus. To be enamoured of the preacher makes for weakness: to be enamoured of the Saviour makes for spiritual strength.

As for Philip, the supernatural way in which he was removed to Azotus did not disturb him. He travelled north to Cæsarea preaching in the cities as he went. Seven times in this chapter is preaching mentioned, and in five of these occasions the word used is one we have carried over into our language as, "evangelize." The occasions are in verses 4, 12, 25 (second occurrence), 35, and 40. In three out of the five it is Philip who evangelizes, so we need not be surprised that presently he is designated, "Philip the evangelist" (21: 8).

The conversion of the Ethiopian was a sign that the time for the blessing of the Gentiles was at hand. He was like the lonely swallow in transit, betokening the advent of summer. In chapter 9, is recounted the call and conversion of the man who is to be the Apostle to the Gentiles. As is so often the case the Lord's choice fell upon the most unlikely person. The arch-persecutor of the saints is to become the pattern servant of the Lord. To this end he was dealt with in an unprecedented way. The Lord Himself dealt with him directly, excluding in all essential things any human instrumentality.

## CHAPTER 9

SAUL WAS STILL filled with furious, persecuting zeal when the Lord intercepted him on the road to Damascus, and revealed Himself to him in a blaze of heavenly light, which shone not only round about him but into his conscience as well. We may discern in the record the essential features which mark every true conversion. There was the light which penetrates to the conscience, the revelation of the Lord Jesus to the heart, the conviction of sin in the words, "Why persecutest thou Me?" and the collapse of all opposition and self-importance in the humble-words, "Lord, what wilt Thou have me do?" When Jesus is discovered, when the conscience is convicted of sin, when there is humble submission to Jesus as Lord, then there is a true conversion, though there is very much that the soul has yet to learn. The Lord's dealings were intensely personal to Saul, for his companions, though amazed, understood nothing of what had happened.

By this tremendous revelation of the Lord, Saul was literally blinded to the world. Led into Damascus, he spent three days which he would never forget, days in which the significance of the revelation sank into his soul. Being blind, nothing distracted his mind, and his thoughts were not even turned aside to food or drink. As a preliminary to his service, Ezekiel had sat among the captives at Chebar and "remained there astonished among them seven days" (Ezek. 3: 15). Saul sat astonished in Damascus for only three days, but his experiences were of a far deeper order. We may get a glimpse of them by reading 1 Timothy 1: 12-17. He was astonished at his own colossal guilt as the "chief of sinners," and even more at the exceeding abundance of the grace of the Lord, so that he obtained mercy. In those three days he evidently passed through a spiritual process of death and resurrection. The foundations were laid in his soul of that which later on he expressed thus: "I am crucified with Christ: nevertheless I live; yet not I, but Christ liveth in me" (Gal. 2: 20).

During the three days Saul had a vision of a man named Ananias coming in and laying his hands on him that he might receive his sight, and at the end of them the vision materialized. Ananias arrived, doing what he was told, and telling Saul he was but the messenger of the Lord, even Jesus, and that he was not only to receive his sight but be filled with the Holy Ghost. By this time Saul was a believer, for only to believers is the Spirit given.

The essential work in Saul's soul having been accomplished, a human servant is used by the Lord. Two things about that servant are worthy of note. First, he was just "a certain disciple," evidently of no special prominence. It was fitting that the only man to help Saul in any way was a very humble one. Saul had been very prominent as an adversary and was soon to be very prominent as a servant of the Lord. He was helped by a disciple who was undistinguished and retiring, yet who was near enough to the Lord to receive His instructions and hold converse with Him. It is often thus in God's ways. Second, Ananias dwelt in Damascus, and thus was one of those against whom Saul had been breathing out threatenings and slaughter. So one of those that Saul would have murdered was sent to call him, "Brother Saul," to open his eyes, and that he might be filled with the Holy Ghost. Saul's evil was requited with good in this overwhelming fashion.

Saul's days of blindness, both physical and mental, were now over: he was baptized in the Name of the One he had formerly despised and hated, and he consorted with the very people he had thought to destroy, for he had become one of them. He had been called as "a chosen vessel," so straightway his service began. Jesus had been revealed to him as the Christ, and as the Son of God, so he preached Him thus and proved by the Scriptures that He was the Christ, to the confounding of his former friends. The friends however speedily became his bitter foes and took counsel to kill him, even as not long before he had thought to kill the saints. He had anticipated entering Damascus with some measure of pomp as the plenipotentiary of the hierarchy in Jerusalem. Actually, he entered as a humbled and blinded man; and he left it in undignified fashion, huddled in a basket, as a fugitive from Jewish hate.

From the outset Saul had thus to taste for himself the very things he had been inflicting upon others. Arrived back in Jerusalem, he was distrusted by the disciples, as was very natural, and the intervention of Barnabas was needed before they received him. Barnabas could vouch for the Lord's intervention and his conversion, and he acted as his letter of commendation. In Jerusalem he witnessed boldly and came into conflict with the Grecians, possibly the very men who had been so responsible in the matter of Stephen's death. Now they would slay the man who held the clothes of those that slew Stephen. In all this we can see the working of the government of God. The fact, that the Lord had shown such amazing mercy in his conversion, did not exempt him from reaping in this governmental way that which he had sown.

Threatened again with death, Saul had to depart to Tarsus, his native city. It may be wondered where came in that visit to Arabia, of which he writes in Galatians 1: 17. We think it was probably during the "many days," of which verse 23 of our chapter speaks, for he tells us that he "returned again to Damascus." If this is so, the flight from Damascus over the wall took place after his return from Arabia. Be that as it may, it was his departure to distant Tarsus that inaugurated the period of rest and edification for the churches, which led to a multiplication of their numbers.

In verse 32 we return to the activities of Peter, that we may see that the Spirit of God had not ceased to work through him while working so powerfully elsewhere. There had been, first, a great work in Lydda through the raising up of the palsied man. Then at Joppa Peter was used to bring Dorcas to life, and this led to many in that town believing on the Lord. It also led to Peter making a lengthy stay there in the house of Simon a tanner.

Meanwhile also the Spirit of God had been at work in the heart of Cornelius the Roman centurion, as the fruit of which he was marked by piety and the fear of God, with almsgiving and prayer to God. The time had now come to bring this man and his like-minded friends into the light of the Gospel. Now to Peter had been given "the keys of the kingdom of heaven" (Matt. 16: 19), so just as he had used the keys on the day of Pentecost to admit the election from among the Jews, now it is his to admit this election from among the Gentiles. This chapter has recounted how God called and converted the man who was to be the Apostle to the Gentiles, the next tells how Peter was delivered from his prejudices and led to open the door of faith to the Gentiles, thus paving the way for subsequent ministry of the Apostle Paul.

## Chapter 10

THE FIRST THING in the chapter is the angelic ministry to Cornelius by which he is directed to send to Joppa and call Peter. No difficulty arose here, for Cornelius immediately did as he was told. The angel, you notice, did not cut a rather lengthy story short by himself telling the message to Cornelius. The *message* of grace can only be rightly told by a man who is himself a *subject* of grace. So Peter must be called. God had respect to the prayers and alms of Cornelius, since they expressed the sincere seeking of his heart after God. If, after hearing the Gospel, he had ignored its message and gone on with his prayers and alms, it would have been a different matter. Then they would not have "come up for a memorial before God."

Next comes the account of God's preliminary dealings with Peter by means of a trance. There was more difficulty here, for he was still bound by his Jewish thoughts, and from these he had to be delivered. The hearers were ready, but the preacher had to be made ready to go. The record is that he "went up upon the housetop to pray," consequently he was in the right attitude to receive the necessary guidance. There was not only a *praying seeker* but a *praying servant* also. Hence remarkable results followed.

The great sheet which Peter saw descended out of an opened heaven. It embraced within its folds all manner of creatures both clean and unclean. It was received up into heaven. Peter was bidden to satisfy his hunger by partaking, and he might have done this by selecting a clean animal for his food. Yet they were all jumbled up together, so he declined. He was told however that God could cleanse the unclean: that in fact He had done so, and what He had cleansed he was not to call common. This happened three times so that the significance of it might sink into Peter's mind. We can see in the vision an apt figure of the Gospel, which comes from an opened heaven, which embraces in its folds a multitude, amongst which are found many Gentiles, who were ceremonially unclean; but all of them cleansed by grace, and ultimately taken up into heaven.

Peter at first doubted the meaning of all this, for ancient prejudices die slowly; but, as he continued to ponder, the situation was cleared by the arrival of the messengers from Cornelius. The Spirit distinctly instructed him to go with them and thus carry the Gospel to the seeking Roman. The "unclean" Gentile was to be saved.

In chapter 8, we saw how accurately God timed Philip's interception of the Ethiopian's chariot. Now we see the servants of Cornelius arriving at the precise moment to clinch the Divine instructions to Peter's mind. The thing was of God, and Peter was irresistibly carried forward.

Arrived at Cæsarea, all was ready in the house of Cornelius. He too was conscious the thing was of God, and so he had no doubt as to Peter coming, and he had called together a number of people who like himself were seekers after God. Verse 25 reveals to us the reverential and submissive frame of mind that marked Cornelius. He carried his reverence too far; still it was no small thing that the haughty Roman should fall at the feet of a humble Galilean fisherman.

Peter now found himself in the presence of a large number of Gentiles, and his opening words to Cornelius show how he had accepted the instruction conveyed to him by the vision. The reply of Cornelius reveals how simply he had believed the angel's message and promptly obeyed it. He had accepted Peter's gentle rebuke when he asserted, "I myself also am *a man:*" yet he knew that *God* was at work and that the meeting was to be held as in His presence. He therefore placed himself and the whole audience as "here present before God," ready to hear from the preacher *"all* things that are commanded thee of God." They were ready to hear ALL. Plenty of folk do not mind hearing pleasant and comforting things, while objecting to the sterner announcements that the Gospel makes.

Peter opened his address with a further acknowledgment that he now perceived that God would have respect to every soul that sincerely sought Him, according to the light he might have, no matter to what nation he belonged. The grace of God was now about to flow richly beyond the boundaries of Israel, though the word which God had sent in connection with Jesus Christ, personally present amongst men, had been addressed to the children of Israel only. Still that word had been well published through Galilee and Judaea, and so Cornelius and his friends knew all about it, being resident in those parts. The things that happened in the life and death of Jesus of Nazareth were well known to them.

So Peter could say, "That word . . . *ye know."* There were however, things that *they did not know;* and these all-essential matters he proceeded to unfold. The death of Jesus had been a public spectacle and everybody knew about it. His resurrection had been witnessed by only a few, and common report denied it, the denial having the backing of the religious authorities, as we learn from Matthew 28: 11-15. Hence Peter now announced the astonishing news that the crucified Jesus had been raised from the dead by an act of God, that he and his fellow Apostles had actually seen Him, eaten with Him, and received from Him a command what they were to preach to others. In verses 42 and 43 Peter made the announcements he was commanded to make.

These verses give us the two themes of his preaching, two announcements which must have come with great power to his Gentile hearers. First, the Jesus, whom men crucified, is ordained of God to be the Judge both of the living and the dead. His crucifixion was the act of both Jew and Gentile. Cornelius must have been familiar with the details, and known some who participated in it, if not actually involved in it himself. He was acquainted with His shame and dishonour and apparent failure. Well, the despised Jesus is to come forth in due season as the universal Judge. The destinies of all men rest in His hands. What an astounding declaration! Calculated to overwhelm every adversary with terror!

But second, before this Judge seats Himself on the judgment throne, all the prophets bear witness that there is forgiveness offered in His Name. That forgiveness is received by "whosoever believeth in Him." Forgiveness through the Name of the Judge! Could anything be more stable and satisfactory than that? The Judge has become the Surety for sinful men, and hence the believer in Him receives the remission of sins, *before* the day dawns when will be held the great assizes for the living and for the dead.

Cornelius and his friends *did* believe. Faith was present in their hearts before ever they heard the message. Hearing it, their faith instantly embraced it, and God signalized that fact by instantly bestowing on them the gift of the Holy Ghost. Their faith leapt forth like the lightning-flash, and was at once followed by the thunder-clap of the Holy Spirit. The Spirit was poured upon these believing Gentiles just as He had been at the beginning upon believing Jews, with the sign of tongues following. The two cases were identical, and in this way "they of the circumcision" who had come with Peter had every doubt dispelled. There was nothing for it but to baptize these Gentiles. If God had baptized them by the Spirit into the one body, men could not deny them entrance among believers on earth by water baptism.

There is just this difference between Acts 2 and this chapter, that there the enquirers had to submit first to baptism by water, and then they were to receive the promise of the Spirit. They had to cut their links with the rebellious mass of their nation before they were blessed. Here God bestowed the Spirit first, for had He not done so Jewish prejudices would have raised a wall against their baptism and reception. So God forestalled them: indeed the whole chapter shows us how this opening of the door of faith to the Gentiles was the moving of God's hand in the fulfilment of His purpose. It shows us too that no rigid law can be laid down as to the reception of the Spirit. It is *always* the result of faith, but it may be *with* or *without* baptism, *with* or *without* the laying on of apostolic hands—see chapter 19: 6.

# ACTS

## Chapter 11

THIS CHAPTER OPENS with the stir which was created in Jerusalem by these happenings in Cæsarea. Those who had strong Jewish prejudices contended with Peter over his actions. This led Peter to rehearse the matter from the beginning and set it forth in order, so that all might see that the thing was distinctly of God. It is remarkable that the Spirit of God has thought it well to put on record Peter's own account, as well as that given us by Luke as an historian, in the previous chapter. This emphasizes the importance of what happened so obscurely in the house of the Roman officer. It was in truth an epoch-making event.

In Peter's account we naturally have his side of the story rather than that of Cornelius. Yet he does furnish us with one detail as to the angel's message to Cornelius, which is not mentioned in the previous chapter. Peter was to tell him "words," whereby he and all his house should be "saved." The law *demands works* from men: the Gospel *brings words* to men, and those words lead them to salvation, if believed. Note also that they were not "saved" until they had heard the Gospel, and believed it; although without a doubt there had been a work of God in the hearts of these people, which led them to seek after God.

In verses 15 and 16 we see that Peter recognized in the gift of the Spirit to Cornelius a baptism of the Spirit, supplementary to that which had been realized in Jerusalem at the beginning. It was God doing for believing Gentiles what He had previously done for believing Jews. God put both on the same footing, and who was Peter or anyone else to withstand God?

This plain and straightforward account given by Peter silenced all opposition: indeed grace so wrought in the hearts of those who had objected, that they not only recognized that God had granted to the Gentiles "repentance unto life," but they glorified God for doing it. They attributed repentance to the gift of God, just as faith is attributed to His gift in Ephesians 2:8.

With verse 19, we leave Peter and pick up the thread from verse 1 of chapter 8. In between, we have had Philip's evangelistic labours, the conversion of Saul, who is to be the Apostle to the Gentiles, and Peter's activities, culminating in his opening in a formal way the door of faith to the Gentiles. We now discover that while the mass of believers scattered by persecution carried the Gospel with them, but preached it only to the Jews, there were some from Cyprus and Cyrene who, arrived at Antioch, began to preach to Greeks, declaring Jesus as Lord, for indeed He is *Lord of ALL*. These men, then, began to evangelize Gentiles, which was exactly the special business which the Holy Ghost now had on hand. As a consequence surprising results followed. God's hand worked with them, though they were men of no particular note, and a great multitude believed and turned to the Lord.

# ACTS

Thus the first Gentile church was formed, and the work speedily reached such dimensions as to attract attention from the church in Jerusalem, and lead them to depute Barnabas to visit them. Barnabas came and instantly recognized a true work of the grace of God. Instead of being jealous that others than himself or the leaders in Jerusalem had been used of God for this, he was glad and he furthered the work by his exhortations. But then he was a good man and full of the Holy Ghost and of faith, and so he cared not for his own reputation but for the glory of Christ. His exhortation was that as they had begun with *faith in the Lord* so they should continue to *cleave to the Lord* with purpose of heart. The working of God's grace was the great thing with Barnabas, no matter through whom it was effected. How good it would have been had the spirit of Barnabas prevailed all through the church's history.

Another thing characterized this good man, Barnabas. He evidently recognised his own limitations. He felt that another than himself was the one to be specially used to instruct these Gentile converts, and so he went off to fetch Saul. Barnabas appears to have been the exhorter and Saul the teacher, and for a whole year they gave themselves to this work. And at Antioch, significantly enough, the name "Christian" first sprang up. It is to be noted how the Lordship of Christ is stressed in this account of the work at Antioch; and where Christ is heartily and consistently owned as Lord, there believers so behave themselves as to provoke the onlookers to name them Christians. By the time chapter 26 is reached we find that Agrippa knows the name. In 1 Peter 4: 16 we find the Spirit of God accepting the name as a satisfactory one.

At the end of this chapter we are permitted to see how freely servants of God, such as prophets, moved about between the various churches. Gifts, granted in the church, are to be used in a universal and not merely a local way. So it came to pass that through Agabus, a prophet from Jerusalem, the church at Antioch was apprized of a coming famine, and took steps in advance to meet the anticipated need of the saints in Judæa. Thus early did the Gentile believers have opportunity to express love towards their Jewish brethren.

## CHAPTER 12

THIS CHAPTER HAS somewhat the nature of a parenthesis. We are again carried back to Jerusalem, to hear of Herod's persecution of the saints, and of how God dealt with him. James the brother of John fell a victim. He was one of the three specially favoured on the mount of Transfiguration, in Gethsemane, and on other occasions. Why the Lord did not interfere on his behalf, as He did for Peter, who can tell? But He did not, and the first of the Apostolic band fell. Herod was cultivating the favour of the Jews, just as Pilate was when he crucified the Lord; and, seeing that the Jews were pleased, he proceeded to arrest Peter. So again we find the Jew playing the part which has brought upon them "wrath . . . to the uttermost," according to 1 Thessalonians 2: 14-16.

Peter's arrest sent the church to its knees. Their appeal was to God and not to man. The last twelve words of verse 5 set forth in a remarkable way the essentials of effectual prayer. It was "to God," and therefore *real* prayer. It was "of the church," and therefore *united* prayer. It was "for him," and therefore *definite*—not wandering away over a hundred and one requests, but concentrated on a special object. It was "without ceasing," and therefore *fervent* and *importunate*—the kind of prayer that obtains answers, according to Luke 18: 1 and James 5: 16. The prayer of the church brought an angel from heaven to deliver.

Herod had his prisoner in the hands of sixteen soldiers, in chains and behind bars and bolts: rumours as to previous deliverances had possibly reached his ears. All these things were as nothing before the angel, and Peter was conducted forth to freedom. Many were still praying in the house of Mary, mother of Mark and sister of Barnabas. Thither Peter betook himself. While they were still beseeching God for Peter's deliverance the delivered man knocked at the door. Lo! the answer to their prayer was there. They could hardly credit it, and in this they were very like to ourselves. God's answer went beyond their faith.

The Jews were disappointed and Herod was baulked of his prey. The only people who died the next day were the unfortunate soldiers responsible for Peter's safe keeping.

But God had not finished with Herod, though Herod was finished with Peter. The wretched king glorified himself before the people of Tyre and Sidon with the throne and apparel of royalty and a public oration. It was a huge diplomatic success, and the people accorded to him, and he accepted, honours due to "a god." At that moment the angel of the Lord smote him. He, a mere mortal, accepted honours that were due to God. Today powerful, yet mortal, men are coming very near to doing the same thing, and we may yet see them also disappear in miserable fashion from the stage of life.

Twice in this chapter do we get the angel of the Lord smiting. He "smote Peter on the side," and in result he "*raised him up*." He smote Herod, and instantly *laid him low;* for "he was eaten of worms, and gave up the ghost." Human flesh has often been eaten of worms after death, but in Herod's case it was before death. A more horrible end could hardly be conceived. With James, Herod was allowed to have his fling; with Peter, he was foiled; and then God made a fool of him, requiring his soul amid scenes of indescribable misery and anguish.

# ACTS

Verse 24 supplies us with a striking contrast. As the worms grew and multiplied in Herod's wretched body so did the Word of God grow and multiply in the hearts of many. When it pleases God to overthrow an adversary He need not exert Himself: a few worms will suffice to accomplish His end. The Word of God is that which accomplishes His end of blessing in the souls of men.

Verse 25 picks up the thread from the last verse of the previous chapter. Barnabas and Saul had gone to Jerusalem with the gift from the Antioch saints, and having fulfilled this service they returned, taking Mark with them. As we open the next chapter, our thoughts are centred once more on Antioch and the work there.

## Chapter 13

THIS LARGE CHURCH, composed mainly of Gentiles, had no less than five prophets and teachers in its midst. Their names are given and prove very instructive; for one had a surname which probably indicates that he was a black man (Niger means Black), one was sufficiently distinguished to have been a foster-brother of Herod, Barnabas was a Hellenistic Jew, Saul had been a Pharisee of the Pharisees, and Lucius may have been a Gentile. Thus it was quite early manifest that race and breeding are not the things that count most decisively in the church, but the gift which is bestowed from on high. These men not only ministered to the saints for their instruction, but also to the Lord in thanksgiving, intercession and fasting; and it was in one of these private seasons that the Holy Ghost gave definite instructions that Barnabas and Saul should be set apart specially to go forth with the Gospel into the Gentile world.

The first and last of the five were chosen for this mission. The others prayed for them and identified themselves with them in their coming service by the laying on of hands. This laying on of hands was not what is today called "ordination," for the two chosen men were already in the full exercise of their ministry. The laying on of hands does uniformly express identification. The others said in effect, "We are entirely with you in your mission;" so that in full fellowship, and without jealousy or rivalry, they sent them forth.

Even so, it was really the Holy Ghost who sent them forth, as verse 4 says; and to Cyprus, the old home of Barnabas, they went first of all, Mark his nephew accompanying them. Arrived at Paphos, they had the encouragement of finding the chief ruler of the island ready for the Word of God; but at the same time they ran into Satanic opposition. Opposition from the powers of darkness is an encouraging sign, rather than the reverse.

Elymas was an apostate Jew, who had sold himself to the service of the devil, and he became the chief opponent of the Gospel at Paphos. But just

# ACTS

as Satan's power was expressed in him, so the power of the Holy Spirit energized Saul, and there was a very striking and drastic proof given that, "greater is He that is in you, than he that is in the world" (1 John 4: 4). The true character of the man was unmasked, and the hand of the Lord laid upon him in judgment. It is striking that Saul should now be used to bring upon another something similar to that which had fallen on himself. After three days the scales had fallen from the eyes of Saul. On Elymas there descended a mist and darkness, which fitly matched the misty darkness of his mind. The deputy believed, and it was the *teaching* of the Lord that impressed him rather than the miracle.

From this point in the narrative Luke gives Saul his new name of Paul (meaning, Little), and at the same time we see the Spirit thrusting him into the leading position in service and ministry, so that in verse 13, "Paul and his company," is the phrase used. There is a designed connection, we think, between the change of name and the change of position. He who is *Little* becomes the *Leader;* and this illustrates the Lord's words in Matthew 18: 4. Did this have something to do with John Mark leaving the company at this juncture, we wonder? Barnabas, his uncle, was being somewhat overshadowed.

At Antioch in Pisidia the rulers of the synagogue invited a message from the visitors, and again Paul is the one to seize upon the opportunity and speak. The record of his preaching is given—verses 17 to 41—so here we have a valuable insight to his presentation of the Gospel to a mixed audience of Jews and proselytes.

He began with God's choice of their fathers in Egypt and His bringing them out of it, and from that point led them up to God's choice of David, and His promise of a Saviour from that man's seed. He then presented Jesus as being the promised Seed, as borne witness to by John the Baptist. Now the tidings of the salvation which is centred in that Saviour was sent to all his hearers, including, "whosoever among you feareth God;" that is, the Gentile proselytes among them.

He then proceeded to speak of the death and resurrection of Jesus: His death the wicked act of the Jerusalem Jews; His resurrection the act of God, and that resurrection amply verified by the testimony of credible witnesses. Hence he brought them "glad tidings," in a twofold way. First there was the good news of God fulfilling His promise in raising up Jesus. The word, "again," should not occur in the middle of verse 33: that verse refers to our Lord's coming into the world, according to the second Psalm. Then, second, there was the good news that when men had consigned Jesus to death, God had raised Him up from the dead, never to die again. Paul found an allusion to resurrection in "the sure mercies of David" (Isa. 55: 3), as well as in the well-known words, he quotes from Psalm 16. The one was written *about* David, and the other written *by* David; but in

# ACTS

neither case did the Spirit of God really refer *to* David, as verse 36 says. David having "in his own age served the will of God," (margin), did see corruption, and the words of his Psalm could only refer to Christ.

Having thus established the resurrection of Christ, Paul brought his address to a climax by the announcement of forgiveness of sins through "this Man," risen from the dead. The announcement was made in oracular fashion as a Divine proclamation. There was no quoting of Old Testament Scripture for this. "Be it known," he said. What he announced they were to know, for really it was God who was speaking through his lips. In 1 Corinthians 2: 13, we find Paul claiming the inspiration of the Holy Ghost for his spoken words; and this being so we have no hesitation in according the same inspiration to his writings, preserved for us in the New Testament. When Paul said, "*Be it known*," then those who believed might *know*. And in just the same way *we know*, when we believe the Holy Scriptures.

Paul not only made plain this general announcement of forgiveness; he also declared the positive result which would follow belief in the Gospel message. By Christ the believer *is justified* from all things. By the works of the law not one of us can be justified at all: by the faith of Christ we are justified from all. We are cleared from every charge that would have stood against us, and invested with "the righteousness which is of God by faith." All this hinges upon faith in Christ, risen from the dead. It is "through this Man," and "by Him."

Paul closed his address with a word of warning, and this was in keeping with what he states in Romans 1: 16-18. In the Gospel "righteousness of God" is revealed, as we have just seen in verse 39 of our chapter; but it is revealed against the dark background of the "wrath of God." Hence his solemn words in verses 40 and 41. The way he quotes from Habbakuk 1: 5 is very striking, for the allusion there is plainly to the Chaldeans. However though the Chaldeans were an immediate fulfilment of the prophecy, it evidently is going to have a larger, ultimate fulfilment in the judgment of the Day of the Lord. No prophecy of the Scripture is of any "private interpretation."

Verses 43-48 show that the Gospel is indeed the "power of God" unto salvation to all who believe. Jews and proselytes were first reached; but when the mass of the Jews, filled with envy, began violent opposition, the Apostles definitely turned to the Gentiles with the offer of salvation, finding in Isaiah 49: 6 a plain command of the Lord to do so. Light and salvation for the Gentiles had been God's purpose from the days of old. Many Gentiles did believe, and thereby it became manifest that they had been ordained to eternal life. *We do not know* who are ordained to eternal life, so we cannot foretell who will believe. When we find anyone really believing, *we know at once* that they are ordained to eternal life.

# ACTS

Not only in Antioch was the Word preached, but also in all the surrounding region; and the prosperity of the work stirred up such a persecution that Paul and Barnabas had to depart. We might have considered it disastrous that these new disciples should *get* persecution and *lose* the preachers. The work in their souls however was of so solid a character that instead of being depressed they were filled with joy and with the Holy Ghost. Without a doubt disciples are more frequently damaged by prosperity than by persecution.

## CHAPTER 14

IN ICONIUM, THE next place visited, the work was similar to that at Antioch. The synagogue was visited and the Word so preached that a multitude of both Jews and Gentiles believed. Again the Jews became the opposers and persecutors, and in view of riotous doings the Apostles fled to other cities.

At Lystra a remarkable miracle was wrought through Paul. A man lame from birth was healed; a miracle almost the exact counterpart of the one wrought by Peter, which we read of in chapter 3. That was done in the very heart of Judaism, and while it gave a great opening for testimony it also brought upon the Apostles the wrath of the Jewish leaders. This was done in the presence of the heathen, who interpreted the wonderful happening in the light of their false beliefs, and would have made an idolatrous festival, had not the Apostles protested, seizing the opportunity to declare to them the true and living God, who is the Creator. The Lycaonians would have done exactly what Paul charges the heathen with doing in Romans 1: 25, saying they "worshipped and served the creature more than the Creator, who is blessed for ever."

The fickleness of men is illustrated in verse 19. The people who would have deified Paul are very easily persuaded against him by certain Jews who followed his footsteps, and they stone him, as they thought, to death. Paul now undergoes the very thing he had helped to bring upon Stephen. In the case of Stephen God did not intervene; in Paul's case He did. Whether Paul was really dead, or whether only battered nearly to the point of death, we have no means of knowing: whichever it was, his restoration, almost in an instant, to ordinary health and strength, was a miracle. The next day he journeyed forth to preach the Gospel in another city, just as though nothing had happened to him.

Their outward journey terminated at Derbe, having been one of evangelistic labours and sufferings. On the return journey they gave themselves to pastoral work, so that the souls of the disciples might be confirmed and established in the faith. It is worthy of note that they did not hide from the disciples that suffering was before them, but rather they told them that it was inevitable. They did not say that we *may* through *some* tribulation enter the Kingdom, but that we *must* through *much* tribulation.

# ACTS

That saying stands true today. We may try to evade the tribulation, but we do not succeed. If through cowardice we shrink from conflict with the world, we get the trouble in our daily circumstances, or even in the bosom of the church of God. The Apostle Paul himself wrote, "Our flesh had no rest, but we were troubled on every side; *without* were *fightings, within* were *fears*" (2 Cor. 7: 5). Today we have to say something similar, only we so often have to reverse the latter clause and say that we have too many fears as to the "without" to do much fighting, and consequently we are too often involved in fightings within the circle of the saints of God—it is, "*without* were *fears, within* were *fightings.*" Either way however the tribulation is ours.

On the return journey they also found that amongst the older converts some were manifesting the character that marked them out as fit to exercise spiritual supervision, and these men they ordained as elders. Apostolic discernment was needed in making the choice, and also a real spirit of dependence on God—hence, prayer—and a refusal of the desires of the flesh—hence, fasting. And when the elders were chosen so that all might recognize them, they did not commit the rest of the believers into the hands of the elders. No, they "commended them to the Lord, on whom they believed." Each believer was set in direct connection and communion with the Lord by faith. Elders were instituted, not to *intercept* the faith of the saints, but to *incite* it to more reality and depth.

Cyprus was not touched on the return journey, and from Attalia they took ship for Antioch direct; and there, the church being gathered together, they told the story of their mission. They had not been sent by the church at Antioch but by the Holy Ghost, yet the church had a very deep interest in these servants who had gone forth from their midst. On their part the servants told what "God had done with them." God was the worker, and they but the instruments He had been pleased to use; and it was God who had opened the door of faith to the Gentiles. The first missionary journey had proved this beyond all dispute.

Yet, though this was so, the manner of their service was not beyond all dispute. No one challenged them in Antioch itself during their long stay there, but then most in that church were of Gentile extraction. When certain men came down from the Jerusalem area, all was changed by the teaching that the observance of circumcision was absolutely necessary for salvation, and Paul and Barnabas had not practised this. When reading the early part of chapter 11, we saw that the Judaizing party in Jerusalem had questioned Peter's action in evangelizing Gentiles, in the person of Cornelius and his friends. Their opposition was overruled, and it was accepted that the Gospel was to go to the Gentiles. The point now raised was that, even admitting that, they must submit to circumcision in order to be saved, and the circumcision must be "after the manner of Moses," thus definitely connecting it with the law system. This new demand was firmly resisted by Paul and Barnabas, and ultimately they and others went up to the Apostles and elders in Jerusalem about this question.

## Chapter 15

FOURTEEN YEARS HAD passed since Paul's first brief visit to Jerusalem three years after his conversion, as recorded in Acts 9: 26-29, and in Galatians 1: 18. The whole of Galatians 2 furnishes us with remarkable insight to what was at stake in the discussion, which was started at Antioch and carried to its conclusion at Jerusalem; nothing short of *the truth and liberty of the Gospel.* We also discover that though in our chapter it says, "they determined" that Paul and others should go to Jerusalem, Paul himself went up "by revelation;" that is, the Lord distinctly revealed to him that he was to go. Also we find that Paul was led to take a very firm line in the matter; giving place to those who opposed him, "by subjection, no, not for an hour;" taking Titus, who was a Greek, with him, and declining to have any compulsion laid upon him as to his being circumcised. The Galatian epistle clearly shows that Paul was fully assured what was the mind of God in this matter, but that it was revealed to him that he should consent to it being referred to Jerusalem for settlement there.

In this of course we see the wisdom and power of God. Had Paul attempted to settle the matter, and act on his own apostolic authority at Antioch, there might easily have been a breach between himself and the other Apostles. As it was, the decision in favour of liberty being accorded to the Gentile converts, was reached in the very place where, had not God controlled by His Spirit, the decision would have gone the other way. But in saying this we are anticipating.

On the journey to Jerusalem the tidings of God's grace to the Gentiles caused great joy to the brethren, but in Jerusalem itself the issue was soon raised. Those who contended for the observance of the law by the converts from among the Gentiles, were believers who belonged to the sect of the Pharisees. For the present they retained their Phariseeism, though believers. This occasioned a formal coming together of the Apostles and elders to go into the question as before God.

There was much "disputing," or "discussion," and then Peter made a decisive pronouncement, by referring to the case of Cornelius, in which he had himself been involved. He pointed out that the heart-knowing God had borne witness to these Gentile converts by giving to them the Holy Spirit, just as He had given Him to themselves on the Day of Pentecost. These Gentiles had been *cleansed*, as the vision of the great sheet indicated, and God had wrought the purification in their hearts *by faith*, and not as a matter of mere ceremonial cleansing. The fact was that God had already decided the point in principle by what He did in the case of Cornelius. We can now understand why so much space is devoted to that case in the Acts; for this is the third time that we have it brought before us.

The law was a yoke, which God had placed upon the neck of the Jew, and both they and their fathers had found its weight to be crushing. To endeavour to impose it upon necks, that had never been subjected to it by God, would be to tempt God Himself. The grace of the Lord Jesus Christ was the only hope of salvation, whether to Jew or Gentile. The way verse 11 reads is quite remarkable. It is not, "they, Gentiles, shall be saved even as we, Jews," but, "we shall be saved even as they." The salvation of the Gentiles could not be on any other ground than grace; and the Jew must come in on this ground too.

Let us not miss the lovely contrast between Matthew 11: 29, and verse 10 of our chapter. The crushing yoke of the law is not to be laid upon our Gentile necks, but because of that we are not left yokeless. We take upon us the light and easy yoke of the blessed Jesus, who has become to us the Revealer of the Father.

From Peter's words it is evident how thoroughly he had learned the lesson he was taught in connection with Cornelius. He pointed out how the thing had been settled there; and so the way was cleared for Barnabas and Paul to rehearse how God had worked in miraculous power among the Gentiles. Barnabas is now mentioned first, for evidently he, free, from any jealousy or envy, could speak more freely of the things done, mainly through Paul. Their testimony was that what God had done *in practice* through them agreed with what He established *in principle* through Peter.

Peter, Barnabas and Paul having had their say, James spoke. He seems to have had a place of special responsibility in Jerusalem, and Galatians 2: 12 indicates that he was noted as holding strict views as to the measure of association that was permissible in the church of God between Jews and Gentiles. Yet he endorsed Peter's declaration, and then pointed out that Old Testament scripture supported it. Amos had predicted how days would come when the Name of God would be called upon Gentiles. If we turn to his prophecy we can see that he had millennial conditions in view, so James did not quote his words as though they were being *fulfilled*, but as being *in agreement* with what they had just heard.

The words in which James summarized Peter's testimony are worthy of special note. "God . . . did *visit* the Gentiles, *to take out of them a people for His Name*." This is God's programme for the present dispensation. The Gospel is not sent forth among the nations with the object of converting them as nations, and so making the earth a fit place for Christ to return to, but to convert individuals, who thereby are taken out from the nations to be His special possession—"a people for His Name." This is a fact of a most fundamental nature. If we are wrong on this point we shall be wrong as to the whole character of the dispensation in which we live. The nations will only be subdued when *God's judgments* are in the earth, as Isaiah 26: 9 so plainly says. The Gospel goes forth in the earth in order that *an election* from both Jews and Gentiles may be called out; and *that election is the church of God.*

Having stated this, James gave what he judged to be the mind of God as to the question at issue. His "sentence," or "judgment," was that the yoke of the law should not be placed on the neck of Gentile Christians, but that they should merely be told to observe certain restrictions in matters as to which they had been notoriously careless. Idolatry and fornication were known as evil, even before the law was given, and so too was the eating of blood, as Genesis 9: 4 shows. God knows from the outset all that He will develop as time goes on. The calling and election from the Gentiles was new to them, but not to God. It was theirs to move on with God; and as for Moses, his words were well to the fore in every synagogue every sabbath day.

The judgment that James expressed carried the whole council with it. They had had before them first, Peter's testimony as to what God had done in connection with Cornelius: second, through Barnabas and Paul an account of God's actings during their missionary journey: third, the voice of Scripture, as quoted by James. *What God had said agreed with what God had done.* They had come together to seek His mind, and by His word and His actions they plainly discerned it; and all were of one accord. Thus a difficult question, which might have divided the whole church, was settled, and ended by drawing them together. When Barnabas and Paul went up to Jerusalem, it was as men whose service was open to challenge and suspicion. When they left they were bearers of a letter in which they were spoken of as "our beloved Barnabas and Paul."

They were also spoken of as "men that have hazarded [or *delivered up*] their lives for the name of our Lord Jesus Christ." To hazard one's life is to risk it, as a gambler risks his money on a throw of the dice: to deliver up one's life is to accept death as a certainty rather than a risk. Anyone who delivers up his life in this fashion should be esteemed as beloved in the church of God. This letter from Jewish believers to Gentile believers breathes throughout a spirit of love and fellowship and unity. They were able to say, "It seemed good to the Holy Ghost and to us;" so sure were they that the Holy Spirit had governed their decision. To put the Gentiles under the law would have had the effect of "subverting" their souls.

All this is very much to the point for us today. The same kind of trouble cropped up amongst the Galatians a little later, and the attempt to mix law and grace is often seen in our day. It cannot be done without destroying the fulness of grace and subverting the souls of those who imbibe such teaching. Verses 30—33 of our chapter show how the vindication of grace and the liberty that it brings, contributed to the establishment and joy of the Gentile believers at Antioch. Also Judas and Silas, the delegates from Jerusalem, exercised their prophetic ministry and strengthened the brethren. This shows how freely those who had gift were permitted to exercise it in any place, and in the presence of men whose gift might be in many ways superior to their own—for Paul and Barnabas were now back in Antioch.

Shortly after, Paul proposed to Barnabas that they take another journey with pastoral work in view. The words of verse 36 breathe the spirit of a true pastor, who desires to see how the believers are getting on. The welfare of their souls is the great point before him. The sad thing was that this excellent proposal became the occasion of a breach between these two devoted servants of the Lord. Barnabas proposed that Mark, his nephew, should again accompany them. Paul, remembering his early defection, was against it, and this difference of judgment generated such warm feeling that they parted company, as unable any longer to work together. Barnabas went to Cyprus, where their first journey had started, and Paul towards Asia Minor, where that journey had extended. Paul found a new companion in Silas, and left after the brethren had committed them to the grace of God. It looks as if Barnabas left hurriedly, before the brethren had time to pray for him.

It ill becomes us to judge these eminent servants of our Lord, but the record certainly seems to infer that Barnabas was too much influenced by natural relationship, and that the sympathy of the brethren lay with Paul. Still the warm feeling and contention lay between them, and the Spirit of God does not hide it. We are not to conceive of Paul as other than a man of like passions to ourselves. He was not perfect, as was his Lord.

## Chapter 16

This chapter opens with Paul back at Derbe and Lystra, back, that is, to the scenes where he had suffered the stoning. In those very places he now finds Timothy, who was to become in his latter years such a comfort to him. A happy illustration of how God's government acts in favour of the godly. We are apt to think of it only as acting against the ungodly. Out of the place of Paul's sufferings sprang one of his greatest comforts.

Now as Timothy's father was a Greek he had not been circumcised, and he would not have been acceptable in Jewish circles. Paul knew this and circumcised him; an action which on the surface seems totally at variance with his attitude in regard to Titus—see Galatians 2: 3—5. But there the whole truth of the Gospel had been made to hinge on the question, whereas here there was no question at all involved. In Timothy's case it was just a matter of removing something which would have been a hindrance in his service for the Lord, and Paul was not concerned to maintain for himself an appearance of consistency which would have been only skin-deep. Here was a God-given helper in the work, and it was expedient to remove all that would hinder his labours.

Paul's somewhat lengthy sojourn in Asia Minor on this second journey is dismissed in five short verses (5—8). It comprised labours of a pastoral sort, for they went through regions where churches were already established through his earlier labours, and these they instructed to observe what had been settled at the conference in Jerusalem, and they were established and increased in number. Then they went into new regions, Phrygia, Galatia and Mysia, and in these of course they did the work of evangelists. This evidently was the occasion when he had so wonderful a reception from the Galatians, to which he alludes in Galatians 4: 13-15. It was also a time in which God exercised very strong control over his movements. When Mysia was reached, Bithynia lay to the north or north-east, and Asia to the south. In both directions he would have gone, if permitted. In the former case he was directly *forbidden* by the Holy Spirit, and in the latter the Spirit did *not suffer* him to go, which apparently indicates guidance of a less direct kind, and more by way of circumstances.

Troas was on the sea coast of Mysia, and here Paul was given positive guidance as to his movements by means of the vision of the man of Macedonia. So here within the compass of five verses we find Divine guidance conveyed to Paul in *three* different ways, twice of a negative sort and once of a positive sort. This should furnish some guidance to any who, very desirous of Divine direction, expect to receive it in some *one* way of their own choosing.

Accepting the vision as giving them God's direction, Paul and his helpers immediately obeyed, and verse 11 shows that God turned the winds in their favour and they had a very rapid passage; for we see, in chapter 20: 6, that when years after he took the journey in the reverse direction it occupied five days. At Troas, Luke, the writer of the book, evidently joined Paul, for in verses 4, 6, 7, 8, it is uniformly "they," whereas in verse 10 the pronoun suddenly becomes "we," and that and "us" continue well into the account of the doings at Philippi.

Philippi had the status of a Roman colony, so the Roman element was strong there, and perhaps correspondingly the Jewish element was weak. No synagogue existed, and all that was to be found was a spot outside the city by a river where prayer to the true God was offered. That spot they sought out, and finding only some women assembled they sat down and spoke to them. That did not seem a very promising beginning, but Paul was the kind of man that accepted and utilized small things. He attempted no formal preaching but just sat down and talked in an informal way. This humble beginning had a great ending. A church was established which above others was filled with grace and was a comfort to him.

## ACTS

The work began in the heart of Lydia, which was opened of God. The words, "which worshipped God," indicate that she was a seeker, and had become a proselyte, and now in the Gospel which Paul preached she found the full thing which she sought. The work was quiet but very real, for she was baptized and her household; and she at once identified herself with the Lord's servants by opening her house to them.

The next incident was the encounter with the female slave who had opened her heart to some dark agent of the devil. She made a pretence of approving Paul and his helpers, and this might have pleased some, who might have argued, "Well, we are servants of God, and if she likes to advertise us, let her!" Paul however was not short-sighted like this. He saw that the devil's patronage is no gain but a disaster, and he refused her testimony by commanding the evil spirit to come out of her. The spirit had to obey, and her masters knew that their money-making scheme was spoiled. This raised their ire, and Paul and Silas were dragged before the magistrates on a charge worded so as to raise Roman prejudice against them. This stirred the crowd, and also moved the magistrates to excited and un-Romanlike action. No proper trial was held; they were flogged and cast into prison.

Under these circumstances even the jailor acted with extra severity, and night descended upon them in this sorry plight. Were they tempted to falter and doubt, thinking that the vision of the Macedonian man had been a little too visionary? Perhaps; for they were men of like weakness to ourselves. But, if they did, faith soon triumphed, and at the darkest hour they were not only praying but singing praises to God. Suddenly God intervened, and not only by the earthquake. Doors are more often jammed tight by earthquakes than opened; and no ordinary earthquake strikes the shackles from prisoners.

Knowing the severity of Roman law in regard to the custody of prisoners, the jailor was on the verge of suicide when Paul's shout reached his ears. The fact that "he called for a light," (verse 29), shows that they were all in the dark. How did Paul know what the jailor was about to do? Paul's sudden call was evidently inspired by the Spirit of God, and it came as a voice from God to the jailor. Here at last was the Macedonian man! He was trembling: he was on his face before his prisoners! Soon he was asking the great question, which since has been asked by millions of convicted sinners. He received the immortal answer, which has been used to the enlightenment and salvation of countless souls.

We often quote Acts 16: 31, but too often we omit the last three words. God loves to identify a man's house with himself and include them in His offer of blessing. Why do we not more often embrace this fact in our faith? We have already had in the chapter the converted woman and her house: now we have the converted man and his house. This surely is most encouraging for all heads of houses who may be reached by the grace of God;

since there is no respect of persons with God, and what He is to *one* He is to *all*.

The jailor believed, and showed his faith by his works without a moment's delay. Then, though it was still night, "he and all his" were baptized straightway. This is pretty clear evidence that baptism is not an ordinance which is *intended* to be a confession of one's faith, and therefore to be observed in public. Had it been that, what an opportunity was missed here! How effectively the thing might have been done the next day when public opinion had veered somewhat in favour of Paul! All must have been confusion in the city after the earthquake, yet the jailor and his house had the links cut with the old life without any delay: for baptism signifies *dissociation*, through the death of Christ.

When the magistrates relented the next day, Paul seized the opportunity to point out to them how they themselves had transgressed, seeing he and Silas were Roman citizens. He did not push the point further, or in any way retaliate. Their way was smoothed however, and they had time to see the brethren and exhort them before taking their departure. From the Epistle to the Philippians we may see how well the work progressed after their departure.

## CHAPTER 17

LUKE GIVES US no details as to what transpired in Amphipolis and Apollonia, but passes on to the happenings in Thessalonica. In this chapter, we notice, the pronoun "we" is not used, so possibly Luke, not being as much involved as Paul and Silas were in the disturbances at Philippi, stayed on there to help the converts further.

Paul first addressed the Jews in their synagogue, as was his custom. Verse 3 gives us the line on which he approached them. He proved from their own Scriptures that the Messiah, when He came, must suffer death and rise from the dead. This established, it was simple to point to Jesus as unquestionably being the Messiah. So in one verse we are given the whole thing in a nut-shell. However long the discourses lasted, the whole point is summed up in these few words, and they stand as guidance for all who would approach the Jew today. Not all believed, but some did, and also many Greek proselytes, and some of the chief women.

At Philippi the riotous proceedings originated with disappointed, money-making Gentiles; at Thessalonica unbelieving Jews were at the bottom of even worse opposition and disorder. In stigmatizing Paul and Silas as, "These that have turned the world upside down," they rendered involuntary tribute to the mighty power of the Gospel, preached with the Holy Ghost sent down from heaven. They might oppose, but they could not stop its advance.

# ACTS

Paul's service in Thessalonica was cut short by this riot, for he served in the spirit of the Lord's instruction recorded in Matthew 10: 23. Hence a move was now made to Berea, where the Jews showed a very different spirit. They had an openness of mind, that is characterized as "more noble," and when Paul showed them what the Scriptures had foretold, they searched them diligently, and thereby many believed. A mind that is ready and free from prejudice, and that gladly bows to Scripture, is indeed *a noble thing*.

Such hostility to the Word of God marked the Thessalonian Jews however that they pursued Paul to Berea, and in the face of further trouble, Paul slipped away to Athens, outwitting his pursuers by a simple ruse. Silas and Timothy remained at Berea, for evidently the animosity was now specially directed against Paul. Hence it came to pass that in his visit to Athens, the great centre of Greek culture and wisdom, Paul was solitary and alone, as far as his service was concerned.

Athens was the great centre of Greek learning and philosophy; it was also full of idols. The highest human culture and the grossest idolatry can exist quite amicably side by side. Into the midst of this state of things Paul stepped, and the sight of it painfully excited his spirit. Though still without his companions he could not rest in the presence of it, and so began to testify to both Jews and Gentiles. In this way certain philosophers had their attention drawn to him, and these men, though belonging to opposing schools and treating him with contempt, had their curiosity sufficiently aroused to desire to hear more. Thus it came to pass that the opportunity was given to him to speak before an assemblage of the most cultured intellects of that time.

We are given a glimpse, in verses 18-21, of the conditions that prevailed in Athens. There was immense mental activity, and an insatiable enquiry into new ideas. They spent their time either in telling or hearing "some new thing;" not, of course, just gossip or tittle-tattle but the newest philosophic notions. Hence Paul's preaching of "Jesus and the resurrection" struck them as a great novelty connected with some deities to which hitherto they had been strangers. The Epicureans believed that the highest good was to be found in gratifying one's desires, and the Stoics that it was in repressing them, but what were these new ideas?

Paul opened his address on Mars' hill by telling them that they were too "superstitious" or "given up to demon worship." Amongst their many shrines they even had an altar dedicated to "The unknown god," lest there should be some demon, unknown to them, that needed to be propitiated. He seized upon this and made it the theme of his discourse, for it was perfectly true that the living God was utterly unknown to them. Paul announced to them the God that they knew not; and if we examine the brief report of his discourse we can see how he set God before them. As regards the things of God these cultured Athenians were simply pagans; so here we are instructed how the Gospel should be presented to the heathen.

Paul began by presenting Him as *the God of creation*. This lies at the foundation of everything. If we do not know Him thus, we do not know Him at all. That is why the evolutionary theory works so disastrously. Its chief attraction to so many is that it enables one to dispense with God altogether, or at least to push Him so far into a remote background as to make Him not worth thinking about. Paul brought Him right into the forefront of the picture he presented; He not only made the world but all things in it. He cannot be contained in men's buildings, nor worshipped as though He needed anything from men's hands. He is Himself the Giver of Life and all things. All men are His creatures, made of one blood, and their times and boundaries determined by Him.

There had remained some glimmerings of light as to this amongst them, and Paul was able to quote some of their own poets as having spoken of mankind as being the offspring of God. In this they were right. Only by faith in Christ Jesus do we become *children* of God, but all men are His *offspring* as His creatures. This being so we ought not to conceive of God as something less than ourselves or as the work of our own hands; and we should be those who seek after Him. His *immanence* is recognized in the words that "In Him we live, and move, and have our being;" yet Paul preached Him as the *transcendent* One, who is Lord of heaven and earth.

But this God of creation is also *a God of forbearance*. Men had not liked to retain God in their knowledge, and so the nations had fallen into ignorance of God. For some centuries the Athenians had been priding themselves on their culture and learning, yet all through they had been in "the times of this *ignorance*,"—this ignorance of God—and Paul told them so plainly. Yet God had "winked at," or "overlooked" this ignorance, acting in forbearance, in view of that which He was going to do through Christ.

But now Christ is come, and God proclaims Himself as *a God of righteous judgment*. He has appointed the day when He will take up the reins of government by the Man of His choice, and the whole earth shall be judged and administered in righteousness. In view of this repentance is the only seemly thing for unrighteous men wherever they may be. It is the only right thing, and God commands it.

The pledge of the coming of this day of righteous judgment has been given in the resurrection of the Man of God's choice. Thus finally Paul set God forth as *the God of resurrection*. Something entirely outside all human calculations had taken place. Jesus had been raised from the death into which man consigned Him! Paul started his work in Athens by announcing

## ACTS

Jesus and the resurrection amongst the *workers* in the market place; he ended on the same theme when speaking to the *thinkers* on Mars' hill.

Their busy brains were revolving in man's world, and hence resurrection lay right outside their field of view. To many of them it seemed an absurdity, and they mocked. Others manifested some interest yet deferred further consideration, as seeing no urgency in the matter. Some however believed, both men and women, and these threw in their lot with Paul. These three classes usually appear when the Gospel reaches any given place: there are the mockers, the procrastinators and the believers.

Paul's stay in Athens was a short one: he did not wait longer there for his companions but went on to Corinth. So it is probable that those who said, "We will hear thee again of this matter," had no opportunity of doing so.

### CHAPTER 18

THE CHAPTER OPENS with Paul at Corinth, and there he met Aquila and Priscilla. The harsh decree of Claudias worked to throw them across Paul's path, and this led to their conversion and then their subsequent service, which earned the high praise of Romans 16: 3, 4. God overruled the decree of expulsion, for good, making the wrath of man to praise Him; and we may hope and pray that He will work in just the same way in regard to modern decrees against the Jews. With this couple Paul abode, and began his work in the synagogue. Here Silas and Timothy joined him, and Paul's testimony became stronger and more direct. Then, the Jews opposing, he turned to the Gentiles.

"He departed thence" (verse 7); that is, from the synagogue; and carried on his testimony in the house of one, Justus, that was close by. Yet a very definite and large work of God took place, even the ruler of the synagogue being converted. By a vision the Lord encouraged him to boldly speak, with the assurance that he should not be molested there, as he had been elsewhere. So for eighteen months he laboured on. There was an attempt made against him, but under God's hand this was frustrated by the cool indifference of Gallio, the Roman proconsul, who treated the whole matter as one of contentions about words and names, and cared for none of these things. So God can utilize the temperament of a governor, as well as the decree of a Cæsar, to serve His ends, and Paul did not leave Corinth till some time after.

With this long stay in Corinth Paul's second journey drew to its end, and he left for Jerusalem and Antioch via Ephesus, where his stay was but short; he promised to return, "if God will." That God did so will, we see in the next chapter. Verse 18 shows us that Paul still observed Jewish customs, as in the matter of a vow.

## ACTS

At Antioch he now spent "some time," an expression which indicates not a very long period: then he was off on his third journey, and first to scenes of former labours in order to strengthen the disciples. This is always a much needed work since there are so many influences which make for the weakening of disciples. We pick up Paul's story in the first verse of the next chapter, and verses 24-28 are a parenthesis dealing with the full enlightenment of Apollos and his happy service, in which we discover that, though Paul had passed so quickly from Ephesus, Aquila and Priscilla had remained there, and through them the Lord furnished Apollos with exactly what he needed.

Apollos possessed the natural endowment of eloquence—he was a master of words. By diligent study he had become "mighty in the Scriptures." Yet, when he came to Ephesus he was not well-informed as to God's intervention in Christ. He only knew of things up to the introduction of Jesus by John's baptism. What he knew, he diligently taught in the synagogue. Aquila and Priscilla, hearing him, at once perceived his lack, and performed the delightful service of showing him hospitality, in order to instruct him more fully in what had come to pass through Christ. Thus God used these saints, of no particular public gift, to fairly launch a very gifted vessel on his career of service. From Ephesus he went to Corinth, and not only did he convince many Jews as to Christ, but also he much helped on the believers. How much of the reward of his effective service will go to the credit of Aquila and Priscilla, who shall say?

### CHAPTER 19

AS WE OPEN this chapter, we find Paul arriving at Ephesus after Apollos had left, and there finding certain disciples, who were in a similar state of ignorance as to the full gospel message. They were truly "disciples," and they had believed as much of the facts concerning Christ as they had heard. The Holy Ghost is given to those who believe "the word of truth, the Gospel of your salvation" (Eph. 1: 13). They had not believed it, because they had not heard it, and consequently they had not received the Spirit. Like Apollos, they had only heard the earliest beginnings of things, connected with John the Baptist, and had been baptised with his baptism. When Paul had instructed them further, and they had been baptised as owning the Lordship of Jesus, and Paul had laid his hands on them, the Spirit came on them and they both spoke with tongues and prophesied. Thus impressive evidence was granted that they had now entered into the full Christian state.

Paul did not in any way blame these twelve men. The transition to the full light of the Gospel was gradual in those days of slow communications. In the beginning of Hebrews 6, we do get things said which imply reproach. There were those amongst the Jewish believers who were blameworthy for not "leaving the word of the beginning of Christ" (margin), and going on to the perfection of the full Gospel. John's ministry had a great deal to say as to "repentance from dead works," and of "baptisms," and of "eternal judgment," but by the time that Epistle was written the full truth of Christ had been sounded abroad, and they ought to have embraced it, even if it cut across many of their Jewish thoughts. There is *no excuse for us*, if we do not go on to perfection.

These men being blessed, Paul turned his attention to the synagogue, where he had briefly testified on his earlier visit, and for three months he reasoned with the Jews, persuading them of the Gospel. At the end of that time he perceived that his work there was finished. The remnant according to the election of grace was manifest, and the rest were hardened, so he made the cleavage complete by leaving the synagogue and carrying the disciples with him, to continue his service in the school of Tyrannus—just as at Corinth he had left the synagogue for the house of Justus. Thereby it was made quite manifest that what God was establishing was not a fresh group of enlightened believers amongst the Jews, but a new thing altogether, embracing both Jews and Gentiles.

So distinct and powerful a work was wrought there that Paul spent two years of labour in that city. God supported him by miraculous manifestations of a special nature, and the whole province was evangelised. As is ever the case, a powerful working of God unmasks the working of Satan, and excites his opposition. The rest of this chapter shows how this came about at Ephesus.

The first move was to oppose by way of imitation. The seven sons of Sceva thought that they too might cast out demons by using the name of the Lord Jesus. But they did not know Him. He was not really Lord to them, and so they could only speak of Him as "Jesus whom Paul preacheth," omitting His title as Lord. The demon at once showed that he did not know them, and he was not deceived by their second-hand use of the name of Jesus. The seven men were utterly discomfited, and their disgrace was known to all. In result the name of the Lord Jesus was magnified.

This led to a great and public triumph over Satan and the dark arts, by which men sought to maintain contact with him. Many that had believed were moved to confess how formerly they had been entangled, and the evil things they had done. Many others moved away from this dreadful evil and publicly burned the books that dealt with these things, in spite of their monetary value. The Word of God grew and prevailed, and this Satanic evil grew less and suffered defeat. It is a sorrowful reflection for us that in our day less attention than formerly is being paid to the Word, and spiritist practices are on the increase.

In these practices Satan approaches men with all the wiles of the serpent. Defeated thus, on this occasion, he had recourse to action in which he revealed himself as the roaring lion. He worked through the cupidity of men. The success of the Gospel had imperilled the trade of the silversmiths, and it was not difficult to attempt to revive their trade under cover of zeal for the reputation of their goddess Diana. Was her greatness to be despised and her magnificence to be destroyed? Here was excellent camouflage for their real concern as to their own money-making prospects!

Their cry of "Great is Diana of the Ephesians!" was a spark that set the whole city alight, for Satan had been at work manufacturing the inflammable material. There ensued the alarming riot, to which the Apostle alludes in his second Epistle to the Corinthians, when he and his friends "were pressed out of measure, above strength, insomuch that we despaired even of life" (1:8). The excited Ephesians were ready to put the sentence of death *upon* Paul, but as he goes on to tell us, "we had the sentence of death *in ourselves*, that we should not trust in ourselves, but in God which raiseth the dead." God did deliver him "from so great a death," but evidently the danger was so overwhelming that Paul likens his deliverance to a resurrection from the dead.

From the account in Acts we can see how God made use of one and another in working the deliverance—certain of the chiefs of Asia; Alexander, who distracted attention from Paul; the town clerk with his diplomatic talk. The majority of the wild demonstrators had no idea exactly why they were demonstrating, and the town clerk reminded them that the Roman authorities might turn the tables on them and accuse them of sedition. It is worthy of note that he was able to say of Paul and his companions, they are "neither temple-plunderers, nor speak injuriously of your goddess" (New Trans.); which shows that they had carefully avoided all that might have given offence. They went in for the *positive* preaching of the Gospel rather than the *negative* work of exposing the follies of idolatry.

This great uproar ended Paul's service in Ephesus, and he departed for Macedonia, as the first verse of chapter 20 records. It is of interest at this point to turn again to 2 Corinthians, and read verses 12 and 13 of chapter 2, and then 5-7 of chapter 7. From these verses we gather that Paul made a short stay at Troas on his outward journey to Macedonia, but owing to his anxiety to meet Titus and hear news of the Corinthian saints, he left for Macedonia, in spite of the open door for service. Arrived in Macedonia, he was still in great disquietude and trouble, yet there Titus did appear and he was comforted. So, evidently the trouble in Ephesus was followed by further trouble both at Troas and in Macedonia. Yet all this side of things is passed over in silence as far as Acts is concerned. Luke could hardly put on record these more intimate details of the Apostle's experiences: we learn of them from his own pen.

# ACTS

## CHAPTER 20

IN ACTS WE are simply told that Paul gave much exhortation to the saints in Macedonia, that he visited Greece, and that to avoid the persecuting Jews he returned through Macedonia on his way back to Asia. Verse 4 gives us the names of his travelling companions on this return journey, though they went ahead across the sea and waited for him at Troas. In verse 5 Luke again uses the pronoun "us," which shows that at this point he again made one of the party. Paul, Luke and others had a voyage of five days, which brought them again to Troas, where not long before "a door was opened . . . of the Lord." The following verses of our chapter show that a great interest in the things of God still was found in that place.

Paul only spent a week in Troas, yet during that time there occurred the memorable meeting recorded in verses 7-12, and we are furnished with a very delightful picture of the simplicity and zeal which characterized those days. It had become the custom of the disciples there to meet for the breaking of bread — the Lord's supper—on the first day of the week. Not the sabbath, but the following day, when the Lord rose from the dead, was selected for this, though it was not a day of leisure, such as the day before would have been for those who were Jews. Hence the Christians met in the evening when the work of the day was done. An upper chamber was their meeting place, "church buildings" being unknown. Paul, with so few days at his disposal, seized the opportunity to discourse to them; and they were so full of interest that they remained all night listening to his words.

It is easy to picture the scene. The crowded chamber; the youth perched in the window opening; the many lights adding to the hot oppression of the drowsy air floating out of the window; the sudden interruption as Eutychus collapses and falls. However the power of God was so manifested through Paul that instead of this episode breaking up the meeting and distracting everyone from Paul's message, their hearts were comforted and confirmed, to settle down and listen till daybreak. The Apostle was now starting his final journey to Jerusalem, the rightness of which may be open to question, but there can be no doubt that the Spirit of God was working through him just as of old. No more remarkable miracle than this was wrought through Paul. The story is marked by the absence of what is ceremonial and official, but it pulsates with power. In popular Christianity today the ceremonial holds the field and the power is absent. Alas, that so it should be!

The day having come, Paul left Troas afoot; Luke and his other companions putting to sea and picking him up at Assos. Arrived at Miletus, he called to him the elders of the church at Ephesus that he might deliver a charge to them, under the conviction that he would not see them again. His touching address seems to fall naturally into three parts.

# ACTS

In the first part he reviews his own ministry among them; this extends over verses 18-27. His first words were, "Ye know, from the first . . . after what manner I have been with you at all seasons." Then, after speaking of *the manner* of his work, he proceeds to *the matter* that characterized it. In both manner and matter we may take him as a model for ourselves.

In the first place his work was *service*. He was not a great ecclesiastical dignitary lording it over the flock of God, but a servant; serving the saints indeed, yet primarily serving the Lord in serving them, and doing it always from the earliest days to the last. Serving moreover with *all humility of mind*, as has been so evident in earlier chapters. He was not a man who expected everyone to give way to him or serve him: he was the helper of others, working with his own hands in order to do so. Again it was with *tears*, and in the midst of many *temptations* which came from the Jews. Tears speak of deep feeling and exercise of heart; whilst the temptations show that he was continually confronted by difficulties and opposition.

He was also marked by *faithfulness* in the declaration of the truth and in its application to the saints. He did not court that cheap popularity which comes from withholding things which may not be palatable, but always aimed at their profit. And further, he did not confine himself to *public* preaching, which often means a good bit of notice and approbation, but gave himself to that *house to house* work, which is much less noticed but often far more effectual. All this shows "what manner" he had been amongst them. But there is also that of which he speaks in verse 24; his utter *devotion* to the ministry committed to him, and to the One from whom he received it. He had delivered up his life for this purpose, and so no anticipation of trouble or even death itself was going to move him. When a servant of God adds to his faithfulness a devotion that does not flinch at death, there is bound to be power in his ministry.

Then as to the matter that characterized his ministry, he mentions three themes. First the Gospel, which had been entrusted to him, and which involved his testifying everywhere and to all, "repentance toward God, and faith toward our Lord Jesus Christ." The Gospel announces "the grace of God," which has been made known in Christ, in His death for our sins, His resurrection for our justification; it leads on our side to repentance and faith. That had been consistently the theme of his preaching.

He had also preached "the kingdom of God," but this had been among, not "all," but "*ye* all." That is, he had everywhere preached the kingdom *amongst the disciples*. This evidently has a present bearing. No doubt he spoke of the kingdom which is to be publicly established, when he spoke of the things to come; but he also kept before them that they had been already brought under the authority of God in receiving Christ as Lord, and he showed them what it meant practically to be subject to God's holy will. It is noticeable for instance that in his epistles Paul is never content with setting forth truth in the abstract; he always proceeded to enforce the conduct which the truth indicated as being the will of God for them.

Then, thirdly, he declared to them "all the counsel of God." He brought them into the light of all that God has counselled for Christ and the church and the world to come. This gave them the knowledge of what hitherto had been kept secret, and showed them that God had higher thoughts than His previously revealed purposes in regard to Israel. This third theme of his ministry was the one that stirred up such furious opposition on the part of many of his Jewish hearers and finally led to his imprisonment. Hence his saying, "I have *not shunned* to declare." If only he had shunned this part of his ministry, he might have had a far more peaceful time in his service and avoided many troubles; for God's counsel involved the bringing in of the Gentiles, according to the truth of the church. He knew this, yet he did not flinch.

An all-round ministry of the Word of God today must include these three themes—the Gospel of God, the kingdom of God, the counsel of God.

In verses 28-31, we find the second part of his address, in which he exhorts and warns them. The Holy Ghost had made them overseers amongst the flock which is the church of God. That flock was not theirs but God's by right of purchase, and they were to feed or shepherd it. But first they were to take heed to themselves, for if a man does not first take heed to himself how can he care for the flock? Moreover they were to watch and be on their guard against the adversaries, remembering how Paul himself had warned them with deep feeling for three years. Is it not a fact that this ministry of warning has almost lapsed through disuse?

Here Paul warns the elders of two main sources of mischief: first, the grievous wolves entering from without; second, the rising up of perverting men within. By "wolves" he meant without a doubt men who were real agents of the devil; the sort that Peter speaks of as bringing in "damnable heresies." How this prediction has been fulfilled church history bears witness; as it also witnesses to the mischief wrought by men who have risen up from the midst of the elders themselves, speaking "perverse" or "*perverted*" things. These are men who very possibly are true believers but they give a *twist* to their teachings which perverts the truth. Thus they make themselves leaders of parties and centres of attraction to those whom they mislead. They attract to themselves instead of leading to Christ. In these words Paul sketched the future of what we know as Christendom.

It is for this reason perhaps that we do not find in the Scripture any instruction as to the perpetuating of the elderhood in an official way beyond the lifetime of the Apostle. If out of the elders are to come these workers of mischief it is as well that we are left to thankfully recognize and accept those whom God may raise up, without their having an official appointment. In the case of men speaking perverted things, their official appointment would only be used to sanction what is wrong.

In the third part of his address Paul indicated the resources that would remain in spite of all that would happen. His *words* were brief and comprised in one verse, but his *matter* of the utmost weight and importance. Our great resource is in God and not in man. He did not commend them to the other apostles: he certainly could not to the elderhood, for he was addressing elders, and out of their midst workers of mischief were to come. God, and God alone, is the resource of His people. But then He has given His Word, which reveals Himself. Formerly He spoke through Moses, as recorded in the Old Testament: that was the Word of *His demand* upon men. Now He has spoken in Christ, as recorded in the New Testament; and that is the Word of *His grace*. To this Word we are specially commended, for it is able to build us up in the faith, and to give us in spiritual power and enjoyment that inheritance along with all the sanctified, which is ours. The inheritance is ours by faith in Christ (see Acts 26: 18), but it is ministered to us in present power by the Word of His grace.

The importance of this thirty-second verse for us today can hardly be exaggerated. God and His Word remain for us, whatever may betide. No power of evil can touch God. He remains, and we may keep in touch with Him in prayer, in communion, in thanksgiving and worship. His Word remains, for He has watched over it in His providence and preserved it to us. Yet, of course, it is the object of ceaseless attacks by the enemy. All too soon it was nearly smothered by the traditions of the Fathers; then it was buried in an unknown tongue and withdrawn from the people; now that it is freely available it is violently criticised, and every attempt is made to destroy its authority. Following in the steps of Judas, great men greet it with a kiss, saying, "Hail, master of beautiful language!" but only to betray it to those who would tear from it every vestige of Divine authority. And, in spite of all, it remains as the resource of the believing and obedient heart.

Paul closed his address by again referring to the uprightness and sincerity that had marked him. Far from desiring to acquire, he had been a giver to others. He put on record a word of the Lord Jesus which is not recorded in the Gospels, and that word he had exemplified. He had earlier spoken of having shewed them as well as having taught them (verse 20), and he repeats that he had shewed them all things. He practised before them what he preached to them. And it is the shewing that tells so effectively.

Paul was called to be a pattern to us both as saint and servant, hence we are given this inspired record of his review of his service, and measuring ourselves against it we are deeply humbled. His words to men over, he went to his knees in prayer with them all, amidst their tears. It must have been an affecting scene. The word used for "kissed" is one which means to kiss ardently, the word which is used for the kisses bestowed by the father on the prodigal in Luke 15. Yet perhaps we detect an element of weakness in the fact that they sorrowed most of all that they could not hope to see him again. Might they not have sorrowed even more that God's fair church was to be ravaged by wolves and damaged by perverting men?

## Chapter 21

As we start this chapter, we see that Luke was still with Paul and his company, and we trace their journey up to Jerusalem. Arrived at Tyre, they evidently sought for disciples, if any were there, and found some. Through these unnamed men the Spirit gave a message to Paul to the effect that he should not go on to Jerusalem. To the Ephesians he had spoken of being bound in his own spirit to go up. Evidently his own inward conviction was so strong that he did not accept the word through the humble men of Tyre. It seems to be a case of his allowing powerful convictions to override the voice of the Spirit reaching him from without. There we must leave it, only observing that if so, we are permitted to see in the succeeding history how God overruled the mistake for ultimate good, though it meant much trouble for Paul.

Leaving Tyre there was another of these beautiful impromptu prayer meetings, just as, arrived at Cæsarea, we have a glimpse of the Christian hospitality of those days. Philip, the evangelist of chapter 8, was their host. His daughters furnish us with examples of women having prophetic gifts, which they exercised doubtless in accord with Scriptural instructions for the service of women.

In that city further testimony was rendered through the prophet Agabus as to what lay before Paul at Jerusalem. Again we see a touching display of affection for Paul, on the part both of his companions and the saints at Cæsarea: a display also of Paul's readiness to lay down his life for the name of the Lord Jesus. Incidentally we see indicated the wise course when a difference of opinion exists which cannot be removed. We all have *to hold our peace*, only desiring that in the matter *the will of the Lord*, whatever it is, may be done.

Having reached Jerusalem, Paul reported to James and the elders what God had wrought through him among the Gentiles. They glorified the Lord in this, for they were prepared to acknowledge them in Christ, in keeping with what had been decided at the conference, of which we read in chapter 15. The Gentiles were not to be put under the yoke of the law. But whether believing Jews should observe their old customs was another question. The Jerusalem brethren urged upon Paul that he should take the opportunity of four men having a vow to associate himself with them, especially as it was alleged against him that he had been teaching Jews to forsake their customs. They felt it was expedient that he should contradict these rumours in this fashion.

Another thing that lay behind the suggestion was that there were now thousands of Jews believing in Christ, but they were all zealous of the law. We should have thought that they would have been zealous of the Gospel and its heavenly hopes, but evidently they had as yet failed to apprehend the true character of that into which they had been brought. It was to such Jewish Christians as these that the Epistle to the Hebrews was written. They were indeed "dull of hearing," and had "need that one teach you again which be the first principles of the oracles of God," needing "milk and not strong meat." They were consequently exhorted to "go on unto perfection" (Heb. 5: 11-6: 2).

The action recommended to Paul, and which he took, was hardly calculated to lead them on to perfection. It was an act of expediency, done to avoid trouble, and as is so often the case entirely failed of its object. It took Paul into the temple where his adversaries were most likely to be found. He ran into trouble instead of avoiding it. The riot against him was fomented by Jews of Asia, men who doubtless had been implicated in the riot at Ephesus. They acted under the supposition that Paul had desecrated the temple by taking into it an Ephesian Gentile. The supposition was evidently mistaken. He had not done this, but he had gone in himself, supposing that thereby he might disarm their prejudice, and this supposition also proved to be mistaken.

Nevertheless the hand of God was over all that happened. The prophecy of Agabus was fulfilled. Paul lost his liberty. Yet by the action of the Roman chief captain he was rescued from the violence of the people. The days of his free evangelistic labours were over—save perhaps for a short time just before the end. Now began the period in which he was to bear powerful witness to the populace in Jerusalem, to be followed by witness before governors and kings, and even before Nero himself. God knows how to make the wrath of man to praise Him, and to restrain the remainder of wrath. He knows also how to overrule any mistakes which His servants may make, and while closing before them certain lines of service to open out other lines, which ultimately may prove to be of even greater importance. It was Paul's imprisonment which led to his writing those inspired epistles which have edified the church for nineteen centuries.

CHAPTER 22

IN ALL THAT happened to Paul in Jerusalem it is not difficult to discern the hand of God controlling behind the scenes. Though the city was in an uproar no one struck a fatal blow until sufficient time had elapsed for the chief captain to intervene. Then the fact of Paul addressing him in Greek

# ACTS

created the favourable impression which led to the permission to address the riotous crowds from the stairs of the castle. Then Paul's choice of Hebrew for his speech led to a complete silence and attention for what he had to say.

It is rather remarkable that we have two full accounts of the conversion of Cornelius in the Acts. In chapter 10, Luke records it as an historian; then in chapter 11, he records how Peter related it. In chapter 15, we have a very short third account of how Peter referred to it in the council of Jerusalem. Again we have three accounts of Paul's conversion. In chapter 9, Luke records it as an historian; in chapter 22, he records how Paul himself related it to his own people, and in chapter 26, how he related it to Gentile potentates. Both conversions were epoch-making and of the greatest significance. In the one case it was the definite and formal calling of Gentiles by the Gospel to the same blessings as Jews and on the same terms; in the other it was the calling of the arch-persecutor to be the chief instrument for the carrying of the Gospel to the Gentile world.

As we read the account in chapter 22, we cannot but see the Divinely-given skill with which Paul spoke. He began by stating what he had been in his early days, when his manner of life was altogether in accordance with their thoughts. He was perfect as to his pedigree, his education, his zeal, and his hatred of the Christians. Then came an intervention from heaven which was clearly an act of God. Now every true conversion is the result of an act of God, yet it usually comes to pass through some human instrument and the Divine act is only recognized by faith. In Paul's case there was no human instrument, but rather something quite supernatural, which appealed to both eye and ear—a great light and a voice of power—so as to cast him prostrate to the ground. He tells the story in such a way as to impress his hearers with the fact that the change in him, which so offended them, had been wrought by God.

The voice that arrested him was the voice of Jesus, and here it is that we discover that the full sentence uttered from heaven was, "I am Jesus OF NAZARETH, whom thou persecutest." The two words are not inserted in chapter 9, nor do they appear when he speaks to Gentiles in chapter 26, but here speaking to Jews, they were full of tremendous significance. They had tacked those words on to His name as a slur and a reproach; and now Jesus *of Nazareth* is in heaven!

From this let us accept the warning not to divide up the names and titles of our Lord in any hard and fast way, though it is very helpful to discern the significance of each. We might have expected Him to say, "I am the One who *was* Jesus of Nazareth in the days of My flesh;" thus relegating that name to His sojourn on earth exclusively. But He did not say, "I was", He said, "I *am*." He does not shed His names, for He is one and indivisible.

## ACTS

Though Paul presents his conversion as being a pure act of God, he relates how Ananias was used of God for the restoration of his sight, and to convey to him the call to be a witness, and to be baptized: also he emphasizes the fact that the said Ananias was a devout and well respected member of the Jewish community in Damascus. Notice that Paul was both to see the glorified Saviour and to hear His voice; and of what he saw and heard he was to bear witness. Hence his speaking of the Gospel he preached as "the Gospel of the glory of the Christ."

Notice too how baptism and the washing away of sins are connected here, just as they are in chapter 2: 38, and as they were in John's baptism. Ananias added, "calling on the name of the Lord," which shows that he pointed to Christian baptism and not John's. Baptism is specially significant in the case of the Jew, which accounts for the prominent place it had on the day of Pentecost and in the case of Paul. These rejectors of Christ must bow their proud heads, and go down symbolically into death, as acknowledging His Name. It was the token of their submission to the One whom they had refused, and only thus could their sins be washed away.

Paul then passed on to relate what happened on his first brief visit to Jerusalem, which is mentioned in chapter 9: 26. No mention is made of this vision in chapter 9, nor in Galatians 1: we only read of it here. It is remarkable that both the Apostles Peter and Paul should have passed into a trance and seen a vision as to their service in regard to Gentiles—Peter, in order that he might break through Jewish custom and open the kingdom to Gentiles; Paul, in order that he should accept the evangelization of Gentiles as his life-work. In this way it was doubly emphasized that the bringing in of the Gentiles was the deliberate will and purpose of God.

Owing to his past, Paul felt that he was pre-eminently fitted to evangelize his own nation, and ventured to tell the Lord this, only to be told that the Jews would not accept testimony from his lips, and that he was to be sent far hence unto the Gentiles. All this he told to the people, and as one reads the record one feels the convincing power of his words. Did he feel that at least *some* of his people must be convinced? Yet there stood that word of the Lord, spoken twenty or more years before, "They *will not* receive thy testimony concerning Me;" and this had been supported by the special messge from the Holy Spirit that he should not go to Jerusalem. At that moment the Lord's words were verified. His mention of the Gentiles becoming objects of the Divine mercy stirred his hearers to frenzy. They *would not* receive his words. They demanded his death with almost uncontrollable violence. When Paul pursued his God-given mission to the Gentiles he was granted the joy of being used to reach the "remnant according to the election of grace" from his own people; when he turned aside, concentrating his attention upon his own people, his words bore no fruit in blessing.

# ACTS

The unreasoning fury of the people coupled with the use of the Hebrew language evidently baffled the chief captain, and examination under the lash was the recognized way of extorting evidence in those days. The mention by Paul of his Roman citizenship checked this, and under God's hand it became the occasion of Paul's further testimony before the leading men of his nation. The Sanhedrin was convoked the next day by the chief captain's orders.

## Chapter 23

As WE OPEN this chapter, we find Paul standing before this august body, and we might have expected him to give the most striking and convincing address of his life. In result however there was a minimum of testimony and a maximum of confusion. Paul's opening remark was bitterly resented, though we can see that it was true. A "good" conscience is acquired and maintained as we sincerely and rigidly carry out all that conscience directs. The zealot with unenlightened or perverted conscience does the most outrageous things in order to preserve his "good" conscience. Thus had Paul acted in his unconverted days, and since his conversion he had with sincerity observed the warnings of his conscience, now enlightened and rectified. How clearly this shows us that conscience is *of itself* no safe guide: it must be enlightened by the Word of God. Its value depends entirely upon the measure in which it is controlled by the Word.

Angry at this opening statement, the high priest ordered that Paul should be smitten on the mouth, thus breaking the law which stipulated that an offender should only be beaten after a proper trial, and then only in a proper way (Deuteronomy 25: 1-3). This manifest injustice moved Paul to a sharp retort; most appropriate, yet not admissible as addressed to the high priest. The council having been summoned in this hurried and informal way, probably there was nothing in his attire to distinguish him; yet, when the error was pointed out, Paul at once acknowledged his fault and quoted the passage which forbade what he had done. He was unable to ask with all assurance, "Which of you convinceth me of sin?" as his Lord had done.

There immediately followed an exceedingly astute move on Paul's part. He presented himself as a Pharisee, and as being called in question concerning the hope of resurrection. Without a doubt he was a Pharisee by birth and early training, and without a doubt resurrection lies at the very foundation of the Gospel. His cry had the effect he anticipated. It rallied the Pharisees to his aid, while violently antagonizing the Sadducees. They were all true party men, viewing everything from a party standpoint. Assuming him to be of their party, the Pharisees swung round in his favour. Truth and righteousness did not count with them, but party did. The same kind of thing is very common today, and Christians are not immune from it; so let us accept the warning which is conveyed to us here.

# ACTS

All through the Acts the Sadducean party appear as the chief opponents of the Gospel. Their materialistic outlook, denying the resurrection, accounted for this. Here we have our last glimpse of them as they furiously protest against the sudden change of front with the Pharisees, and use such physical vigour that Paul might have been pulled in pieces. Their violence defeated their purpose, for it forced the chief captain to intervene, and Paul was for the second time rescued from the hands of his own people.

How very beautiful verse 11 is! We are not told anything as to Paul's feelings, but the Lord's message to him of good cheer certainly infers that he was depressed. We cannot help thinking that the whole of this Jerusalem episode had fallen below the high standard that had characterised all his earlier service; yet he certainly had testified of his Lord. His gracious Master fixed upon that fact, acknowledged it, and told him he was yet to bear witness in Rome — Jerusalem the religious centre, Rome the imperial and governmental centre of the earth of those days. What a refreshment for Paul's spirit!

The next day there was hatched the conspiracy on the part of more than forty men to kill Paul. The nature of the curse under which they bound themselves testifies to the ferocity of their hatred, so it looks as if they were of the Sadducean party who had been baulked of their prey the day before. The chief priests also were of that party, and so were nothing loth to implicate themselves in the business. They were to pretend that they wished to examine him further, and the forty men were ready to kill him.

Again we find the hand of God frustrating their devices. The story—as ever in Scripture—is told with brevity and restraint. We discover that Paul had a sister and a nephew in Jerusalem, but how the young man got information of the plot we are not told. God saw however that it reached his ears, though only concocted a few hours before, and also gave him the courage to reveal it. That he had such easy access to his uncle, and that Paul's request for his nephew to have access to the chief captain should have met with so courteous a response, we trace to God's overruling; though very probably the outrageous behaviour of the Jews had provoked a reaction in the mind of the chief captain in favour of Paul. In result he not only listened to the young man but took him at his word without any hesitation, and immediately took steps to frustrate the plot.

The remainder of the chapter gives us a glimpse of the efficiency that marked the Roman military system. The chief captain acted with the utmost promptness in his decision to remit Paul to the civil governor at Cæsarea. He took care also to run no risks. He knew the vindictive fury of the Jews when matters of a religious sort were at stake; so he did not make the common mistake of underestimating the danger. The force that took charge of Paul must have numbered practically five hundred men, a ratio of twelve to one against would-be assassins. Every consideration was given to the prisoner, even to the extent of providing beasts for him to ride.

# ACTS

## Chapter 24

THE LETTER WRITTEN by Claudius Lysias is quite a typical document, in which he presented his own actions in the most favourable light; but on the other hand it entirely exonerated Paul of anything really evil or worthy of death. The only accusations against him were as to "questions of their law." Thus it is made clear that the first Roman official into whose hands he fell was quickly convinced that the charges against him were as to his faith, and there was no fault in him as to matters of conduct. God evidently took care that this should be made abundantly plain.

Thus it was ordered that the forty men failed in their purpose in spite of their vow and curse. Paul was safely in the strong hands of Rome, and in due time would be able to state his case in a calmer atmosphere, and bear the Name of his Master before "the Gentiles, and kings," as well as the children of Israel, as had been predicted to Ananias. First of all he had to appear before Felix, the governor.

The arraignment of Paul before him bears all the marks of bitter animus and prejudice. That not only elders but even Ananias the high priest should have thought it necessary to go down to appear against him, shows the importance they gave to his case. Then they employed an advocate who, to judge by his name, was a Roman and not a Jew. Tertullus, they doubtless felt, would know better than themselves what would appeal to the Roman mind, and so be more likely to secure a conviction. Tertullus *did* know, and began with fulsome flattery, for the account given of Felix's administration in secular history is in flat denial of what he stated. This he followed by a fourfold charge against Paul. All four charges were vague, particularly the first, that he was a pest, and the second that he was a mover of sedition. Vague charges were preferred, for he knew they could not be easily disproved as plain definite charges often can be.

The third and fourth charges were a little more definite. The fourth, as to profaning the temple was false, as the previous chapter showed: the third was the only one with some semblance of truth. He had proved himself a leader amongst the Christians, who were known by the Jews as the sect of the Nazarenes. They were indeed followers of the despised Nazarene, but they were emphatically not just a new sect amongst the Jews. The book of Acts was written to show us they were not this but rather something entirely new. The world never understands any genuine work of God.

Tertullus took care to present the action of Lysias in an unfavourable light, since he had baulked the violence of the Jews; and the Jews supported the assertions of their advocate. The Jews supplied the animus and used the Gentile as their tool, as they did in the case of the Lord.

Paul's answer was in every way a contrast to the oration of Tertullus. He acknowledged that Felix had had many years experience as judge among the Jews, but he refrained from flattery. He avoided vague assertions, denying explicitly any disputations and sedition, and pointing out that only twelve days had elapsed from the moment he had set foot in Jerusalem. He showed that while they had made plenty of accusations they had furnished no proofs, and could not do so. Then by making a plain and simple confession of what had characterized him, and what lay really at the bottom of their hostility, he threw into relief that which lay at the foundation of the Gospel that he preached. They called it heresy, but it was the very foundation of the truth.

In this skilful way did Paul announce his belief in all that had been written in the Old Testament, and show that all Christian hopes are based upon the resurrection, which of course has been verified in Christ. And it is just as certain that there shall be a resurrection for the unjust. That was evidently a shot directed at the conscience of Felix, as well as all others present. No one shall remain buried in the grave to escape the mighty hand of God in judgment.

Having proclaimed his faith in the Scriptures and in the resurrection, Paul went on to affirm that his conduct had been in keeping with what he believed. His conscience was clear, and he had only come up to Jerusalem on a mission of mercy, and when in the temple his behaviour had been perfectly orderly and correct. It was the Jews from Asia who stirred up the tumult, not he; and now that there was opportunity for them to present their charges against him in an orderly way, they were not there to do so.

But there were Jews present who had seen him appear before the council, and he knew that they found no fault in him, save that he avowed his belief in the resurrection. Paul knew no doubt that it was the Saducean faction who were pursuing him so relentlessly and appearing against him, and he took care to make it very plain to Felix that his belief in the resurrection of the dead, as verified in the resurrection of Christ, was the real matter at issue. It may be also that Paul wished to acknowledge that the way in which he had cried out in the council had not been quite free from blame.

Felix, as we learn from verse 24, had a Jewess as wife, and so was well informed as to things, and realized at once that there was nothing evil in Paul. He adjourned the court under pretext of waiting for Lysias the chief captain, so once more the accusers were foiled, especially as the adjournment was *sine die*, as our courts put it. Meanwhile Paul was given an extraordinary measure of liberty, in which again we may see the overruling hand of God.

There is no record of Lysias coming down, but we are told how Felix, with Drusilla his wife, sent for Paul and gave him a private audience while he testified of the faith in Christ. This was a great opportunity, and Paul evidently knew the weak and crooked character of the governor, and so he emphasized righteousness, temperance, and judgment to come. We may take *righteousness* as summing up the Gospel message, as Romans 1: 16, 17, shows so clearly. Temperance or *self-restraint* is the result of the Gospel in the life of the one who receives it; and *judgment to come* is what awaits those who refuse it. So though the summary given of Paul's address is exceedingly brief, we can see that the three words are such as cover the salient facts of the Gospel.

There was great power with the message and Felix trembled, yet he deferred the matter to that "convenient season," which so often never comes. It was so in this case. Though two years passed before Felix was superseded by Festus, and during that time there were a number of interviews, nothing came of them, and Felix left Paul bound in the effort to curry favour with the Jews. The real canker at the heart of Felix was the love of money. His case strikingly illustrates how there may be a powerful working of the Spirit through the Gospel *from without* upon a man, but how any working upon heart and conscience *within* may be smothered by some active lust, such as the love of money. True conversion takes place when the Spirit's work from without is supplemented and answered by the Spirit's work within.

## Chapter 25

FESTUS HAVING ARRIVED, he went up to Jerusalem after three days, and such was the animosity against Paul that at once the high priest and other leaders accused him, and asked Festus to have him brought to Jerusalem. Though years had passed they would still fulfil their vow and wreak their vengeance. Such is religious rancour! Festus however declined this, so once more his accusers had to journey to Cæsarea. This second hearing was practically a repetition of the first, as is shown in verses 7 and 8. Paul had merely to rebut a large number of unproved assertions. Now Festus, as the next chapter shows, had not got any intimate knowledge of Jewish things; still, knowing them to be a people difficult to handle, he wished to gain their favour, and so suggested that after all Paul might go up to Jerusalem for his final trial.

In this sudden change on the part of Festus we may see the hand of God. During the night that followed the uproar in the council the Lord had appeared to Paul and told him that he must bear witness to Him in Rome, and now He controls circumstances to bring this to pass. The suggestion from Festus led Paul to appeal to Cæsar, a privilege that belonged to him as a Roman citizen. Paul knew that the proposed change of place was the prelude to his being handed over to his enemies, though Festus knew very well that he had done no wrong. If Festus began yielding to the clamour in order to placate the Jews, he would end by yielding everything. Paul's appeal settled everything. Having appealed to Cæsar, to Rome he must go. This is the third occasion on which we find Paul taking his stand on his Roman citizenship, and here most evidently it was made to serve and work out the purpose of his Lord.

The coming of Agrippa and Bernice to salute Festus became the occasion for Paul to bear a third testimony before governors and kings, and we are now given a much fuller insight into the mighty way in which he presented the truth. He had not failed previously to convey even to Festus that which lay at the heart of the whole matter, for in speaking to Agrippa of his case, Festus stated the controversy to rage around, "one Jesus, which was dead, whom Paul affirmed to be alive." This shows that, pagan though he was with no real understanding, he had grasped the central fact of the Gospel. The death and resurrection of Christ are at the basis of all blessing, and the full declaration of the love of God. We know something of this, while he know nothing of it. Still, Paul had made it plain.

That it was all a mystery to Festus, in spite of his having rightly seized the point at issue, is evident from his address to Agrippa, when the court had assembled and, Paul being brought forth, the proceedings commenced. He had no certain thing to write to his lord, the emperor in Rome. He hoped that Agrippa with his superior acquaintance with Jewish religion, might be able to help him to understand more clearly what was at stake, and know what to say.

## Chapter 26

On this occasion there were no tedious preliminary proceedings. Agrippa immediately gave Paul permission to speak for himself. Thus set free, he was able to dispense with all mere details of self-defence, and come straight to the message with which God had entrusted him, after acknowledging Agrippa's expert knowledge, and beseeching for a patient hearing.

He began by stating that he had been brought up in the strictest form of Judaism amongst the Pharisees, and that what was now charged against him was in connection with the hope that all Israel had entertained from the days when God gave His promise. That hope they still held, but Paul maintained there had been a fulfilment of it in Christ, and particularly in His resurrection. So from the outset of his address he kept the resurrection well to the fore, as being the main point at issue. Yet resurrection lay beyond men's thoughts, whether Jewish or pagan; hence his question, "Why should it be thought a thing incredible with you, that God should raise the dead?" It would be *utterly incredible* if only men were in question: bring God in—the real, true, living God—and *it is incredible that it should not be*.

In this third account of his conversion we find the Apostle greatly emphasizing the determined and furious opposition to Christ which

# ACTS

characterized him at the beginning. He was indeed "a blasphemer, and a persecutor, and injurious," as he told Timothy: he carried it to the point of being "exceedingly mad" against the disciples, and persecuting them even to distant cities. This was the way in which he did the many things "contrary to the name of Jesus of Nazareth." It was at midday, when the sun shines most strongly, that another light brighter than the sun arrested him on the road to Damascus, and the voice of the Lord was heard. The uncreated light threw the created light into the shade.

Several interesting features, not mentioned in the earlier accounts, appear here. The light from heaven brought the whole company down into the dust, and not Paul only. Further, the voice was in the Hebrew tongue. This is remarkable, for we have been told earlier that though his companions heard the voice it conveyed nothing to them. It was in their own language, yet they did not understand. They were affected *physically*, but only Paul was affected *spiritually*. The essential element in conversion is not great sights, nor wonderful sounds, but the life-giving work of the Holy Ghost. Jesus was manifested only to Paul, and that in such a way that he discovered Him to be his Lord.

When he owned Jesus to be his Lord, he was told plainly what he was to do as regards his own personal salvation. That we learned from the earlier accounts. Here only are we told that at the same time the Lord told him with equal plainness, that He was apprehending him to make him the servant of His will in a very special way. He was to be a witness to others of that which had just been revealed to him, and of further things that yet were to be made known to him by the Lord. Here only do we learn of the way in which the Lord commissioned him from the outset, and what the terms of that commission were. They are very striking, and they account very fully for the remarkable career which we have been tracing in the earlier chapters.

The Lord's purpose was that he should be "delivered", or "*taken out*" from among the people, and the Gentiles; that is, he was to be separated both from his own people, the Jews, and from the Gentiles, so as to stand in a place distinct from both. It has often been said that the Lord's words, "I am Jesus whom thou persecutest," were the first intimation that the saints were His body: we may perhaps say that the words we are now considering were the first intimation of the distinct place the church occupies, called out from both Jew and Gentile. Paul started by himself being put in the place into which were brought all those who believed the Gospel that he was commissioned to preach.

But, as the end of verse 17 says, he was specially sent to the Gentiles. As we have before noticed, he was blessed to many Jews as long as he followed his commission in the Gentile world; it was only when he turned aside from this to address himself specially to his Jewish brethren, that he failed to reach them. How fully this warns us that our Master must be supreme, and that our wisdom is to abide by His plan for our lives and service. To the Gentiles he was to go, that he might "open their eyes."

This was a new departure in God's ways, for hitherto they had been left to go their own way. They had been in darkness and ignorance, but now their eyes were to be opened.

If, through Paul's labours, their eyes were effectually opened, they would turn from darkness and the power of Satan to light and God. This is what we mean by conversion. It must of course involve conviction of sin, for none of us can come into the light of God without that conviction being wrought in us. But then as the result of turning there is the reception of forgiveness. There is the Divine act of forgiveness in which we may rejoice, and not only so, but we also enter into an inheritance which we share in common with all those who are set apart for God. Forgiveness is what we may call the *negative* blessing of the Gospel and the inheritance is the *positive*. Forgiveness is a loss rather than a gain—the loss of our sins; of the love of them as well as of the penalty they entail. The inheritance is what we gain.

And all this is "by faith that is in Me." Here we have the way in which the blessing is reached. Not by works, but by faith; and of that faith Christ is the Object. The virtue is not in the faith but in the Object in whom faith rests. Thus from the very moment of his conversion Paul's future course and ministry was marked out for him, and by revelation from the Lord he was given the message that he was to preach. We have then in verse 18, a complete summary of the blessings that the Gospel brings to the one who receives it in faith. The eyes of his heart and mind are opened to the truth; he is brought out of darkness into light, and from Satan's power unto God; his sins are forgiven and he knows it; he shares in the inheritance common to those who with himself are set apart for God.

Having received these instructions, Paul had been faithful to his commission, and beginning where he was and widening out to the nations, he had showed to men everywhere what their response to the Gospel should be. They should repent; they should turn to God; they should do works in keeping with the repentance they professed. Repentance involves that coming into the light which enables one to see and judge one's own sinfulness, and then the confession of it before God. Now the more we see our own sin, the more we distrust ourselves; the more we distrust ourselves, the more we learn to trust in God: consequently turning to God follows this turning from ourselves. All this is an inward process of mind and heart of a more or less secret nature, but if it is real it soon produces actions and works in keeping with it. If there be no "works meet for repentance," we may be sure that the repentance professed is not the genuine article. Paul insisted on all three things, and he knew of course that not only are they God's appointed way in which the blessings of the

Gospel are received, but they are themselves produced by the Gospel, where it is received in faith.

Now it was just this which had so stirred up the animosity of the Jews, for if this was the way of entrance into God's favour, it was as much open to the Gentile as to the Jew. But he made very plain to Agrippa that what had been predicted by Moses and the prophets lay at the foundation of all that he had preached. He announced the suffering of Christ; His resurrection; and that as risen He should bring the light of God to all mankind —not only Jews, but Gentiles also. How clearly this last point is stated in Isaiah 49, just as the death and resurrection of Christ are predicted in Isaiah 53.

In verse 23 then we have a plain testimony rendered to Agrippa, Festus, and all others present, as to *the glorious basis of fact on which the Gospel rests*. Indeed we may say that primarily the preaching of the Gospel is the declaration of those facts, and we need to keep them in the forefront of our preaching today as much as in Paul's day. Then, as we have seen, verse 18 gives us *the blessings that the Gospel confers;* and verse 20 *the way in which the Gospel blessings are received*.

To the pagan mind of the Roman the idea of resurrection was simply incredible, as Paul had anticipated at the opening of his address, so the mention of Christ risen from the dead moved Festus to a loud exclamation. How often through the centuries has the Christian been charged with madness! Here is the first recorded instance of the taunt being flung by the man of the world. Yet it was not vulgar abuse, for Festus was a polished Roman. He did at least attribute Paul's "madness" to an excess of study and learning. But mad he thought him nevertheless!

Paul's reply was moving in its dignified simplicity. He addressed Festus in a way that became his high estate, and then asserted that on the contrary what he had said were "words of truth and soberness." To Festus it was all the romance of an intoxicated mind, for the gods that he venerated wielded no powers beyond the grave. Feeble man can kill and bring down to the grave—that is an easy thing: only of the living God can it be said, "The Lord killeth, *and maketh alive:* He bringeth down to the grave, *and bringeth up*" (1 Sam. 2: 6). Let us all aim so to declare the Gospel that our hearers may recognize that we are speaking *the sober truth*.

Having answered Festus, Paul launched an appeal to Agrippa, knowing that he professed to believe the prophetic Scriptures, and would therefore know that what he preached as fact had been foretold there. The appeal evidently went home. Agrippa's answer, we fear, was not a confession that he was very nearly convinced of the truth of the Gospel, but rather an attempt in a semi-jocular way to throw off the effect of the appeal. He said in effect, "In a little you will be making a Christian of me!" From his words it is evident that the term "Christian," first coined at Antioch, had by now obtained wide currency. By it the disciples were very accurately described.

About Paul's rejoinder there is a moral elevation which is not easily surpassed. A poor prisoner stands in the midst of great pomp and magnificence and desires for his august judges that they might be just as he himself is, save for his bonds! As the angels looked down on that sight they saw an heir of everlasting and supernal glory standing before potsherds of the earth robed for a brief moment in tawdry display. Paul knew that, and that there was nothing better for any man than to be almost and altogether such as he was.

This closed the session. Paul had the last word; and we rejoice to note how, filled with the Holy Ghost, he is standing in the full height of the great calling that had reached him—the calling that has reached us too.

Once more also is his innocence declared by competent authority. Had he not appealed to Cæsar he might have been free.

CHAPTER 27

WHILE AT EPHESUS Paul had "purposed in the spirit" saying, "I must also see Rome" (19: 21); and, what is more important still, it was the Lord's purpose for him—"so must thou also bear witness at Rome" (23: 11). We have just been tracing God's ways behind the scenes bringing to pass that "it was determined that we should sail into Italy." Again Luke uses "we," showing that he was now again a companion of Paul as they started on this journey, which was to be so full of disaster, and yet have so miraculous an ending.

Looking at second causes, Paul might have bitterly regretted his appeal to Cæsar, when Agrippa declared that but for it he might have been set at liberty. Looking to God, all was clear, and Paul with other prisoners started on the voyage. Yet though the journey was thus ordered of God, it did not follow that everything moved with ease and smoothness. The very opposite; for it is put on record from the beginning that "the winds were contrary" (v. 4). The fact that circumstances are against us is no proof that we are out of the way of God's will, nor do favouring circumstances necessarily mean that we are in the way of His will. We cannot safely deduce from circumstances what may or may not be His will for us.

Circumstances continued contrary and progress was tedious, "the wind not suffering us" (v. 7), and the dangerous time of year arrived when it was customary to suspend voyages in some safe harbour. The place called Fair Havens was reached, which in spite of its name was not a suitable spot, and here a conflict of opinion developed. The skipper was desirous of reaching Phenice, while Paul counselled that they were about to run into disaster and loss, not only for ship and cargo but also to their lives. The Roman centurion, in charge of the party of prisoners, held the casting vote, and having listened to the voice of worldly wisdom and nautical skill on the one hand, and that of spiritual understanding on the other, he decided in favour of the advice of the skipper.

Any ordinary person, without a doubt, would have decided as did the centurion; and when suddenly the wind veered and blew gently from the south, it looked as though God was favouring the centurion's decision. But again we see that circumstances furnish no true guidance; for they set sail only to be caught in the dreaded Euroclydon, which upset all their plans. They proceeded by sight and not by faith, and all ended in disaster. They took all possible measures to work out their own salvation, but without effect, so that ultimately all hope was abandoned. It is easy to see that all this may be effectively used as a kind of allegory; representing the soul's struggles for deliverance, whether from the guilt or the power of sin. Nothing was right until God intervened, first by *His word* through Paul, and then by *His power* in the final shipwreck.

It was when they were nearly starved and quite hopeless that the angel of God appeared to Paul. Nearly a fortnight had passed since the storm began, and until this point Paul had not had anything authoritative to say. But now the word of God had reached him, stating that he must appear before Cæsar, and that he and all sailing with him were to be saved. God having spoken Paul could speak with authority and the utmost assurance. After a fortnight's tossing on the wild seas the feeling of one and all must have been deplorable and depressing. But what had feelings to do with the matter? *God had spoken*, and Paul's attitude was, "I believe God," in spite of all the feelings in the world.

All the probabilities of the situation also would have given a negative to what the angel had said. That a small sailing vessel, packed with 276 people, should be wrecked and destroyed, in days when there were no friendly lifeboats, and yet every one of the 276 be saved, was so highly improbable as to be pronounced impossible. But God had said it, so Paul laughed at the impossibility and said, "It shall be done." Moreover so strong was his faith that not only did he say this in his heart but he also said it aloud in the way of testimony to the other 275 people on board. His exact words were, "It shall be even as it was told me." The salvation of all had not yet happened, but he was as sure of it as if it had.

Faith has very simply been defined as "Believing what God says, because God says it," and this is well supported by Paul's words, "I believe God." In this case *feelings, reason, experience*, the *probabilities* of the situation, all would have contradicted the Divine statement, but faith accepted what God said, though all else denied it. Faith in our hearts will speak in just the same way. The Divine testimony to us deals with matters far greater than a salvation for time only, and it reaches us not from the mouth of an angel but through the holy and inspired Writings, which we

ACTS

now have in print in our own tongue; but our reception of it is to be equally definite. We simply believe God, and thus set to our seal that God is true.

Verses 34-36 show us that Paul's attitude and actions corroborated his brave words of faith. Thus we see him exemplifying what James so stresses in his epistle: faith, if it is alive, must express itself in works. If, having uttered words of faith, he had remained depressed and dejected like the rest, no one would have paid much attention to his words. But rather, having announced words of good cheer, he was himself most evidently of good cheer. He gave thanks to God, he partook of food, and exhorted the others to do the same. His works thus attesting the reality of his faith, all were impressed by it. They too were of good cheer and took food. As yet the circumstances were not altered, but they were altered as the confidence of faith found a place in their hearts, for it furnished them with "the substantiating of things hoped for, the conviction of things not seen" (Heb. 11: 1. N. Trans.). The whole episode is an excellent illustration of what faith is and how faith works.

It illustrates also how faith is vindicated. God was as good as His word, and every soul was saved. His promise was fulfilled literally and exactly, and not approximately and with tolerable accuracy, as is so common amongst men. We may take Him at His word with absolute certainty. Yet this does not mean that we can become fatalistic, and ignore ordinary measures of prudence. This also is illustrated in our story. After Paul had announced that all should be saved, he did not permit the sailors to flee out of the ship, since their presence was needed; and later, when all had eaten enough, they lightened the ship still further by casting the wheat into the sea. They did not fold their arms and do nothing as fatalism would have decreed, but took the ordinary measures of prudence, while trusting in God's word. The ending was really miraculous. In one way or another all were saved.

CHAPTER 28

WE STILL SEE the protecting hand of God stretched over Paul and his companions when they had landed on Malta. Though the inhabitants were "barbarians" according to Roman thoughts, they showed exceptional kindness to the shipwrecked party, and things were so over-ruled that they soon discovered that one of the shipwrecked visitors was no ordinary person. Paul was busily engaged, doing what he could to help, when a viper fastened itself on his hand. The superstitious islanders placed their interpretation on this, but when the expected did not follow they changed their minds, jumping to the opposite conclusion. Superstition never comes to right conclusions. To Paul doubtless it was a very minor happening, seeing he had been through the long list of adventures which he catalogued

## ACTS

in 2 Corinthians 11: 23-28. And when he wrote that list it was still unfinished. He had not, for instance, been through the shipwreck of which we have been reading. He had been shipwrecked three times before this happened. There are not many who have survived four shipwrecks, we venture to think, even if professional sailors, which he was not.

The chief man of the island taking a kindly interest in them in their need, Paul was enabled to repay him by prayer and the healing of his father. We do not read of any testimony that Paul rendered, yet his praying must have shown to all that the healing power he wielded was not his own but connected with God. The islanders, finding that the power of God was in their midst, were not slow to seek it for their bodies, and seeking they found it. All this, in the providence of God, led to a time of comfort after the fortnight of terrible testing, and even to a time of honour, and this lasted for three months. The Apostle has put on record, "I know both how to be abased, and I know how to abound" (Phil. 4: 12). These three months proved to be a time of abounding.

The same might be said of the rest of the journey, when it was resumed. All went favourably and arriving at Puteoli, and finding brethren there who begged Paul might be with them for a week, the visit was happily arranged. By this time evidently the centurion in charge had taken the measure of his prisoners, and was disposed to accord him remarkable liberty. On the overland journey too, brethren came to meet him, having heard of his approach, and this was a great cheer to Paul. Spiritual man though he was, and thoroughly in touch with God and dependent upon Him, he was not above thanking God and taking courage from the love and fellowship of saints, whose spiritual stature may have been much beneath his own. It is striking to see this, and very encouraging for us. Let us be very careful not to despise, or even underestimate the value of the fellowship of saints.

Thus Paul arrived at Rome. His circumstances were very different from those that he had visualized when he wrote in advance of what he purposed to do (see Romans 15: 22-32), but he *did* come to them with a certain measure of joy by the will of God, and he *was* marked by "the fulness of the blessing of the gospel of Christ." God's hand was still over him, for though a prisoner he was permitted to dwell by himself under guard, and this gave him a measure of liberty for service and testimony.

Only three days after his arrival he was able to call together the chief of the Jewish colony in Rome and lay something of his case before them. He made it plain that he had no wish to be an accuser of his nation, but that his whole offence in Jewish eyes was connected with the "hope of Israel;" that is, the long promised Messiah. The Jews on their part professed ignorance of his case, but they knew of the Christ whom Paul preached, and to be a Christian meant to them belonging to a "sect . . . everywhere . . . spoken against." *Everywhere,* be it noted; not only amongst the Jews but amongst Gentiles also. Genuine Christianity never has been popular, and never will be. It cuts too deeply across the grain of human nature.

Still they professed a desire to hear what Paul had to say; and so a day being fixed, many came, and for a whole day he was able to expound and testify and persuade. His theme was the kingdom of God and Jesus, as the One in whom that kingdom is centred and established; and all that he had to say was based upon the law of Moses and the prophets, for there all had been typified and foretold. The three verbs are worthy of note. First he *expounded* the Sacred Writings, showing what they had to say and making their force plain. Then he *testified* of Jesus, relating doubtless what he knew personally of His glory in heaven, and showing how exactly He had fulfilled all that the Scriptures had said concerning His advent in humiliation. Lastly he set himself to *persuade* his hearers of the truth of all he advanced. Paul did not preach what has been called a "take it or leave it" Gospel, but laboured with loving zeal to reach the hearts of those who listened, and secure a response in faith from them. Let us see that we imitate him in this, for we have to remember that though nothing short of the working of the Holy Spirit in the hearts of men is effectual, the Spirit is frequently pleased to work through the persuasiveness of servants of God, who are filled with love and zeal.

It was so in this case. The record here is that while some remained in unbelief, "some believed the things which were spoken." When the Word is preached it is nearly always thus. Only in the Acts—when Peter preached to Cornelius—do we find everybody converted; but that is not the usual thing, for at the present moment God is calling an election out from both Jew and Gentile.

To the unbelieving Jews, ere they departed, Paul spoke a final word, quoting the passage from Isaiah 6, which the Lord Himself quoted in Matthew 13, and John quotes in chapter 12 of his Gospel. This sad and terrible process of hardening and spiritual death had set in even in the days of Isaiah some seven centuries before Christ. It was far more pronounced when Christ was on earth; and now the final stage was reached. Paul pronounced these words, realizing that during this Gospel age Israel's day as a nation was over. Nationally they are blinded and without understanding in the things of God, though very acute as to the things of the world. This does not of course conflict with the fact that God is still calling out a remnant according to the election of grace, as Romans 11 states.

It is worthy of note that in quoting this passage Paul says, "Well spake *the Holy Ghost.*" If we turn to Isaiah 6, we find the prophet saying in regard to this message, "Also I heard the voice of the Lord," referring to *Jehovah of Hosts;* and turning to John 12, we find the comment, "These things said Esaias, when he saw *His* glory, and spake of *Him*," and we have only to look at the preceding verses to discover that the "His" and "Him" refer to

*Jesus.* How plain it is then that Jehovah of hosts is to be identified with both Jesus and the Holy Ghost—three Persons, yet one God.

Verse 28 gives us the last words of Paul, as recorded in the Acts. They are very significant, as giving us the point to which the book has conducted us. He proclaims as a definite message from God that His salvation is now sent to the Gentiles as the result of the blindness and hardness of the Jew; and he adds "they will hear it." This does not mean that all of them will do so, but rather that in contra-distinction from the Jew, a hearing ear is going to be found there. This, thank God! has proved true throughout the centuries.

When the Lord spoke to the Syro-Phenician woman about the children and the dogs, the poor woman, seeing the point, took the place of being but a Gentile dog, and yet claimed that God was good enough to permit that there should be some crumbs of mercy for her. She was right: the Lord called her faith great and honoured it by granting her desire. But here we find something more wonderful still. The children having despised and rejected the good things provided, not the crumbs merely but the whole meal is sent to the dogs. As Paul himself puts it in Romans 11, "the fall of them" is "the riches of the world, and the diminishing of them the riches of the Gentiles . . . the casting away of them . . . the reconciling of the world." This does not mean that all the world is definitely reconciled, but that God has now turned in favour towards the world, offering His salvation to all men.

Paul was still a prisoner, yet he was allowed to hire a house and dwell there and receive all who wished to see him. Thus he had opportunities for testimony, and the word of God was not bound. As far as this book is concerned we take leave of him spending two whole years preaching the kingdom of God and teaching the things concerning the Lord Jesus Christ without any restraint. His trial was delayed in the providence of God, and a door of utterance was thus opened to him. During this time Onesimus was converted and doubtless others also; some of his Epistles also were written.

Closing the Acts, we finish apostolic *history:* passing to Romans we begin apostolic *doctrine.* It is the doctrine which enables us to understand the *significance* of the history; while the history enables us to appreciate the *authority* and *weight* of the doctrine.

www.ingramcontent.com/pod-product-compliance
Lightning Source LLC
Chambersburg PA
CBHW020730160426
43192CB00006B/171